W9-AHL-681

www.wadsworth.com

wadsworth.com is the World Wide Web site for Wadsworth and is your direct source to dozens of online resources.

At *wadsworth.com* you can find out about supplements, demonstration software, and student resources. You can also send email to many of our authors and preview new publications and exciting new technologies.

wadsworth.com
Changing the way the world learns®

State and Local Government:
Public Life in America

George H. Cox
Georgia Southern University

Raymond A. Rosenfeld
Eastern Michigan University

WADSWORTH
™
THOMSON LEARNING

Australia • Canada • Mexico • Singapore • Spain
United Kingdom • United States

Political Science Publisher: Clark Baxter
Senior Developmental Editor: Sharon Adams Poore
Assistant Editor: Jennifer Ellis
Signing Representative: April Lemons
Marketing Manager: Diane McOscar
Permissions Manager: Bob Kauser
Print Buyer: Barbara Britton

Interior Design: Jennifer Dunn
Cover Design: Ellen Kwan
Cover Photographs: (large) PhotoEdit; (inset) PhotoDisc
Photo Research: Susan Friedman
Production, Copyediting, Graphics, & Composition:
    Summerlight Creative Book Production Services
Printer: Courier, Kendallville

Wadsworth/Thomson Learning
10 Davis Drive
Belmont, CA 94002-3098
USA

For information about our products, contact us:
Thomson Learning Academic Resource Center
1-800-423-0563
http://www.wadsworth.com

International Headquarters
Thomson Learning
International Division
290 Harbor Drive, 2nd Floor
Stamford, CT 06902-7477
USA

UK/Europe/Middle East/South Africa
Thomson Learning
Berkshire House
168-173 High Holborn
London WC1V 7AA
United Kingdom

Asia
Thomson Learning
60 Albert Street, #15-01
Albert Complex
Singapore 189969

Canada
Nelson Thomson Learning
1120 Birchmount Road
Toronto, Ontario M1K 5G4
Canada

ISBN 0-534-55540-3

This book is dedicated to
Ann Cox and Janelle McCammon,
our long-suffering yet supportive wives.

Contents

Foreword   xi

Introduction   xiii

CHAPTER 1

The Power of Place:
*Society, Culture, and Popular
Government   1*

Constitutions and Sovereignty   3

The Power and Sense of Place   5

  Regional Cultures   5

  Urbanization and Mass Culture   6

  Place as Personal Property   7

The People Called "Americans"   8

  Race and Racial Consciousness   9

  Diversity's Policy Implications   13

  Immigration and Migration   13

Political Culture   16

Technology and Civic Culture   19

  *Technology and Generational
  Change   20*

  Technology and the Individual   21

  Enjoying Leisure Life   22

  *Technology's Effect on Place, Time,
  and Culture   22*

Chapter Conclusion   23

CHAPTER 2

**Power Sharing in
a Federal System:**
*Theoretical and Practical
Balance   27*

Constitutional Federalism   28

  A Confederation of States   28

  A More Perfect National Union   28

  Judicial Interpretation   30

  Citizenship and Voting Rights   33

  *National Supremacy More
  Generally   38*

  *Conclusions About Constitutional
  Federalism   38*

Programmatic Federalism   38

  *Policy and Program
  Development   39*

  *Policy or Program
  Implementation   42*

  Policy or Program Evaluation   44

Issues in Federalism   47

  Revenue Sharing   47

  Unfunded Mandates   47

  Policy Preemption   47

Local Government Home Rule   48

Chapter Conclusion   49

Capital City Players:
*Everyday Politics
in the States   53*

State-Level Political Parties   54

  State Party Organization   54

  *Parties' Organizational
    Effectiveness   56*

  *Party Organization
    and Discipline   56*

  *The Character of State Political
    Parties   57*

  State Partisan Elections   58

  *Regulation of Campaign
    Finances   59*

  *State Parties
    in the Government   61*

State-Level Interest Groups   62

  Interest Group Activities   64

  Regulating Interest Groups   64

Media in the State Capital   64

  News Services   65

  Capital City Newspapers   65

  Broadcast Media   66

State Political Systems   67

Chapter Conclusion   72

State Legislatures:
*Policy Roles and Procedural
Rules   75*

Public Policy Decision Making   76

Direct Democracy   77

Representative Democracy   80

  Public Expectations   80

  *Representation in State
    Legislatures   81*

  Election Campaigns   83

  Legislative Sessions   84

  Legislator Profile   84

Legislative Life in the State Capital   86

  *Legislatures and Political
    Players   87*

Legislative Leadership   88

  Chamber Leadership   88

  Party Leadership   89

Passing State Laws   89

State Legislation   93

  Public Education   93

  Crime Control   94

  Welfare Reform   94

Legislative Oversight   94

  Program Review   95

  Budgetary Oversight   96

  Regulatory Oversight   97

Chapter Conclusion   98

State Executives:
*Leadership
and Accountability   101*

State Governors   102

  Gubernatorial Elections   103

  *Results of Recent Gubernatorial
    Elections   105*

  Governors Taking Office   107

  *The Governor as Legislative
    Leader   108*

  *The Governor's Immediate
    Staff   109*

  *The Governor as Budgetary
    Leader   110*

  *The Governor's Appointment
    Powers   112*

Lieutenant Governors   112

  Appointed Agency Heads   114

State Managers   116

Reforming Executive Branch
  Government   117

Chapter Conclusion   119

CHAPTER 6

Bureaucrats and Regulators:
Delivering Services and
Protecting Consumers   *121*

The Bureaucracy of Service
   Delivery   123

Specialization
   and Professionalism   125

Civil-Service Protection   126

Hierarchy and Communications   127

Evaluating State Government
   Professionalism   129

Bureaucracy Conclusion   130

Regulators and Consumer
   Protection   131

Selecting the Regulators   132

Corporate Regulation   132

Professional Licensing   133

State Public Service Commissions   135

Organization and Powers   135

Public-Service Issues   137

The Future of Public Service
   Commissions   138

Regulation: Some Answers   138

Chapter Conclusion   139

CHAPTER 7

State Courts:
The Rules and Boundaries
of the Game   *141*

American Justice   142

Criminal Trials   142

Civil Trials   143

Court Structure in the States   144

State Trial Courts   144

State Appeals Courts   144

Serving as a State Judge   145

The Administration of Justice   147

Issues Before the State Courts   149

Crime-Control Concerns   150

Crime Control and the Courts   151

Correctional Supervision
   and Incapacitation   152

Juvenile Crime   155

Criminal Justice   155

Civil Justice   156

Chapter Conclusion   158

CHAPTER 8

Local Communities:
Politics Where We Live *161*

A Community of Neighborhoods   163

Neighborhood and Tenants'
   Associations   165

Neighborhood Issues   165

Neighborhood Politics   168

Business and Labor Organizations 170

Local Business Issues   173

Business's Political Power   174

Labor's Political Power   175

Civic Clubs   176

Civic Issues   177

Civic Clubs and Politics   179

Religious Congregations   179

Religious Issues   180

Faith-Based Organizations
   and Politics   182

Special Issue Organizations   183

Typical Special Interest
   Organizations   183

Special Interests and Politics   183

Interpreting Community Groups   184

Elite Theory   185

Pluralist Theory   186

Regime Theory   187

Chapter Conclusion   188

CHAPTER 9

Taking the Next Step:
Local Political Participation 191

Local Elections   193

Popular Votes on the Issues   194

Electing City Officials   194

Mayoral Elections   198

Local Judicial Elections   200

Variations on the Representative
Government Theme   201

Voter Turnout   202

Other Forms of Participation   205

Interpreting Local Participation   206

Chapter Conclusion   209

CHAPTER 10

Navigating City Hall:
How Local Government
Is Structured *211*

The Big Picture of Local Government
Structure   212

Historical Background of Local
Government Structure   214

Political Machines   215

Progressive Reform Movement   217

Conclusion to History of Local
Government Structures   220

Municipal Government Structure   220

Strong Mayor Form   221

Council–Manager Form   222

Commission Form   224

The Choice of Form   225

Townships   226

Duties of City Officials   227

City Councils   227

City Mayors   228

City Managers   233

Mayoral Leadership   235

Local Government Bureaucrats   237

Chapter Conclusion   237

CHAPTER 11

Counties, Special Districts,
and School Systems:
Politics Beyond City Hall   *241*

States and Their Counties   242

County Geography   242

County Demographics   243

County Authority   243

The Commission Form
of Government   244

County Administrators   245

Other Elected County
Officials   245

County Executive   246

County Courts   247

County Services   248

Consolidated Services   248

County Government Capacity
Building   249

Special Service Districts 251

Governmental Powers of Special
Districts   252

Chicago's Special Districts   253

Water-Quality Districts   253

Concerns About Special District
Government   254

Independent School Districts 255

State Educational Policy   255

Local School Policies   255

School District Politics   256

Confidence in Public Schools   257

Education Policy Innovation   260

Local Education Policy
Making   262

Chapter Conclusion 263

CHAPTER 12

Metropolitan Government:
Accommodation
and Reform   *267*

The Growth of the Metropolis   268

Technical Change   268

Governmental Factors   269

Cultural Forces   270

The Debate over Metropolitan
Government   271

Advantages of Multiple Local
   Governments   272

Disadvantages of Fragmented Local
   Governments   273

From Fragmentation
   to Coordination   278

Councils of Government   278

Informal Cooperative
   Agreements   279

Interlocal Service
   Agreements   279

The Lakewood Plan   279

Tax-Base Sharing   279

Two-Tier Systems   280

City–County Consolidation   281

Other Options   282

Transportation Policy and Metropolitan
   Areas   284

The Local Government View
   of Transportation   284

The National Government View
   of Transportation   286

Transportation Policy Issues for State
   and Local Governments   286

Chapter Conclusion   287

CHAPTER 13

Local Government Policy:
Decision Making Close
to Home 281

Local Ordinances 292

Code Enforcement 293

Mandated Programs 294

Raising Public Revenues 295

Land-Use Regulation 296

Land-Use Plans   297

Zoning Ordinances   297

Subdivision Regulations   297

Building Codes   298

Housing Codes   298

Eminent Domain   299

Conclusions about Local
   Policy Making 299

Balancing Priorities and Making
   Trade-Offs 300

Development and Preservation 301

Economic-Development
   Strategies   301

Community-Preservation
   Strategies   304

Balancing Development
   and Preservation   306

Public Safety and Social Justice 307

Public Safety Strategies   307

Ensuring Social Justice   309

Mobility and Sprawl 311

Personal Mobility   311

Urban, Suburban, and Exurban
   Sprawl   312

Balancing Mobility
   and Sprawl   312

Excellent Services and
   Modest Taxes 313

Quality Public-Service
   Strategies   313

Keeping Taxes Modest   314

Balancing Service
   and Taxation   315

Chapter Conclusion 315

Appendix
Neighborhood Survey **319**

Glossary 323

Name Index   337

Subject Index   341

Foreword

I am writing this foreword with a great deal of enjoyment and pride. The enjoyment is in seeing the development of an interesting and potentially quite important book in state and local government in the United States. The pride is in the accomplishments of George Cox and Raymond Rosenfeld, both of whom I had the opportunity to teach as graduate students at Emory University. They bring complementary talents and experiences to bear in writing this book and the mixture of their talents has proven quite fruitful.

State and local government in the United States remains too lightly regarded in American political science, condemned to be stereotyped (often along with public administration) as "manhole counting" and unworthy of the arsenal of analytical and methodological tools developed by the discipline. The denigration of this field has been unfortunate for some time but is even more so in the contemporary era. Much of the recent innovation and development in American government has been at the level of the states and their localities. The innovation can be seen in the public policies being adopted, but perhaps even more clearly in terms of changes in public management. No longer are the states and localities following the lead of Washington, but rather practitioners from Washington must move beyond the Beltway to find out what is happening in American government.

Perhaps the most interesting feature of what is a more genuine New Federalism is that the changes in the contemporary era are driven from the bottom up, rather than from the top down. Numerous attempts by Washington to invigorate state and local government have largely failed, but the more recent changes appear successful because there is some autonomous development at these levels of government. Executive and legislative leaders in state and local government have been innovators and entrepreneurs who have reversed, probably forever, the somnolent image of many state capitols.

In addition to changes in leadership, the bottom-up character of the changes has been enhanced by the development of a more active citizenry. Americans may appear to participate little in government when voting alone is considered, but the growth in citizen participation through other means should not be forgotten, especially at the local level. This participation may be directly with government or with nonprofit organizations that become involved in delivering public services, but the public cannot be considered as inert as critics of American democracy might have us believe.

This book captures well the changes that have been occurring in state and local government, including those occurring in the formal components of government. The authors focus a good deal of attention on citizens and their roles in the public sector. The various chapters point out the multiple roles—citizen, consumer, advocate, and so on—played by state and local residents, and they point to the complexity of public action. Although it deals with complexity, the book remains accessible to students and any reader who wants to understand more about the processes of governing beyond Washington.

It has been several decades since George, Raymond, and I were together on the Emory campus. It is very rewarding to see that the friendships developed then—both intellectual and personal—have survived those years and have, in this case, borne considerable fruit.

B. Guy Peters
Maurice Falk Professor
of American Government
University of Pittsburgh

Introduction

Welcome to *State and Local Government: Public Life in America.* Now that your professor has adopted this textbook and used the first part of the title to identify your course subject, we can talk a little about the subtitle, *Public Life in America.* As time goes by, you will develop a public or civic dimension to your personal and professional life. Having taught for twenty years, we have heard about it many times from alumni. We know it is hard for many of you to see that civic aspect of your future now. This is why we are providing this introduction.

Most of your attention is now taken up with your private life. Campus life is full of new friends and new experiences. Your schoolwork seems abstract, and it's hard to see connections between studying and your future. If you work, then it is likely at a "job" that you have taken only for the money that it brings in. On the social, educational, and occupational fronts, it is hard to see what lies ahead after graduation. Let us help you visualize some of the realities that our alumni report; these will be your concerns all too soon.

Let's start with the *occupational aspect of life.* Many of you are training for publicly regulated occupations or professions. State governments regulate many professions to ensure consumer protection, including banking, real estate, public utilities, contracting, building, and insurance. Your state licenses nurses, architects, teachers, pharmacists, veterinarians, speech therapists, psychologists, and many other professionals. Attorneys must be examined, licensed, admitted to the state bar and then required to assume responsibilities as officers of the state courts. In professions such as teaching, there are multiple layers of regulation: national grant guidelines, state department of education regulations, school board rules, and county health and safety codes. Our point is that there is a world of difference between a job and a profession. Professionals have the power to help or harm the public, so state and local regulations and regulators are there to make sure they act responsibly.

Every year, your profession will face the prospect of new laws and regulations. Again, the case of schoolteachers is illustrative. Congress, the state legislature, the city council, the school board, the school superintendent's office, and perhaps others will consider policy issues about your work. The same is true for virtually every profession. Should optometrists be allowed to write prescriptions? Can school nurses treat children who have chronic illnesses? Can builders use new insulation materials to reduce the cost of home construction? New policies are always being proposed. Your profession will have to lobby public officials to make sure that the policies—laws, regulations, and rules—regarding your group are fair and effective. The price of inattention will include considerable inconvenience and lost earnings.

Finally, some of you will be the regulators, not the regulated. Public service is an important and demanding calling. State and local officials must deal with a tremendous range of threats to citizens and the public interest. They also must protect the legitimate interests of corporations and professions. Elected officials, civil servants, and government contractors undergo highly specialized education and training in their areas of specialization. If you are a public official in state, county, or municipal government or in a special district, then you will be under close media attention. Your judgments will resonate or clash with public opinion on issues of the day. The rewards of public service are great, but the demands of these professions are considerable. You will need to be a clever strategist and a lifelong learner to keep up with changing times.

In the *personal sphere of life*, you will face other civic challenges. You will want to own your own home if only because it is an essential tax shelter. If you build or remodel a house or condominium, then you and your contractor will face a host of permitting agencies, codes, building inspectors, and mortgage regulators. Once you move in, you will be concerned that zoning, pollution, noise, and traffic regulations protect your neighborhood or condo development because this home is the largest investment many of us make in a lifetime. If the resale value of your home is diminished, then you are in deep financial trouble.

If you marry, you will need a marriage license. If you have a child, you will get a state birth certificate. When your child goes to school, you will be concerned with immunizations, transportation, curriculum, school safety, and a many other concerns that are regulated by or discharged by public employees. Your family's safety will be in the hands of public police officers, firefighters, and emergency medical staff members. Taxes—income, sales, gasoline, property, and utility—and user fees not only fund worthy services, but also reduce your family wealth. In public life as in private life, you only get what you pay for. The amenities that make your community a pleasant place to live and work depend on you being involved enough in civic affairs to shape the policies and the budgets that will have such huge effects on your life.

There is no place to run and no place to hide. In the real world, you will have many demands in your public life. The only question is whether you will handle these challenges competently or incompetently. If there is one thing that we know after twenty years of talking with alumni, it is the importance of *civic competence*. There are winners and losers in the game of state and local politics. Which one will you be?

Organization of the Book

The chapters are organized in a way that you will get to know some of the people (or players) before seeing how they interact and produce policy results. In this regard, note Chapter 3 on "Capital City Players" and Chapter 8 on "Local Communities" (pages 53 and 161). In addition, every chapter contains boxes that tell real-life stories about community activists, state and local politicians, and innovative public servants. There will be many opportunities in the course to discuss the politically active people in your own state and communities.

The book starts with a general orientation to social and geographic context of state and local government in the United States. We also introduce you to the principles of federalism through which several layers of government share power in this country. We then devote considerable attention to state governments. It is important to first understand how state governments work because local governments depend on their states for many of their powers and programs. Then we look at the various types of local government in the United States. We provide important details on how they work and what issues are being addressed at the local level. The overall plan of the book is to give you solid foundations in both state and local government.

Policy Coverage

We are both policy guys, and every chapter has plenty of policy content. We haven't separated it and put it in the back of the book. You will become practicing professionals and possibly community activists somewhere down the road. Now is a good time to start scanning for threats and opportunities in the policy actions that governments take. Government is a means to achieving shared goals, and your occupation and your family often require public means for addressing your concerns. We all have to learn how to secure the policies that will protect our work and home. We place the policy discussions where we hope they will illustrate government structures and processes. That way, you get two payoffs: You learn policy content and nail down organizational principles.

Value Orientation of the Book

Every textbook has a value base whether or not it acknowledges it. Our book is no exception. Considerable contemporary sociology and social criticism literature are cited in the text. We *believe in* the public life of American states and communities. We are broadly inclusive in the types of civic involvement we survey. We treat interest organizations and civic associations with respect because they and many other social institutions structure our public lives. We are not particularly sympathetic with Americans who want to retreat to secure lifestyle enclaves and write off the broader community. We favor active and involved citizens and creative and determined public officials. We want to declare this "bias" right up front.

Features of the Book

To implement an *active learning approach* to state and local government, we have included features in the book that will help you get to know the state and community where you live. "Exploring on Your Own" is a feature that suggests specific relevant activities outside of class. The activities will help you get the feel of state and local government and improve your ability to visualize the processes we describe in the textbook. The "Collecting Your Thoughts" exercises will help you focus and develop your own ideas. With notes on your clearer ideas, you can be a more effective class participant. Pay attention to the "Elsewhere in the World" features not only because they are interesting, but also because you will work in an internationalized marketplace. These examples of state and local government in other countries will broaden your horizons and help you prepare for a more internationalized future. Yet perhaps the greatest resource you will have in the course is your instructor. He or she tunes into many of the processes we describe. Take advantage of the opportunity that class discussions afford to get the instructor's help with interpreting the book's themes in terms of your *own* state and local governments.

Other Resources

Throughout the textbook, we have identified Web sites of interest. The end of each chapter lists several InfoTrac terms. InfoTrac College Edition offers students four months' free access to this online database of current political events. The Wadsworth Political Science Resource Center includes information on all of Wadsworth's political science texts in fields as wide-ranging as American, comparative, and international politics; constitutional law; and Texas politics. The Resource Center contains information on surfing the Web, links to general political science sites, a career center, news sites, election updates, and a discussion forum. Wadsworth Publishing also maintains a special Web site at <*http://www.wadsworth.com/politics/cox_rosenfeld/index.html*>.

We hope you will use this state and local government course as an opportunity to train for future success. Each chapter is written in a conversational voice, and we have provided links to other resources that you may want to explore. The study of state and local government is not overly abstract or theoretical. State and local officials and the community's civic leaders are right out the door and down the street. Get to know them and broaden your civic competence right here, right now.

Acknowledgments

We greatly appreciate the leaders at Wadsworth Publishing for giving us this splendid opportunity to bring new excitement to the study of state and local government. April Lemons recognized an opportunity when she visited one of our state and local classrooms and saw students having fun. Clark Baxter and Sharon Adams Poore at Wadsworth and S.M. Summerlight of Summerlight Creative schooled us in writing strategies and helped us learn the craft. Both Clark and April have been loyal professional and personal mentors over the life of the project, and we appreciate their unwavering support.

We also acknowledge the time and sincere remarks of the reviewers who helped guide us in revisions of the text: Cynthia J. Bowling, Auburn University; Marvin K. Hoffman, Appalachian State University; Marilyn Howard, Columbus State Community College; Aubrey Jewett, University of Central Florida; Janet B. Johnson, University of Delaware; Quentin Kidd, Christopher Newport University; F. Glenn McNitt, State University of New York at New Paltz; and Samantha Mannion, Housatonic Community College. Without their valuable input, we would not have emerged from the writing process confident of the contributions this textbook provides to student learners.

Special thanks to B. Guy Peters who taught us (and many other political scientists) so much about politics and policy. He encouraged us to take the contract for the book and nurtured us through the rough spots in the writing process. His mentoring of former graduate students is a model for all senior faculty members, and his foreword to the text itself is a pearl of great price.

Good luck with your studies in state and local government. We hope that *State and Local Government: Public Life in America* serves you well. We look forward to getting to know many of you through the Web site and professional conferences. Let us know what you think about the book. Alas, all errors of fact and interpretation in the textbook are our own.

George H. Cox
Savannah, Georgia

Raymond A. Rosenfeld
Ypsilanti, Michigan

The Power of Place: Society, Culture, and Popular Government

- **Constitutions and Sovereignty**
- **The Power and Sense of Place**
- **The People Called "Americans"**
- **Political Culture**
- **Technology and Civic Culture**
- **Chapter Conclusion**

Today, we find ourselves at a political crossroads in the United States. Do we want to be a homogeneous people with global reach, or do we want to be empowered individuals with local clout? Our national identity is strong. We are a prosperous and creative society known and imitated around the world. In many ways, our language, dress, and music are hardwired into a new international culture of middle-class expectations. Mass communications takes "America, Inc." all over the world. If you were to look through the eyes of Europeans, Latin Americans, Africans, or Asians, you would easily recognize an American, even at a distance.

At the same time, we are increasingly focused on our immediate environment. We long for greater control over our careers, our homes, and our neighborhoods. We resist conformity and assert our individual power as professionals, consumers, and citizens. As professionals, we want to have more personal control over our workplaces, our work hours, and the technologies that make us more creative employees. As parents, we want to have more control over school choice, textbook adoptions, teacher evaluations, and disciplinary policies. We join professional organizations and neighborhood associations to make our wishes known beyond our offices and households. Step up to the mirror, and see our individual uniqueness. We can see broad diversity where outsiders see sameness.

This tension between our national identity and subnational identities has powerful political implications. Most Americans want to have a responsible

In this painting by George Catlin, former U.S. President James Madison addresses delegates to Virginia's Constitutional Convention of 1829–30.
Source: Courtesy of the Virginia Historical Society, Richmond, Virginia

national government that can defend our national interests, manage our growing economy, and coordinate national priorities such as technology and space exploration. On the other hand, empowered people expect to be heard and have their wishes respected by local officials and state representatives. Big government within the Washington, D.C., beltway is distrusted, and its budgets are under attack by political conservatives. At the same time, state and local governments are under tremendous pressure to produce more and better services at the lowest possible cost. Neither the national government nor state and local governments can afford to rest on their laurels in these times of high expectations. Do we expect Washington officials whom we dislike and distrust to lead us to new cultural and economic heights? Or do we want more reliable state and local officials to work miracles with strangled powers and ravaged budgets?

This tension between the politics of nation building and the politics of local control is not new. At many points in American history, we have stood at similar crossroads. The national government of the United States of America was constituted by the states in 1787. Their representatives met and drew up a constitution that provides for a central government while stipulating the need for separate state governments. The delegates to the constitutional convention expected to establish and maintain a balance between the overall needs of American citizens and the unique needs and wants of people living in particular states. To help implement this balance, many of the same founders who wrote the national constitution also wrote *state constitutions*. Since that time, every state that has entered the union has done so after writing its own state constitution.

In this chapter, we examine some of the reasons for the development and persistence of subnational government in the United States. Specifically, we look at constitution making as a claim of state sovereignty over a state's land, its people, and ultimately its problems. Then we will explore differences among the states' land and population that have led to differing approaches to government structure and policy. After reading the chapter and exploring some of our suggestions for further research, you will be prepared to evaluate the importance of social and cultural differences in understanding why state and local governments sometimes act decisively to solve their social, economic, and political problems. Prepare yourself to answer questions such as these:

CHAPTER 1 The Power of Place: *Society, Culture, and Popular Government*

- As Americans, are we one people or many different peoples?
- Why has so much attention been given to the debate of national citizenship versus state citizenship?
- What regional differences among the states are state and local politicians working so hard to protect?
- What relevance do subnational governments have in an international, electronic information age?

The answers to these questions are important if we expect Americans' powerful but stressful loyalties to their nation and subnational states and localities to be balanced in the twenty-first century. But first we turn our attention to some basics.

❧ Constitutions and Sovereignty

The United States of America is founded on a few basic principles. One is that "governments are instituted among men, deriving their just powers from the consent of the governed" (Declaration of Independence, 1776). Believing this to be a universal principle, the founders of the United States and the authors of the thirteen state constitutions gathered in representative groups to constitute governments in the name of the people.

Before the American Revolution severed the ties of the thirteen North American colonies and the British Crown, ordinary people were considered to be subjects of their lawful government. The British king ruled his lands and colonies through a gradually eroding doctrine of the divine right of kings (Kantorowitz, 1957). Under this feudal system, the Crown was hereditary, and people were bound to their king by mutual bonds of duties and obligations. If you violated the arrangement, you literally became an "outlaw," a person living outside of the king's protection. So long as you honored your responsibilities, the king would honor your land claims, inheritance rights, and other legal privileges of that system. Granted, the British Parliament was working to restrain the abuse of power by the monarch during the late eighteenth century, but no political rights yet existed beyond those of that slowly reforming feudal system. The king was your sovereign, and he held the claim to control over the land and people within his domain. The not-very-gifted King George III was particularly stubborn about this matter, and it cost him most of Great Britain's North American colonies and eventually the respect of many of his subjects at home.

Take away the sovereign, and where do a country's **sovereignty** claims stand? This was the fundamental question that the founders of the American republic had to address. Some Scottish, English, French, and native-born American theorists held that the basis for sovereignty over a land and its people rested in the will of the people themselves. It was the sovereign right of like-minded people to control their own social, economic, and political destiny. The people constituted their government, not the other way around. They were **citizens,** not subjects. Some theorists saw this as a divine principle and others as a natural law. In either case, people were not meant to be ruled by anyone other than their own representatives on terms other than what they, the people, prescribed. *Constitution writing* therefore was seen as the act of creating a government that would have lawful sovereignty over a country and a people.

Developing a national constitution for the United States presented many practical difficulties. Even though the founders were all middle-aged or elderly white males, they represented different ideologies and different constituencies. A great deal of scholarly attention has been devoted to the political faction that called itself the **Federalists.** Alexander Hamilton and James Madison were among these men who argued for a relatively strong central government. It is fitting that we study these thinkers because they prevailed in establishing a national framework of government we still enjoy. Other prominent thinkers such as Thomas Jefferson and Patrick Henry, however, were deeply suspicious of a strong national government. These **Anti-Federalists** argued for strong state governments and broad personal liberties, sometimes at the expense of the national government. They were concerned about centralized power such as that exercised by the British government over its colonies in North America. They viewed state governments as a popularly accountable counterbalance to the newly formed United States government.

Some of the differences between constitutional convention delegates reflected the sizes of their respective states. States with large land areas and growing populations such as Virginia and New York wanted more power than small-area states such as Delaware and Connecticut. These differences led to famous compromises such as a *bicameral* or two-chambered Congress in which citizens were to be represented by total population in the House of Representatives but the states were to have equal representation in the Senate.

Many other issues divided the founders, including some that arose from the distinctive lifestyles of various states and the growing frontier communities (Rakove, 1996). The people of New England were different from the people of the Southern states in certain important respects. New England's economy was based largely on manufacturing and trade, and its political elite was from a merchant class. The South's economy was based on large-scale agriculture, and its political elite was mostly from landed gentry. New England's elites were critical of the use of slave labor in the South. The Southern elites were afraid of being exploited by cash-rich New Englanders. Both regional elites vied for control of the Western territories that would soon enter the union as sovereign states. Certain compromises thus were reached in this area as well. House seats were apportioned based on population, but only three-fifths of all slaves were counted when the numbers of House seats were determined for slave-holding states (Article I, Section 2).

Even with these compromises, some states, including Virginia, remained reluctant to approve the national constitution. They insisted on a formal Bill of Rights as a condition for their approval. The Bill of Rights could address several specific state worries about the national government, such as the Third Amendment, which prohibited any federal government from housing soldiers in citizens' homes without the citizens' permission. Perhaps the most important amendment for the states was the Tenth: "The powers not delegated to the United States by the Constitution, nor prohibited by it to the States, are reserved to the States respectively, or to the people." This **reserved powers clause** has been a bulwark of states' protections against intrusion by the national government. Even today, federal courts often take note of this constitutional provision when hearing cases that concern national versus states' rights.

Concerns about domination by a national government and economic and social differences among the states persisted long after the founding of the

United States. In fact, the controversy over the rights of the states as opposed to the prerogatives of the national government continues to this day, some of it related to regional differences. Are Westerners different from Easterners? Has the cowboy West disappeared, or do remnants remain? Is there a distinctive New England culture? Is the Southeast the Old South, a New South, or just the Sunbelt? Questions that arise from political geography and its role in our government and politics need our attention.

❧ The Power and Sense of Place

The United States is a vast land. Some Americans feel drawn to the wide open spaces of Nebraska's prairies or Arizona's deserts. Others crave the vistas of Tennessee's mountains or the Oregon shoreline. Many of us feel loyal to the part of the country where we spent our childhood years. Some of us prefer an urban landscape to rural peace and quiet. Whether as college alumni going back for homecoming or retirees eager to return to the land of their youth, many Americans feel place-bound in one sense or another.

This painting by Edward Beyer shows the idyllic landscape surrounding Salem, Virginia, in 1855. Roanoke College stands in the center.
Source: Lora Robins Collection of Virginia Art, Virginia Historical Society, Richmond, Virginia

This *sense of place* is nothing new in American history. Many European colonists came to North America seeking land to farm and the freedom that went with self-sufficiency. A frontier heritage was shaped as Americans moved westward seeking new challenges and opportunities. Native peoples were displaced by Indian resettlement programs and faced new lands with unfamiliar terrain, vegetation, and hunting potential. The national and state governments offered veterans and immigrants generous homestead grants. In virtually all generations, the American landscape has shaped us as we have tried to shape the land.

Regional Cultures

Distinctive state and regional cultures developed as settlers interacted with their environments. "Texicans" were said to view everything in the grand panoramic terms of their cattle herds, while New Englanders were described as thrifty and cautious as they struggled through their long, severe winters. Midwesterners became known for their openness, and the phrase "Southern hospitality" entered the American vocabulary. Stereotyping people based on their region is easy. Nevertheless, both positive and negative personality traits are linked to regional differences in individuals' minds and in our popular culture.

The U.S. Civil War was a watershed for many issues of regional loyalty. When Southern states tried to secede from the Union in 1861, among the divisive issues were slavery or its abolition, regional economic fears, and states' rights. The United States government sought to reclaim the seceding states, and a long and bloody war ensued as Northern and Southern state militias organized themselves into opposing armies. The outcome of the Civil War may have been inevitable, however. The southern tier of states that formed the short-lived Confederate States of America had little other than agriculture to sustain themselves and their troops. The northern tier of states that remained as the United States had not only agriculture but also manufacturing and international trade—and a U.S. Navy to protect shipping and blockade the South. Clearly, the Civil War led to the abolition of slavery and the submission of states' rights to national sovereignty.

After the victory of U.S. forces, the country's attention became more clearly focused on the West. Veterans from both armies traveled there to seek a new life. Former slaves became buffalo soldiers and served in U.S. Army units in the West, as did former Union and Confederate soldiers and recent European immigrants. Gradually, investments in Western ranches, mines, and railroads brought prosperity to many Americans. More and more Americans became workers in an industrial and increasingly urban economy, and mobility became a hallmark of the American worker. We underwent a shift in our perspective of place: from region of the country to urban or rural environment.

Urbanization and Mass Culture

Other shifts in the American concept of place also would take place. Families and individuals moved from rural to urban environments during the first half of the twentieth century. Cities offered industrial jobs and a more cosmopolitan lifestyle. Opportunities dried up in rural areas, and huge migrations to cities such as Chicago sent urban population figures soaring. We will have a great deal more to say about urban politics in later chapters. For now, it is sufficient to note that urban migrations broke down some Americans' regional loyalties.

The urban workforce was more literate, and Americans began to read newspapers, then listen to the radio, then watch television, and then surf the Internet. The products and services that were available to consumers were increasingly national rather than local. A mass culture arose in which Americans in many parts of the United States shared a common lifestyle and a common political outlook. Educational and employment opportunities led more and more Americans to migrate several times within the United States over the course of their lives.

Mobility. In 1990, only 62 percent of all Americans resided in the state in which they were born (see Table 1.1). The range of the native-born state residents varies considerably. In some states, the overwhelming majority of residents were born in-state; in others, fewer than one-third. It thus becomes difficult to generalize about the population's *mobility*. Such mobility and mass culture have added to the breakdown of regional identities, and many Americans now identify themselves more in terms of the cities or metropolitan areas in which they work or live. We often feel less loyal to the states in which we were born or now live—and the two are often different.

Even more recently, suburban vistas have replaced urban ones for some of us. Smaller cities and towns have had a renaissance. Some Fortune 500 com-

Table 1.1
Birth State as Current State of Residence, 1990

Rank	State	Percentage of Current Residents
1	Pennsylvania	80.2
2	Louisiana	79.0
3	Iowa	77.6
4	Kentucky	77.4
5	Mississippi	77.3
*	*	*
*	*	*
*	*	*
46	Wyoming	42.6
47	Arizona	34.2
48	Alaska	34.0
49	Florida	30.5
50	Nevada	21.8

Source: U.S. Bureau of the Census online.

panies have relocated from major metropolitan areas to places where land is cheaper and labor costs are lower. The electronic superhighway has made it possible for white-collar workers to work from home or their cars. This makes the physical sense of place almost irrelevant for these workers, yet they can feel urbane even though they no longer live in urban centers. Media bring the world to us: National and international news, sports, and cultural events are available at the push of a button on the television remote.

Each phenomenon has affected some but not all Americans. For example, the *gentrification* of older urban neighborhoods has brought some suburbanites back into the city. Rural schools have satellite dishes that bring the world into the most remote classroom. In other words, we have many newer senses of place, all of them developing at once. In today's society, we are aware of place but do not feel controlled by it as in years past. As some of us move from place to place, we take our ideas and values with us. We acquire others when we arrive at our new place. So, at the same time that each locale is becoming more diverse, we as individuals are becoming more expansive in our thinking. Most states are therefore experiencing important social and political changes. And the pace of change is accelerating. There are fewer true New Englanders or Southerners or Texans or Californians. The political institutions of the states may govern the same territory as they did twenty-five or fifty years ago, but the human dynamic has made the meaning of place new.

Place as Personal Property

Americans may be more mobile and less place-bound than ever before in our history, but this does not mean we are totally rootless. In fact, we are strongly anchored to our physical environment in the form of property.

People who valued private ownership of property founded the United States. The right to own property means that we claim to have exclusive rights to hold or use a place or thing. Most of us pride ourselves in our clothes, automobiles, home furnishings, and other consumer goods, and home ownership is a goal for most if not all Americans. Whereas *property* in the seventeenth and eighteenth centuries simply meant land to many of America's early settlers, we

Take a few minutes and write down your fondest memories of place and then answer these questions.
1. Where did you grow up? What were your favorite vacations? Did you have good times at summer camp?
2. Now visualize your ideal space as an adult. Are you a mountain or a beach person? Do you like urban excitement or rural peace and quiet? Is weather important or irrelevant to you?
3. If you could live anywhere you wished (and still earn a good living), where would that be?
4. Would you like to work from your home? Or is home a place where you can get away? Is where you live an important part of who you are?
Bring your notes to class for discussion.

now also recognize proprietary claims to our possessions and the fruits of our labors. In fact, today we even talk about "intellectual property rights" when we claim exclusive control over the fruits of our professional creativity.

In the European tradition, property rights are entwined with the notion of liberty (Pipes, 1999). People have liberty to the extent that they are free to come and go, to acquire and to dispose of their property as they see fit. As a core value, private ownership of property gives people security and a sense of freedom in a country where citizens are not place-bound. Throughout our study of state and local government, we will alert you to significant liberty interests that are expressions of the cultural value that we attach to property. Because Americans are a materialistic and acquisitive people, the private ownership of property is a bedrock social value. Its acquisition and enjoyment are part of who we are as a people.

❧ The People Called "Americans"

The United States is home to people from all over the globe. We enjoy Spanish music and Japanese cuisine. African art sits beside Scandinavian furniture. Each of us fills our personal space with the sights and sounds of treasured legacies. We are many diverse peoples, and yet we are all one people: Americans. Our language, art, film, and music express both the rich traditions of our ancestors and the vibrant amalgam of what people all over the world call the "American lifestyle."

Diversity can be interesting and exciting. One advantage that Americans enjoyed when choosing city life was the excitement of varied cultures. We actually could make lifestyle choices about how to dress, where to live, and what to eat. Different friends and work associates brought us tastes of their cultures, and we could share ours with them. At its best, diversity fosters understanding and tolerance. Diverse experiences and tastes, not skyscrapers, make us cosmopolitan.

Diversity also can be divisive, though. Around the world, ethnic and religious conflicts abound. Serious tribal wars rage in central Africa and southern Europe. In the Middle East and in Northern Ireland, ethnic intolerance ravages the countryside. Racially motivated church burnings are the shame of what many Americans consider the New South. Differences may be interpreted as positive or negative, and human beings often fall short of seeing the beauty of our diverse colors, faiths, tongues, and politics. We also often fail to see how our diversity has made us what we are.

Race and Racial Consciousness

Race or *ethnicity* is socially defined. There are many different colors of people in the world, but it is we who describe one group as white (based on skin color), others as African American or Asian American (based on geographic origin), others as American Indian (based on a widely accepted historical misnomer), and yet others as Hispanic (based on culture). These are not only imprecise terms, but also transient descriptions. During this century, Americans of African heritage have been labeled "Negroes," "people of color," "blacks," and now "African Americans." The notion of a Caucasian race was not even fabricated until 1775, and Irish, Italian, Slavic, and other immigrant groups often were considered nonwhites under the laws of some states and national immigration policies (Jacobson, 1998). At any point in time, people share no better than a hazy understanding of what racial terms such as *black* and *white* mean.

Language concerning "mixed race persons" is also part of the American experience. We have been very creative in trying to distinguish the various shades of color in this country (see Table 1.2). Even several categories fail to record, for example, the many subgroups of "mulatto" that have at times been important to some Americans. Old race laws in Mississippi and biting contemporary social commentary in Spike Lee movies attest to the continued American fascination with color.

Table 1.2
Common Racial Terminology

Term	Definition
Caucasian	Eighteenth-century misnomer referring to Russian skull type
white	Shifting description of certain European immigrants
black	Crude skin-tone description of various African groups
mulatto	Mixture of African and European
mestizo	Mixture of American Indian and European
Eurasian	Mixture of European and Asian
Afroasian	Mixture of African and Asian
mixed race	Unspecified mixture (African assumed)

Source: Various sources plus Jacobson (1998).

Overall, Americans are 13 percent African American and 12 percent Hispanic American (as estimated by the U.S. Bureau of the Census for 2000). We are 4 percent Asian American and not quite 1 percent American Indian. Seventy-two percent—almost three-fourths—of all people in the United States are European American. However, these relative proportions are changing. By the year 2050, the United States is projected to have a population that is 15 percent African American, 24 percent Hispanic American, 9 percent Asian American, and 53 percent European American (see Figure 1.1).

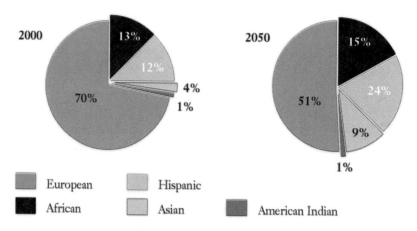

Figure 1.1 Shifting demographics in the United States
Source: U.S. Bureau of the Census

Of course, the ethnic composition of certain states or cities may be quite different from the overall total. Mississippi's population is more than one-third African American, and south Florida has a large Hispanic American population—principally Cuban Americans. In California, roughly one-fourth of all residents are Hispanic Americans. Californians of Hispanic origin come mostly from Mexico, while Florida's Hispanic population results more from immigration from Central America and the Caribbean. Again, vague racial or ethnic labels often mask important cultural details.

Supposedly, observations about ethnic diversity help us understand the different states or cities and their unique cultures. This may be true to a limited extent. For example, many Americans view race and poverty as being closely related. There are many more poor minority neighborhoods than there are poor white neighborhoods. There are states with large welfare populations and states where the numbers are quite small. And we place a racial or ethnic stereotype on poverty in many parts of this country. The profile of poor people, however, is similar when two communities are compared head-to-head.

At the micro—or neighborhood—level, poverty is remarkably similar no matter where it is. A recent study, though, found differences when comparing white slums with African American slums (Mincy, 1997). The unemployment rate experienced by African Americans was 23 percent compared with 14 percent for whites. Thirty-four percent of African American families received welfare, compared with 17 percent of white families. But this does not mean that poverty is a totally different experience for different races in the United States. For example, the percentage of residents in Mincy's two neighborhoods who lived below the poverty line was an identical 53 percent. High school dropout rates were virtually identical: 18 percent for whites and 20 percent for African Americans. Fifty-eight percent of the white men were not in the labor force, while 61 percent of the African American men were outside of the mainstream labor pool. By these criteria, poverty looked remarkably similar.

We hasten to add that the Mincy study compared black and white low-income neighborhoods. He is not suggesting that the *prevalence* of poverty in the United States is the same for blacks and whites. At the macro—or socie-

CHAPTER 1 The Power of Place: *Society, Culture, and Popular Government*

tal—level, we should ask questions about why we have so many more poor minority neighborhoods. Social policies to address this inequality are important in virtually every state and city.

Civic Equality of the Races. Our political system places a high value on the worth and liberty of individuals. That is another basic American principle that was discussed at the nation's founding. We commonly think of civil equality of the races as a product of the civil rights movement of the 1960s, but its roots are much deeper. For many generations, at least some Americans have voiced commitment to the civic equality for all individuals. Some states never countenanced slavery, and some states extended citizenship rights to all free landholders before the Civil War. Of course, many national laws and Supreme Court decisions have been needed to bring the ideal of civil equality anywhere near reality nationwide.

It is not that we as a people don't understand the consequences of racial discrimination for African Americans and other minorities. For two centuries, scholars and social activists have made it clear that having black, yellow, or red skin has serious repercussions in the United States. Abolition did not end discrimination, and neither did outlawing segregation in schools and the workplace. Open-housing laws did not end discrimination, and neither did simply monitoring voter-registration offices. Efforts at freeing the individual from the effects of discrimination have been slow to take effect because it is the group that is the target of racism more so than an individual.

To overcome what one observer has called the problem of the "Two Americas" (Lipset, 1996: 113), we have had to explore "group remedies." Affirmative action, minority contractor set-asides, and other racial preferences are group-level solutions that have been tried in several states. These macrolevel approaches to dealing with racism try to remedy the cumulative ills of the past by facilitating opportunities today. Such remedies have drawn criticism from both European American and African American scholars. Some perceive that racism must be combated at the personal level (e.g., Carter, 1991: 216), and others criticize specific group solutions as unfair "reverse discrimination." This makes the question a lingering political issue in state and local government.

From the perspective of minority group members, the United States may look very different than it looks to majority group members. Race has defined social status and limited economic prospects for many Americans. The African American population of the United States has suffered almost uninterrupted discrimination since the first Africans were brought here as slaves in chains (McClory, 1981: 50–52). In each generation, they have found relatively fewer opportunities than have European Americans or virtually any other racial or ethnic group. For them, skin color has been a life-defining characteristic. (See also **Box 1.1.**)

Social Expressions of Diversity. America has many small cultural enclaves, from Hispanic neighborhoods to African American business districts, where distinctive social customs are followed. Within these enclaves, residents may resist what they perceive to be "outsiders." The African American neighbors of Asian merchants, for example, may feel reluctant to spend their consumer dollars at a "foreigner's" shop. In this way, difference can become divisive "as our nations and neighborhoods [fragment themselves] into smaller and smaller

BOX 1.1 *American Indians Have Their Own Perspective on the Land*

For most of our history, mainstream European American culture ignored or denied the value of Indian culture. Granted, some of our earliest European settlers lived among the Indians and adopted their lifestyle of cooperating with nature. Many more settlers, however, wanted to push Native Americans off their land and take it for their own farming, mining, or development. The United States also has been accused of practicing genocide during some periods of Indian removal and resettlement.

Today, the American Indian Movement (AIM) speaks out on issues that are important to our Indian populations. Some of the viewpoints concern preserving the land, and others relate to Indian rights under treaties and current laws. There is a wide variety of issues on which there is an identifiable and valuable Indian perspective. Learn more about AIM and its particular agenda by visiting its Web site at *<http://www.aimovement.org/>*.

loyalties and clans. And those clans are increasingly sealed off from one another by ethnic and political loyalties of dubious human value" (Price, 1995).

On the other hand, appreciation for diversity is touted in cultural forums and taught in many schools and universities. All cultures contribute to the wealth of our national art, music, sport, literature, and wisdom. There are African American art festivals, Hispanic American music festivals, and Polish American dance festivals. Throughout the United States, community-wide concerts reserve spaces in their programs for jazz, blues, and Tex-Mex tunes.

Such *multiculturalism* is controversial in some sectors of American public opinion and in social commentary. Some media commentators have reported that we are locked in "culture wars." Former Reagan administration official Bill Bennett champions Western (European) civilization and laments what he terms "political correctness" that places all social and political ideas in a relativistic framework (Bennett, 1992: 171–173).

Racial or ethnic identity obviously has its own virtue. Americans who emigrated from Cuba have a culture of which they are justifiably proud. African Americans have succeeded in retracing and rediscovering their African heritage, and that culture too has much of which to be proud. There is more to white racial

Diversity—ethnic, racial, and cultural—is a profound element of modern life in every state.
Source: © SuperStock

pride than genealogy or celebrations of St. Patrick's Day (Irish), Columbus Day (Italian), or Bastille Day (French). The Arcadians of Maine, for example, have a distinctive French American culture that they are working to preserve. And Haitian immigrants in Florida have a different French (or Creole) culture that they enjoy, one that is different still from the French American culture of the Louisiana bayous. So, not only are white subcultures different, but also even distinctive immigrant subcultures are different.

Many Americans identify strongly with their ethnic groups; others do not. A citizen who politically promotes his or her own racial or ethnic group is practicing **identity politics** (Welch, Gruhl, Comer, Rigdon, & Steinman, 1999: 11). Such behavior can be seen in candidate selection, voting, and lobbying activities, and it is increasingly common in American politics. Although understandable, identity politics does raise questions about whether we can define a *public interest* that is broader than particular group interests. Can we support a group's interests based on principles of fairness or justice—even when the benefits do not flow to us personally? Are there occasions when we should rise above and transcend race and ethnicity altogether? Perhaps we can strike a balance between public service and self-service.

Ethnic Strife

News accounts are full of reports of tribal violence in the former Yugoslavia, the former Palestine, Central America, Indonesia, Northern Ireland, and Central Africa. In fact, the post–Cold War political world seems to be dominated by sectarian (religious) and ethnic violence. The United States is remarkably fortunate to have as little violence of these types as we have. That we are all socialized to respect the Constitution and ordinary laws is certainly one reason. In the absence of any such social glue to hold a civil society together, it may fall apart. You and your classmates may want to discuss current world affairs and speculate whether or in what ways the United States is or is not exceptional.

Diversity's Policy Implications

In this age of mass media, preserving cultural identity is no small task. Language is often a key. Should young school children in Maine or Florida or Louisiana be allowed to speak French at school, or should they be "forced" to master and use English? Should teachers in California be encouraged to support African American students' use of Ebonics, the variant of English that incorporates words and expressions from the black experience? And should government conduct its business in Texas and California in Spanish as well as English? Some states have felt so strongly about the issue that they have passed "English-only" statutes. Languages other than English are thus relegated to "foreign" language classes and "harmless cultural events" such as concerts. On one level, the language spoken in the home and neighborhood is an expression of valued cultural diversity. On another level, though, the integration and cohesion of the country may be tied to the common use of a single language—English, in our case.

Immigration and Migration

The population of the country changes as a result of natural increase, or new births, and as a result of immigration, new arrivals to American shores. Internally, regions grow or contract as a result of natural increase, immigration, and migration. These demographic phenomena have important implications for the policy agendas of state and local governments.

The words *immigration* and *migration* sound similar but mean very different things. Immigrants are people who come to this country from overseas, often in search of improved economic conditions and more personal and political liberty. Some obey our immigration and naturalization laws, and others do not and thus enter the United States illegally. In either case, they are new to the American scene. *Migration* refers to the way in which people within the United States move around. In a free society, people are able to move to another state or another city whenever they wish. They may seek better opportunities or simply want a change of scenery.

Since 1990, more than five million persons have immigrated to the United States from other countries around the world (U.S. Bureau of the Census online). These immigrants have settled throughout the country, but some states have been favored over others. In a typical year, more than 200,000 immigrants enter California and more than 150,000 move into New York state (see Table 1.3). This level of immigration strains state and local government services and social programs. How can the state of Florida, for example, provide for the needs of Haitian immigrants while also trying to care for its other residents? This is especially true when state officials have no control over illegal immigration that pressures such states as Florida and California with their large immigrant populations. Sometimes, native resentments of such pressures lead to the passage of public referenda such as the one in California that directed state government to cut off welfare services even for legal immigrants.

Table 1.3
International Immigration by State, 1997

State (Rank)	Number of Immigrants
1. California	203,305
2. New York	123,716
3. Florida	82,318
4. Texas	57,897
5. New Jersey	41,184
6. Illinois	38,128
7. Virginia	19,277
8. Maryland	19,090
9. Washington	18,656
10. Massachusetts	17,317

Source: U.S. Immigration and Naturalization Service.

As people settle into life in the United States, they often migrate from the place where they initially settled to other locations. Perhaps employment prospects are better elsewhere, or maybe they want to relocate where the cost of living is lower. For whatever reason, long-term residents and immigrants alike take their cultures with them in their journeys to new places. This draws our attention to the fact that culture persists and evolves, is concentrated and dispersed, and is place-specific and mobile.

Not all areas of the country grow at the same pace. In fact, some lose population while others gain. In recent years, it has been the southern tier of states from Arizona to Florida, the so-called Sunbelt, that has grown (see Table 1.4). This movement has affected our national character and politics. The migration to the southern tier of states has meant increased prosperity for that region as businesses relocated south. In the South itself, companies could operate at a lower cost because the wages that employees expect are lower than in other regions of the country. The cost of doing business is also lower when it comes to land costs, taxes, and regulation. Some native-born Northern workers have followed the job market south.

Table 1.4
Regional Growth in the United States, 1990–1998

Census Region	Net Change (Millions)
Northeast	+0.85
South	+9.70
Midwest	+3.10
West	+7.20

Source: U.S. Bureau of the Census.

Climate has been another inducement for southward migration. Retirees, sports enthusiasts, and other lifestyle-oriented Americans are interested in warm climates as well as the relatively low cost of living in the South. Their savings or investment income will go further in Southern states than elsewhere in the country.

Culturally, the South has become far more diverse as a result of migration. People of many different ethnic backgrounds now live in that region. In many respects, this migration is like earlier movements of Americans. Once, California or the West Coast more generally was the hot destination. Earlier, people flocked to the Midwest to participate in boom economics. Even earlier, the Northeast held the great promise of success. Population always ebbs and flows. Americans are and always have been on the move. And immigration plus this mobility certainly stirs the ethnic and cultural mix of the country (Elazar, 1994: 253). (See also **Box 1.2.**)

BOX 1.2   *The Bureau of the Census Gathers Demographic Data*

The Constitution of 1787 requires that the nation's population be enumerated, or counted. When the census establishes how many people live in each state, seats in the U.S. House of Representatives can be apportioned to the states based on each one's population. The Bureau of the Census in the U.S. Department of Commerce is the actual agency that conducts the count.

Other national laws have been passed that distribute funds based on population. The size of grants to states and localities for services to elderly citizens are tied to how many older people live in an area. Similarly, housing dollars are tied to the extent and severity of substandard residences in a state or city. The census bureau tries to collect demographic data to address these kinds of informational needs.

Some political figures and some vocal citizens have objected to the number and personal nature of some questions on the 2000 census. They resist the requirement that sampled families who get the "long form"—a more detailed questionnaire—must report personal information, as well as information on their finances and property. The census takers keep all such information strictly private, but some Americans nonetheless do not want to participate. This places census takers and policy makers in a bind because they may not have the information needed to operate valuable programs. Some states and cities may not get the representation and funds to which they are entitled.

Politically, the South has gained considerable influence. Southern states now have more congressional districts and presidential voters than before. Campaign contributions flow more easily from the region. Because many Southerners are socially conservative, the Republican Party has benefited from the growth of congressional seats and increases in presidential voting strength. Many Southern states send predominantly Republican congressional delegations to Washington, D.C., and Republican candidates do well in presidential races. Many Southern states now have Republican governors, and Republicans hold the majority in at least one chamber of most Southern state legislatures.

Americans with different cultures do manage to learn the common civic practices of democracy. We manage to speak English and do business in the mixed capitalist economy of this new century. Somehow, perhaps through our schools, we stay Americans despite our diversity. Sometimes, Americans fear that we are losing our distinctive culture, but those who travel abroad often change their minds. We are surely more alike than we often realize.

Collecting Your Thoughts *Surveying Ethnic Diversity*

Make some notes about the diversity you see around you on campus. Specifically, look around your larger classes at the many different colors of people. Now answer these questions.
1. Can you tell a person's nationality by his or her skin color?
2. Are the foreign students somehow obvious because of their dress or speech?
3. How many states and countries may be represented in your bigger classes? Keep your notes to discuss with classmates in your state and local government class.

❧ Political Culture

Up to this point, we have suggested that historical patterns of settlement and features of the land affect public expectations of government. We have explored the ethnic diversity of the United States and noted the increased mobility that Americans have as they go off to school, change jobs, and retire. In this way, regional differences in social values and political preferences probably will gradually fade away. Distinctive New England or Southern or Midwestern cultures will weaken with the constant arrival of new neighbors and the onslaught of mass media.

Attitudes about public life that develop in one place—for example, country of origin or a specific region of the United States—may be portable. We need a concept that describes people's belief systems in a way that is not tied to a specific place. Here is where the concept of *political culture types* becomes useful. We can then consider the need for government that reflects citizens' cultural values and policy preferences.

Social mores (pronounced "mo-rays") are customs or folkways that develop over time and take on the status of behavior codes or even laws. Segregation of the races was a social more in the South that was reflected in laws that created so-called separate but equal schools for blacks and whites. This system of racial separation was practiced from the 1940s through the 1960s in the Southern states and was much like the late apartheid laws in South Africa. Because we take **politics** to be the means and processes by which societal decisions are made and carried out (Plano & Greenberg, 1997: 100), **political culture** is the set of mores that shapes the laws and lawmaking in a state or locale.

The most often-utilized political culture types originated in the study of political geography. Regional differences in political attitudes were noted for the South, New England, the Midwest, and so on. Daniel Elazar was probably the most famous contemporary scholar who studied political culture types in the United States. He argued that "each subculture is strongly tied to specific sections of the country, reflecting the streams and currents of migration that have carried people of different origins and backgrounds across the continent in more or less orderly patterns" (Elazar, 1984: 115). The most common political cultures are the traditionalistic, the individualistic, and the moralistic.

Elazar's *traditionalistic political culture* is rooted in the nation's agricultural history. In the eighteenth century, land was the measure of value, social standing, and political power. In this type of political culture, social relationships are stratified—that is, a class system has developed. The wealthy, landed gentry rule over the propertyless classes. They perceive that making political decisions is *noblesse oblige* (literally, a noble's obligation) for the upper social classes. Passivity is all that remains for the lower classes.

Traditionalistic political cultures developed mostly in the South, where large-scale agriculture dominated the economy. Slavery was a widespread practice, and tenant farming kept poor farmworkers, both black and white, tied to the land after abolition. Education was reserved for the sons and daughters of plantation owners and perhaps their cousins who lived in such Southern seaport cities as Charleston, South Carolina; Savannah, Georgia; and New Orleans, Louisiana. Politics was the occupation of the gentry, and its members ran things to suit their interests. Government was small and unobtrusive, taxes were low, and conservative social values were rigidly enforced.

The social mores of this Southern agricultural society persisted for many generations. As time went on, fewer people lived in rural areas, but the social mores of class structure and segregation persisted. Urban businessmen were willing to overcome their *nouveau riche* (that is, newly rich) reputations and take their place among the educated and privileged elite. Poorer people who remained on the land or who worked for wages either were kept out of politics or became pawns of political bosses who could control their votes.

Traditionalistic values are *conservative* in the sense that they try to preserve the virtues of the past along with the privileges of those on top of the social pyramid. For example, harsh prison sentences are more likely for crimes committed in states dominated by traditionalistic political culture (Cox, 1984: 12). When the civil rights movement came to the South, researchers found that welfare benefits were lower and social service programs for the poor were weaker in states with this type of political culture (Dawson & Robinson, 1963). Public policy reinforced the social system.

Individualistic political cultures are quite different. These political cultures are common to the mid-Atlantic states and the Midwest. The history of settlement in the mid-Atlantic states of Maryland, Pennsylvania, and New Jersey is quite different from that of Virginia, Georgia, and Tennessee. The former have always favored commerce, and their political culture is that of the entrepreneur. In individualistic political cultures, capitalism reigns. The seaboard states developed mores that supported the acquisition and investment of capital, and settlers took these values with them when they migrated to the Midwest.

Under capitalism, people can create their own futures. The individual is valued as the potential inventive genius or marketing guru who may be rich and powerful tomorrow. In the individualistic political culture, every consideration is given to personal initiative, and class distinctions are relatively unimportant. It's "what you know," not "who you know" in the individualistic political culture. Citizens in these states would consider traditionalists from the South as archaic remnants of a bygone era.

Government in the individualistic political culture states often operates through contracts. If the state wants something done, it is likely to contract for the service with a private corporation. Taxes are viewed as incentives more than obligations, and the tax structure is expected to support individual initiative and achievement. To follow our previous examples, prison use would be selective because it is expensive; private providers might develop a wide range of community supervision alternatives. Welfare would look more like workfare, and every effort would be made to keep social service bureaucracies to a minimum.

Social relations in the individualistic political culture are far more democratic than in the traditionalistic political culture. The economic system is much more open to achievers regardless of ethnicity or immigrant status. The common faith is that the system works, so there is relatively little perceived need for government intervention on behalf of people in need. The marketplace of buyers and sellers and the marketplace of inventive new ideas will sustain the society.

People who grow up and live in *moralistic political culture* states do not share that faith in market forces. The moralistic political culture is found in the upper Midwestern states of Minnesota, Wisconsin, and Iowa and in much of the Pacific West. Immigrants from northern Europe, especially Scandinavia, settled the Midwest, and subsequent migrations took the culture west. In the moralistic political culture, government has a positive obligation to help people develop. Most people want to achieve, and government should be optimistic and proactive. A *commonwealth* of interests binds citizens together in broad social enterprises. To the moralistic American, we all are in one boat together. We sink or survive by virtue of our commitments to each other.

Moralistic political cultures tend to develop liberal social policies. Government is large, and taxes are high. If you want to achieve broad social goals, then you have to spend money. Crime is a symptom of social ills that need to be addressed. Every effort should be made to prevent crime and rehabilitate offenders in community-based programs. Those prisons that are necessary should be clean and stress the rehabilitation of the offender. Welfare payments should be compassionate and try to address families' real needs. Where work is required, training and childcare should be provided. Government has a positive obligation to help people lift themselves out of poverty.

Moralistic political cultures promote values that most Americans would consider activist. The mores of these communities are very civic-minded, and the level of volunteer participation in community-improvement projects is quite high. States with moralistic political cultures do not simply and unthinkingly spend more money. They also marshal citizen action to combat social problems, and they sincerely expect social problems to improve in response to efforts to make life better for everyone.

Few states have a pure political culture of one type or another. The typical state might have a dominant political culture that is one type or a hybrid of two types with one being dominant. This is sometimes expressed at the substate level where enclaves of political culture exist that are different from the overall dominant state pattern. For example, in the 1980s, Florida was a state with a strong traditionalistic political culture, especially in north Florida. Individualistic political culture was found as a secondary trait in central and coastal areas of the state, and the Miami area was actually dominated by moralistic political culture with a secondary individualistic influence.

Obviously, not all states are *homogenous*. As migrations bring new people into a state, the political culture stirs in a new mix of people with different values and policy preferences. Nevertheless, political scientists who try to explain policy variations in the states stress the importance of political culture for state politics and policy. Researchers have found that differences in political cultures explain much of the variation around the country in policies from crime control to welfare reform. Levels of political participation vary by region and by political culture zone within regions. For this reason, many state and local government researchers in the United States study Daniel Elazar's work.

⮞ Technology and Civic Culture

We have noted the importance of mass media in breaking down regional differences in the values and politics. Other obvious connections between our increasingly national character and technology include the automobile, which has transformed our landscape and revolutionized our sense of personal liberty (Kay, 1997), and the World Wide Web or Internet, which allows us to explore the world from our desktop computer. Throughout our history, Americans have been fascinated with the technology that could give us more control over our future.

No one loves drudgery. We are always exploring new and better ways of getting things done. We Americans love our stylish automobiles and fast home computers. To the extent we can use science and mechanical genius in producing new technology, we will have more effective work and more lavish free time activities to enjoy. For many Americans, both our quality of life and our personality as Americans are linked to our enthusiasm for technology.

Technology and Generational Change

It is important to realize that each generation has had its powerful technologies. In the eighteenth century, for example, when the continent was being settled, the rifle replaced the musket. This technological breakthrough involved creating grooves within the barrel of the gun. The bullet would spin in a way that made its flight more predictable and accurate, and the round, tumbling musket ball was a thing of the past. Hunters could now kill game from much longer distances.

Nineteenth-century agricultural economy benefited tremendously from technology. Inventions that made planting and harvesting of crops easier became available every few years. Cyrus McCormick, for example, invented the reaper that bears his name. Manufacturing technology then sprang up in cities to meet the demand for each new agricultural device. Those industries in turn required machine tools. At every level of the U.S. economy, technology was shaping the economy as far back as two hundred years ago.

Our modern highways link millions of people in ways that previous generations could not have imagined. Here the freeways of Denver, Colorado, connect downtown and the deep suburbs in just minutes.
Source: © SuperStock

In the twentieth century, we built on the technological foundations of the past. Transportation in particular proved critically important in the development of the U.S. economy. The railroads linked agricultural and ranching centers with the heavily populated East. Trolleys and subways allowed people to move about in our congested cities. The automobile further revolutionized American culture. With urban streets and rural highways, Americans could move about freely. And behind each transportation breakthrough stood layers of manufacturing industries. (See also **Box 1.3**.)

Late in the twentieth century, telecommunications and the computer ushered in what became known as the Information Age. Telephone technologies, especially cellular telephones, now allow instantaneous voice and data communication. Television and its cable and satellite offspring make sharing images with sound equally immediate. The continent and indeed the world have become much smaller places in the wake of this revolution in information technologies. We each now have the world at our fingertips.

We always have been a technologically creative people. In the frontier-settlement period, we were interested in better guns, traps, and plows. During the taming of the land, we constantly invented new agricultural tools and machinery. In urban life, central heat and elevators made indoor living more comfortable, and cable cars and streetlights made outdoor life more conven-

CHAPTER 1 The Power of Place: *Society, Culture, and Popular Government*

NASA has proposed a new kind of transportation that can help solve problems of air-traffic congestion, travel delays, and wasted commuting time. The Smart Air Transport System (SATS) envisions a new generation of small, economical aircraft that can land at the 5,400 public-use airports in the United States that are underused. If these small airports were equipped with all-weather traffic-control devices, then travelers would be able to avoid the current air-transport network of seventy huge airports that serve as national hubs and 410 regional airports.

Such a system would also help travelers avoid congested and overused interstate highways. Thus, taxi jets could take vacationers and business travelers directly to specific destinations in less time than it would take to drive. These new aircraft would be quiet, efficient machines that also could deliver cargo, emergency teams, and perishable medical supplies to virtually any community in the United States.

Frederick Hansen has written about the potential for this SATS technology in the March 2000 issue of *PA Times*, a publication of the American Society for Public Administration. See also NASA at *<http://sats.nasa.gov>* and *<http://www.unomaha.edu/~unoai/sats>*.

ient. And nothing changed our lifestyles as much in the twentieth century as the personal automobile and then the personal computer.

Technology and the Individual

Technology assumes a knowledge base. The sciences of physics, geology, and chemistry inform construction technology and this in turn underpins much of what is taught in architecture schools. Certain people are drawn to the foundation sciences, others are interested in technological invention, and yet others want to apply the knowledge to everyday life. The flowering of technological economies brings with it the ascendancy of knowledge and learning.

One consequence of the value placed on knowledge has been the relatively equal access it offers both genders and people of different ethnic groups. A first-rate architect can be a European American male or an African American female. Technology, in effect, is a new frontier in and of itself (Elazar, 1994: 93). Brainpower is what drives the U.S. and indeed the world economy. And a talent for invention has never been more prized than it is today.

However, knowledge and talent are not equally distributed across the entire population. Just as we have the technologically able, we also have the technical-

Exploring on Your Own   Diverse Views and Web Browsing

Go to our Web site—*<http://www.wadsworth.com/politics/cox_rosenfeld/index.html>*—to find links to several of today's "empowered voices" that are available to you through Web technology. You will find a link to the American Indian Movement (AIM), an independent voice of activists from many American Indian tribes. Our site also offers a link to River Watch, a program that works with the Illinois state government to monitor river water quality in that state. You may find many other voices on the Web. Simply use a Web search engine to locate groups by key words that describe the issues in which you are interested: civil rights, immigration laws, and so on. We do not endorse any one particular group or any particular side of an issue. We invite you to explore the diversity of ideas on your own.

ly ignorant. In the workplace where information technology plays a major role, what do the computer-illiterate do? This leads to the larger question of whether we are becoming economically two Americas within the United States (Reich, 1991: 208). Even our fabled technology is a double-edged sword.

Yet another effect of U.S. technological development has been the proliferation of relationships (Gergen, 1991: 49). From approximately 1850 to 1950, the nation witnessed the invention or popular use of the railroad, postal service, print media of all types, buses and automobiles, the telegraph and the telephone, and motion pictures, radio, and television. All of these technological advances brought social change. People had more and varied relationships. Much more time was spent interacting with others and less time spent alone.

One would think that technology would make people feel happier and more secure. By the 1950s, many Americans had everything they ever dreamed they could want: automobiles, nice houses, and many of the labor-saving appliances we enjoy today. Yet there was widespread anxiety and discontent among the American middle class (Ehrenreich, 1989: 30). Contemporary Americans experience needs and longings that do not have technological fixes. In fact, the technology we so treasure may have made our expectations of life unreal.

Enjoying Leisure Life

The opening lines of the seminal study of American character, *Habits of the Heart*, reads "Living well is a challenge" (Bellah, Madsen, Sullivan, Swindler, & Tipton, 1985: 3). As Americans, we aspire to work shorter hours and earn higher pay and thus explore the finer things of life. We want to vacation in the Caribbean and play golf on the weekends. There is nightlife for the gregarious and robust cable or satellite television for the sedentary. We are entering an era in which recreation and entertainment are major growth industries.

In each preceding century, labor-saving technology has offered relief from constant work. Fewer pioneers died of attacks by wild animals after efficient rifles were invented. Farmers wore out their bodies less with the introduction of agricultural technology. The time required to get from one place to another decreased with modern transportation forms. And today, one office worker can do the tasks that would have taken many employees to accomplish a few short decades ago. Simply put, work may consume less of our energy and time—if we keep it within reasonable parameters.

One good use of the freed time is *civic involvement*. Contrary to popular belief, Americans volunteer more of their time than do the citizens of most other industrialized democracies. Sixty percent of all Americans perform voluntary service in their communities compared to 47 percent of all Canadians, 35 percent of the French, 26 percent of the British, and 27 percent of the Japanese (Lipset, 1996: 279). For some citizens, volunteer service may be with the local Red Cross; for others, it may be with their children's Little League. Overall, technology frees up time, and Americans choose to invest at least some of it in civic life.

Technology's Effect on Place, Time, and Culture

The Information Age is changing us in ways we are only beginning to appreciate. Television is spreading a mass culture throughout the United States and even around the world. Computer literacy and access to the World Wide Web are providing vast stores of information to more and more people. Virtual reality in cyberspace makes it possible for engineers to thoroughly test machines that have not yet even been built. Political pollsters can work overnight and tell us what we think about an issue when their sample data were collected only yesterday. The list goes on and on.

The effects of the Information Age's mass culture on localized cultures throughout the United States include everything from more uniform fashions to common expectations about year-round schooling. The great public opinion and advertising industries try to shape our values and preferences using ever more subtle media. It leads one to ask, is our culture being homogenized?

On the other hand, low-cost but high-powered computer and communications technology can give voice to segments of the population that have been drowned out by media in the past (Lappé & DuBois, 1994). For example, gay rights advocates can sponsor home pages, Christian fundamentalists can respond with computerized mailings, and each state's political parties can survey public opinion to see how members should vote on same-sex marriage legislation. Neighborhood associations, environmental groups, and consumer associations can have their own small-scale but high-quality technologies—that get better and cheaper all the time.

If some technology forms tend to homogenize our culture while others give an ever-greater voice to diverse subcultures, then it is hard to generalize about where our fascination with technology is taking us. Perhaps we are taking the technology and using it for our own ends. The possibility that sophisticated technology *may* enslave us does not mean that it *will*. From a political perspective, we might benefit from seeing it as a form of empowerment. There is power in the slick advertising of candidates and issues, but there also is power in being aware of the sales pitch and feeling able to resist or even answer it. Americans are notorious channel surfers! Passivity has always led to victimization. Taking charge of our lives means taking charge of our technologies. If we can combine our technological competence with our civic impulses, we can accomplish great things in politics, economics, and societal relations.

❧ Chapter Conclusion

In this chapter, you have read about how states and the nation exercise constitutional sovereignty over their lands and people. However, in a democratic society, it is the people who should shape government policy, not an isolated political elite. Our representative form of democratic government provides for the representation of a wide variety of interests. We have examined just a few.

- Our sense of place leads us to treasure the ecological uniqueness of the land where we live, work, and recreate. Each state and city can be expected to have its own environmental issues and policies.

- Our diverse ethnicity raises issues in human relations that are specific to particular areas of the country. Long-standing issues of racial equality, immigrant rights and responsibilities, and shifting internal migration suggest different policies for different states and cities.

- Political culture has become mobile and is evolving into many hybrid subcultures that have spread throughout the United States. Policy preferences of the past are challenged as each state and city becomes more and more of a blended culture of old and new residents.

- Technological change at an ever-increasing pace brings possibilities of a more homogenized culture and more empowered diverse voices. Depending on the locale and the issue, policy may be shaped by efforts at spin control and efforts to give equal time to differing viewpoints.

Specific government policies and programs are subject to the shifting population, culture, and technology. You have read about how English as the official language has become an issue in states with high immigration levels. You may have noted how state social service policies consider immigrants' rights and responsibilities, and how specific political cultures favor different solutions to crime control. The level of welfare benefits also depends on a state's political culture. In other words, social policies reflect the preferences and sometimes the prejudices of the society that makes them.

Of course, our federal system has checks and balances that keep states and cities from being excessive. That is the theme of our next chapter. Nevertheless, the best way to understand the great variety of state and local policies is to start by appreciating the diversity of places and people that make up American society. We are many different peoples, and we are one people. At its best, providing for powerful subnational governments—state and local governments in our system—allows for diversity within unity.

Key Words for InfoTrac Exploration

civic involvement   political culture   racially mixed people   urbanization
multiculturalism

Sources Cited

Bellah, Robert N., Richard Madsen, William M. Sullivan, Ann Swindler, and Stephen M. Tipton (1985). *Habits of the Heart: Individualism and Commitment in American Life.* Berkeley: University of California Press.

Bennett, William J. (1992). *The De-Valuing of America: The Fight for Our Culture and Our Children.* New York: Simon & Schuster.

Carter, Stephen L. (1991). *Reflections of an Affirmative Action Baby.* New York: HarperCollins.

Cox, George H. (1984). "Values, Culture, and Prison Policy." *The Prison Journal, 64*(2) (Fall–Winter): 5–15.

Dawson, Richard E., and James A. Robinson (1963). "Inter-Party Competition, Economic Variables, and Welfare Policies in the American States." *Journal of Politics, 25:* 265–289.

Ehrenreich, Barbara (1989). *Fear of Falling: The Inner Life of the Middle Class.* New York: Pantheon.

Elazar, Daniel (1984). *American Federalism: A View From the States* (3rd ed.). New York: Harper & Row.

——— (1994). *The American Mosaic: The Impact of Space, Time and Culture on American Politics.* Boulder, CO: Westview Press.

Gergen, Kenneth J. (1991). *The Saturated Self: Dilemmas of Identity in Contemporary Life.* New York: HarperCollins.

Hansen, Frederick D. (2000). "Congestion, Rage, and Modern Transportation." *PA Times 23*(3) (March): 3.

Jacobson, Matthew Frye (1998). *Whiteness of a Different Color: European Immigrants and the Alchemy of Race.* Cambridge, MA: Harvard University Press.

Kantorowitz, Ernst H. (1957). *The King's Two Bodies: A Study in Medieval Political Theology.* Princeton, NJ: Princeton University Press.

Kay, Jane Holtz (1997). *Asphalt Nation: How the Automobile Took Over America and How We Can Take It Back.* New York: Crown.

Lappé, Frances M., and Paul M. DuBois (1994). *The Quickening of America: Rebuilding Our Nation, Remaking Our Lives.* San Francisco: Jossey-Bass.

Lipset, Seymour Martin (1996). *American Exceptionalism: A Double-Edged Sword.* New York: W.W. Norton.

McClory, Robert J. (1981). *Racism in America: From Milk and Honey to Ham and Eggs.* Chicago: Fides/Claretian.

Mincy, Ronald (1997). "Methodology and Policy." In Thomas D. Boston (Ed.), *A Different Vision. Volume 2—Race and Public Policy.* New York: Routledge.

Pipes, Richard (1999). *Property and Freedom: The Story of How Through the Centuries Private Ownership Has Promoted Liberty and the Rule of Law.* New York: Alfred A. Knopf.

Price, Reynolds (1995). "Introduction." In Toni Morrison, *Song of Solomon.* New York: Alfred A. Knopf.

Rakove, Jack N. (1996). *Original Meanings: Politics and Ideas in the Making of the Constitution.* New York: Random House (Vintage).

Reich, Robert B. (1991). *The Work of Nations: Preparing Ourselves for 21st Century Capitalism.* New York: Alfred A. Knopf.

Welch, Susan, John Gruhl, John Comer, Susan M. Rigdon, and Michael Steinman (1999). *American Government* (7th ed.). Belmont, CA: Wadsworth.

Power Sharing in a Federal System: Theoretical and Practical Balance

✢ **Constitutional Federalism**

✢ **Programmatic Federalism**

✢ **Issues in Federalism**

✢ **Local Government Home Rule**

✢ **Chapter Conclusion**

The features of the American land, the characteristics of its people, and new technologies shape this society and its institutions. Political institutions—the structure and powers of government—are likewise shaped by state constitutions and the national constitution. As we noted in Chapter 1, the legitimacy of government at both levels is linked to popular sovereignty. Public representatives draft constitutions, and the public approves them in referenda. The variety of state constitutions and laws enacted under them reflect the variety of public values and policy preferences across the United States. But basic questions arise about the balance of power between the national government and the fifty state governments:

- Are the states constitutionally free to enact any laws they choose?
- Have the states and the federal government worked out a division of labor in which each specializes in certain kinds of policy and takes different roles in implementing programs?
- Are there legitimate duties and prerogatives reserved to local governments in the United States?

These questions require that we look more closely at the U.S. Constitution, especially its Tenth Amendment, the provision that reserves broad political powers to the states and the people. That amendment and U.S. Supreme Court's decisions about its meaning define the balance of power between the states and the national government in the United States.

❧ Constitutional Federalism

During the American Revolution, the states collaborated in fomenting a rebellion. In 1776, they issued a joint Declaration of Independence from Great Britain. The rebellious states sent their representatives to a conference, or congress, that could make policy on their behalf. They needed to stick together—to be the *united* states—if they were to win the war of national liberation against the British Empire's global reach and power.

A Confederation of States

The first document that the delegates wrote called for a confederation. A **confederation** is a league of independent states. A central government's only power is to coordinate those activities that its member states delegate to it (Plano & Greenberg, 1997: 34). Such confederacies exist even now. This format for government was not intellectually revolutionary.

The states called their pact the Articles of Confederation and Perpetual Union. The pact severely limited the role of the central government:

> Each state retains its sovereignty, freedom, and independence, and every power, jurisdiction, and right, which is not by this Confederation expressly delegated to the United States, in Congress assembled. The said states hereby severally enter into a firm league of friendship with each other, for their common defense, the security of their liberties, and their mutual and general welfare, binding themselves to assist each other, against all force offered to, or attacks made upon them, or any of them, on account of religion, sovereignty, trade, or any other pretense whatever. (Articles II and III)

The states would cooperate under the terms of the articles, and they initially believed that such an agreement would be adequate for their long-term needs—that is, as a "perpetual union." The delegates to the convention who drafted the confederation and union articles did not want a stronger form of association, fearing that it would threaten each state's rights.

The Articles of Confederation and Perpetual Union were prepared in 1776 but not approved by all thirteen states until 1781. The United States then operated under an officially confederated system for eight years: 1781 to 1789. Under the Articles, each state had one representative in a single-chamber legislative body. The confederation had neither an independent executive nor a national judiciary. The approval of nine states was required for the national government to exercise any of its limited powers. The national government had no taxing power, and it could not apply its laws directly to citizens without state action to implement its decisions. Amendments to the pact required a unanimous vote. Obviously, the "United States" had an extremely minimal and weak government when they operated as a confederation.

A More Perfect National Union

A new constitution was drafted in 1787 and approved two years later. This new pact created a limited but more viable national government: It had the powers to tax and otherwise directly regulate the behavior of U.S. citizens. Certain powers were given to the national government—making treaties and waging war, organizing a postal system and a common currency, and managing interstate commerce—to strengthen the union so that it could withstand any future attempt by European powers to control North America. According to many

CHAPTER 2   Power Sharing in a Federal System: *Theoretical and Practical Balance* scholars, *dual sovereignty* existed under which both the national government and the state governments had unique powers and responsibilities.

Several of the powers of the new United States government were simple responsibilities that could only be accomplished by a national government. The states occasionally had border disputes, and these were to be settled by a United States Supreme Court (Article III, Section 2). As noted, the national government would coin money, regulate interstate commerce, operate a postal system, and regulate trade with foreign countries and the Indian nations.

The states cooperated in letting the fledgling national government get on its feet. They were all too aware that commerce had to function and the country had to be defended. It was in their interest to let a group of experienced political leaders attend to national concerns while state leaders got on with the responsibilities of everyday government. After all, the states still enjoyed a special status under the Constitution of 1787. They retained their state constitutions and managed most of the daily business of government.

As a practical matter, more and more states were entering the Union (see **Table 2.1**). As they did so, certain pressing matters demanded the attention of state political leaders. Harbors, roads, and bridges had to be built and maintained. Criminal and civil law had to be established along with a system of ordinary courts. Public health regulations had to be established to protect the citizenry from pestilence. Compared with these pressing and practical obligations, a national government's more distant and vague concerns seemed remote.

Table 2.1
The "Second Thirteen" States of the Union

State	Year Entered Union
14. Vermont	1791
15. Kentucky	1792
16. Tennessee	1796
17. Ohio	1803
18. Louisiana	1812
19. Indiana	1816
20. Mississippi	1817
21. Illinois	1818
22. Alabama	1819
23. Maine	1820
24. Missouri	1821
25. Arkansas	1836
26. Michigan	1837

Source: Compiled from *The World Almanac, 2000:* 566.

The authors of the new Constitution of 1787 envisioned a federated or **federal government,** one in which the people act on their popular sovereignty by establishing both national and subnational, or state, governments. Both types of government are supreme in their own "proper sphere of authority" (Plano & Greenberg, 1997: 40). Federal governments require a compromise on the question of citizen loyalties. Citizens are free to identify with their own regions while still being loyal to a national union of states. Federal systems are found around the world today: Canada, Mexico, Switzerland, Germany, Australia, and India are good examples. The United States is somewhat different from other modern federal republics in that states' authority is not delegated by or derived from the national government. Instead, the authority for each level of government is constitutionally fixed in the Constitution of 1787's Tenth Amendment.

A review of state constitutions completed in 1989 concluded that these documents balance the national constitution, and they reflect important independent polities or political units within the country (Advisory Commission on Intergovernmental Relations, 1989). In one sense, the study of state and local government is the study of the practice of self-government under these fifty distinctive state constitutions. Many Americans are unaware of the governmental innovations and citizenship rights included in these state documents.

Historically, the states have cited *sovereignty claims* when it suited their purposes. The Southern states argued that they were free to practice slavery because the national Constitution had not prohibited it and they enjoyed considerable reserved powers (Tenth Amendment). Their critics would answer that the Constitution claims for itself the right to be the *supreme law of the land* (Article VI). Issues such as slavery finally led seventy years later to the American Civil War, which resolved some of the most strident arguments between state sovereignty and national sovereignty proponents. However, the power of culture and the constitutional argument concerning dual sovereignty persisted long after the Civil War.

During the twentieth century, we had cycles of centralization and then state or local government autonomy. These swings in the federal–state relationship reflected the constitutional thinking and powerful policy issues of their times. The national government was strong during the Civil War, the Great Depression, and the Cold War. The state governments were strong in the periods between these grand national emergencies. Despite sometimes being disappointed by state governments' provincialism on issues such as civil rights, many Americans remain protective of the powers of their state and local self-governments.

Judicial Interpretation

Practically, federalism is whatever the U.S. Supreme Court says it is. The Constitution is a general document, and much of what it means depends on the specific justices who sit on the U.S. Supreme Court. Presidents appoint justices to the Court, and those justices appointed by our more conservative presidents often have strongly asserted states' rights views. Gradually, a given group of justices on the Supreme Court can hand down many decisions about state and national government authority that are sufficient to establish a clear "law of the land." The resulting *judicial doctrine* holds until changing national priorities and changing Court membership reinterpret federalism some other way. Lesser federal judges tend to follow the Supreme Court's lead in handing down their own decisions—and state and local courts *must* do so.

Justices who take a narrow and literal view of the powers of the national government are typically called **strict constructionists,** and those who treat the Constitution as a living and evolving document are often termed **judicial activists.** States tend to consolidate more power when strict constructionists are on the bench. State authority tends to erode when activist judges seek to apply new national rights or broaden national powers to policy terrain that has heretofore been the province of state and local governments.

The current Supreme Court has made clear its views on American federalism. Chief Justice William Rehnquist, a strict constructionist, leads the Court majority. In many 5–4 decisions that have covered different policy areas, the Rehnquist court has articulated its states' rights rationale.

The Commerce Clause. During the era of U.S. civil rights legislation—roughly 1955 to 1975—the Supreme Court allowed a broad interpretation of the U.S. Constitution's **commerce clause** (Article I, Section 8). Federal authorities reasoned that interfering with a person's freedom of movement was a constraint of free commerce. Segregated bus, train, and airport terminals were therefore illegal because local customs were intruding on the constitutionally protected rights of all American citizens. A similar line of reasoning could be argued for discrimination in banking and credit. As we are about to see, other applications of the commerce clause were more of a reach. Education and housing are primarily state and local matters, but no one in Congress or the White House wanted to slow the progress that was being made in extending full civil rights to all citizens.

U.S. Supreme Court Chief Justice William H. Rehnquist leads a court that now includes two female associate justices, Ruth Bader Ginsburg (left) and Sandra Day O'Connor.
Source: © Corbis Sygma

In the Gun Free School Zone Act of 1990, the national government made taking a firearm onto school property a crime. A Texas youth did so anyway, and he was arrested and convicted under the new law. His attorneys appealed the conviction, arguing that the federal government had no authority over schools. The states operate public education, and the reserved powers clause suggests that state control over schools is consistent with "the intent of the framers." The attorneys for the federal government responded that the Gun Free School Zone Act was a valid application of the commerce clause. In other words, the clause that had been invoked so successfully to cover federal intervention in cases of Southern racial segregation also might extend into other areas. Not so, said the Supreme Court. Schooling is *not* interstate commerce, and thus the Court declared the Gun Free School Zone Act unconstitutional. Texas and other states, of course, are free to pass their own state laws prohibiting firearms on school property.

The majority of Supreme Court justices used the same reasoning in May 2000 when they ruled that provisions of the 1994 Violence Against Women Act are unconstitutional. Gender-based violence may be a social ill that everyone wants to correct—for example, thirty-seven state attorneys general support the law—but assault is not commerce. States alone have jurisdiction in such criminal justice matters.

Associate Supreme Court Justice Antonin Scalia is particularly straightforward about his views on the U.S. Constitution. He explicitly rejects the proposition that it is a living document. "The Constitution does not change in its meaning. What it approved back in 1789, or 1791 if talking about the Bill of Rights, it approves of now. What it forbade then, it forbids now." He calls himself an *originalist* rather than a strict constructionist. When asked about the evolution of social issues, he responds, "How come societies only mature—they never rot?" (quoted in Labbe, 2000).

Reserved Powers. Congress passed the Brady Handgun Control Act in an effort to control convicted felons' access to firearms. The law requires a background check of anyone trying to buy handguns and declares that local law enforcement officers will conduct the check until such time as a national database is available to screen prospective handgun buyers.

A sheriff in New Mexico and other law enforcement officials complained that they did not have the resources to complete a background check and that the federal government had no authority to compel them to do so. In 1997, one Brady Act provision—which required local officials to complete a task without being provided the federal funds to pay for the task—was stricken. This type of "unfunded mandate" has long been a sore point with state and local officials, and the Rehnquist Court drew another line to restrict federal domination of the states.

The Religious Freedom Restoration Act (RFRA) was passed in 1993, and the Supreme Court struck down portions of it in 1997 after the city of Boerne, Texas, sought to restrict renovation of a historically significant church on the grounds that the 1923 structure was an architectural treasure. The bishop of the diocese wanted to expand the building to meet the needs of a growing congregation. The church's attorneys argued that the RFRA protected the congregation from the burden of local historic landmark laws. The Rehnquist court disagreed, holding that the RFRA was too broad and nonremedial. The free exercise of religion to which the law referred was a vague reference to an unclear problem in state and local law. In effect, the Supreme Court ruled that the intrusion into local affairs was unwarranted. Any such law would need to be narrower in relieving a specific problem. Otherwise, Congress exceeds the limited powers that the Court sees as appropriate for the national government.

These two cases have a common feature. In each one, the Supreme Court has expressed a view that the powers of the national government are limited and that the Constitution articulates the occasions for proper intrusion into state affairs. Strict constructionists resist the efforts of judicial activists to make new constitutional law without amending the Constitution to permit new intrusions.

For the current Supreme Court, the national government must be able to show a compelling reason to exert its authority in a situation in which the states have exercised legitimate powers under the Tenth Amendment. Today's Court members, in fact, appear to take the amendment *itself* seriously. A string of decisions in 1999 and 2000 ruled that several workplace protections afforded by the national government do not pertain to state employees. For example, state workers cannot sue their employers for age discrimination under existing federal statutes. The Rehnquist court reasons that if they could, then states would have no sovereignty, even over their own employees. (See **Box 2.1**.)

University professors and librarians in Florida and Alabama have sued their state governments under provisions of the federal Age Discrimination in Employment Act of 1967 as amended in 1974. They alleged that the state universities had failed to provide a previously agreed-upon pay raise. The effects of reneging on pay raises hit senior employees hardest. In what has come to be known as the Kimel Case, the U.S. Supreme Court ruled 5–4 that age is not protected in the same way as race and gender. In fact, they said, the Congress lacks the authority to override states' immunity from federal lawsuits when it comes to age (Nicholson, 2000). Now, the only recourse that state employees who allege age discrimination have is to complain to their state Equal Employment Opportunity Office, which means that protections vary from state to state. The amount of damages for successful complainants will usually be less than they would be under federal law. Needless to say, advocacy groups such as the American Association for Retired Persons and public employee unions are concerned about the ruling effectively defederalizing age discrimination.

Source: Nicholson, Trish (2000). "Ruling Stirs Criticism: State Employees Lose Ground in Age Bias Cases." *AARP Bulletin, 41*(3) (March): 16–17.

The current Court does not seem willing to look the other way when the federal government uses the commerce clause or federal statutes to move into an area that constitutional conservatives believe should be reserved to the states. This strict constructionist perspective may give the states the room they want to take the initiative in many areas of government programs. This will take us to the topic of programmatic federalism in due time. For now, however, we note that many Americans have reservations about greater state power. They recall the many decades in which some politicians used "states' rights" arguments to protect their states' racial segregation laws. The term *states' rights* has a bad connotation to some people, and they want us to remember why. The judicial activists get their turn at bat on the issue of voting rights.

Citizenship and Voting Rights

We can see the shifting role of federalism in the actions of the federal government and state governments on almost any issue (Weissert & Schram, 1996). Voter registration is a particularly interesting case in federalism because the Constitution declares that people born in the United States or naturalized as citizens here are "citizens of the United States and of the State in which they reside" (Fourteenth Amendment). The right to vote—which political scientists call the enjoyment of the **franchise**—is therefore one of several basic constitutional rights that could be defined by the national or state governments. Does the national government determine voter eligibility, or do the states retain that right and responsibility?

Registering to vote is a fundamental act of citizenship. Susan B. Anthony, an early women's rights advocate, called it "the pivotal right." Prominent theologian Theodore Hesburgh termed its exercise "the civic sacrament" (Eigen & Siegel, 1993: 675, 679). Yet the twentieth century witnessed struggles in many states as citizens tried to establish their eligibility to vote. Some states erected barriers to registration such as discriminatory rules that barred minorities from voting, while others passed what seemed to be benign state and local regulations that were supposedly designed to protect the election systems from abuse.

States' Role in Citizenship. Citizenship is defined in the U.S. Constitution in such a way that the franchise is exercised at the state level with oversight by the national government (Article IV, Section 2). State legislatures proscribe the criteria for eligibility to vote and specify the procedures for registering. Counties or other offices that are subordinate to state-level offices administer the state laws and actually register voters.

The practice of registering prospective voters is designed to prevent electoral abuse. Without a system of certifying eligible voters and then confirming their eligibility at the polls, states might find that individuals who are not citizens would vote or eligible people might vote more than once. We consider subversion of registration laws to be election fraud, and preventing abuse is seen as a positive measure that enhances civic life.

The states began to experiment with formal **voter registration** in the early nineteenth century. Urbanization made it impossible for local poll officials to know each prospective voter personally, so a formal means for identifying individuals was needed. Massachusetts enacted an official registration law in 1800, and several New England states soon followed suit. The practice gradually expanded to more and more states and then quickened after the Civil War. By 1890, most states had adopted some form of official voter list (Reitman & Davidson, 1972: 31).

Over time, state laws and their enforcement have reflected changing social and political mores. At the turn of the century, James Bryce commented, "I cannot attempt to describe the complicated and varying election laws of the different states" (Bryce, 1911: 146). He reported that many states were striving to overcome *machine* control of electoral systems—that is, the manipulation of local government by political bosses. Election fraud, in fact, was not rare in the United States during the nineteenth and early twentieth centuries. Humorist Mark Twain wryly called votes "the only commodity that is peddleable without a license" (Eigen & Siegel, 1993: 684).

Women were acknowledged as having the right to vote in Wyoming before the territory's admission to the union as a state in 1889, and territorial leaders refused to enter the union without preserving *women's suffrage* (Welch, Gruhl, Comer, Rigdon, & Steinman, 1999: 167). By 1910, four states had recognized the right of women to vote. Finally, in 1920, the federal Constitution was amended to grant women the franchise. We should not forget that in the lifetimes of many of our own grandparents, states denied women the right to vote.

Well into the 1960s, Southern states manipulated their registration requirements to disenfranchise African Americans. They erected barriers such as poll taxes, literacy tests, citizenship tests, moral character criteria, and similar devices to empower voting registrars to turn away African Americans who wanted to register. These states also tried to sidestep every congressional and federal court effort to extend the franchise to all citizens (Claude, 1970: 105).

Federal Intervention. The national government has stepped in on many occasions to ensure that the state and county interpretation of citizenship is consistent with national citizenship protections. In this way, enjoyment of the franchise by African Americans was enacted by the national government and extended to the states by the Fifteenth Amendment to the Constitution. The exercise of the franchise by women was exercised by innovative states and then adopted by constitutional revision nationally by the Nineteenth Amendment. Poll taxes were outlawed by the Twenty-Fourth Amendment, and voting age was lowered to eighteen by the Twenty-Sixth Amendment.

Enforcement of citizenship rights in general and enjoyment of the franchise in particular has often been the subject of specialized national legislation. The 1957 Civil Rights Act prohibited registrars from intimidating prospective minority voters in federal elections. The Civil Rights Act of 1960 extended the powers of the federal attorney general to include actions against discriminatory state governments if the discriminating registrars themselves resigned, otherwise became unavailable, or obstructed consent decrees declaring individuals eligible to register. The act also allowed the federal government to appoint referees who could register African American voters. The 1964 Civil Rights Act disallowed any "pattern or practice" in a state that discriminated in voter registration and also prohibited different registration standards for different segments of the community, as well as irrelevant disqualifying standards (Claude, 1970: 88, 97, 101–102).

Despite these federal enactments and decisions, the states of the former Confederacy had made little progress in opening voter registration to African Americans by the mid-1960s. In 1965, the U.S. attorney general reported to the House Judiciary Committee that relatively few African Americans were registered to vote in the South (Claude, 1970: 107). The estimated percentages ranged from 6 percent in Mississippi to 19 percent in Alabama to 37 percent in North and South Carolina. Only three Southern states had as many as half of voting-age African Americans registered: Florida (51 percent), Texas (58 percent), and Tennessee (70 percent). Efforts by the Department of Justice—even those that extended to sending registrars to the South—had proved relatively ineffective.

The **Voting Rights Act of 1965** added new teeth to the federal government's efforts to enfranchise African American citizens in the South (Lowenstein, 1995: 31). States and localities in which less than half the voting-age population voted in the 1964 presidential election were singled out for special treatment: Alabama, Georgia, Louisiana, Mississippi, South Carolina, Virginia, and large areas within North Carolina. Section Four of the act prohibited these jurisdictions from using literacy tests or other devices to preclude African Americans from registering. Any qualification or prerequisite had to be cleared first with the justice department. The Voting Rights Act effectively broke segregationist control of Southern voting. By 1967, 60 percent of all voting-age African Americans were registered in Mississippi. In an area specially targeted by the law, the percentage rose to 57 percent. The gap between the registration rates of African American and white populations in the South was reduced from 44 percentage points in 1965 to 11 points in 1972 (Lowenstein, 1995: 32). The Voting Rights Act would be extended and strengthened in 1975 and 1982, and official barriers to African American registration in the South continued to disintegrate.

Contemporary Barriers. The historical record clearly shows that states have tried to manipulate the registration process to the detriment of citizens other than Southern African Americans. Language minorities, including large Hispanic populations in some states, were addressed in the 1975 amendments. Nevertheless, this has not prevented states from continuing to maintain barriers to voter registration, although on a less discriminatory basis. For example, the federal judiciary has allowed states to mandate registration cutoff dates of thirty to fifty days. Other states make it easier to register individuals by allowing them to mail in their registration applications. Research suggests that patterns involving political culture and voter-registration barriers continue (Cox & Thacker, 1994, 1998).

In 1989, former Democratic Party Chair Ron Brown argued, "You've got to jump through all kinds of hoops to vote in America" (Eigen & Siegel, 1993: 676). Roughly two-thirds of the voting-age population of the United States is registered to vote. That figure is lower than those in other Western democracies, and the differences worry some observers. Other social critics such as conservative columnist William F. Buckley have not been concerned. In 1970, he tersely commented, "Too many people are voting." Twenty years later, he was still questioning the common wisdom about voter registration and asking, "Why do we want dumb votes?" (Eigen & Siegel, 1993: 676).

During the late 1980s and early 1990s, approximately thirty states experimented with *agency-based registration* (Cloward & Piven, 1996). These laws authorized registration in a variety of government offices, such as social services agencies and departments of motor vehicles, where people could register to vote when they came in to conduct other business. In 1976, Michigan was the first state to allow such registration; by early 1990, six states and the District of Columbia permitted registration at the time of driver's license application or renewal (Smolka, 1990: 226). In 1993, the Congress passed the National Voter Registration Act (NVRA), a statute based on these apparently successful state experiments. Because voting registration at the time of driver's license renewal was the clearest example of agency-based registration, the NVRA has been nicknamed the "Motor Voter Law." The NVRA also mandates mail-in registration, requires periodic purging from voter rolls of people who have moved or died, and maintains that people moving into a jurisdiction must be allowed to register even if cutoff dates would otherwise have made them ineligible. Although the NVRA technically pertains only to federal elections, the law changes state procedures for federal elections and clearly seeks to shape voter registration and participation in state elections.

Some states resisted the NVRA, claiming that voter registration is a purely state prerogative. California and South Carolina, for example, argued that the federal government was imposing an unreimbursed cost on the states for a federal election activity (Lowenstein, 1995: 54). Other states have moved to bring their state laws into compliance rather than maintain two parallel registration systems.

The initial eighteen months of the new law increased registration rolls by nine million people in forty-three states and the District of Columbia (Cloward & Piven, 1996), although with considerable variances by state. Illinois reported an increase of only 4 percent, while Louisiana increased by 13 percent and both North Carolina and Missouri rose by 15 percent. These fig-

---

Exploring on Your Own Campus Voter Registration

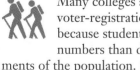 Many colleges and universities conduct voter-registration drives on campus because students register to vote in lower numbers than do all other eligible segments of the population. Sometimes, these drives are sponsored by Young Republicans and Young Democrats, and at other times they are sponsored by the student government association or the community voter registrar. What is the status of such efforts on your own campus? Discuss what you find with your classmates. You may decide to organize a voter-registration drive yourself. Remember, as the Reverend Jesse Jackson said, "If you don't vote, you don't count."

ures suggested that the NVRA might expand the registration rolls and ultimately voter turnout.

Patterns of Voter Registration. Before the Motor Voter Law was passed, traditionalistic political culture states had many more registration barriers than did either individualistic or moralistic states. After the passage of that law, the three types of states were more alike (see **Table 2.2**), which was just what backers of the national law intended.

Table 2.2
Political Culture and Registration Barriers

| Culture Type | *Number of Official Barriers* | |
	1992	1996
Traditionalistic	7.1	3.3
Individualistic	5.4	3.5
Moralistic	4.1	2.1

Note: Barriers are scaled using *The Book of the States* data.

Source: Previously unpublished data from Cox & Thacker, 1994, 1998.

In terms of actual voter registrations, rates rose very slightly. Before Motor Voter, the moralistic political culture states distinguished themselves by having most of their voting-age population registered (see **Table 2.3**). The traditionalistic and individualistic states were more than 10 percentage points off the pace set by moralistic states such as Minnesota.

Table 2.3
Political Culture and Actual Voter Registration

| Culture Type | *Percentage by Year* | |
	1992	1996
Traditionalistic	72.5	74.6
Individualistic	70.0	76.3
Moralistic	85.2	81.8

Note: Registration % = number of registered voters divided by total voting age population.

Source: Unpublished data from Cox & Thacker, 1994, 1998.

Between 1992 and 1996, the traditionalistic and the individualistic states closed that gap to 5 percentage points. The impact of Motor Voter appears to have been most dramatic in the individualistic states and least in the traditionalistic states. Already, observers have speculated about why results that may be modest for most states. What role do modern barriers to registration actually play? Are the ones removed by the NVRA really the most significant ones? Or are citizens motivated by other factors such as disinterest in politics and politicians? Many questions remain about the NVRA's efficacy.

Like most other Americans, members of minority groups need to protect their ethnic and cultural heritage at the ballot box.

Source: © Sam Sargent / Liaison International

National Supremacy More Generally

Other aspects of the Constitution of 1787 nurture a strong national government. According to the document's preamble, its purpose is to "promote the general welfare." Congress is to take steps that are "necessary and proper" for carrying out its assigned powers (Article I, Section 8). This is sometimes referred to as the *implied powers clause.* The *supremacy clause* (Article VI) suggests that acts of the national government are binding on citizens and the states. Judicial review makes state laws subject to approval by federal courts (*Marbury* v. *Madison,* 1803). Together, these constitutional doctrines give the national government the power it needs to lead and supervise the states *if and when* it has the political will.

Conclusions About Constitutional Federalism

We have briefed you on the current Supreme Court's stand on important aspects of the federal relationship. Strict constructionists would take heart that the Rehnquist court seems to be scrutinizing national intervention in state affairs. The Court's rulings regarding the commerce clause and the Tenth Amendment suggest that it is quite conservative in interpreting the powers of the national government.

We also have given you background on what happens when states' rights theory runs amok. The history of abuse of Americans' citizenship rights should alert you to the dangers of immoderate swings to the right. For judicial activists, the Constitution must remain a living document, with such concepts as citizenship and voting rights allowed to evolve as society evolves. Judicial activists hasten to remind us that the U.S. Constitution is still the supreme law of the land, and states have rights only within that context.

The civic culture of the states is interesting to legal scholars. But why should all of us be interested in shifts in thinking about the role of the national and the state governments? Because social problems lead to new social policies and programs. A *social policy* is an official decision about how to approach a problem. Then come specific *social programs* from which people receive the services they need in order not to suffer from the problem. Poverty, for example, is one social problem that leads to one or more welfare policies that authorize programs such as workfare and food stamps. But who makes the policy and prescribes the programs that are needed? The national government? The states? The answer depends on which cycle of federalism is in vogue at the time.

❧ Programmatic Federalism

Social policy is developed at both the national and the state levels. In this section, we take an overview of the development of social policy in the states. There are important federalist interactions between what the states are doing

Now that you know something of the constitutional history of
states' rights and national voters' rights, give some thought to
where you stand on the citizenship issue. Is your American citizenship basic to you? Do you feel that the federal government
will continue to work to protect your political rights? How do you feel about
state and local officials when it comes to ensuring your voting rights and
other forms of participation in our democratic system? Do you trust them as
well? If appropriate, discuss individual thoughts with your classmates.

and the policies being considered by the U.S. Congress. We then explore how
public policy is implemented in the form of state programs. Local governments are also important partners in service delivery. Finally, we examine the
need to evaluate social policies in terms of their efficiency and effectiveness.
The public expects its tax money to be spent in a prudent and responsible manner. For that reason, all levels of government involved in the federal system are
challenged to fine-tune social policies until they actually solve or at least ease
the problems that led to the passage of the enabling legislation.

Policy and Program Development

In 1932, Supreme Court Justice Louis Brandeis called states the "laboratories
of democracy" (quoted in Osborne, 1988). Each state experiences a social
problem such as poverty in its own context of land, people, and culture. For
example, rural Southern and Midwestern states have pockets of poverty caused
by subsistence agriculture that may fail in times of flood or drought. Northeastern urban states have congested ghettos of unemployed and underem-
ployed wage workers. Western states have American Indian reservations where
yet another kind of dependence and poverty are found. Being poor means different things in different parts of the country. The land itself provides a context for defining poverty.

Poverty Amid Plenty. People are poor, and groups experience different
rates of poverty. In the South, for example, there are high proportions of
African Americans in the population. Following the abolition of slavery, many
blacks remained tied to the land through tenant farming. Today, in parts of
rural Mississippi, Alabama, and Georgia, as much as half of the population is
made of poor black farmers. Color as well as economic condition marks their
poverty. In the Southwest, Hispanic Americans experience high levels of
poverty. Their language and heritage mark their poverty as much as does their
economic condition. Similar issues confront American Indians, recent Asian
immigrants, and Third World immigrants more generally. Poverty is a complex social problem that involves individual and group expectations, lack of
resources, racial discrimination, and powerful social labeling that is applied to
people in economic need.

Each state's political culture interprets the poverty within its boundaries.
In the traditionalistic political cultures of the South and West, income inequal-
ity is commonly viewed as a fact of life: The poor have always been with us.
They form the lower social stratum that has traditionally served the landed or

moneyed elite. The poor are not without virtue, but elites in the traditionalistic political culture expect people to accept their lot in life. The government certainly should not intervene in this natural differentiation of people. The individualistic political culture views poverty as a lack of opportunity or an unwillingness to take advantage of economic opportunities. Individualists see the economy as a marketplace in which employers and workers meet to determine wages. People who are paid low wages will be motivated naturally to improve their work skills to earn more. Low-wage earners who do not strive to become more employable are reasonably relegated to the ranks of the working poor. Even today's technological economy needs menial labor. Only in the moralistic political culture states is societal responsibility for the poor really shouldered. Moralists believe that the government has a positive obligation to help each person develop his or her maximum potential and that it should offer programs of employment readiness, job-skills training, and subsidized entry-level work. If individuals cannot work in the competitive workplace, then they should be supported at public expense. Society would be remiss if it refused to care for its indigent citizens.

Underlying these different approaches to poverty are basic facts of life that define what it means to be poor in one of the most affluent countries in the world. More than one-fourth of all African Americans and Hispanic Americans live below the poverty line (see Table 2.4). States with large proportions of their populations living in such poverty have both high levels of need and low levels of tax resources. For example, in 1998, one person in five in Mississippi and New Mexico lived in poverty, and social welfare programs had to try to serve this large proportion of the population. At the same time, this one-fifth of the population paid relatively little into the state budgets that financed the welfare programs. Only a large influx of federal welfare funds kept this relationship of high need and low resources from starving those in need on the one hand or bankrupting the poorer states on the other.

Table 2.4
Poverty and Ethnicity in the United States, 1998

Racial Group	Individuals Living Below Poverty Level (%)
European Americans	10.5
African Americans	26.1
Hispanic Americans	25.6
Asian Americans	14.6

Source: The World Almanac 2000: 393; Statistical Abstract of the United States, 1996–97: 48–50.

Another fact of life about poverty in the United States is that the welfare population is made disproportionately of children, the elderly, and disabled persons. Eleven percent of all people living in poverty in 1994 were ages 65 years and older; an additional 20 percent were children; and yet another 9 percent were disabled to the point that they could not work (*Time Almanac 2000:* 833; *Statistical Yearbook of the United States, 1996–97:* 472–475). This means that almost half of all poor people in the United States are children, old

Many inner cities are marred by poverty, decay, and graffiti, expresses despair and hopelessness. Members of the so-called welfare class may feel such alienation every day.

Source: © Stephen Ferry / Gamma Liaison

people, and disabled adults. Few people in these groups can be expected to leave the ranks of the poor by getting mainstream jobs. If family members become gainfully employed, then the children and elderly may rise above poverty with them. A *social safety net* may always be needed to catch Americans who are not candidates to become a part of the regular workforce.

Finally, the family member who stays home with a child or an elderly person is almost always a woman. Mothers of young children must find affordable child care if they are to find jobs and go to work. Caregivers of elderly people and disabled people may have similar needs. Added to this restraint is the lack of education and work experience that is common to many women on welfare who have stayed at home to care for family members. One-fourth of adult welfare recipients never finished high school, and only 13 percent have marketable work experience (Statistical Abstract of the United States, 1996–97: 476). Most important, perhaps, is that these figures are national averages. The employability of welfare recipients in some states is much worse than the average.

From Welfare to Workfare. These facts of life about poverty in the United States have not discouraged state governors and legislatures. In some states, expenditures for social programs per recipient have steadily increased. In most states, though, governors and legislatures have been trying to change the nature of their welfare programs. State officials call the new approaches to easing poverty "reforms," although some critics charge that they are merely retreats from state responsibility for low-income people in need.

New Jersey has sought to be a leader in rethinking social welfare policy and programs. In 1992, the legislature *capped welfare benefits.* Now, children born after a family goes on welfare do not increase the family's welfare award (Lemov, 1995: 30), which makes having more children a disincentive for parents that is much like the disincentive of cost already experienced by many middle-class American families.

Other states have taken different approaches. Arizona and Wisconsin, for example, have been *privatizing* welfare eligibility and payment programs (Lemov, 1997). Indiana uses private contractors to help welfare recipients find jobs, and Texas has automated its entire benefits eligibility and payment system. These state innovations show how willing governors and state legislators are to experiment with new and cheaper approaches to social welfare policy.

Related Issues. There have been some problems with changing welfare's purpose and policies. Mothers who have to leave children at home or who cannot care for them after school need *child-care* programs. Private child-care and after-school programs are expensive, and subsidized programs often have waiting lists. Yet the clock is running on the mother's eligibility to receive welfare payments and provide care herself. In an era in which many middle-class mothers are declaring that it is good to stay at home with preschool children, it is interesting that poor mothers are expected to abandon their children's care to low-paid strangers.

Another problem has been *transportation* to and from work. Many of us Americans work some distance from our homes. If our income is sufficient, then we can afford the automobile, the gasoline, and the parking fees. Poor workers, however, often have to rely on public transportation to reach their jobs in distant parts of a city or the suburbs. The transportation costs are greatest for the people who can least afford them.

Finally, the kinds of jobs that former welfare recipients can secure often lack *benefits.* These workers have no health insurance when they or their children get sick. They have no retirement benefits when they are too old to work anymore. Any education benefits are geared to their employers' needs, not their own. Moreover, employment for the working poor is not a rich and secure experience as our professional careers are likely to be. In fact, they may work long and very hard hours only to end up worse off that they were when on welfare. Certainly, some poor people do climb out of poverty, but we should not assume that declining welfare rolls are a sure sign of success for these workers.

Policy or Program Implementation

President Bill Clinton—himself a former governor—has cooperated with the states in experimenting with welfare reform (Weissert & Schram, 1996: 8). The federal government has offered *waivers* of national welfare regulations to states that want to try new approaches. These waivers allow specific regulations to be suspended for a time while new rules or techniques are explored. The federal government has even been willing to subsidize some state experiments with grants for pilot workfare and child-care projects. The Clinton administration's philosophy has been that pilot programs may lead to new and more effective social welfare policy. In the era of federal budget cutting before budget surpluses developed in the late 1990s, both the White House and Congress were interested in any innovation that would reduce the financial burden of welfare to the national government and the states.

National Governors' Association. State governors meet and often speak as a group when it comes to social policy. In 1995, the National Governors' Association proposed a national welfare reform package, suggesting that welfare as an entitlement for able-bodied adults be phased out in the United States. In response, President Clinton and Congress cooperated to repeal the Aid to Families with Dependent Children (AFDC) program. AFDC was replaced by Transitional Aid for Needy Families (TANF). The TANF program features *workfare*, the requirement that able-bodied adults work for their welfare benefits. It provides job-readiness training and job-placement services. Public agencies may serve as employers if there are not enough private jobs for all of the new workers. Program participation is limited in total years of eligibility.

Everything about the program emphasizes that public assistance will be a temporary bridge from poverty to private employment.

National Welfare Politics. President Clinton has been interested in the TANF idea because it responds to the major public and media criticisms of traditional welfare. Many Americans believe that we have created a permanent welfare class. Several generations of welfare recipients may live in one household, and none of the adults may ever have known the responsibility and the rewards of employment. Absent fathers may not pay for the support of their children, even when the courts have ordered child-support payments. Over time, more children may be born into the household and thus perpetuate the cycle of poverty. The question then arises, would the war on poverty ever be won?

Many members of Congress would like to see the cost of welfare further reduced or eliminated from the national budget. They are asking the states to do more and pay more of the costs of welfare programs, although perhaps with some national funding through block grants. Congress decided to balance the federal budget and so placed domestic expenditures for welfare, education, housing, and other social programs on the chopping block. Governors of both major parties are interested in having more control over state welfare and workfare programs. (See also Box 2.2.)

BOX 2.2   *The Medicaid Program: A Federal–State Partnership*

The Medicaid program was created in 1965 as a part of President Lyndon Johnson's War on Poverty. This jointly funded federal–state program assists states in providing adequate medical care to eligible needy persons. It covers approximately 36 million individuals; it cost $170 billion in 1998 ($100 billion in federal funds, and $70 billion in state funds). Within broad national guidelines provided by the federal government, each state:

1. establishes its own eligibility standards;
2. determines the type, amount, duration, and scope of its services;
3. sets the rate of payment for services; and
4. administers its own program.

Thus, the Medicaid program varies considerably from state to state, as well as within each state over time. Initially, Medicaid was the medical-care extension of federally funded income-maintenance programs for the poor. Recent legislation expands Medicaid coverage to more low-income pregnant women, poor children, and some Medicare beneficiaries. Legislative changes focus on enhanced outreach toward specific groups of pregnant women and children, increased access to care, and improved quality of care.

In addition to more beneficiaries from new legislation, the most pronounced Medicaid service–related trends in recent years have been the continued sharp increase in expenditures for intensive acute care and for home health and nursing facility services for the aged and disabled. Long-term care is an important and increasingly used provision of Medicaid—especially as our nation's population ages. Almost 45 percent of the total cost of care for persons using nursing facility or home health services in the United States in recent years is paid by the Medicaid program. The data for 1996 show that Medicaid payments for nursing facility and home health care totaled $40.5 billion for more than 3.6 million recipients—or an average of more than $12,300 per long-term care recipient. With the percentage of our population who are elderly, or disabled, or both increasing faster than the younger groups, the need for long-term care is expected to increase. This trend places substantial pressure on state governments whose Medicaid expenditures often seem out of their control. (For more on this, see <http://hcfa.hhs.gov/medicaid/mover.htm>.)

National Action. Subtitled the "Personal Responsibility and Work Opportunity Reconciliation Act," the Welfare Reform Act of 1996 required that the head of every family on welfare had to go to work within two years or lose benefits. Further, the law limited lifetime welfare benefits to five years for all but a small number of hardship cases. It permitted welfare payments to unwed teenage mothers only if they were living with their parents and enrolled in school. It allowed states to prohibit subsequent children from being included in the welfare calculation, limited food stamps to three months for unemployed adults without small children, and reduced awards to mothers who did not establish paternity and seek child-support collection. It also denied welfare to all future illegal immigrants and required illegal aliens already in the country to secure citizenship or lose their benefits (Plano & Greenberg, 1997: 527).

Like AFDC, TANF is a set of fifty state welfare programs. The national government itself does not operate welfare offices, hire social workers, or print welfare checks. Instead, it provides money to the states through **block grants.** Each state then sets up and operates its own statewide welfare agency that meets the federal requirements. Counties—administrative subdivisions of state government—operate welfare offices that are consistent with federal and state law. This is *programmatic federalism* at work.

State Implementation. Many state welfare programs are huge enterprises. California's, for example, serves 918,000 families a month—or roughly 60 percent of the state's poor population. The average monthly benefit for a family of three is $556. For three-fourths of California families on welfare, this check is their only source of income. The national government and the state each pay half of the cost, which totals more than $6 billion per year (Anderson, 1997).

A change in policy at the top sends ripples throughout state and local government across the country. Every state has instituted its new TANF program, and detailed state rules and guidelines have been established. County welfare workers within each state have been applying the new rules. They have been trained to implement workfare at the local level. Still, many questions at the local, state, and national levels remain to be answered: Who will locate jobs for welfare recipients? How will employers who are willing to train and hire welfare recipients be compensated? Who will orient the recipients to the demands and benefits of regular employment? How will the child-care, transportation, and health-insurance needs of mothers going to work be accommodated? Who will counsel the client who claims that no one will hire her? Determining what it takes to make the program work and measuring the degree to which it does or does not succeed is the process of *policy* or *program evaluation.*

Policy or Program Evaluation

Program evaluation is the process of making informed judgments about program effectiveness and efficiency (Rossi & Freeman, 1993). *Informed* in this sense means the use of factual data. The process is judgmental in the sense that decision makers must ultimately use the information to determine a program's future. Program evaluation answers questions such as: Does the program work—that is, does it produce the desired effect on a problem? Is the program effectively run—that is, do services reach the clientele? Is the program operated efficiently—does it spend money wisely? The answers to these and related program-evaluation questions are important to many players in the political system.

Shaping the Evaluation. Policy makers are interested governmental *stakeholders* when evaluating the effectiveness and the efficiency of social programs. Congressional committees, federal bureaucrats, and White House staff members are all concerned with program success or failure. Congress has an oversight responsibility to review programs and spending to determine if reauthorization and continued appropriations for a program are warranted. The federal agencies that disperse the funds and White House staff members who often champion a program have a vested interest in its success or failure. Parallel to these national policy makers are state-level decision makers who are legitimately concerned about a program's track record. The state legislature, state bureaucrats, and the governor's staff also discuss how well the program is working within their state. They may have program-evaluation information that reflects the effectiveness and efficiency of the state program, data that the federal government may aggregate for many or all of the states. For example, audits may capture information on check-payment errors. Overpayment and underpayment are problems in government programs. With the data, goals can be set for reducing or eliminating these errors. These data are typically captured by a state or local agency's management information system (MIS).

Client- and employee-advocacy groups and public-interest organizations also want to evaluate social programs. Client groups want to determine if needed services are actually reaching the people who need them and whether clients are underserved. Do services reach all areas of the state or nation? Does service provision treat all racial groups and both genders fairly? Interest groups who represent employees of social service programs want to protect their members' reputations and income. Consumer groups also are interested in these questions and more. Public-interest organizations want to know if tax dollars are being wasted. Are social service workers making themselves comfortable while underserving people in need? Is money being properly accounted for? Are service decisions based on objective priorities or political expediencies? Client, employee, and consumer groups rely on the testimony of clients, employee experts, and whistle-blowers for their evaluative information. The groups themselves rarely have the financial resources or access to agency operations that would be needed to gather more complete numerical information.

Interpreting the Results. The media also want to participate in the program-evaluation process. Investigative reporters look into rumors about program shortcomings, fraud, and client abuse. Whistle-blowers contact the media with insider information about ineffectiveness and inefficiency. Arguing that the public has a right to know what is being done with tax dollars, the media have a *watchdog function* for the state or nation. Reporters also keep score on specific political leaders, Congress or state legislature, and the federal and state bureaucracies. For the media, failures in several program areas may be like blood in the water to sharks, bringing more and more reporters and commentators to question a policy.

Public opinion is usually passive until sensational events or election year politics trigger interest. Policy makers want to be sure that the citizenry provides a base of support for a program. To secure their reelection, most officials will avoid unpopular programs or those that have been compromised by scandal. Of course, the only way to find out what the public thinks is to ask, so private polling companies, interest groups, and public-service universities frequently conduct public-opinion polls. Political players sometimes commission such polls, with "favorable" results usually finding their way to the media. These polling data then become a part of the program's evaluation. Unfortunately, the public rarely distinguishes a scientifically sampled poll with fair questions from a biased set of questions asked of mall shoppers. Genuine insight into what the public thinks absolutely requires the former.

Political parties evaluate social programs using all of the information that is available to them. Incumbent parties want to be able to document a sound track record, and their opponents want ammunition to assail them. This drama is acted out not only in Washington, D.C., but also in all fifty state capitals. Our two-party competitive political system thrives on platform promises and failed programs. The public is offered a choice based to some degree on the promises that the group in power could deliver certain results.

The social scientists who are typically contracted to evaluate social programs often are caught in the riptide of program-evaluation politics (Peters, 1996). Factual information on social programs such as those constituting welfare reform is rarely unambiguous. Most programs have both successes and failures. Successful models may encourage the sponsors and champions of a program, while examples of failure may fuel the criticism of detractors. Unfortunately, program-evaluation results are often used selectively. The painstaking collection and analysis of data may be lost in the partisan or ideological conflict that surrounds many social programs.

Some Preliminary Findings. Welfare rolls have fallen in most states. Overall, the number of family-assistance recipients fell by one-third from 1995 through 1997 (Rom, 1999: 363). Because many individuals lose their eligibility if they don't find employment, the numbers will continue to decrease. A healthy economy has helped moderate the number of new applicants and stimulated at least some jobs for people who must find work. The U.S. economy, in fact, has grown in each consecutive quarter for more than seven years! Indeed, overall levels of poverty in the country have improved (see Figure 2.1). However, if and when the economy cools off, applications for assistance will increase as work opportunities go down. At that point, it may be hard to isolate the effects of welfare reform.

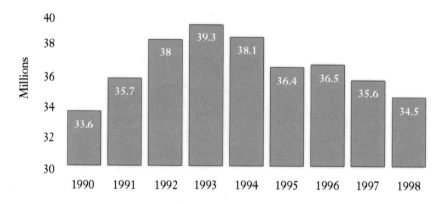

Figure 2.1 Poverty in the United States: Number of People Living Below the Poverty Level
Source: U.S. Bureau of the Census, reported in *World Almanac, 2000:* 393

CHAPTER 2 Power Sharing in a Federal System: *Theoretical and Practical Balance*

❧ Issues in Federalism

Three serious and persistent concerns have developed in the federal relationship between the national and state governments, as well as in the relationships between some states and their local governments: revenue sharing, unfunded mandates, and policy preemption. Many state and local officials believe them to be intertwined and inseparable.

Revenue Sharing

Considerable money flows into Washington by virtue of the national income tax and its collection by the Internal Revenue Service (IRS). With revenue sharing, some of that money flows to the states through grants and is distributed to the local governments that deliver welfare, public health, and other services. When the economy is flush, there is enough revenue to balance the federal budget or even generate a surplus. When the economy is lean or congressional representatives insist on tax cuts, the federal revenues dry up. Paradoxically, the states may get the least money when their needs are greatest. In the past, deficit spending enabled Washington to pump more money into the pipelines despite modest tax revenues. Balanced budget laws have slammed that door.

Competition for increasingly scarce federal revenue dollars may make for adversarial and sometimes vicious state and local relations. Cities want and need revenue and see little "value added" in the state governments' pass-through of the funds. States, however, want to shape local programs by making policy about how the funds should be used. The relationship may be amicable in good times, but it is fractious in lean times.

Unfunded Mandates

One of the most contentious issues is federalism has been *unfunded mandates*, or the federal government's practice of requiring certain state actions without providing funds to the states to implement those actions. Requirements vary by policy area. One especially unpopular unfunded mandate has been the Americans with Disabilities Act (ADA). Although most state officials support the goals of the act, they do not appreciate being required to change buildings, revise policies, and provide new services by a federal government that itself provides no funds for the effort. After all, the federal government has far more resources than do state and local governments. Yet the important citizenship rights of access and accommodation that ADA mandates are apparently not important enough to Congress to warrant paying for them.

Governors resent these unfunded mandates. Major efforts have been made by the National Governors' Association to convince Congress and the president to curb the practice. Although recent Congresses and presidents have paid lip service to ending unfunded mandates, they have not followed through. Reaping the political capital from passing decisive legislation without providing revenues to get the job done may simply be too tempting. Unfortunately, the states are left holding the bag.

Policy Preemption

Related to unfunded mandates is the matter of *policy preemption*. Federal regulatory agencies are often accused of issuing rules that supercede existing state regulations. For example, a federal regulator may issue a rule that requires new standards for environmental protection in sensitive habitats. Some states may have been doing nothing to address the environmental problem singled out by the regulators. But what about the states that have been actively pursuing their own strategies of environmental protection? Suddenly the efforts of many years are superceded by federal regulation.

Governors, legislators, and state agencies are understandably upset when the federal government steps in and preempts their authority in a policy area. The federal government seems to call on the states to innovate and experiment and then drops a regulation on them—and often without the new funding needed to implement the regulation. To many state officials, the federal government speaks of its support for policy *devolution*—leaving more authority at the state level—from one side of its mouth, then turns around and declares a preemptive policy from the other side.

Power in the federal relationship between the national government and the states swings back and forth. Sometimes, policies and programs are nationalized; this was the case, for example, during the 1960s when Great Society programs tried to win the federal War on Poverty. At the same time, major new civil rights laws were passed and the country was undergoing a major military buildup and increasing deployments in Vietnam. The current reaction to this concentration of power and resources in Washington has been the "devolution revolution," with policy and programs returned or handed over to the states. Pressures for large national programs have declined as more Americans seek more effective solutions closer to home. The chorus of support for devolved powers is not without its detractors, however (see, e.g., Donahue, 1997). Not all social problems may be amenable to fifty separate solutions, and federalism's purpose is not the dissolution of the union but problem solving at the level where action can be most effective and efficient. It is therefore incumbent on state and local governments to form partnerships to "get the job done." Nothing less will satisfy a demanding public and critical media.

❧ Local Government Home Rule

Counties were created as the administrative subdivisions of state government and still serve that purpose. You will note that the names of many county departments are exactly the same as the names of corresponding state agencies in the state capital. This is because agencies such as the county health department and county welfare department are administering the state's programs in those areas. They take many of their policy directions from state officials. Yet counties have become much more than administrators of state programs. Today, **home rule** laws permit elected county officials to develop their own policies and programs in areas such as public recreation, environmental protection, and solid-waste disposal. In these programs, counties often mix state and local funds to provide services that are priorities for local citizens, becoming more like general-purpose local governments (Berman, 1993). In fact, in rural areas of the United States, they *are* the general-purpose local governments.

A city gets its governmental powers through a city charter that has been issued by the state legislature. The charter authorizes the particular municipality to collect certain taxes and provide certain services. Cities can exercise only those powers explicitly granted them by the state, a principle that has been enshrined as **Dillon's Rule.** Historically, this sort of delegated power served the interests of some cities some of the time. State legislatures would pass local bills to relieve particular problems that might arise when a city lacked a specific power needed to operate a program. However, this proved to be an awkward and inefficient process. As a result, some states have passed home-rule provisions. These provisions in state law may grant some or all local governments the power to deal with purely municipal or local matters without recourse to state lawmakers. Other states broadly provide that locals may make ordinances and operate programs except where explicitly prohibited from doing so by state law (Berman, 1993). Of course, most local governments would love to have broad home-rule powers, but many state legislatures are reluctant to let go of their authority over local affairs. Suffice it to say that most municipalities must cling to their charters as their source of legitimacy.

Local governments in the United States are not as powerful as the national or state governments. Any type of public enterprise that depends on another level of government for its legitimacy is vulnerable. We will look at the issues involved in effective local governance in later chapters.

---

elsewhere in the world

Swiss Federalism

Switzerland has twenty-three cantons, three of them subdivided. These cantons are diverse in terms of land, language, and culture. Each subnational "state" as we would call them has its own social welfare programs. Only those powers that must be exercised by the national government are centralized. The Swiss therefore call their system of government the Swiss Confederation. Learn more about the government of Switzerland by visiting its home page at <http://www.ethz.ch/swiss/Switzerland_Info. html>.

Swiss Cantons and Welfare

Switzerland's welfare program is explicitly targeted at helping the poor achieve self-sufficiency and has devolved welfare policy to the canton level. Unless a person is seriously handi-

capped, the canton government is responsible for public assistance; if the person is totally disabled, then the national government steps in. Motivated to limit the cost of such programs, most cantons offer counseling and social services that are geared to getting a family functioning on its own. The amount of aid is determined by a caseworker. Relatives can be required to help the needy family, and fathers are held strictly accountable for child support. Several cantons also have created poverty-prevention programs for their youth.

Feel free to explore and learn more about other important nations that use federal systems of government. India, Nigeria, and Germany, for example, are interesting because they also experiment with a balance of state and national power. Yugoslavia is an interesting example of what happens when federal relationships fail.

❧ Chapter Conclusion

The pendulum that swings back and forth between devolved power at the state level and nationalized power in Washington, D.C., currently favors the states. Without the Cold War or international economic depression, pressures for strong national power have lessened, and demands for subnational responsibilities have become stronger. In the United States, as elsewhere in the world, devolved power is common. Nevertheless, the arrangement does have detractors (e.g., Donahue, 1997). Not all problems are amenable to fifty separate solutions, they say, and the purpose of federalism is not the dissolution of the union. Rather, federalism seeks to place problem solving where it can be most effective. State and local governments thus must get the job done in the policy areas where they have asserted their prerogatives.

Federalism is a cornerstone of self-governance at the state level. In this regard, we have noted the following:

- Both congressional actions and Supreme Court decisions currently favor a growing role for state governments in the federal relationship. Political leaders hope that state powers will not lead to another era of so-called states' rights in which citizenship rights were abridged.
- Americans enjoy citizenship rights at *both* the national and state levels, even though the superior claims to rights as an American must sometimes be used to correct state restrictions of civil and political rights.
- Programmatic federalism provides a framework through which the national government can share some of its wealth with the states. States, however, want to put their own imprints on programs.
- Concerns have developed about the fairness of the federal–state relationship when funds are cut, unfunded mandates are issued, and federal regulations preempt state laws.
- Local governments are the "poor relations" in the federal system. They depend on state law for their powers, even when limited home rule is allowed.

Specific government policies and programs get caught in these shifting currents of American federalism. We examined four specific cases of the Supreme Court's strict constructionist outlook on federalism: school safety, violence against women, handgun regulation, and religious freedoms. Voter registration laws—and the question of protecting voting rights—are a classic study in balance between state and federal authorities. Welfare programs can be tailored to meet specific state needs and preferences. You also may have noticed that political culture shapes state voter-registration policy. Moreover, the social characteristics we profiled in Chapter 1 were evident in the contours of modern federalism in this chapter. Our governmental structures cannot escape who we are as a people—and as many diverse peoples. Only a system of relationships as flexible as federalism could accommodate so much variation within an overall national government. Our political system needs federalism to make it work.

Collecting Your Thoughts *What Do You Think Is the Proper Balance?*

You have read the basic arguments for "strict constructionism" versus "a living constitution." Do you think that we need to read between the lines of the original document in order to apply ideas to today's problems? Or do you believe that the Constitution says what it means and means what it says? Should we be concerned that states' rights may threaten our national citizenship rights? Or is the historical erosion of states' rights a legitimate concern for the twenty-first century? Either way, remember that many countries face the same problems of federalism. Sketch your ideas and bring them to class for discussion.

Key Words for InfoTrac Exploration

judicial activism   unfunded mandates   voter registration   workfare programs

Sources Cited

Advisory Commission on Intergovernmental Relations (1989). *State Constitutions in the Federal System.* Washington, DC: Author (A-113).

Anderson, Eloise (1997). "Blunt Instrument." *Governing,* 10(6) (March): 72.

Berman, David R. (Ed.) (1993). *County Governments in an Era of Change.* Westport, CT: Greenwood.

Bryce, James (1911). *The American Commonwealth,* Vol. II. New York: Macmillan.

Claude, Richard (1970). *The Supreme Court and the Electoral Process.* Baltimore: Johns Hopkins University Press.

Cloward, Richard A., and Frances Fox Piven (1996). *The Impact of the National Voter Registration Act (NVRA): January 1995–June 1996, The First Eighteen Months.* New York: Human SERVE Campaign for Universal Voter Registration.

Cox, George H., and Patti Thacker (1994). "Scaling the Barriers to Voter Registration." *Comparative State Politics,* 15(5) (October): 1–5.

——— (1998). "More on State Barriers to Voter Registration." *Comparative State Politics,* 19(1) (February): 26–31.

Donahue, John D. (1997). *Disunited States.* New York: Harper Collins (Basic Books).

Eigen, Lewis D., and Jonathan P. Siegel (Eds.) (1993). *The Macmillan Dictionary of Political Quotations.* New York: Macmillan.

Labbe, Jill R. (2000) "Seeing the Constitution as Enduring, Not Living." *Fort Worth Star-Telegram,* May 16.

Lemov, Penelope (1995). "The End of the Baby Bonus." *Governing,* 8 (April): 30–34.

——— (1997). "The Rocky Road to Privatizing Welfare." *Governing,* 10 (July): 36–37.

Lowenstein, Daniel H. (1995). *Election Law: Cases and Materials.* Durham, NC: Carolina Academic Press.

Osborne, David (1988). *Laboratories of Democracy: A New Breed of Governor Creates Models for National Growth.* Boston: Harvard Business School Press.

Peters, B. Guy (1996). *American Public Policy: Promise and Performance* (4th ed.). Chatham, NJ: Chatham House.

Plano, Jack C., and Milton Greenberg (1997). *The American Political Dictionary* (10th ed.). Fort Worth, TX: Harcourt Brace.

Reitman, Alan, and Robert E. Davidson (1972). *The Election Process: Voting Laws and Procedures.* Dobbs Ferry, NY: Oceana.

Rom, Mark Carl (1999). "Transforming State Health and Welfare Programs." Pp. 349–392 in Virginia Gray, Russell Hanson, and Herbert Jacob (Eds.), *Politics in the American States, A Comparative Analysis* (7th ed.). Washington, DC: CQ Press.

Rossi, Peter H., and Howard E. Freeman (1993). *Evaluation: A Systematic Approach.* Newbury Park, CA: Sage.

Smolka, Richard G. (1990). "Election Legislation." *The Book of the States, 1990–91.* Vol. 28. Lexington, KY: Council of State Governments.

Time Almanac 2000 with Information Please. Boston: Family Education Company.

U.S. Bureau of the Census (1997). *Statistical Abstract of the United States, 1996–97.* Washington, DC: U.S. Government Printing Office.

Weissert, Carol S., and Sanford F. Schram (1996). "The State of American Federalism, 1995–96." *Publius: The Journal of Federalism,* 26 (Summer): 1–26.

Welch, Susan, John Gruhl, John Comer, Susan M. Rigdon, and Michael Steinman (1999). *American Government* (7th ed.). Minneapolis: West.

World Almanac and Book of Facts—2000. Mahwah, NJ: World Almanac Books.

Capital City Players: Everyday Politics in the States

⚜ **State-Level Political Parties**

⚜ **State-Level Interest Groups**

⚜ **Media in the State Capital**

⚜ **State Political Systems**

⚜ **Chapter Conclusion**

A vast network of political players lives in your state capital, whether it is Tallahassee, Florida; Sacramento, California; or Albany, New York. Many hundreds, even thousands, of individuals are involved. This network within the capital community is made of political party officials, interest group leaders and lobbyists, and members of the capital city media corps. They know each other and do business with each other on a daily basis. What these players share in common is a deep fascination with politics. What distinguishes them from one another is that their agendas differ. Their stock and trade is information, specifically information about politics and policy. They never tire of talking about personalities, bills, or news stories that feature political players. To them, all of it is exciting and important. As a result of this almost full-time attention to politics, these political players have influence far beyond their numbers.

In this chapter, we will look at each group of political players: the activists who run the major political parties, the lobbyists who try to shape policy, and the broadcast and print media representatives who investigate and report political events. We will explore the following basic questions:

- Is it *what* you know or *who* you know that affects political careers?
- How does money become a powerful tool of influence in state politics?
- What or who controls the content and flow of information that shapes state policy?

We will try to isolate the behavior of the essentially private players—party officials, lobbyists, and reporters—from the behavior of elected and appointed

The Massachusetts State Capitol building is a significant Boston landmark and a venue for wide-ranging political discussions.

Source: © Frank White / Liaison International

officials who actually conduct the public's business. The reason for this separation is that we want to distinguish the players in the political environment who make demands for action from other state government players who (in their official capacities) actually decide public policy issues. This distinction will be important later when we examine state legislators, governors, bureaucrats, and judges who staff the public agencies of state government. This latter group is supposed to act "in the public interest." Political actors such as party officials, lobbyists, and news reporters have more narrow constituencies. They are professionals at politics, while public officials are professional politicians.

Also in this chapter, we introduce the concept of political systems. Systems analysis allows us to relate the behavior of many political players to the actions of state decision makers. We learn to analyze who presses for what issues and with what result. Systems theory also is a useful device for explaining policy decisions. It relates the content of demands made by political players to concrete laws, executive orders, and judicial and regulatory decisions adopted by state government officials. For these reasons, **a systems analysis of political life** is a powerful tool in understanding the players and their game.

ꙮ State-Level Political Parties

Political parties are private associations whose purpose is to work to secure elective public office and then facilitate governance by its members within government. The legal status of political parties at the state level is that they are heavily regulated corporations. For example, Democrats in Georgia are organized as the Democratic Party of Georgia, Inc. Political activists throughout the state are card-carrying members of their party, and their high level of interest in the party sustains its organization, fund-raising, and electioneering activities.

State Party Organization

The articles of incorporation for each state political party are filed with the secretary of state. These articles or by-laws declare the party's purposes, identify its office locations, and describe its administrative organization. State political parties typically have a party chair elected by the state's party activists. As a practical matter, the governor anoints this individual if he or she is of the same party. Otherwise, the party chair would be someone who is liked and respected by ranking elected officials of the party and chairs of the county party affiliates.

Party activists, elected officials, and county party leaders are organized into a central committee that organizes the party's convention, manages fund-raising drives, and maintains public-relations activities (Bibby & Holbrook, 1996: 80–81). Nowadays, details about the organization of political parties in your state typically are available on their Web pages. Annual reports filed with the secretary of state stipulate those who serve as officers of the organization, their terms of office, and their legal addresses. Many of the organizational and fund-raising activities of the major parties are geared to securing elective office. Reports also provide details of the party's finances, but we will have more to say about regulation of party funds later in this chapter.

Most of the party offices of both the Republicans and Democrats in each state are located in the state capital near the centers of government. These offices are maintained near the state capitol building, where they are convenient to the successful party officials who serve as legislators and executive branch officials. Statewide political activity spreads out from these headquarters. In many ways, the fifty state political organizations and their affiliated county organizations form the bedrock of U.S. party politics (Jewell & Olson, 1982: 75).

State political parties and county affiliates must attend to many duties. They have to *recruit* new political talent—new political blood—throughout the state. Today's party leaders and the elected officials who are the party's best-known standard bearers will not be around to lead the party forever. Party officials and office holders who value their party roots travel their states, meeting new people in the party. Local civic leaders, church deacons, business innovators, and student government presidents may be promising candidates for the party to promote in future elections. These people must be identified and trained in the arts of politics, especially public speaking, fund-raising, and teamwork.

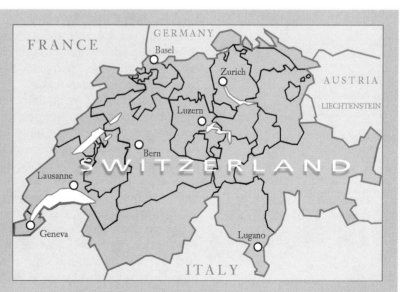

Swiss Political Parties

The Swiss Council of States consists of forty-six member who represent twenty-three cantons. Each canton elects two members, and each half canton elects one. Election procedure is determined by cantonal law and varies: Jura uses proportional representation, while the others use some form of the majority system. Switzerland has eleven major and minor political parties ranging from Social Democrats to an Evangelical People's Party. Again, consult the Swiss home page (*<http://www.ethz.ch/swiss/Switzerland_Info.html>*) and those of specific cantons for more details.

The party leaders must also *raise funds*. Political parties are private associations, and they receive little public funding. We can safely assume that members and friends raised any resources enjoyed by a state party. Money will be needed for helping under-resourced candidates who are new to politics, holding statewide conventions or meetings, advertising the party's platform, and deferring party officials' travel expenses. A state political party conducts many, many activities, and they all cost money. So, the fund-raising never stops.

Parties' Organizational Effectiveness

Strong state party organizations are relatively recent. In today's political environment, state parties are well organized, well funded, and quite busy influencing state government and policy. They were not so strong in the 1970s and 1980s. Historically, weak parties were the rule because of a lack of real two-party competition. The Republican Party dominated many Midwestern states, and the Democrats controlled most Southern states.

In hindsight, one-party dominance weakened many of the state parties in power. Because there was no threat from the other party in the November general election, ambitious politicians typically turned their criticism on fellow party members in the partisan primary. This *intraparty*—within the party—*competition* at primary election time often was savage (Nice, 1983: 371–372). As a result, state parties often knew little cohesion or harmony within them, and there was little common purpose in fund-raising and other basic party responsibilities.

The dynamic of two-party competitive political systems now makes each party battle hard to stay abreast of its competitor. Ambitious candidates must maintain harmony within their own party's ranks, reserving their sharpest criticism for the other party's candidate in the general election. This has led to more party cohesion and a healthy solidarity within the state party organizations. State Republicans and Democrats each now work within their respective parties to get elected and govern thereafter.

Party Organization and Discipline

The state party leadership has the responsibility of getting things done and keeping the peace. The party chair has the unenviable job of encouraging cooperation and compromise. Even in the best of times, politicians may be tempted to violate what some call the Eleventh Commandment: "Thou shall not criticize thy fellow party member, especially in public." The chair often has to be the principal peacemaker.

One device for forging unity can be the **party platform.** State party officials hope that harmony can be maintained if the party gives each standard bearer some of what she or he wants. Of course, individual candidates nowadays go into media campaigns with their own takes on issues. They may accept general guidance from the party, but the influence of state party officials will only be proportional to the state party's percentage of a candidate's campaign fund. And many candidates raise much of their own campaign funds.

The same strategy might be used in making working arrangements among the party faithful for passing legislation. One person's pet bill would have everyone's support today, and he or she would be expected to back others' bills later. When it works, this type of **logrolling** can keep everyone happy for a time. However, individual legislators usually have made promises to individual constituents and interest groups in order to get elected back home. Party *whips* (vote counters) and the *governor's floor leader* (personal spokesperson) may bring the message of party unity on a vote, but the ultimate decision on how to vote is an individual official's decision.

The Character of State Political Parties

The United States has a **two-party competitive** political system at both the state and national levels. Only Nebraska has a nonpartisan election for its unicameral (one-chamber) legislature. In every other state, the Republican and Democratic Parties compete for control of the state legislature and other state offices. To distinguish themselves and their party, candidates and party regulars communicate moderate **political ideologies** that describe where the party stands on the issues of the day.

The **Republican Party** in most states is the "Party of American Business," just as it is at the national level. Republican candidates and supporters are primarily white suburban professionals. Many Republican campaign themes promote the financial issues of lower taxes and smaller government, industrial development, and free trade. On social issues, most state Republican Parties are conservative: They promote welfare reform, strict law enforcement, and a modest level of social services.

The **Democratic Party** in most states is a coalition party of liberals, African Americans, women, and organized labor. Typical Democratic campaign themes are civil rights, environmental protection, and employee protections in the workplace.

Of course, no two state organizations of either party are the same. Party philosophy at the state level varies a great deal. Southern Democrats are more conservative than Northeastern Democrats. New York Republicans and Texas Republicans hold different views on many issues. Important regional issues and themes are found in both Republican and Democratic campaign messages.

Third parties are rare and short-lived in U.S. politics at both the national and state levels. Election districts are set up for winner-take-all elections, not proportional representation. Even a popular third party would be hard-pressed to win 51 percent of the vote in an entire electoral district and then hold that district in subsequent elections. If we had proportional representation, then third parties could earn seats equal to their percentage of the total popular vote in the state. As we are, however, our system simply is not friendly to third parties.

Two particular parties, however, have had more popular if not electoral appeal in recent years. The **Libertarian Party** is organized in several states. Libertarians propose that government should intrude as little as possible in the lives of private citizens. They favor a "small government" that levies few taxes and regulates few personal and corporate behaviors. Libertarian candidates can get on statewide ballots because they have entire states within which to collect signatures or record a percentage of previous votes to get them on the ballot. They also may have more luck in larger cities. However, they are hard pressed to win 51 percent of the vote in most legislative districts where there are Republican and Democratic opponents.

The **Reform Party** also advocates "small government." Its only real victory has been the election of Jesse Ventura as governor of Minnesota in 1998, although he subsequently quit the party. Reform candidates advocate what they believe are more creative approaches to social problems. They support public–private partnerships, cooperation with philanthropic agencies, and local community empowerment.

Even in states where one party dominates, the parties still have factions. For example, even while the Democratic Party dominated politics in the South, urban African American politicians could only keep an uneasy alliance with rural whites of the same party. Now, with Republican Party fortunes on the rise, we often see a membership of conservative retirees in alliance with suburban business owners and ambitious urban lawyers. Because different factions' interests are at stake in many policy debates, Democrats may tend to fracture along an urban–rural fissure while Republicans fracture along age or ideological lines. Sharing a party label and even sharing a suite of state party offices does not guarantee harmony and bliss in partisan politics.

State Partisan Elections

Political parties have two basic duties in U.S. democratic practice. They electioneer—that is, they try to get their candidates elected—and they govern as a team within state offices once they are elected. **Electioneering** takes the party's and the candidate's message to the people. Candidates are the standard bearers of their party—that is, they are expected to espouse its philosophy and promote its programs. Candidates also shape their states' party platforms by bringing new ideas and approaches to state government. The party regulars campaign for their party's candidates, help them raise funds to keep the campaign going, and keep an eye on the opponent's camp.

The election of a governor and other statewide elected officials is a partisan process in which candidates compete within a **party primary** so that the winners of the opposing parties can face each other in a general election in November. The dates for a state primary can range from as early as May (Kentucky) to as late as September (Wisconsin) (*The Book of the States, 1998–99:* 161–162). The specific rules for party primaries—or the less common primary in conjunction with party caucuses or conventions—vary by state (see Table 3.1).

Table 3.1

Method of Selecting Candidates, 1998

Selection Method	Number of States (%)
Primary election	37 (74)
Convention, then primary	9 (18)
Split convention and primary	4 (8)

Source: Compiled from *The Book of the States, 1998–99:* 159–160.

The primary is the most popular way of selecting party candidates for statewide office. Several states provide decision rules to account for results in which primary candidates do not win a clear majority. Others allow for minor party candidates to get on the general election ballot by convention or petition, whereas the two major parties must go the primary route. In nine states, party conventions select entries for the primary ballot. Four states use the primary for selecting governor and lieutenant governor candidates but retain the convention for nominating other statewide elected officials such as the secretary of state or state treasurer. However, the typical pattern is for interested party members to vie for public attention in media-based primary campaigns. Registered voters go to the polls in the primary election and select the standard bearer for each party.

Some citizens think that party primary laws are too rigid because states regulate who can vote in party primaries. Roughly one-half of the states limit voting in the primaries to people who are registered members or who "are affiliated with" a specific party (Gray & Eisinger, 1997: 96). This is called a *closed primary*. Other states allow anyone to vote in either primary so long as they declare which ballot they want when entering the polling place. This method has been called a "modified closed primary" by some and an "open, but selection of party" primary by others. Other states allow people to vote on a mixed primary ballot that allows the voter to jump around, voting for some candidates in the Democratic Party primary and other candidates in the Republican Party primary. This is called an *open primary*. Only one state, Louisiana, holds a nonpartisan primary!

Controversy arises from the fact that the parties have traditionally chosen their own candidates for public office. They once used meetings of party regulars called **caucuses** for this purpose, but the primary steadily gained popularity in the states. Allowing voters a direct role in candidate selection seemed like a good idea. A party could see how well each prospective candidate came across with the public while also building voter interest in the party for November's general election. Now the public has become used to deciding on candidates in May or September as well as choosing between the parties' candidates in November. In fact, many voters now see themselves as "independent voters." They want to participate in either or both of the parties' decisions. Having agreed to the primary system, state legislators cannot go back to party caucuses without seeming undemocratic. Parties are therefore left with no alternative but to appeal to independents as well as their party members in the media-oriented primary campaigns.

Regulation of Campaign Finances

State and federal law regulate the political parties. They are monitored in terms of campaign practices, especially *campaign financing*. The age of blatantly buying votes and bribing elected officials is behind us in most states. Laws govern the management of the polls and require all campaign spending to be reported. Statements concerning the source and amount of state money received are typically filed with the secretary of state's office.

Campaign contributions from individuals are regulated differently than contributions from organizations, many of which are interest groups. To keep anyone from trying to "buy an election," *dollar limits* have been placed on the amount of money that individuals or organizations can give to a particular candidate. Roughly two-thirds of the states limit the amount that can be given to any individual candidate. Florida, for example, caps the amount at $500 and Maine allows $5,000. Other states control the total of contributions from any individual to candidates; for example, New York allows an aggregate of $5,000 per year, and Wisconsin permits $6,000, none of which can come from corporations or labor unions (*Book of the States, 1998–99:* 178–185). Few states try to control how much a candidate or his or her family can spend from personal funds. The U.S. Supreme Court has warned that any such limitation would be a constraint on free speech (Chi, 1993: 285).

Contributions by organizations are watched closely. Corporations are prohibited from giving to candidates in almost one-half of the states, and companies typically have dollar limits much like those imposed on individual contributors in the remainder of the states. Labor unions typically are treated much the same as corporations, but states may require that they set up a separate **political action committee** (PAC) to channel and report their giving.

Money that is contributed to an individual candidate is regulated differently than money given to a political party, or so-called *soft money*. Remember that political parties are private organizations, and they can assert that, like all other private associations, they provide a variety of services to their members. They may fund general party ads, and their contributions to candidates are unlimited in most states.

Campaign-finance reform movements have been established in several Western states (excluding California). In these states, the actual costs of most campaigns have been low. The average for legislative races in Oregon, Washington, Idaho, Montana, Wyoming, Utah, Nevada, and Alaska during the early 1990s was approximately $20,000 for a state house seat and $40,000 for a state senate seat (Sanchez & Bender, 1993). Nevertheless, big contributors dumped considerable money into selected state races to shape results that were favorable to their own interests. In Nevada, for example, winning candidates got 42 percent of their traceable campaign funds from gambling interests, while losing candidates garnered only 13 percent of their funds from the same sources (Sanchez & Bender, 1993: 2). Other big campaign investors were the resource-development industries such as timber in Washington and Oregon and mining and grazing in Montana. They gave 10 percent of traceable contributions for a total of almost $5 million. Other big contributors were public and private labor unions, professional associations, and the construction and real-estate industries.

Controversial campaign finance is not peculiar to the West. In Georgia state senate races, the average cost to run for office increased from $36,000 in 1992 to more than $41,000 in 1996. The outlay by 1996 winners was four times that for losers. Many of the winners were incumbents who are allowed by state law to carry over funds from one campaign to the next. Some did not even have opposition, a comfortable state of affairs caused at least in part by their large war chests. Candidates typically chipped in less than $5,000 of their own money, but two individuals bankrolled themselves with $94,000 and $84,000 campaign funds, respectively. Small contributors of $100 or less gave only 18 percent of the total. Major contributors were the Georgia Medical Association and the Georgia Realtors Association.

One state that has tried campaign finance reform is Oregon. Measure 9 was adopted by popular initiative in Oregon in 1994. It imposed $100 limits on contributions to legislative candidates: $200 per cycle of primary and general elections for the 1996 elections. Two-thirds less money came into candidates, and one-third more contributors began to participate in the process. Organized labor's giving was cut by 93 percent, and gifts by lawyers declined by 55 percent. Some givers "bundled" their individual gifts to avoid tripping over the limitation, but the role of money in campaigning seemed to diminish. However, a recent evaluation of the impact of Oregon's campaign finance reform showed no shift away from incumbent advantage, no increase in independent or third-party candidates, and no increased interest in open seats (Sanchez, Bender & Casey, 1997).

Your school probably has Young Democrats and Young Republicans on campus. Check them out. Pick the group whose politics is closest to yours if that will make you feel more comfortable. Attend a meeting, read the group's literature, and (most important) study the leaders. These young men and women probably have political ambitions. They may hope to be discovered in the statewide talent search that always seems to be taking place. You don't have to

be a "pol" yourself to appreciate the gifts (and limitations) of this "type" of student. Also keep an eye out for any factions in the group, and if you get a chance, observe if the two party groups "snipe" at each other. This kind of firsthand observation can teach you a lot about politics. You don't have to become one or even admire "the type" to understand them. Compare your impressions with those of others in your class.

Some states have really clamped down on contributors, and some have even experimented with more publicly financed elections. The goal of all such state legislation is to minimize the influence of campaign contributions on policy making. If wealthy individuals and interest groups can buy an elected official, then popular government in the United States will be in great trouble. Political parties are heavily regulated to ensure that election to public office remains in voters' hands.

State Parties in the Government

The end of the election season brings us to the second function of political parties: *governing as a team.* Once a political party gains control of a chamber of the state legislature, then it has the authority to select the chamber's presiding officials and committee chairs. Party members hold majorities on all of the committees where the important work of crafting policy is carried out. In other words, a party controls the legislature to some degree or another and is accountable to its regulars and the electorate for producing the policy results that were promised during elections.

Control of the state legislatures is a central goal for the Democrats and the Republicans in each state. In recent years, the Republican Party has made major inroads into what was the Democratic domination of politics at the state legislature level (see **Figure 3.1**). By 1996, Republicans had gained rough parity with Democrats in terms of the total number of legislative seats that each enjoys nationwide. In 1998, the Democrats stemmed the tide, gaining forty state legislative seats nationally.

Republicans traditionally have been strong in New England, the Midwest, and the Western states. They have been making major advances in the Southern states where they have gained control of at least one body of the legislature in many states.

It is not unusual for an election to place a divided government in control of the state. Some executive branch officials are Republicans, and others are Democrats. One party does not control the legislature. Instead, there may be overall parity in both chambers, or one party may hold the upper house while the other controls the lower chamber. This type of divided government is becoming more common, perhaps because it does not make the average citizen at all uncomfortable (Squire, 1993). After all, we have had divided government in the nation's capital for decades.

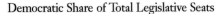

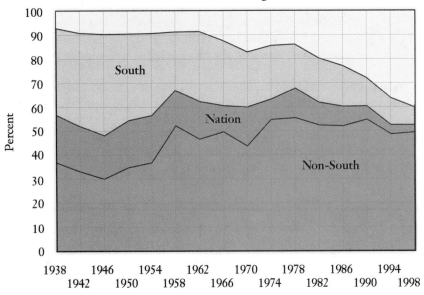

Figure 3.1 Partisan control of state legislatures

Source: National Conference of State Legislatures online (*<http://www.ncsl.org/>*)

❧ State-Level Interest Groups

State legislators respond to their constituents because that is their duty as elected officials and because they cannot hope to be reelected unless the public finds them responsive. Corporations and associations are constituents, too. People organize themselves to compete and succeed in the economy (corporations), and people organize themselves to promote and protect their occupations, philosophies, and groups (associations). These **interest organizations** are concerned about state laws and regulations that may help or harm them. It is only reasonable that they would lobby state officials to protect and promote their interests.

Revenue to support state interest groups comes mainly from membership dues (Lowery & Gray, 1997: 14–15). The organizations provide a variety of benefits in return: conferences, contacts with officials, publications, and participation opportunities. These services are provided in addition to the advocacy and lobbying that we have come to expect from state and national interest organizations.

State capitals are blanketed with the offices of interest organizations ranging from utility companies to schoolteachers' unions to hospital associations. Some states have more interest group activity than do others (see Table 3.2). **Lobbyists** working out of these offices wine and dine state legislators in their efforts to influence legislation. Surveys have been made of which kinds of interest groups are most active in state politics. Individual corporations, business and trade associations, utility companies, banks, hospital associations, builder and contractor groups, and insurance associations have lobbyists in virtually all state capitals (Thomas & Hrebenar, 1996: 127). Other groups that are

Table 3.2
States with Most Registered Lobbyists

State	Number in 1996	Change Since 1988
1. Arizona	5,500	+1,000
2. Illinois	3,500	+2,900
3. New York	2,000	+410
4. Florida	2,000	-2,000
5. Ohio	2,000	+500
6. Missouri	2,000	+1,000
7. Virginia	1,600	+800
8. Michigan	1,300	-400
9. Minnesota	1,300	+200
10. Texas	1,200	+400

Source: Council of State Governments, *The Book of the States, 1998–99:* 484.

almost always represented are local government associations, public employee unions, and schoolteacher organizations. **Public-interest organizations** are advocacy groups for causes rather than agents of direct self-interest. Environmental groups are one such public-interest organization, and they have established themselves in many states.

Examples of interest group activity at the state level can be drawn from any state. One interesting example of interest group activity is the monitoring done by area Chambers of Commerce in Vermont. The Lake Champlain Regional Chamber of Commerce, for instance, issues a weekly newsletter that details the legislative deliberations and votes in Montpelier, the state capital. Specific legislators are identified so that local chambers can contact them concerning important bills.

Another interesting situation developed in the 1998 session of the Georgia General Assembly. Garden clubs made political news when they took on the state's billboard industry. The companies that maintain these signs wanted a state law that would allow them to cut down trees that blocked motorists' view of their advertising. Garden clubs objected that the roadside landscape should be spared. State legislators took the garden club members—16,500 people organized into 550 chapters—seriously.

Lobbyists represent a wide variety of interest groups, and it is not unusual to see these representatives waiting their turn to see state government leaders.
Source: © Paul Conklin / PhotoEdit

Interest Group Activities

Some interest organizations have been rated as extremely effective in getting their preferences adopted by state legislatures. School teachers' groups are perhaps the most effective interest organizations, followed by general business groups such as Chambers of Commerce and utility companies (Thomas & Hrebenar, 1996: 149). Some of this success is because skilled and hardworking lobbyists provide information to legislators, help draft bills, testify before legislative committees, and communicate group concerns to key lawmakers. It would be naive to assume that the impact of teachers' votes or utility companies' campaign contributions play no role in influencing state policy. Politicians respond to pressure from interest groups just as they react to their party leadership and local constituents. All sorts of inputs may affect a legislator's decision on how to vote on a particular bill.

Regulating Interest Groups

State governments take measures to control the political activities of interest groups. One simple but effective measure is to require that lobbyists *register* with the secretary of state or other designated official. In registering, a lobbyist must provide a name, address, photograph, and employer name. This information becomes a part of the public record, open to the press and citizens alike. Thereafter, when the individual is on state grounds such as the legislature, an identification badge must be worn. This badge lets legislators and staff members know that the person is a lobbyist.

Beyond registration, *periodic reports* also must be filed. In all but ten states, lobbyists must declare the type of legislation or administrative action they seek to influence. In forty-two states, the reports also will disclose all expenditures being made that benefit public officials or employees. In roughly one-half of the states, each lobbyist's compensation and its source or sources also must be reported (*The Book of the States: 1998–99:* 381–382). Lobbying regulation has small but beneficial effects (Gray & Lowery, 1998). Rules make the lobbying process more transparent, or more open to public view. Such regulation does not seem to harm even small and new groups that want to be a part of political life in the state capital.

❧ Media in the State Capital

Citizens rely on print and broadcast media for political news. Some people like to sit down with the morning newspaper; others prefer to listen to state and

New Jersey Governor Christine Todd Whitman prepares for a press conference with members of the capital media corps.

Source: © Laura Pedrick / Corbis Sygma

local news on the car radio on their way to and from work. Regardless of the medium we choose, many of us want access to current information about our political officials and their actions.

News Services

Each state capital has its *news bureaus.* These agencies hire reporters who provide detailed news about state government to newspapers, news magazines, and radio and television stations. With the growing interest in the devolution of policy to the states, these agencies often provide news feeds to national magazines and networks. More and more coverage of state government is available to interested students or constituents.

Print stories about state government are often picked up and printed in *Governing* magazine. This national monthly newsmagazine is focused on the concerns of state and local governments. Another good source of information about the states and their political issues is *State Legislature*, a monthly newsmagazine targeted at state elected officials.

Increasingly, mainstream national newsmagazines are covering state politics, especially governors. The personal story of a state's chief policy maker makes good reading for a national audience. Chapter 5 gives more attention to the relationship between the governors, their press secretaries, and the media.

Capital City Newspapers

The most important news source is the state government desk of the major daily newspaper in the state capital, at least according to prominent state officials themselves (Beyle & Lynch, 1993: 35). An experienced journalist or team of journalists who keep track of political events in state government staffs this newspaper desk. This detailed coverage is of interest to some newspaper subscribers, depending on individual tastes and preferences. However, the political players and state officials in the state capital are attentive readers. They are anxious to see how their issues and activities are being covered in the paper.

Several sections of the capital's major newspaper are of particular interest to politicians. *Feature articles* on state issues are certainly important. What sort of coverage is given to an issue like deteriorating state highways or unsafe school bus inspections? If an issue gains visibility with the public, then elected officials and career state civil servants will feel pressured to act. Daily news reporting is also important, especially during legislative sessions. This coverage names proponents and opponents of key bills and repeats the charges and countercharges of political parties about how bills are being treated. It reports on the activities of lobbyists who support or oppose particular pieces of legislation. All players look for their names in the newspaper. They are human enough to want to see their motives and actions cast in a positive light.

The *editorial pages* are another important section of the capital city news daily. On these pages, the paper's management takes stands on the major policy issues of the day. Many of these issues involve state government operations, bills before the legislature, cases before regulatory commissions, and other state policy matters. Again, political players are named and characterized in the editorials. Many readers can be swayed by editorial opinion, so political players prudently read and respond as needed to newspaper editorials.

Finally, newspapers also run purely *political analyses*. Media representatives tend to keep score in political races, assess the fortunes of the major political parties, and examine the careers of individual politicians. It is important when they state that an individual's political stock is rising, and it can be dangerous when they declare a candidacy dead. Judgments about the overall success of a party in the legislature or in the election season also can be important pronouncements. The average citizen has little firsthand knowledge of candidates, parties, or politicians. The declared momentum of a candidate or party can sway the independent voter, and the casual financial donor can be scared off by an unfavorable media evaluation of a candidate, party, or officeholder. In other words, political analyses may not need to be challenged, but they can never be ignored.

Not everyone in the state or even the state capital reads the daily newspaper, but most politically influential people do. The major capital city newspaper informs, advocates, and evaluates politics. It is a major player.

Broadcast Media

The state public radio and television networks often cover the state legislature in great detail, and many even have daily coverage while the legislature is in session. Commercial radio and television also give routine coverage to state politics and government. However, the broadcast media treatment given to state politics and policy is different than that provided by newspapers. Broadcast news is generally more superficial, more dramatized, and more focused on consumer-oriented issues. In fact, few state political leaders seem to take television seriously (Beyle & Lynch, 1993: 38).

Public radio and television are funded by a combination of national and state grant money plus contributions from individual and corporate supporters. Because state money is involved, public radio and television commonly provide detailed and even-handed coverage of state government. For example, public

---

Exploring on Your Own **Media Scan**

Go to the library and get the major newspaper from your state capital. Scan the paper for articles, editorials, cartoons, and other materials pertaining to state government. If you are taking this class while your state legislature is in session, then there should be lots of information. Also locate alternative media such as newspapers published by African American activists or newsletters issued by specific interest groups. How does advocacy journalism differ from commercial media? Bring your notes back to class for discussion.

radio might broadcast live the governor's State of the State Address, and public television would probably carry highlights and analysis of the speech that evening. During the legislative session, public radio and television might provide nightly coverage using a newsmagazine format. The ability of public television to bring visual images into homes is a major advantage for that medium. The public can literally see legislators at work. We can see them interviewed in some depth about the issues before the legislature. Video clips can contrast the positions on issues held by the majority and minority parties. The governor can comment on legislation, and legislators can comment on the effectiveness of state administration. The public can get a great deal of information through the medium of public television. Unfortunately, most people are more interested in commercial media than in public media.

State and local news on the *commercial networks* is limited in most media markets. Some news of the legislature's deliberations or the governor's policy programs does find its way onto the daily news broadcasts of local radio stations and network television affiliates, but state news always competes with national feeds of late-breaking political developments in Washington, D.C., and sensational local news programs. The state government share of this type of news coverage is quite small.

Feature-length coverage may be found if local stations develop special features on state politics issues. These issue-oriented programs are similar to national network news specials. In-depth interviews with state newsmakers may be produced if coverage in the print media seems to draw public comment. Although their production may be less polished, the content does reach attentive members of the public. Some *public-service programming* can be found on cable-television channels. Live or taped coverage of state government activities may be carried on public-access cable, although, like network affiliate coverage of state issues, it suffers lower viewer ratings than does entertainment programming.

Talk radio has become popular as controversial personalities such as Rush Limbaugh and Gordon Liddy have launched their own nationally syndicated shows. State capital radio stations have tried to piggyback on this success with their own talk-radio programming, with the host interviewing newsmakers in state politics and citizen callers questioning guests. Talk-show programming may not be news media per se, and many have a theatrical point of view, but they do represent a medium of communication with the public.

The influence of state media is hard to measure. A few surveys of state officials have been made, but we really do not know how political leaders weigh media comments in their decision making. A particular issue may capture the media's attention and hasten its listing on the political agenda. An embarrassing scandal may be uncovered by a news organization acting as a watchdog for the public interest. The political fortunes of candidates and officeholders can be scored, and administrations evaluated. Nevertheless, the public has much less information about state government than about national or local government. State news is largely the province of the specialist and the activist.

❧ State Political Systems

State governments respond to political pressures. They live and function within a robust political environment of personal and group ambition. Because politics affects policy and policy makers, we think it important to relate the many pressures and players to one another. David Easton's model of the political system allows us to deal with many political influences and their interactions (see Easton, 1965).

A *model* is a picture or metaphor that helps us conceptualize a real-world phenomenon. The model is an intentional simplification, not a description of any specific person's behavior or any particular state's politics. After a model is fully developed, evidence can be collected to see how the model applies to various situations.

The systems analysis of state politics begins with a statement about structures rather than processes. David Easton, one architect of political systems theory, uses a box in the center of his model to represent decision makers. The structure of decision making that takes place within the box is really another kind of study. To the systems analyst, the *decision-making structure* in the box could be a legislative committee, the governor's office, a court deliberation, or a regulatory board. In any case, the decision-making locus itself—the box—is irrelevant. All political decision making in the democratic American political milieu is influenced by dynamics that come out of the *political environment*. It is these processes, not the decision-making structures, that are of interest to the systems analyst.

Conceptualize the decision-making box as being afloat in a sea of politically relevant opinions, needs, and ambitions. These private-sector phenomena constitute the *political environment*. For example, many citizens who are interested in improved education have similar reform ideas. They talk about them informally over coffee, at the barbershop, or at the pool. This is private, constitutionally protected speech. If the comments are critical of the school board or state school regulations, so be it. The citizens' thoughts and speech reflect their free exercise of political liberty.

If these and other citizens want something—say, improved public education for their children—they can come together to discuss their concerns and possibly form an interest organization. The purpose of the group is to advance the cause of better schools. This is still private, protected behavior. Is it political? Well, that depends on where we draw the boundary between a political system and its environment. For the moment, imagine that the new education reform group usually sits on the boundary of politics. It could resist the impulse to make demands on the school board, or it might become politically active and make demands of policy makers to reform the schools.

This brings us to the first dynamic of the systems model—*demand*. Systems theorists represent the relationship between a political demand and a government decision maker with a causal arrow (see **Figure 3.2**). Any political action by a private interest organization brings that group into the domain of the political system. It may still have purely private activities, but it has become a political player. For example, the local Chamber of Commerce will still have its luncheon meetings, encourage and welcome new companies, and privately deal with customer complaints. These private activities in no way disqualify the

Figure 3.2 System demands

CHAPTER 3 Capital City Players: *Everyday Politics in the States*

organization from taking a seat at the political table when it comes to state legislation, business regulation, or campaigns for the governor's office.

Most politicians would like to respond to legitimate demands for action. An effective demand received in person, through correspondence, or through the media gets the ball rolling. However, political action requires more than just a demand for action. If all that was needed for a political decision maker to act was a demand, then welfare rights organizations would have succeeded in making welfare benefits generous in every state. Obviously, all demands are not equally effective. Some demands come from "weak" groups—that is, organizations with little money, prestige, or votes to deliver. Other demands get filtered out of the flow of politics by the media. They judge an issue to be irrelevant, inappropriate, or trivial. As a result, the issue gets no publicity, and no pressure builds for the demand to be taken seriously. However, even an issue those politicians find interesting may fail to get acted upon. This is because a second factor, support, is also needed for action to take place.

Political *support* takes the form of adequate resources and supportive public opinion. The systems theorist represents support in the system model with a second causal arrow alongside demand (see **Figure 3.3**). To act, political decision makers must have certain *resources*. Revenues come into government from taxes, fees, and other sources. Some demands for policies or programs would be expensive, and the resources may not be there to enact the program being demanded. In this case, the politician faces an unpopular choice with voters: raising taxes or charging new fees. On the other hand, if meeting the demand would not be costly, then it has a better chance of being enacted.

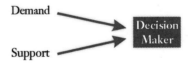

Figure 3.3 Demand and support

The other support is positive *public opinion*. Most public opinion is not active. If the public was aggressively insisting on a particular position on an issue, then that would be demand. The demand would be expressed by many groups and be acted on accordingly. However, most of us are not extremely opinionated about most issues. In fact, we are often ignorant of many issues altogether. What the politician has to "consult" is really the underlying public feeling about an issue. If the official is fortunate enough to find opinion poll results on an issue, then the underlying public sentiment may be uncovered. The politician or an interest group may even pay to have an opinion poll conducted, although most politicians must rely on their own perceptions of where the public stands on an issue.

Reasonable demands that are made in a context of positive public opinion and adequate resources will be placed high on the political agenda of a government body. The politics of **agenda building** (Cobb & Elder, 1983) in the states is therefore a boiling stew of competing demands and shifting supports. Political parties are valuable at this stage in the political system. They can filter and rank a long list of demands. In this way, politicians pool their cumulative expertise in deciding what is feasible and desirable. They are astute judges of how the public will react to their actions. They are skillful in crafting compromises that give many competing interests some of what each one wants. Although most systems models do not diagram the screening process of the media and the ranking function of political parties, we certainly can (see **Figure 3.4**). Obviously, the media and political parties play important intervening roles in our variant of the political systems model. The newspaper editors, radio commentators, and television or cable reporters place a certain "spin" on the issues. They may find merit in some problematic demands for action, and they may show little interest in other worthy issues. By covering an issue, political media give it credibility. Media also interpret what the public thinks about an issue with or without solid public-opinion poll data. The very language they use to describe revenue problems shapes the future of an issue that requires considerable public revenue. Not everyone reads the state pages of the major newspapers and magazines, but politicians do.

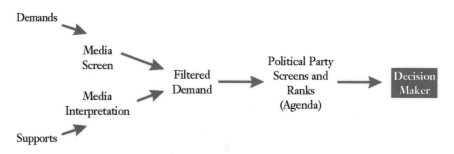

Figure 3.4 Filtering and ranking demands

The question inevitably arises about what role campaign financing plays in this model. Private groups certainly do contribute to political parties and individual campaigns. You will recall that they often have PACs that are totally devoted to dispensing such assistance. Does the money from a private interest group come with no strings attached? Probably not. Politicians and groups try to come to some acceptable but soft understanding about issues. A particular candidate may be endorsed by an interest group, or a given political party may be a regular recipient of financial support from an interest organization. This is not to say that interest groups buy politicians. Many groups give to many candidates of both parties and may regularly give money to both state party organizations. They are prudent investors. But to say that a candidate would refuse the endorsement or financial support of all interest groups is to say that he or she has no issues or is weak on taking positions on the issues. Few refuse the money.

In reality, a legislative session or a gubernatorial campaign is chaotic. There are so many groups, and each has numerous needs and wants. Without the screens of the media and political parties, an agenda for action would probably never get built. There are simply too many demands. A considerable influence on the ultimate agenda is the interest of the politician or candidate.

People who seek or hold public office have their own personalities and priorities. This is clearly true in the case of judges, political officials whose judicial philosophy guides much of the policy they make. But governors and legislators and regulators are individuals, too. They will elevate certain issues and the groups that advocate them by virtue of a personal belief in the cause. And yet the systems model draws our attention to the interplay of many forces that influence policy making, helping us describe a basic fact of American political life: Influence is plural, not unitary. No single power elite controls the politics of our state governments. Granted, some people and some groups have more influence than others. But various groups vie for influence, and almost all get their way at least some times. They therefore stay in the game. We call this interpretation of American politics *interest group liberalism* or **pluralism.** It is an interpretation of state politics that is quite consistent with the systems model of political behavior.

Winning takes the form of system *outputs.* To win at the game of pluralist politics is to get a bill passed or secure a favorable executive order, judicial decision, or regulatory ruling. In a constitutional democracy in which law is supreme, issues get resolved for the time being when a lawful decision is made. This is why David Easton calls politics "the authoritative allocation of values." Many groups with many values compete for influence, and someone wins. The state law on touchy matters such as abortion can say one and only one thing about legal behavior at this point in time. The law may change tomorrow. Some groups obviously hope so. They will work tirelessly to have their own views adopted. But the law can say only that single thing on an issue such as abortion at any given time: It's the law, and citizens must conform to its authority. Otherwise, a pluralistic democracy cannot survive.

Systems theorists represent policies as decision outputs with causal arrows coming out of the decision-making box (see Figure 3.5). Decision outputs can be any policy ranging from a legislative act to a governor's declaration, a court decision, or a regulatory agency ruling. The key aspect of the decision is that it is an *authoritative policy decision.* In other words, it has the force of law. Regardless of the interplay of demands that lead to the decision, some resolution is made. For the moment, the issue is resolved: Some people win, and others lose. Of course, victory is transitory. Losers do not give up. Next time, they may be the winners.

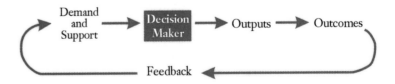

Figure 3.5 System outputs, outcomes, and feedback

Decisions have consequences or decisional *outcomes.* Outputs produce outcomes when the decisions hit the system's task environment. The policy will have some effects. They may be the ones envisioned when the policy was adopted, or they may be unintended consequences. The outcomes are experienced in the politicians' task environment, the very place where problems (inputs) originate. The policies may have effects on the problems they were designed to solve. To some extent, the policy decisions have results, and the policies are judged as effective or ineffective depending on their outcomes. We will have more to say about actual policy outputs and their outcomes in the chapters on state legislatures and governors.

When the outcomes of policies become known, new demands will arise and old demands will be reshaped. In systems terms, this process is called *feedback*. Media help this part of the process by reporting on the effectiveness of government policies and programs. Citizens and funding agents pick up on the news about a program's outcomes, and the level of support for future decisions in that policy area is affected. In other words, feedback makes the whole systems analysis *dynamic*. If it were static, then a program would be implemented and would succeed or fail. That would be that. But social problems do not usually just go away. Policy making is a long process of fine-tuning policies and programs until some reasonably satisfying outcomes are achieved. Over time, political systems adapt, perhaps even learn. In that sense, a state political system is not just a collection of players, but a system within which the capital city players may thrive or wither. They are interwoven in a network of dynamic political relationships.

✎ Chapter Conclusion

In this chapter, you learned about everyday politics in the state capital. The political party officials, interest group lobbyists, and media personalities interact with government officials in an elaborate drama. The stakes of this political game are high. Citizens' lives will be affected by the decisions made in their state capitals. The following points are worth noting:

- Many conversations over lunch or drinks will ultimately shape public policy. There is nothing particularly sinister about this process of influencing government decisions. After all, interest groups and political parties are just another way of citizens voicing their concerns.
- The media have their jobs to do as well. They believe they serve the public interest when they scrutinize and sometimes sensationalize public affairs. This may indeed be the case. The media are not quick to publicize whether citizens find their reporting credible. State officials are a different matter.
- State elected and appointed officials ascribe moderate influence to print media and somewhat less influence to broadcast media. The major state capital newspaper and the news services are particularly important to politicians.
- The point of this chapter is not to glorify or condemn the way politics works. Rather it assumes that "politics is." If we return to our questions about whose influence counts in state politics, you will have to make some judgments for yourself.
- Personal influence or reputation carries weight for a distinguished few. Money can influence decision makers, especially if the politicians do not have the resources they need to seek reelection.

- Our task as citizens and political science students is to try to understand politics and relate to the process in effective ways. Political officials and the other people who are politically active in the state capital are still people. They have all of the vanities and limitations we all have. They are simply living in a fishbowl.

Key Words for InfoTrac Exploration

campaign funds	political party platforms	Reform Party (United States)	talk shows

Sources Cited

Beyle, Thad, and Patrick Lynch (1993). "Measuring State Officials' Views of the Media." *Comparative State Politics*, *14*(3) (June): 32–42.

Bibby, John F., and Thomas M. Holbrook (1996). "Parties and Elections." Pp. 78–121 in Virginia Gray and Herbert Jacob (Eds.), *Politics in the American States: A Comparative Analysis* (6th ed.). Washington, DC: Congressional Quarterly Press.

The Book of the States, 1998-99 (1998), Vol. 23. Lexington, KY: Council of State Governments.

Chi, Keon S. (1992). "Financing State and Local Elections: Trends and Issues." *The Book of the States, 1992–93* (Vol. 29). Lexington, KY: Council of State Governments.

Cobb, Roger, and Charles Elder (1983). *Participation in American Politics*. Baltimore: Johns Hopkins University Press.

Easton, David (1965). *A Systems Analysis of Political Life*. New York: Wiley & Sons.

Gray, Virginia, and Peter Eisinger (1997). *American States and Cities* (2nd ed.). New York: Longman.

Gray, Virginia, and David Lowery (1998). "State Lobbying Regulations and Their Enforcement: Implications for the Diversity of Interest Communities." *State and Local Government Review*, *30*(2) (Spring): 78–91.

Jewell, Malcolm, and David Olson (1988). *Political Parties and Elections in the American States*. Chicago: Dorsey.

Lowery, David, and Virginia Gray (1997). "How Similar Are State and National Interest Organizations?" *Comparative State Politics*, *18*(1) (February): 1–15.

Nice, David (1983). "Revitalizing the States: A Look at the Record." *National Civic Review* (January): 371–376.

Sanchez, Samantha, and Ed Bender (1993). *The Price of Democracy: The High and Hidden Costs of Politics in the West*. Portland, OR: Western States Center.

Sanchez, Samantha, Ed Bender; and Linda Casey (1997). *Campaign Finance Reform in Oregon: The Impact of Campaign Finance Reform on the 1996 Oregon Elections*. Helena, MT: Western States Center.

Squire, Peverill (1993). "Divided Government and Public Opinion in the States." *State and Local Government Review*, *25*(3) (Fall): 150–154.

Thomas, Clive S., and Ronald J. Hrebenar (1996). "Interest Groups in the States." Pp. 122–158 in Virginia Gray and Herbert Jacob (Eds.), *Politics in the American States: A Comparative Analysis* (6th ed.). Washington, DC: Congressional Quarterly Press.

4

State Legislatures: Policy Roles and Procedural Rules

- ❧ **Public Policy Decision Making**

- ❧ **Direct Democracy**

- ❧ **Representative Democracy**

- ❧ **Legislative Life in the State Capital**

- ❧ **Legislative Leadership**

- ❧ **Passing State Laws**

- ❧ **State Legislation**

- ❧ **Legislative Oversight**

- ❧ **Chapter Conclusion**

If you drive your car today, you are required by law to have a valid driver's license, title or other proof of ownership, automobile insurance, and a current license tag. The driver's license documents that you have passed state-mandated tests of your driving knowledge, your physical ability to see and control the car, and your practical skill in operating the vehicle. State laws and regulations specify that the title to the vehicle must be onboard, and most of us keep it in the glove compartment. Most states also require you to carry an insurance policy that protects others from dangers caused by your driving—and, hopefully, protects you as well. Finally, yet another state law requires that you pay state taxes on the value of the vehicle and display a state-manufactured license tag with tax stickers on the vehicle.

If you need them, you must not drive without your glasses or contacts. You must not exceed the posted speed limits on streets and highways. You must slow down in all school zones, turn down the music in a hospital zone, and pull to the side of the road at the sight or sound of an emergency vehicle. You must not drive after consuming alcoholic beverages. And in some states, you may not operate a telephone, computer, or other distracting device while driving.

Violate any of these or a myriad of other state driving regulations, and your driving privilege will be restricted or withdrawn. All of this state law is involved in the simple act of driving to class!

In many hundreds of ways, the state in which we live affects our daily lives. State law regulates your workplace, assesses taxes on your department store purchases, and imposes sanitary restrictions on the sandwich shop where you have lunch. Few Americans appreciate how much responsibility has been given to state legislatures. We have ignored the range and complexity of state law too often.

In a democratic society, public policy (or law) is made by properly selected representatives of the people. In state government, the key elected representatives are the state legislators. Representative government is designed to reflect the will of the people while simultaneously providing a cushion of protection for established rights already in the law. In its simplest terms, both the people as a mass public and people organized around their vested interests are to be represented. State legislatures try to respond to both individuals and groups.

In this chapter, we will define public policy and discuss how it is made. We briefly describe direct public action on policy issues. We then examine the election of state representatives, what they are like as policy makers, how they accomplish their work, and what the workday is like in the state capital. We also note some of the key issues in state legislative policy making as examples of legislative work products.

In the process of learning about the basic structure and operation of state legislatures, we will answer some important questions about how democratic the policy-making process may be.

- Is public opinion more accurately expressed in direct democratic action or through the deliberations of the people's representatives?
- Whose long-term interests are best served by protracted legislative attention to laws, budgets, and regulations?
- Do the political parties, various interest groups, and the media vie for influence and ultimately balance each other out? Does any single elite dominate state government?
- What key policy issues face state legislatures today? Who are the winners who most benefit from changing policy?

By the end of this chapter, you should have a clear idea of how state legislatures make so many policies that affect our daily lives. You also may be prepared to answer for yourself basic questions about how democratic your state government really is.

❧ Public Policy Decision Making

The state policies that are passed by legislators are called **statutes** or statutory law. Laws are binding on individuals and corporations within the state, and particular laws address specific needs or problems. State law is full of thousands of detailed statutes and regulations that control behavior, award benefits, allocate resources, and shape the everyday lives of citizens and corporations. State law regulates everything from birth certificates to drivers' licenses, high school diplomas, and marriage licenses.

The great majority of statutory law continues year after year. During any one legislative session, only a tiny fraction of state laws can be examined, updated, amended, or repealed. Great volumes of state statutes are collected in *codebooks*. Many professionals spend years of education and more years updating their knowledge of the details of state law and how each one is applied. In fact, this is a core responsibility of being an attorney-at-law.

State law must conform to the state constitution, the federal constitution, and relevant national laws. According to legal scholars, this *corpus*, or body, of state law exhibits regularities and patterns in its code. It is organized into topical code chapters and annotated with special abbreviations that locate each provision within the larger body of law. Tradition and custom steer lawmakers in predictable directions. It is no accident that the legislative leaders in most states are attorneys. Even when the leadership comes from different backgrounds, stables of staff attorneys keep the form and substance of state law consistent.

BOX 4.1   *Lawyers at Work*

If you plan a career in law, you will probably become part of the specialized "priesthood" of lawyers who try to master the state codebook (along with many other subjects). Relatively few lawyers practice before the federal bench.

The overwhelming majority of attorneys practice within a state bar, a group of attorneys who have been examined and found knowledgeable. Of course, the exam is the state bar exam. Each state's laws are different, so you must be licensed in the state where you wish to practice law. After passing the bar exam, you apply for admission to the state bar. Your license permits you to practice civil and criminal law in the state. You can keep your license only so long as you abide by the rules that govern lawyers' behavior. You will probably join the state bar association so that you can lobby for favorable state laws that govern attorneys.

Laws are enacted in many ways. A *constitution* might be adopted by a convention of the public's representatives or through a popular referendum. Normal *state laws* might be passed by the legislature; *regulations* are issued by state regulatory agencies. Governors issue *executive orders*. State Supreme Court Justices make *rulings*. All have the power of law. We focus our attention now on the public's role in policy making, because it is the public's interest that is at stake in capital city politics.

◆ Direct Democracy

In small local communities, people may be able to influence policy decisions directly or decide specific matters themselves. We call this **direct democracy.** In a neighborhood or in a small township, the people may be willing and able to come together to make decisions that affect them all (Lappé & DuBois, 1994). In New England, this activity is called a *town hall meeting*, a term that has been picked up and used by politicians all over the country. But even medium-sized cities must rely on *indirect democracy*—that is, elected officials—to make public policy. States, on the other hand, have always seemed too large to be governed through direct democracy, especially before the

Citizens such as these at an incorporation hearing in Laguna Niguel, California, can meet to either determine for themselves or greatly influence policy decisions made by elected officials.
Source: © Spencer Grant / Stock · Boston

development of fiber-optic computer networks and electronic data processing.

There have been two notable exceptions to the generalization that indirect democracy rules: (1) the popular referendum and (2) the initiative. A **referendum** is a public vote on a policy issue. Some states use referenda to decide constitutional questions or issues that require popular consent under the state constitution. Referenda also are used to resolve policy questions that politicians are unable or unwilling to decide on their own. The **initiative** is a legislative proposal from the public that will later be decided by the public (the direct initiative) or the legislature (the indirect initiative). The subject matter of the initiative may be either the state's constitution or ordinary laws.

The referendum is used for different purposes in the twenty-six states where it is allowed (see **Table 4.1**). In twenty-three states, a *statutory referendum* functions as a veto of bills that have been passed by the state legislature, although typically not budgetary items. For ninety days following passage of a bill, citizens may file their completed referendum petition with the state's secretary of state. The completed petition must show a number of signatures that is equal to between 4 and 10 percent of the voter turnout in the most recent gubernatorial election (each state's target is different). The bill's implementation is suspended until a referendum vote can be held. If a majority of those who vote disapprove it, then the bill is killed.

In twenty-one of these same states and in two others, the legislature may place a bill on a popular referendum ballot. This type of legislative referendum can be binding or advisory. If the latter, then the advisory referendum represents an effort by the legislators to gauge public opinion on a controversial issue.

Table 4.1
State Referenda Laws

Type of Action	Number of States
Citizens petition to review bill	23
Legislature submits bill to public	23
(Both types of bill action)	(21)
No legislative referendum	27
Constitutional change	49

Source: Compiled from *The Book of the States, 1998–99:* 210

CHAPTER 4   State Legislatures: *Policy Roles and Procedural Rules*

Take a few minutes and sketch your vision of teledemocracy in the year 2010. Use what you know about the World Wide Web, electronic mail, and computer analysis of numerical data to inform your vision. What will the quality and stability of decision making be like in 2010 if we decide more and more issues directly? Will everyone be a part of the decisions? What groups within U.S. society will be able to use this tool for their own ends? Be prepared to discuss these issues with your classmates.

Constitutional revisions are adopted by referenda in every state except Alabama. Because state constitutions are relatively specific documents compared with the national constitution, these popular votes often involve important policy decisions. Eighteen states allow citizens to initiate a constitutional change through either the direct or the indirect initiative process.

The *direct initiative* allows a citizens' petition to place a substantive policy issue on the ballot, even without the agreement of the state legislature. Seventeen states permit the direct initiative, most of them in the West and Midwest. Other states allow an *indirect initiative*, or a petition that forces the state legislature to take up the issue. Only eight states use this approach, and four state constitutions allow both direct and indirect initiatives.

Some of the important issues that states have decided through the popular referendum are quite controversial. California seems to lead the way in using referenda to enact laws that catch the attention of the U.S. news media and public. Proposition 13, for example, was a constitutional issue on the California ballot in 1978 that rolled back property taxes and stimulated a taxpayer revolt in other parts of the country.

Another example of the important measures that have been enacted through popular initiative are the term-limits laws for state officials that passed in California, Colorado, Oklahoma, and Oregon. Popular movements in those states led to restrictions on the number of terms that a state legislator may serve. Many voters agreed that politics was becoming a lifelong profession for some of their representatives. As we will see later, however, these public reactions may seriously affect the future of legislative leadership, the relative strength of interest groups, and many other important aspects of life in the capital city.

Citizens have used the popular initiative technique to place other important issues on the legislative agenda, and important matters clearly get decided in popular referenda. As we noted in Chapter 1, the prospects for greater use of direct democracy are enhanced by the new technologies of computerized communications and fast electronic data processing. It may soon be technologically feasible to submit many or even most public policy decisions to popular referenda. It may be easier and easier to log in petition names and more readily secure a popular initiative for the electronic ballot. So far, though, direct democracy is the exception rather than the rule in the United States. We still primarily rely on representative government—or indirect democracy—for our policy making.

❧ Representative Democracy

American democratic theory provides criteria for representative democracy. It holds that the method of selecting representatives is critical to the **legitimacy** of government. Fair and open elections should be held on a regular basis. This regularity and openness provide the public with an opportunity to support or remove incumbents and screen the appeals and accusations of challengers for elected office. In state government, the boundaries of electoral districts and terms in office for the legislature are particularly sensitive issues. Many people also are concerned about campaign financing and the advantages that incumbents have in the legislative elections.

Democratic practice also should require open access to decision makers by the public, interest groups, and the media. People should have a say in the particular policies being considered by the legislature. It would be unfair to consider a law that affected a person or company and not let that party study and comment on the proposal. By the same token, ordinary people cannot comment on prospective legislation unless they know about its existence. The news media help keep people informed about potential new laws.

Public Expectations

Citizens' expectations about how they are to be represented vary. Some of us want our representatives to vote our own preferences, not theirs. This has been called the **delegate orientation** model of representation (Wahlke, Eulau, Buchanan, & Ferguson, 1962). We have delegated our say in policy matters to the elected individual, but we want to keep him or her on a short leash. If the representative goes against the wishes of constituents, then a person who holds the delegate orientation feels betrayed. Another model of representation is the **trustee orientation.** Under this model, people are elected to represent their constituents because local voters trust their judgment. Many of us have little knowledge about the policy issues that the representatives must consider. More important, we may have little time and interest to explore them on our own. Given these parameters, we are happy to let people who we trust vote their own best judgments and consciences on the issues.

Finally, some of us have a mixed view on the issue of representation. We may wish our representatives to vote their own views sometimes and consult us at other times. This will involve the representative having the good political judgment to know which issues do and do not require constituent consultation. We call this the **politico orientation** to representation. It probably comes closest to matching the orientation of most voters because it is flexible and practical.

Again, we are brought back to the central role that policy decisions play in our orientation to representative government. Policy making is the foremost duty of representatives because of the need for problem solving in the workaday world. John Quincy Adams once remarked, "Democracy has no forefathers, it looks to no posterity, it is swallowed up in the present and thinks of nothing but itself" (quoted in Rakove, 1997: 366). The practical need to resolve issues takes democratic practice out of the abstract world of theory and into the everyday world of satisfying people's needs and wants. We do not expect our elected officials to bring us all or even most issues to decide. Instead, we simply expect our state legislators to get the job done.

The primary method of establishing or revising state law is the *legislative act.* Bills are introduced into the state legislature, discussed and debated there, and either passed or rejected by our elected state representatives. We should understand who these legislators are, how they came to be elected representatives, and how they do their work. It is also important to know about the interplay of political influences in the state capital. Policy is not made in a vacuum, and a clear understanding of state lawmaking requires an appreciation of how organized interest groups, political parties, and news media interact around key public policy questions. If citizens understand how policy is made at the state level, then they can hold politicians and others involved in the process accountable for what is and is not enacted into state law.

Representation in State Legislatures

The legislatures of the fifty states represent the basic form of popular representation in the policy-making circles of state government. U.S. democratic practice uses what is called the **single-member district** form of representation. In other words, voters elect one politician to represent their locale in the state. Within each single-member district, the elections are strictly "winner take all." No silver medal is given for second place in a legislative race.

A second basic feature of state legislatures is that they are almost always **bicameral.** Every state except Nebraska has a bicameral legislature. This means the legislature has two chambers, one typically called the State House of Representatives—or less commonly the House of Delegates—and the other the State Senate. In terms of names, this practice obviously follows the national model. However, the basis of representation for state houses and state senates is *strictly population.* Unlike the U.S. Congress, the two chambers do not have different bases for representation. (Recall that the U.S. Senate comprises two senators for each state, while members of the House of Representatives are elected from districts with equal populations.) Both state senators and state house members are elected from population-based districts. Because the state senates have fewer members, their districts are larger.

Finally, state legislators are elected for **fixed terms** of office. Unlike parliamentary systems in other countries, U.S. elected officials do not serve under the pressure of removal from office. In parliamentary systems, a no-confidence vote can bring new elections anytime. The typical term of office for state senators is four years; the term for state house members is two years (*The Book of the States,1998–99:* 68). Twenty states limit the number of terms a state legislator may serve. State senators, for example, might be limited to two four-year terms and state house members to four two-year terms (Patterson, 1996: 200). People who distrust elected officials and believe they represent special interests view these **term limits** as reforms.

The rationale for having larger state senate districts and allowing longer terms for the senators is to protect them from wildly shifting public opinion. The larger district makes it harder for a small core of disaffected voters to oust them, and having elections only every four years brings the senators under fire less often. By way of contrast, state house members are always running for office. Their tiny constituencies force them to stay close to popular sentiments because they must face voters every twenty-four months. The dual systems protect established interests and respond to public opinion at the same time. In theory, at least, that is the difference between senate and house representation.

Selecting Representatives. State legislators are almost always elected from single-member population-based districts. These districts each represent roughly the same number of the state's citizens or **constituents.** The districts are drawn by the legislature or by a board that reports to the legislature. They must be redrawn every ten years to reflect changes in population that are documented by the national census of population. This process is called **redistricting.**

Typically, urban districts are geographically small because population is denser in cities. Rural districts may be quite large geographically. The process of "districting" may require combining the populations of more than one county to equal the same population of a few square miles in an urban center. The key criterion is that each legislator represents the same number of people.

Drawing district lines is a highly political process. The legislators who draw the lines each want to preserve their own power bases. They also want to advance the fortunes of their own parties, caucuses, or ideologies. If one political party is dominant, then it will try to preserve its dominance. If minorities have held key seats in the past, they will struggle to maintain them or add new minority seats to the legislature. Suburban conservatives will try to advance their numbers at the expense of urban liberals. Many different political interests are represented in redistricting committees or boards. A great deal of bargaining takes place in negotiating the redistricting maps following each census.

Voting rights laws have had to take note of redistricting by state legislatures. These legislatures also redistrict U.S. House seats, but the national government has had some influence in approving redistricting plans because of the Voting Rights Act of 1965, which requires that legislatures in states with histories of racial discrimination submit their plans to the federal Department of Justice for clearance before they are implemented. In the 1950s and 1960s, Southern state legislatures would draw electoral districts in such a way that minority candidates had no chance to win. That practice was called *racial gerrymandering.*

In the 1980s and 1990s, the argument was made that some proposed districts were so oddly drawn that *only* a minority candidate could win. North Carolina, Georgia, and Louisiana all saw lawsuits over their congressional districts. Yet other critics have claimed that making some districts safe for minorities has meant making neighboring districts safe for white incumbents. The arguments and counterarguments became very complex. Of course, the federal courts ultimately have to rule on these cases because they involve civil rights complaints. The current U.S. Supreme Court appears to want districts in which factors other than race are considered. For example, districts should be reasonably compact and not stretch in narrow bands across a state. People who share a district should have something in common other than just their racial makeup (*Miller* v. *Johnson*, 115 S.Ct. 2475; *Bush* v. *Vera*, 116 S.Ct. 1941; *Shore* v. *Hunt*, 116 S.Ct. 1894).

Looking across the states, we can see the effects of internal migration patterns (discussed in Chapter 1) on state legislative districts. Remember that Americans move around based on many personal preferences and professional needs. Some states have become more densely populated as a result. California had roughly 32 million people in 1996, and its state senate had forty members (data from National Conference of State Legislatures [NCSL], 1998), which means that a single state senator represented almost 800,000 people. Prospects for any one of 800,000 constituents to have personal access to a state senator are slim. In Indiana, by contrast, each state senator represents "only" 117,000 constituents—just 15 percent of the constituents a California senator has. This is an important point, because researchers have found that helping constituents, or **casework,** is increasingly important in keeping an officeholder an incumbent (Freeman & Richardson, 1994). It is a clear way in which population dynamics affect state politics.

Candidate Qualifications. An individual who would like to run for a state legislative seat will need to meet the state's minimum qualifications. Most state constitutions specify that candidates be at least eighteen or twenty-one years of age to run for the lower state house (see Table 4.2). The age qualifications for state senate are typically higher: Roughly half the states require that candidates be older than twenty-one. The data also show interesting regional patterns. Southern states, for example, require that a person be twenty-one for service in the state house of representatives and twenty-five or even older to serve in the state senate. This may reflect the conservatism of state laws in these states. In contrast, California and New York both have eighteen-year-old requirements for house and senate members. This may reflect their more inclusive, reform-minded politics.

Table 4.2
Age Requirements for State Legislature

Minimum Age	Number of State Houses	Number of State Senates
18 years	18	16
21 years	24	7
22–25 years	8	20
26–30 years	0	7

Source: Compiled from *The Book of the States, 1998–99:* 71–72.

Other requirements to serve in the state legislature involve citizenship and residency. Nineteen states require U.S. citizenship to serve in the state legislature. Arkansas and Maine specify that the U.S. citizenship shall have been in effect for a specified number of years—three and five years, respectively. Legal residency in the state is required in thirty-two states, and several of them have set time of residency requirements of six months to five or more years. Some states take a different approach. Twenty-eight require that the candidate be a qualified voter in the state.

Election Campaigns

Some state legislatures have virtually no turnover. In fact, in the time frame 1994–96, Alabamans returned all 140 of their state legislators, and Maryland voters returned all of their 188 (NCSL, 1998). Other states have had a bit more change: California's turnover was 40 percent, and Maine's was 42 percent. However, the national average is only 20 percent. In most cases, challengers have an uphill battle if they want to unseat an incumbent, who has the advantages of name recognition, relevant issues, and campaign funds. This is why so many incumbent state legislators run unopposed and why term-limitation movements are so enthusiastic in some states.

You probably live in a college community. The campus has its own values and needs, and these may be different from other areas of town and the rest of the state. Should students try to elect a fellow student to the state legislature? What allies might you seek if you tried? Do you even know who the state legislators are who represent your area? Make some notes about where you stand on the issue of representation. Bring them to class for discussion.

Legislative Sessions

The typical state legislature convenes in January. Every other year, the session will follow right after the November elections in even-numbered years. The legislative session may last for a specific period of time, or the state constitution may allow the body to meet until all of its business is completed. State legislative sessions have gradually gotten longer and longer. In the 1940s, legislatures met every other year; then states changed to meeting for a short time each year. Many now meet almost year-round (Saffell, 1984: 155). More policy making is expected of the states, and the volume of work has steadily expanded.

Even for so-called part-time legislatures, there is work to do before the session actually begins. Budget and revenue committees meet in the fall to plan for the upcoming year. Study groups and standing committees often convene to consider policy changes that will be on the legislative agenda. The party caucuses gather to discuss political strategy. In other words, even part-time legislatures have a calendar that keeps them busy for most of the year.

Legislator Profile

The types of people who want to be state legislators is an interesting issue to explore. Conventional wisdom once held that rural landowners wanted to get elected so that they could protect the agricultural industry within a state and do so in short winter legislative sessions—typically January through March—when little could be done on the farm. Another group of people who seemed to want to serve was lawyers. They could gain a great deal of visibility and many contacts from serving in the state legislature. Their work also permitted them to be away from the office for the several weeks required by the legislative session.

Data from 1993 and 1995 suggest that the occupations of state legislators are quite varied (Gordon, 1994; *Governing*, 1995: 17). Today, fewer than 10 percent of all state legislators are farmers, and roughly 15 percent are lawyers. Other professions such as teaching, medicine, engineering, and the clergy combine for another 18 percent. The business professions—owners, managers, real estate agents, insurance salespeople, and more—total 28 percent.

As legislatures become full-time, year-round ventures, there typically is a shift from part-timers of various professions to full-time professional politicians. Approximately 15 percent of all legislators consider themselves full-time politicians. The remaining 14 percent are homemakers, retirees, government employees, and union workers.

The National Conference of State Legislatures has characterized whole legislatures in terms of their degree of *professionalism*. Professionalized states

Texas legislators meet in caucus on the House floor to decide legislative strategy.
Source: © Bob Daemmrich / Stock · Boston

such as California, New York, and Florida have full-time legislators with large staffs, relatively high pay, and stable membership. The "citizen" legislatures in such states as Maine and Georgia are part-time bodies with small staffs, low pay, and high turnover. Many states have "hybrid" legislatures that fall between the two extremes.

The combination of increasing workload, demographic shifts, and migration among states has resulted in more diverse state legislatures. As a journalist who covers state politics recently noted, "A generation ago in America, more than a few legislatures did an admirable job of feeding the regional stereotypes their states conjured up in peoples' minds" (Ehrenhalt, 1995: 7). He observed that distinctive regions such as New England, the West, and the South now have a "wide assortment of styles and subcategories" of legislators.

One change in legislator demographics has been diversification in race. As recently as 1980, minorities held tiny fractions of legislative seats, even in states with large minority populations. In 1995, however, 25 percent of all Alabama legislators were African Americans. Other states with more than 15 percent African American representatives were Louisiana, Mississippi, Georgia, and South Carolina (NCSL, 1996). The non-Southern states of Illinois, Ohio, New Jersey, and Michigan also have significant African American representation in their legislatures of more than 10 percent. More than one-third of the New Mexico legislature is Hispanic American. Other states with significant Hispanic representation—again more than 10 percent—are Arizona, California, and Texas. Two-thirds of Hawaii's state legislators are Asian Americans.

German State Legislatures or *Landtag*

In the Federal Republic of Germany, the Basic Law (national constitution) requires that the structure of the *Land* (state) government must "conform to the principles of republican, democratic, and social government based on the rule of law." Twelve states are governed by a cabinet led by a minister president together with a unicameral legislative body called the *Landtag*. The legislators are popularly elected, typically for four years, and the minister president (governor) is chosen by a majority vote among Landtag members. In the state of Hesse, for example, fifty-five legislators are selected from districts, and fifty-five from state or party lists. The main responsibilities of state government include cultural affairs, schools, administration of justice, police, and public health. The states work with the federal government in other areas, including university construction, the improvement of regional economic structures, agrarian reform, coastal preservation, educational planning, and the promotion of science.

elsewhere in the World

Alaska and Arizona both have significant numbers of Native Americans in their legislatures: 10 percent and 11 percent, respectively.

The numbers and percentages of women serving in the state legislatures also has increased dramatically. The Washington legislature is 40 percent female. Other states with more than 30 percent female legislators are Nevada, Colorado, and Arizona (NCSL, 1996). Alabama has made special provisions for teachers—a female-dominated occupation—to hold legislative office. Now, nationwide, one legislator in five is a woman.

~ Legislative Life in the State Capital

The physical settings for legislatures is also interesting. State capitals were most often established with meetings of the legislature in mind. If you look at maps of the states, you will notice that many capitals were placed in the geographic centers of their states because eighteenth-, nineteenth-, and even twentieth-century legislators had to travel considerable distances to attend sessions. Cities such as Sacramento, California; Little Rock, Arkansas; and Springfield, Illinois, grew up as strategically placed governmental centers.

Walk the streets around your state capital and you will see how the layout of streets and offices supports legislative activities. Initially, you will notice that the immediate area of the capital is filled with government buildings, parks, and civic memorials. The architecture of the capitol buildings is sober and impressive. The clear message is that serious people gather here to make important decisions. Parks surround the capitol buildings to give space and nature's beauty as support for the center of the state's government. Citizens feel invited to stroll around the capitol grounds and take pride in their state. Various civic monuments complete this impression. Some statues may recognize famous "founding fathers," significant governors, or key legislators in the state's history. Other memorials honor the state's war dead. Each generation tends to add its heroes to the group of past state residents honored at the state capital.

Wander farther from the capitol building itself and you will see the offices of state government agencies. Dozens of buildings usually are required to accommodate the state departments of health, social welfare, education, highways, corrections, and labor. Scattered among them also are the headquarters of many organizations that do business with the state. Councils for mentally handicapped citizens, teachers' organizations, municipal leagues, union offices, and insurance and banking associations are all represented in the typical downtown district. The restaurants and bars near the capitol are filled with government officials and lobbyists Mondays through Thursdays but deserted on weekends when the legislature is not in session.

If you visit with the legislators from your own part of the state, you will find that they have their own legislative offices. As recently as ten to fifteen years ago, many states did not provide individual offices for their elected representatives (Howard & Walker, 1985: 72, A-98). The legislators were limited to the workspace on their desks in the legislative chamber itself. Only senior committee chairs and the leadership of the state house and the state senate had offices, staff, and the technological support such as fax machines and computers needed to get work done. Increasing workload has led to more time being spent at the capital, and even part-time legislators have demanded a workplace where they and their staff can meet constituents and lobbyists, manage their correspondence, meet with colleagues, draft legislation, and complete the myriad other tasks expected of them.

Legislatures and Political Players

Once a political party gains control of a chamber of the state legislature, it has the authority to select the chamber's presiding officials and committee chairs. The party holds majorities on all committees, which is where the important work of crafting policy is carried out. In other words, the party controls the legislature to some degree or another, and party leaders are accountable to regulars and the electorate for producing the policy results that were promised during elections.

In Chapter 3, we discussed the shift in the pattern of partisan control from one-party dominance to two-party competitiveness in the states. This shift is the result of two factors. One is the *partisan realignment* of voter preferences favoring Republican candidates. This national phenomenon has carried state legislatures along with the change in control of Congress. It is also the result of many Southern Democrats switching parties. It has been politically convenient for some to do and thus get closer to what they perceive to be the public's or their constituents' sentiments. It also offers them opportunities to govern as a part of the dominant conservative regime.

State legislators respond to their constituents because it is their duty as elected officials and because they cannot hope to be reelected unless the public finds them responsive. Corporations and associations are constituents, too. State capitals are blanketed with the offices of interest organizations ranging from utility companies to schoolteachers' unions to hospital associations. Lobbyists working out of these offices wine and dine state legislators in their efforts to influence legislation.

Each state capital has its newspapers, news bureaus, and news-oriented broadcast media. These organizations provide the public with news about the legislative session through syndication to other newspapers, newsmagazines, and radio and television stations. We earlier noted that an important news source for legislators is the state government desk of the major daily newspaper in the state capital. One or more experienced journalists carefully track political goings-on in the legislature. Newspapers in the state's smaller cities may cover the legislative session in the state capital as well. The state public radio and television networks also often cover the state legislature in great detail, and many even have daily coverage while the legislature is in session. With the growing interest in the devolution of policy to the states, these state news organizations often provide news feeds to national magazines and networks. More and more coverage of state government is available to the interested student or constituent.

The influence of state media on legislators is hard to measure. An embarrassing scandal may be uncovered by a news organization acting as a "watchdog" for the public interest. Legislators certainly don't want to be caught by surprise by an eager reporter, and many legislators and most legislative leaders will have learned how to handle the media. Mutual consideration goes a long way in helping both media and legislators as each tries to do their jobs.

✒ Legislative Leadership

There are two types of leadership in the state legislature, and both are critically important for getting legislative work done. Both the state's senate and house of representatives have chamber officials in addition to party officials. These chamber officials are responsible for the overall operations of the chamber in which they serve.

Chamber Leadership

The primary chamber official in the state senate is often the **lieutenant governor.** Forty-two states have lieutenant governors who are elected statewide, and they preside over the state senate in twenty-six of these states. In this role, the lieutenant governor assumes the additional title of president of the senate and may break tie votes in twenty-five of these states. In six of these twenty-six states in which lieutenant governors preside over the senates, the officeholder also appoints committees. Five of the six are Southern states. In twelve states, the lieutenant governor assigns bills to committees, and half of these states are in the South. Obviously, in that part of the country, lieutenant governors are powerful legislative officials.

A state without a lieutenant governor presiding over the state senate has a separate *president of the senate* elected by members to serve as their presiding officer. State senates also have a *president pro tempore* who presides over the chamber when the president of the senate is unavailable.

The presiding officer of the state senate is responsible for the chamber's smooth operation and decorum. State senates are relatively small groups, and a premium is usually set on pleasant interpersonal relations. Nevertheless, the presiding officer must be in charge, recognizing speakers, controlling debate, and ruling some comments or conduct out of order in order to preserve the decorum of the chamber. This is especially important to elected officials when their proceedings are televised across the state. In three-fourths of the states, the senate president or president pro tempore will refer bills to committees and schedule their debate. In the other states, this is handled through the chamber's rules committee or a similarly named committee of the senators. Presidents or presidents pro tempore of the state senate appoint committees and name chairs in twenty-eight states.

The **speaker** is the chief presiding officer of the state house of representatives. He or she is elected by the mem-

The late Lieutenant Governor Robert Bulloch (left) was a powerful presence in the Texas legislature.

Source: © Bob Daemmrich / Corbis Sygma

bership to preside over the house's deliberations during a given session. Because the state house is usually a very partisan body, the majority members will typically choose one of their own as speaker. Seniority is one attribute that is taken into consideration, but the members also want someone who can maintain order in these often-unruly chambers. In all but a half-dozen cases, the speaker refers bills to committee. In forty-four state legislatures, the speaker also makes committee appointments and names the committee and subcommittee chairs.

Party Leadership

Party leaders constitute another major group of legislative officials. Both the state senate and state house of representatives have a *majority leader* and a *minority leader.* These party officials are responsible to their respective party's members for legislative action in support of the party's platform. They speak for their party in negotiations with the other party or with the governor. They are public spokespersons when the media cover party matters in the state capital and throughout the state. Assisting the majority and minority leaders in each chamber is a *party whip*, an individual charged by fellow party members with keeping members advised of important committee and floor votes. The whips help deliver the votes that the party leadership is counting on at key moments in the legislative session.

The governor has a *floor leader* in each chamber. Because governors may only attend those special sessions of the legislature to which they are invited—such as the State of the State Address—they must have legislators who speak for them. The governor's floor leaders are often but not always members of the governor's party. They speak for the governor's bills and give the governor's viewpoint on other legislation. These loyal supporters are expected to suppress their own viewpoints and espouse the governor's outlook on policy and politics. Why would the governor need a floor leader when his or her party has a party leader and whip in each chamber? The answer may be that political parties or party factions do not always stand with their governors on particular policy issues. The governor may need another way of making his or her legislative leadership effective.

Chamber officials and party officials help bring order to the chaos of legislative politics. Without strong presiding officers, the agenda would be lost and relatively little could be accomplished. Without mature and responsible party leaders, members could engage in intemperate behavior or fade through inactivity or fatigue during a session. Both types of leadership are needed to make the legislature work as envisioned in the state's constitution.

❧ Passing State Laws

Sponsors are members who introduce bills in the state legislature. Any type of bill can be introduced in either chamber with the exception of appropriations bills, which must originate in the house of representatives. In fact, members can file at least some bills even before the legislature actually convenes in all states except Michigan, North Carolina, and Wisconsin (*Book of the States, 1998–99*: 93).

If you were a member of the state legislature and had a specific piece of legislation you wanted passed, you would wisely consult with other members and the leadership before submitting the bill. You could pick up valuable suggestions about how to strengthen the bill, and several members might agree to serve as cosponsors of the legislation.

You would find out how long you would have to get the bill in shape and submit it for consideration because each chamber's rules give deadlines. A typical deadline might be a certain number of days into the session or a certain number of days before its expected adjournment. After that, you will need a supermajority vote of the members to get your bill introduced. For example, a three-fifths or two-thirds vote might be required.

One reason for deadlines is the sheer volume of bills that are being introduced in today's state legislatures (see **Table 4.3**). The number of bills being introduced produces a blizzard of paperwork for state legislators and their staffs. Individuals are sponsors or cosponsors of scores of bills. Each party has extensive lists of bills that it considers as priority legislation. The governor's bills alone could fill a large notebook. Everyone sees the writing on the wall by the midpoint of the legislative session: There are far more bills than can be intelligently considered. Some constituents and valued interest group supporters are going to be disappointed. But committees are booked solid trying to introduce and pass the most important pieces of proposed legislation. And floor debate goes on later and later each evening. The clock is running down, and the vast majority of bills that have been introduced will never see the light of day.

Table 4.3
Number of Bills Introduced and Enacted in 1996–97 Legislative Sessions

State	Bills Introduced	Bills Enacted
New York	32,263	1,566
Massachusetts	15,020	912
Hawaii	7,351	698
Mississippi	7,039	878
Minnesota	6,656	422
Illinois	6,522	812
New Jersey	5,814	653
California	5,391	2,125
Florida	5,052	853
Pennsylvania	4,764	377

Source: Compiled from *The Book of the States, 1998–99:* 105–106.

After your bill is submitted, the clerk of the chamber will read it into the record for the first time: This is the official birth of your proposed legislation. Then the presiding official of the chamber, or less commonly a rules committee, will refer it to an appropriate committee for study and discussion. Rules governing the referral of bills vary by chamber, even within the same state. Of the one hundred state legislative chambers in the United States, fifty-six have rules that require an appropriate referral to a relevant committee. In the other half of the chambers, your bill is more at the mercy of the presiding official or leadership.

Like their counterparts in most states, Texas legislators spend a lot of time on the floor of the House as well as in their offices meeting with constituents and representatives of various groups.
Source: © Bob Daemmrich / Stock · Boston

An unfavorable referral can send your bill to an untimely death or, perhaps more commonly, a long period of neglect in an uninterested committee. In thirty states, you have the entire biennium of the legislative session to get your bill through. However, if you did not introduce until the second year of the two-year session, you will need help in hurrying the bill along. Remember: Time is of the essence!

Fortunately for bill sponsors, legislative committees have staff members who can work up a bill for the committee chair and members. Only Alabama and Georgia do not have professional staffers assigned to the standing committees of their legislatures (*Book of the States, 1998–99:* 112). The committee chair and the staff will schedule discussion of your bill.

Whether or not hearings need to be held on the bill depends on its complexity and importance. In virtually all states, committee meetings are open to the public and the media. This means that interest groups will want to be present to defend their group's interests. In fact, opposing groups may show up and all want to speak. The committee chair has the unenviable job of structuring committee discussion of the bill. It may or may not allow time for public comment or questions. As a practical matter, the attention that is given a bill may turn on how much media attention it is receiving. It is hard to give a bill short shrift with television cameras in the committee room.

Three things can happen to a bill in committee. It may be voted out with a recommendation that it pass. Or it may be amended so that the committee can support an altered version or a committee substitute if the changes are extensive. Most commonly, bills die a quiet death in committee. They go in, but they never come out.

To be reported out of committee, the bill must receive a positive vote of committee members or, under extraordinary circumstances, a discharge petition from the members on the floor. As a sponsor, you want the bill to come out of committee in recognizable form. You and your cosponsors want to speak for the bill from the well—or podium—of the chamber. When the bill comes back from committee, it receives its second reading and is then scheduled for floor debate.

Floor debate is certainly the most colorful activity of state legislatures. A bill is read for the third time, then proponents and opponents debate its virtues and limitations under the tight control of the presiding officer. If you watch the televised floor debates or even read news summaries about them, you will appreciate how heated and personal remarks can become. Partisan differences, an urban–rural difference, philosophical differences, and even gender and racial differences are vented in the name of debating particular legislation. And sometimes *bipartisan cooperation* takes place as legislators come together and overcome their differences in the name of the public interest. The whole spectrum of human emotion gets expressed in legislative floor debate.

One frequent bone of contention among legislators is the projected costs of state projects and programs. Cost considerations can inflame partisan, ideological, and regional differences—all over the same bill. To get reliable cost figures, state legislatures require the preparation of **fiscal notes** on pending legislation. These notes estimate a proposed action's direct and indirect costs, and they identify the specific sources of revenue needed to fund the activity. The fiscal notes also identify resultant costs to local governments in the state. Fiscal notes are required of all bills in twenty-six states, and they are available on request of legislators in most of the others (*Book of the States, 1998–99:* 103). The notes are distributed to appropriations committee chairs and legislative budget office staff in roughly half of the states.

To allay worries of future obligations and never-ending expenses, some states have begun to enact **sunset legislation.** Sunset laws provide for the demise of state projects or programs if they are not reauthorized on a specific timetable. State sunset laws take several forms (see Table 4.4).

Table 4.4
Scope of State Sunset Laws, 1997

Type of Coverage	Number of States
Comprehensive	8
Regulatory	10
Selective	18
Laws repealed or inactive	10
No sunset laws	4

Source: Compiled from *The Book of the States, 1998–99:* 123–125.

Comprehensive sunset laws apply standard time limits to broad categories of bills. The maximum time limit is six years in some states, ten years in others. The *regulatory* sunset law states incorporate audits or reviews of state regulatory agencies into the legislature's oversight activities. Time limits before these reviews also may run as long as ten years in some states. *Selective* sunset laws attach provisions to only selected legislation. The states commonly perform this sunset activity in a piecemeal fashion; they have no comprehensive sunset legislation.

Interesting to note is that several states that enacted sunset laws have subsequently repealed them. Arkansas ended a one-time review in 1983, the same year that Connecticut suspended its process until the year 2000. Mississippi repealed its law in 1984, and New Hampshire followed suit in 1986. In other words, several states have tried sunset provisions for legislation only to terminate or suspend their use. Informal reports suggest that these states were discouraged by the sheer magnitude of the legislative workload involved.

Most states record vocal or electronic *roll call votes* in the final determination of a bill (*Book of the States, 1998–99:* 116–120). Regular legislation requires a simple majority approval. An important exception is the two-thirds majority

CHAPTER 4 State Legislatures: *Policy Roles and Procedural Rules* required in most states to override a governor's veto of a bill. Votes taken one day may be revisited on a subsequent day if the members agree to suspend the rules. In their haste to meet their closing deadlines, legislators simply claim that they made a mistake on the previous vote. It gets that chaotic.

ꞏ❧ State Legislation

The fifty state legislatures make laws regarding a wide range of issues. We could not even begin to catalog all of the new laws that are coming out of the states. The states are particularly active now in enacting legislation that addresses issues of education, crime control, and public welfare. These three sample policy areas will give you some idea of the kinds of issues that are being debated and decided in state legislatures. A trip to your own state legislature's Web site will reward you with lots of details about the policy issues that are being considered close to home.

Public Education

State legislatures have been challenged to make school funding equitable between locales within their states (Perlman, 1995: 24). Increasingly, wealthier school systems have supplemented state basic grants to education with local tax revenues. This has resulted in pockets of poorly funded schools in sparsely populated rural areas and lower-income urban neighborhoods. Courts in states from Arizona to Rhode Island have handed down decisions that seem to require legislatures to equalize educational opportunity within their states. Some states—notably Michigan, Texas, and New Jersey—have responded by overhauling their school-tax laws. Texas capped taxable property in any given school district and redirected "excess" revenue to poorer districts; Michigan repealed much of the local school board authority for taxing property and replaced the revenue with increased sales and cigarettes taxes (Lewis & Maruna, 1996: 457). The goal of such legislation is funding equity to remove the advantage of localities that have large numbers of wealthy residents and a lot of valuable property to tax. Of course, such legislation is also of interest to legislators who are concerned with tax reform as a larger issue.

Another education policy question involves quality and accountability in public schools. Educational outcomes can be measured in terms of the test scores and employability of students who are schooled in a state. Some observers believe that schools need to compete with each other to improve their performance (Osborne & Gaebler, 1992: 93–104). State legislatures have been considering two policies: open enrollment of students regardless of school district and vouchers that parents may use to purchase the education they believe their children need.

Child-development programs are yet another education issue. Many states are looking at preschool and kindergarten programs that can better prepare children for entering school. Education may begin in the home, but busy families continue to rely upon child-care providers for assistance. To reassure parents, many state legislatures now mandate the licensing of child-care providers.

These are only a few of the many education and child-care issues that are facing the states. We will have more to say about public education in Chapter 11's discussion of school districts and the many political and policy development challenges they face.

Crime Control

There is no shortage of crime-control rhetoric in state legislatures. Everyone wants to appear to be hard on crime, and legislators' rhetoric often seems aimed at constituents back home who are leery about personal safety and the security of their property. Legislators from the inner cities and those from the suburbs play to the cameras when this hot button issue is mentioned. Some policy areas such as environmental protection and health-care reform may require special knowledge, but everyone feels like an expert on crime control.

The legislators' rhetoric has often been backed up by legislative action. In recent years, many states have abolished parole and required mandatory prison terms for repeat offenders. Youth are increasingly being tried as adults because of the serious crimes that underage offenders commit nowadays. When you examine your own state's legislative agenda, the session probably will be replete with measures that are hard on crime and criminals.

We will have more to say on crime in Chapter 7 when we look at the facts of crime trends and the crime control efforts of state courts. Suffice it to say that the "common sense" approach of many legislators belies the complexity of criminal behavior and its practical control.

Welfare Reform

Welfare reform has been a pet project of the governors. State after state has passed legislation that requires recipients to work for their benefits and get off welfare within a specific number of years. President Clinton and Congress cooperated with the governors' welfare reform agenda, adding momentum to policy change efforts. Pick up any national magazine that covered state and local government, and you would find many "innovative approaches" to reforming the welfare system at the state level.

In Chapter 3, we showed the intricate web of intergovernmental relations that are involved in changing public assistance in the United States. Clearly, state legislatures are constrained by federal law in this area, and unless a state wishes to refuse federal welfare funds, it will "color within the lines" that Washington has drawn. Nevertheless, some states launched innovations in transitional aid that merited the attention of intergovernmental planners and neighboring states.

If we have learned anything about state policy making in recent years, it is that state legislatures become caught up in policy fashions or fads. They will shamelessly copy each other in a rush to seem responsive to public demands for better schools, safer streets, and more effective social welfare programs. Perhaps we should not judge them harshly. These issues would not have the currency they enjoy today if the public, the media, political parties, and interest groups did not find them interesting agenda items. However, it is also fair to note that many worthy issues may be displaced when state legislatures play to the media. The legislative agenda is filled with less colorful and "newsworthy" concerns.

❧ Legislative Oversight

Lawmakers do not escape responsibility for state policies and programs once laws and budgets are passed, so they may conduct periodic reviews of state agencies under the guise of determining compliance with the legislature's intent in authorizing and funding the agency's programs. Some legislators see oversight in a positive light and seek to fine-tune state programs for better performance. Other legislators are more cautious, wanting to fund only those programs that work while also reducing the size of state government in general. In other words, oversight means different things to different people.

Program Review

State agencies' policies and programs are controlled through authorization and appropriations legislation. Programs are authorized when enabling legislation—or an **authorization** bill—is passed that declares the state's intent in creating a new program, outlines its mission, defines its scope of responsibilities, and relates its duties to other, existing state policies and programs. Once the program is authorized, it can receive an **appropriation** through which the state provides funds for the program to operate. A small section of the overall state budget is devoted to supporting the new program. The funds are placed in the appropriate state agency for administering the program.

State legislatures pass laws authorizing statewide programs in the hope that social or economic problems will respond to policy actions. For many of the types of programs we have mentioned, this is a long-term expectation that often must be updated. A state might pilot a child-development program, for instance, with only a few sites and a limited budget. After a year or two of operation, the program may have been evaluated by the responsible state agency, by independent evaluators from a university or the private sector, and by the press. The legislative committee that has oversight of that area of state law would probably conduct a program review to determine if the *pilot program* was effective and efficient.

Based on the program review, the existing child-development programs may be funded statewide. The success of the pilot program apparently justifies a larger statewide program. If problems are uncovered during the review, the pilot program might be revised and extended with another tentative appropriation. This sort of *fine-tuning* may create a pilot program that meets legislative expectations. In the unlikely event that a review shows the approach to be worthless, then the existing pilots can be closed and perhaps a new strategy considered. In any event, legislators will have some idea of what the state is getting for its money.

Sunset laws are an extreme variant of this type of oversight process. If legislators have reason to believe that a new state program may not succeed, then they may place a time limit on the initial program's authorization. If the sunset provision is for five years, say, then a program review is triggered in year four. Program supporters will have to return to the legislature to get the program extended beyond five years or it closes down. This type of provision is increasingly popular in state legislatures.

Hearings on bills that *reorganize* an agency or change its mission are another means of oversight. If constituents or interest groups have complained about a state agency or its programs, then legislators may direct policy change by rewriting the authorization legislation. This type of major program surgery may be necessary when a scandal has revealed serious defects in approach or administration. A child-care program plagued with child abuse scandals, for example, would probably undergo this type of searching review. The legislature simply could not stand by and allow such a program to continue unchanged.

Budgetary Oversight

Budget hearings for each state agency are another, more routine way of monitoring the effectiveness and efficiency of state programs. Agencies must return each year to the legislature to get new funds, and funding requests give legislators an excellent opportunity to quiz agency heads about policies and programs.

With one exception that we discuss below, the legislature only considers budgets for the following year. Experts tell members approximately how much money they will have to spend the next year. These budget estimates consider the tax code and the economic forecast for the near future. A simple formula for determining the next year's state revenue is tax rate multiplied by tax base. If the state relies on an income tax, then the income tax rates multiplied by the gross taxable income that should be earned the following year equals expected revenue from that source. The motor fuel tax rate multiplied by the expected gallons sold equals revenue from that source. States sales tax rate multiplied by projected gross retail sales equals revenue from that source. The grand total is the state's **revenue estimate.**

Each state agency wants its share of the next year's budget. The agency heads will appear before the budgetary committees of each chamber, reporting on their agencies' successes and identify their agencies' resource needs. At this time, individual legislators may exercise their prerogative to interrogate the official and ask questions about alleged waste, inefficiency, or fraud—which can mean time in the hot seat for an agency head who has suffered bad media coverage, disgruntled employees, dissatisfied clients, or unhappy constituents.

Actually, each year brings two budget packages. Before the following year's budget can be built, the state legislature must amend the current year's spending. The current budget probably was passed many months ago, and events have overtaken many state agencies. For example, some agencies have had more demand for services than they expected when their original requests were made. Others have been overtaken by price increases for key goods and services they purchase. The midterm correction for a current year's budget is commonly called the **supplemental budget.** This optimistic term assumes that more revenue has been coming into the state's coffers than was projected. It assumes that the state treasury has more money to hand out to state agencies in need. This may or may not be the case. In some states, the supplemental budget actually has included cuts in agency budgets. Revenue has not met projections, and the legislature must reduce the funds that are available to agencies for the rest of the year.

Individual legislators try to satisfy constituents back home by protecting local operating units of state agencies. A legislator would not only try to keep positions from being cut at the local office of the state employment security agency, for example, or the youth detention facility in his or her hometown, but also try to get improvements at these branches. Again, the constituents can be viewed as individuals and organizations. Many groups who operate with state funds at the local level are dependent on state appropriations. The local affiliates of the state association for handicapped citizens and the local teachers who belong to the state federation of teachers have group interests to be protected.

Other balancing considerations include the legislator's own conscience, partisan commitments, partisan ideology, and trade-offs made with other legislators, to name but a few. Budget decisions not only are about "bringing home the bacon," but also constitute a high-stakes game that seasoned representatives play very well. Incumbents stay in power for a reason. We will have more to say about the budgetary process in Chapter 5 when we explore the concept of executive budgeting and how governors try to exercise budgetary leadership.

Regulatory Oversight

Legislative review of administrative regulations is a growing area of legislative oversight. The state's constitution and its statutes may provide that any state regulatory rule be approved by the legislature within a prescribed time period. In Idaho, for example, a standing committee of the legislature reviews all pending rules. Rules that impose fees must be approved, and other rules may be implemented if the committee does not object. In Washington state, committee disapproval triggers a public hearing process. Other than publishing its disapproval, the legislative committee has no power to overturn the state's regulatory rule. The procedures of all states are idiosyncratic. Yet all but nine of them exercise legislative review of administrative regulations in some form.

State regulators make decisions every day that financially benefit some citizens and disadvantage others. A state public service commission rule that requires local telephone companies to notify customers or get their permission before changing long-distance service benefits the consumer by potentially saving individuals the additional cost of the new service. However, the notice and agreement procedures cost the telephone companies a lot of time and money. Benefits flow from one party for the benefit of the other party. This common regulatory fact of life, in fact, makes regulation controversial.

Consumers and consumer advocacy organizations lobby hard for what they see as needed reforms. Reporters love to cover heart-rending human-interest stories about cheated and abused consumers. Businesses complain about unnecessary and expensive government regulation. And remember that there are more business lobbyists in the state capital than any other kind of interest representative. This makes for volatile politics. We will look at state regulatory agencies in more detail in Chapter 6. At this point, suffice it say that legislators are not immune from being drawn into these conflicts. Regulatory reform is an agenda item in many state legislatures each year.

Oversight of one form or another is virtually continuous in state government. Along with the authorization and appropriation duties, it is a mainstay of state legislative life in the state capital. Legislators simply cannot forget about a policy or program once it has been passed. Neither can they ignore the actions of state bureaucrats and regulators who implement their legislative acts. Political responsibility is much broader than that. In fact, it is remarkable that even some state legislators view their responsibilities as a part-time job. It takes talented politicians to manage the legislative agenda even when they give it their undivided attention.

Exploring on Your Own **Interning at the State Capital**

Ask your instructor or your college's internship coordinator about opportunities to spend a term working at the state capital. If you take such an opportunity, you will be assigned to a particular representative or committee. You will learn a great deal about the legislative process and bills before the chamber. It also counts as great work experience on your resume!

❧ Chapter Conclusion

We have developed many new themes about state legislatures in this chapter. We have looked at the role that legislative leadership and procedure play in governing the state. We have examined some of the tools legislators use to craft and revise public policy. We have even reviewed safeguards that state legislatures have put in place to keep decent checks and balances vital in state government. It has proven to be a considerable task.

We have also woven into the discussion some of the purely political concepts that were introduced in Chapter 3: Political parties, interest groups, and the media are intertwined with the structure and process of the state legislature. Nothing takes place without some partisan dimension to it. No law is passed that is devoid of interest group wins and losses. And nothing escapes media attention.

You now have more information about how policies on issues such as education, crime control, and welfare reform are actually made. You understand the legislative process from passage of legislation to oversight of agencies and policies. This will prove valuable when we look at these issues in even more detail later in the book. Now it is time to take stock. We need to ask ourselves the following basic questions about where we stand today with our representative democracy:

- Is the Information Age making direct democracy more possible or more attractive? Do we want to trust our elected representatives to pursue the public interest in any broad terms, or are we really interested in a delegate model within which we can use the tools of direct democracy to trump any wayward thinking?

You will have to decide for yourself whether direct democracy will lead to better decisions than representative democracy. The technology will probably be there. We will have to decide whether the public will take the time to study policy questions and act intelligently. There *is* potential there, but is there also real concern?

- Are we committed enough to the protection of our own professional interests that we will allow others' interest groups to have a say in their futures as well? Or are we just political consumers who want more for less from our state government?

Long-term professional success will require *some* governmental role. We will look at how regulation sometimes benefits occupations in Chapter 6. In the meantime, we must look at the role legislatures play in helping both their corporate and citizen constituents. The general consensus is that business fares well at the hands of most state legislatures. But do state laws do enough to give business the environment it needs to compete and succeed in the world marketplace?

- Finally, what are political reforms really accomplishing? Will term limits displace all of the mature chamber and party leadership in the state capital? If so, then will interest groups, legislative staffers, and political "spin doctors" replace them in the leadership roles? Do we really want to trade in our representative democracy for a weakened "ad hoc-racy"?

Perhaps we need to place some checks on our reform fervor and encourage able people to run for state elective office. They will not likely do so if we belittle the work of government institutions such as the state legislature. The daily deluge of bills may bore them, and the constant chatter of lobbyists may tire them, and the fishbowl may frighten them. But do we really want them to give up? If the citizen legislator *does* give up, then we know that the politics of vested interests is waiting in the wings to take over.

Key Words for InfoTrac Exploration

apportionment (election law)

referendum

school funding

welfare reform

Sources Cited

The Book of the States, 1998–99 (1998). Lexington, KY: Council of State Governments.

Ehrenhalt, Alan (1995). "Twilight of the Bubba Era." *Governing, 8*(10) (July): 7.

Freeman, Patricia K., and Lilliard E. Richardson, Jr. (1994). "Casework in State Legislatures." *State and Local Government Review, 26*(1) (Winter): 21–26.

Gordon, Dianna (1994). "Citizen Legislators—Alive and Well." *State Legislatures, 20* (January): 25.

Governing, 1995: 17.

Howard, S. Kenneth, and David B. Walker (1985). *The Question of State Government Capability*. Washington, DC: Advisory Commission on Intergovernmental Relations.

Lappé, Frances M., and Paul M. DuBois (1994). *The Quickening of America: Rebuilding Our Nation, Remaking Our Lives*. San Francisco: Jossey-Bass.

Lewis, Dan A., and Shadd Maruna (1996). "The Politics of Education." Pp. 438–477 in Virginia Gray and Herbert Jacob (Eds.), *Politics in the American States* (6th ed.). Washington, DC: Congressional Quarterly Press.

National Conference of State Legislatures (1996). Online: <*http://www.ncsl.org/programs*>.

Osborne, David, & Ted Gaebler (1992). *Reinventing Government: How the Entrepreneurial Spirit is Transforming the Public Sector*. Reading, MA: Addison-Wesley.

Patterson, Samuel C. (1996). "Legislative Politics in the States." Pp. 159–206 in Virginia Gray and Herbert Jacob, *Politics in the American States* (6th ed.). Washington, DC: Congressional Quarterly Press.

Perlman, Ellen (1995). "Ten Legislative Issues to Watch in 1995." *Governing, 8*(5) (February): 24–25.

Rakove, Jack N. (1997). *Original Meanings: Politics and Ideas on the Making of the Constitution*. New York: Random House.

Saffell, David C. (1984). *State Politics*. Reading, PA: Addison-Wesley.

Wahlke, John C., Heinz Eulau, William Buchanan, and Leroy C. Ferguson (1962). *The Legislative System*. New York: John Wiley & Sons.

State Executives: Leadership and Accountability

- ❧ **State Governors**

- ❧ **Lieutenant Governors**

- ❧ **State Managers**

- ❧ **Reforming Executive Branch Government**

- ❧ **Chapter Conclusion**

Imagine yourself as a young journalist working in the state capital. You have been on the job for only a few weeks, and the state legislature is about to convene. The sights and sounds of popular government getting underway will hit you like a tidal wave. There will be so many voices clamoring for press and public attention that you can count on being confused and frustrated. Surely there must be someone who can rein in the runaway impulses of state government! There must someone who can at least articulate an agenda, a list of priorities from which everyone can work. There must be someone who can focus our attention on the major issues that really matter to the people of the state. Fortunately, there is. One statewide elected official may command this type of attention and respect: the governor.

Individual state legislators each represent a small constituency within the state. Each interest group speaks for a relatively narrow set of issues that concerns its members. The major political parties are broad coalitions, but even they have limited ideological agendas. The governor, however, is elected by all of the people—or at least a majority of voters. His or her party has won the big prize in state elections. The governor can try to speak for all the people and pursue the public interest rather than narrow professional or partisan interests.

Beyond the matter of political leadership, some public official must take responsibility for the daily operations of state government, and it is fitting that it is the governor. The executive branch is by far the largest and most expensive sector of state government. Virtually all state tax dollars go to support executive branch activities, so great responsibilities should go with these tremendous resources. Most state agencies operate professionally and competently, but sometimes things go wrong. Programs or people may fail to measure up to public expectations. If a state disaster-relief program is sluggish and storm victims suffer, then media exposure is likely to bring a public outcry. If a state employee commits an unethical act under cover of office, then there will be demands for disciplinary action, dismissal, and perhaps criminal prosecution. Someone must be politically accountable for every state program and every state employee. Ultimately, that one accountable person is the governor.

In this chapter, we explore the growing importance of the executive branch of state government. We seek to understand the answers to these important questions of politics and policy:

- Who are the new breed of U.S. governors and what are their interests and concerns?
- How does a modern governor lead an enterprise as large and complex as state government?
- What are the responsibilities of the lieutenant governor, state agency heads, and top-level state agency administrators in helping to get the job done?
- Are there systems of goal setting and information management that can bring coherence and accountability to state government?

After reading this chapter, you should understand how governors try to lead the policy-development process in their states. You also should understand how adopted public policy is implemented in state government. Along the way, you may develop a greater appreciation for the skyrocketing demands of citizens, who always want more and better services for less and less money.

❧ State Governors

It must be clear to you by now just how noisy and confusing political life in the state capital can be. Each state legislator has his or her own agenda, constituent demands, party concerns, and constant pressures from interest groups. The chamber and party leaders may quiet the chaos, but they are also subject to discordant needs and impulses. As each legislator or legislative leader clamors for attention, the political noise can be deafening. What's more, little may get done. There needs to be a focus, some overall *leadership*. This has become the responsibility of the state's governor.

Early state governors were intentionally weak figures. The framers of the state constitutions wanted most of the authority of state governments to be concentrated in the hands of the state legislatures, in part because some framers had suffered under oppressive royal governors. Others simply subscribed to the revolutionary ideal of personal liberty protected by extremely limited, maybe even impotent, government. There was little interest in a strong and powerful governor to lead a state. Two hundred years of trial and error would be needed to evolve a system of state government that was ready and able to deliver efficient and effective public services. Once state government became accountable for getting great things done, effective political leadership became essential.

Today, governors lead their states. They are the central political leaders and chief executives of state government. The people elect them to lead their

Alaska's Tony Knowles is like most governors: He wants good relations with members of both political parties so he can see his legislative agenda enacted.
Source: © Michael Penn

states and take responsibility for state government operations. They are expected to have the political savvy of a president and the managerial expertise of a corporate chief executive officer. All governors try to live up to these exalted expectations, and some governors even succeed. But it is a very big job, and many others fail to meet the public's high expectations.

Gubernatorial Elections

Governors usually are elected to serve four-year terms. Only Vermont and New Hampshire have governors who serve two-year terms. Governors often are limited to two consecutive terms or a specified number of years in office (see Table 5.1). In other words, the majority of them govern under some form of **term limit.** This gives the typical successful governor only eight years to make his or her imprint on the state. The term-limit restriction seeks to prevent any individual from getting control of the governor's office and holding onto it indefinitely. In the early twentieth century, several states had corrupt political machines that gained and kept control of their respective governors' offices for many years.

Table 5.1
Governors' Term of Office

Term of Office	Number of States	Percentage of States
Two 4-years terms	28	56
Limited number of years	6	12
Unlimited 4-year terms	14	28
Two-year terms	2	4

Source: Compiled from *Book of the States, 1998–99:* 33–34.

The Republican and the Democratic Parties have been highly competitive in trying to win the governorship in most states. Historically, there have been only a few states dominated by one party; most of the states today are *two-party competitive political systems.* This means that career paths of ambitious public officials are always under development in the state capital. Not surprisingly, the state legislature is one source of promising gubernatorial candidates. Leaders of the state senate or house of representatives have many political contacts and are familiar with the issues that face state government. Politicians who have served a region of their state in the U.S. House of Representatives also may be attractive candidates. Other excellent staging posts for potential governors are statewide elected positions other than governor such as the secretary of state, state school superintendent, state treasurer, or lieutenant governor. In these positions, a person may have had an opportunity to develop voter appeal and fund-raising skills, as well as name recognition, an important consideration in an era of poorly informed and independent voters. Finally, there are always political outsiders who want to run against the established interests. These individuals may be wealthy businesspeople, media personalities, or other men and women who enjoy high visibility and name recognition. Overall, the primary field of candidates may have several of these different types of politicians: state legislators, statewide elected officials, current and former federal representatives, and self-styled outsiders. This variety adds interest to each party's primary election.

In the **general election** for governor, both parties will spend a great deal of money on consultants, polling, advertising, and travel (see Table 5.2). The national parties may assist the gubernatorial candidates by supplementing the financial resources of the state party organization. The state and national party organizations also can provide expertise and endorsements. Few politicians have the personal resources to fund a campaign themselves, so they must depend on financial support from their party, individual citizens, and interest groups. The exception to the rule might be the millionaire outsider candidate who funds his or her own campaign.

Table 5.2
The Five Costliest Gubernatorial Races, 1994

State	$ Million
California	60.6
Pennsylvania	36.1
New York	32.3
Tennessee	28.0
Texas	26.4

Source: Council of State Governments in Beyle, 1994: 50.

Issues play a role in gubernatorial elections. Incumbent governors who seek reelection will have to run on their records. Challengers from both within the party (usually until the primary is decided) and from the other party will question that record. If no incumbent is running in the race, then the retiring governor's party will have some obligation to defend his or her—and the party's—record in office. This can be either an advantage or a liability. Issues are often reduced to media sound bites, which can take on lives of their own.

One example of this type of oversimplified issue is the abolition of parole. On the surface, the issue seems to be one of severity versus lenience in sentencing offenders. Those who advocate abolishing parole argue that convicted criminals should serve their entire sentence. Early release violates "truth in sentencing" and interferes with the offender getting his "just deserts." It also violates the victim's and the community's rights. However, to abolish parole would be to let convicted felons return to the streets unsupervised. It is parole officers who keep tabs on ex-convicts after they are released from prison. Abolition of parole also would remove one of the few tools that corrections officials have for motivating convicts to behave in prison and perhaps rehabilitate themselves. The issue obviously has at least two sides. Yet imagine how difficult it is for an incumbent or a party in power to defend parole against its glib detractors. It is an example of a *challenger's issue*, or an easy way to make the party in power an electoral whipping boy.

Someone wins the primary, and someone wins the general election. That is the one inevitability of our democratic system. The margin of victory will likely not be large in an era of two-party competitive politics. There will be little in the way of a clear message from the electorate, a so-called **mandate** from the people. Issues will remain complex, and the leadership challenge for the new governor will have just begun. There is far more to leadership than winning an election.

Results of Recent Gubernatorial Elections

The 1998 elections for governor in states with open seats were an interesting and exciting lot. In California, Governor Pete Wilson, a Republican, had reached his two-term limit and could not run for reelection. A Democrat, Lieutenant Governor Gray Davis, was elected. California is a large and influential state; its state policies are often used as models by other states. The Democrats also gained control of both chambers of the California legislature. This Democratic control in California should have important political ramifications at the national level as the Democrats try to regain control of the U.S. House of Representatives (Shields, 1998). When the 2000 census is completed, California may pick up three or four House seats; these and all of the other California House seats will be given districts created to their own advantage by the California Democrats.

In Florida, Jeb Bush—the younger son of former President George Bush—became the first Republican governor of that state since Reconstruction. Florida's popular Governor Lawton Chiles, a Democrat, had reached Florida's two-term limit. Bush defeated Lieutenant Governor Buddy MacKay in a race with another populous and influential state on the line. The Florida state legislature is in Republican hands. Because Florida also has gained population since the 1990 census, new and existing House seats will be at issue there just as in California. However, in Florida, it is Republicans who hold all of the cards.

In Minnesota, professional wrestler and Reform Party candidate Jesse Ventura beat both the Democratic and Republican candidates: one a former mayor and the other the state's attorney general. He became only the second governor who is neither a Republican nor a Democrat (Maine's governor, Angus King, won reelection as an independent). Ventura's election has left many political pundits baffled. By making a direct appeal to the voting public, he bypassed many of the customary linkages to the major parties in the electorate and in the legislature. His legislative program drew considerable media attention, and state legislators were soon entertaining his populous proposals for tax cuts and other antiestablishment measures. Early in 2000, the governor left the national Reform Party because he did not want to be associated with some of the personalities who were running under the party's banner. The saga of Jesse Ventura continues!

Figure 5.1 Partisan winners of the 1998 gubernatorial elections
Source: Data compiled from National Governors' Association Web page.

All in all, thirty-six states held gubernatorial elections in November 1998. Republican candidates won in twenty-three of the states; eleven Democrats and the aforementioned third-party and independent candidates won the other contests. Republicans were able to maintain their control of the majority of governorships (see Figure 5.1).

Republican strength is widespread, but much of the party's success in capturing governors' offices in the 1990s has been in the South. Republicans held onto the governorships in Texas, Tennessee, and Arkansas while adding Florida to their ranks. Virginia, North Carolina, Mississippi, and Louisiana already had Republican governors who did not face reelection in 1998. Only a few years ago, a Republican governor was almost unheard of in the South. The Democratic Party considered the region to be safe territory. They did not expect the *voter realignment* that took place in the South beginning with the presidency of Ronald Reagan. Although Democrats have managed to wrest South Carolina and Alabama away from Republicans and hold onto Georgia and the border state of Maryland, the Republican Party has a strong hold on Southern governorships.

The Republican Party is also strong in the Midwest and West. In Ohio, Robert Taft secured the governorship for his party, and Michigan's Governor John Engler was returned to office to keep the position Republican. The Democrats enjoyed a surprise victory in Iowa when liberal State Senator Tom Vilsack defeated a better-known and financed conservative. Farther west, Republicans held onto governorships in Illinois, Nebraska, Kansas, Oklahoma,

CHAPTER 5 State Executives: *Leadership and Accountability*

South Dakota, Idaho, Wyoming, and Arizona. Arizona's Jane Dee Hull was reelected as governor. She stands with New Jersey's Christine Todd Whitman as the nation's two Republican women governors. New Hampshire's Jeanne Shaheen is the sole Democratic woman governor in the United States.

New York's Republican Governor George Pataki also was reelected. New York is a large state with influence far beyond its borders. The New York state legislature is split, with Republicans controlling the senate and Democrats controlling the house. It is unclear which way the winds of political change are blowing in the Empire State.

The general popularity of the national Republican Party in the 1980s and 1990s and the steady and relentless realignment of the South raised Republican hopes in the last few elections. However, the gubernatorial elections of 1998 gave Democrats cause for cautious optimism. The Republicans still control the majority of governorships, but state legislatures are more equally divided between both parties, and split control is common. The Democratic Party nationally gained forty state legislative seats in 1998, a considerable accomplishment in an off-year election.

Governors Taking Office

In the few weeks between a general election and the swearing in of a new governor, the winner and his or her transition team try to put their administration together. In many instances, the individual who is leaving the office tries to smooth the way. Thirty-five states have specific legislation on the books that provide for and fund gubernatorial transitions (*The Book of the States, 1998–99:* 29). Priorities for a *transition team* may include communicating about the current year's budget and spending by state agencies, legislative priorities and their budgetary impacts, and collaboration about any pending state emergencies such as flood or drought relief and court scrutiny of prison overcrowding. If the departing governor and incoming governor are of the same political party, then obviously more collaboration takes place than if they were from different parties. In fact, if the governor's office is changing occupants and not parties, then some of the outgoing governor's staff members may even stay on in the new administration.

Inauguration day comes early in the new year. It is an exciting time for the new governor, his or her family, and supporters. There are solemn ceremonies, fancy dress parties, and constant media events. Citizens come to the state capital from all over the state to see and to be seen. Few celebrations can match the glamour of inauguration week festivities.

As the governor and his or her family and staff settle in, it is easy to overlook the important ceremonial role that state governors play. Once elected, governors and their families move into the *governor's mansion*. Here, the governor and his or her spouse host visiting dignitaries, celebrate important state holidays, and conduct award ceremonies for local heroes and outstanding state employees. These ceremonies are important to award recipients, their families, and their friends. They are also important civic exercises for public officials. The general public cannot be aware of the contributions of the state's outstanding citizens unless public recognitions are celebrated and covered in the news media.

Governors' mansions are virtual palaces that are well suited for entertaining. A visiting foreign minister or European bank president would be comfortable indeed if he or she came to visit on a trade mission. This type of lavish hospitality is also extended to visiting federal officials, national leaders of the governor's party, and other governors. The public may take pride in the positive image that the governor and the first spouse project for their state. No one wants guests to find their state's hospitality to be shabby. The expenses seem to be born cheerfully in most states.

The Governor as Legislative Leader

The incoming governor has one month to prepare a major policy address, the **State of the State Address**. State constitutions follow the example of the national constitution in allowing the governor to address a joint session of the legislature. The purpose of the State of the State Address is to outline the governor's priorities for the new legislative session. Obviously, this is a great opportunity for a new governor to exercise political leadership by identifying and defining problems in this address. For example, violent crime may be a growing problem in the state, and anything from weakened family structure to chronic unemployment may be a cause. The governor can list his or her priorities for addressing the problem, especially those that require a new legislative act or new budget item (see Table 5.3).

Table 5.3
Content Analysis of State of the State Addresses, 1998

Social Concern or Policy Issue	Highlighted in Speeches (%)*
K–12 education	88
Public safety	74
Children's issues	72
Environment	65
Tax relief	60
Economic development	37
Higher education	37
Transportation	23

*Percentage is for number of states out of forty-three analyzed (seven states were excluded: Arkansas, Montana, Nevada, Texas, Florida, Louisiana, and North Carolina).

Source: Condensed and tabulated from Council of State Governments, "State Government News." Reprinted in *Book of the States, 1998–99:* 483.

On the day of the State of the State Address and in the impressive venue of a joint legislative session, the governor has the undivided attention of both the legislature and the media. It is a critical opportunity to lead the state. On that day, the governor stands before the television cameras as the focus of government politics and policy. It is an opportunity that few governors waste.

There is relatively little regional variation in gubernatorial priorities found in the content of these State of the State Addresses. Of the four gubernatorial addresses that failed to highlight education from kindergarten to twelfth grade, one each were from the East, South, Midwest, and West. Higher education and public safety were featured more often in Southern and Western states, and tax relief was discussed in Midwestern and Southern states. Party alignment in a state may affect the agenda as well. For example,

Governors such as Alaska's Tony Knowles can set their legislative agendas early in their tenure in their State of the State Addresses.

Source: © Michael Penn

we have noted that Midwestern and Southern governors are disproportionately Republican, and tax cuts are a favorite policy issue for that party. In any case, governors target issues that they believe are of interest to their citizens and the legislators. Their policy addresses should not be assumed to be laundry lists of all conceivable social concerns. Governors are seeking specific policy outcomes.

Follow-up to the State of the State Address takes many forms. Legislative members of the governor's party will introduce his or her *legislative program*. The governor's **floor leaders** will interpret the new bills as they are introduced in each chamber and link them to the governor's overall program. The party officials—majority or minority leader, depending on the governor's party affiliation, and the party whip—will all work to pass the governor's bills. Every effort is usually made by fellow party members to secure passage of the governor's program because the party succeeds when the governor succeeds. He or she is both the state's leader and the party's leader.

The opposition party in the state legislature may agree with the governor's definition of problems but not with the approach to solving them. The minority party members ran for office proclaiming their own approaches to the state's problems. Their legislative program will reflect the values and priorities of their political party. The party officials in the state legislature will answer the State of the State Address and match the governor bill for bill on major policy options. Relatively little bipartisan cooperation can be assumed in two-party competitive states. Exceptions might include disaster relief, new education spending, and popular tax-reform measures.

The governor also must take his or her program to the people. One power that state legislators respect is the power of public opinion. If the governor can rally the public around his or her approach to solving the state's problems, then party members will stand strongly behind him, and he may even forge a bipartisan coalition for certain bills.

The Governor's Immediate Staff

One key to influencing public opinion is access to and good relations with the news media. The press secretary is the key staff member in the governor's office who is responsible for maintaining such a good relationship. He or she does this by providing members of the media with accurate and timely information. Reporters and other media representatives are pressed for time and

You live in a state and may or may not go to school in that state. For this exercise, choose one: your home state or the state in which you are in school. Spend a few minutes thinking about the issues you wish the governor would highlight in the next State of the State Address. Don't be intimidated by the list of what other state governors have done in the past. Come up with your own list of concerns that the state government ought to be addressing. Jot down your short list and be prepared to discuss how your priorities compare with those of your classmates.

challenged by their competitive industry, so trust is essential in their relationship with this staff member. A press secretary who misleads reporters or makes them look bad will wound the governor (Nigard, 1998). If the press secretary can convince them that he or she will cooperate with them as much as the governor will allow, then members of the media are much more likely to treat the governor and his or her programs kindly.

The media and the public are interested in what the governor has to say about the state's problems. For their part, the media want a good story. For citizens, the concern is often for personal prosperity and safety. Governors might typically couch their public appeals in terms of economic development and crime control. Economic development policies involve attracting new industry and retaining existing businesses, as well as addressing infrastructure needs such as quality public education and good roads. Crime control policies may include strict laws, severe penalties, and new prison construction. Of course, good schools and new prisons cost money. The public wants quality public goods and services but at a bargain price, and there is often an underlying belief that government spending is wasteful and that public services are ineffective. Governors therefore often must express their appeals in terms of efficient and effective public services.

Fragmentary evidence suggests that the public is satisfied with how governors are able to manage the affairs of state government. In 1994, Thad Beyle compiled data from the National Network of State Polls at the University of North Carolina. These polls reported that twelve governors held approval ratings of 60 percent or higher; another fifteen scored in the 50 percent to 59 percent approval range (Beyle, 1996: 227). In other words, more than half of all governors scored a positive rating of at least 50 percent. Ultimately, the important approval rating is that given in the polling booth. Even governors with relatively low approval ratings have been reelected to office.

The Governor as Budgetary Leader

While only the legislature can tax and spend, governors must lead in budget planning if they hope to fund their priorities. They must show that tax revenues will be available to implement their programs. They also must coordinate the budget requests by the myriad of state agencies to which annual appropriations are life's blood. Governors may have to propose new revenue sources. This issue was behind the move by several states to legalize and organize lotteries to pay for new educational services. This strategy permits a state

New York Governor George Pataki works closely with staff members to shape the agenda and address issues that are important to both the citizens of the state as well as his own party.
Source: © Les Stone / Corbis Sygma

to take in new revenue without raising taxes, and that could be an important component of a governor's overall economic development strategy.

The governor's staff member who is most responsible for funding state programs is the director of planning and budget, whose primary job is to analyze how the existing and proposed revenue streams would affect state education programs for several years. Only then would the governor and the public know whether the economic development game plan was a good one.

The governor's office requires that state agencies submit their budgetary requests to the office of planning and budget for review and consolidation. The governor prepares an **executive budget** or at least drafts the budget in forty-one states. In the process of developing the consolidated budget, governors inevitably cut agency requests. In fact, many state legislators consider this to be the first line of defense against *budget creep*, the gradual but steady growth in the total state budget.

Once a budget passes his or her legislature, governors in forty-one states can veto budget items, a power known as a **line-item veto.** Governors use their line-item veto powers to remove items that seem excessive or unnecessary from the budget bill passed by the legislature. These are often what are known as *pork barrel projects*, and they may have been placed in the budget to bring some highly local and frequently unnecessary benefit to a legislator's constituents such as a state park or an office building. Local contractors, of course, can make a great deal of money at the state's expense. Using this type of veto, a governor can establish budgetary leadership early and late in the budget-development process. Provisions for overriding such vetoes vary by state, but a typical provision would require a two-thirds majority of both chambers of the state legislature to override the veto.

Other budget-related gubernatorial powers might include hiring freezes when funds are running low or employee layoffs when true economic hardship straps state government. The latter procedure, sometimes referred to as a *reduction in force* (RIF) is a nightmare because of employee seniority rights, so governors try to avoid it. If an individual's position is abolished—or "RIF'ed"—he or she may "bump" a less senior employee in another state agency and take that individual's job. The ripple effects can be devastating to productivity and morale.

The press secretary and the planning and budget director are only two of many staff members who work with the governor. There are large staffs of policy analysts and budget analysts. State government is complex, and governors must address a wide range of policy areas: agriculture, recreation, tourism, economic development, and education, among others. Reporters may ask for details of the governor's plans in any of these areas at any time. The state legislature may initiate new policy on any topic at any time. Governors have to keep up with a wide range of issues, and most have large staffs to help them do just that.

The Governor's Appointment Powers

One of the most important powers a governor enjoys is an *appointment power*. To a considerable extent, governors only are able to develop and implement their policy agenda if they have their own handpicked administrators at the head of state agencies. Otherwise, state agencies may head off in different directions or ignore the governor's efforts at policy leadership.

Some **constitutional offices** in state government are commonly filled through elections. During the same November elections that decide the governor's race, the public usually elects state attorneys general, state school superintendents, and secretaries of state (see Table 5.4). State constitutions declare that these officials and their departments shall have some independence from the governor. However, should the state's planning and budget director and the state's director of economic development be elected? Most states do not think so, so their constitutions provide for gubernatorial appointment of most agency heads. Thus, the appointment and removal power gives governors authority within state government. Agency heads must respect and follow the governor's lead in making and implementing state policy. We will return to a discussion of appointed state agency heads after discussing the role of the lieutenant governor in state government.

Table 5.4
Other Statewide Elected Officials, 1998

Statewide Elected Officials	Number (%) States Holding Elections
Attorney general	41 (82)
Treasurer	39 (78)
Secretary of state	34 (68)
State school superintendent	15 (30)
Agriculture commissioner	13 (26)
Insurance commissioner	11 (22)
Public utility commissioner	8 (16)
Labor commissioner	6 (12)

Source: Compiled from *Book of the States, 1998–99:* 22–23.

❧ Lieutenant Governors

All but eight states—Arizona, Maine, New Hampshire, New Jersey, Oregon, Tennessee, West Virginia, and Wyoming—have lieutenant governors (*Book of the States, 1998–99:* 47). Conventional wisdom holds that governors have ready-made emergency successors and helpers, their lieutenant governors, in much the same way the president has an emergency successor and helper in the vice president. If the U.S. Constitution and the state constitutions were used as a guide, then both the vice president and the lieutenant governors of half the states would seem to divide their time between two types of duties. They would serve as a chamber official in the upper legislative chamber—the U.S. Senate and the state senate, respectively—and as second in command to the president or the governor.

Actually, the U.S. vice president works more closely with the president than does the lieutenant governor with the governor. Modern vice presidents preside over the U.S. Senate only on ceremonial occasions—such as the State of the Union Address—or when their vote might break a tie in the Senate. The president pro tempore of the U.S. Senate presides over that body's everyday business. Otherwise, the vice president is properly viewed as an executive branch official. Many recent vice presidents have had important policy assignments from the president. For example, Vice President Al Gore was a spokesman for the Clinton administration on environmental issues and "reinventing government" efforts to reduce the size, cost, and complexity of the federal government.

Many lieutenant governors more often keep to their state senate duties. They preside over state senate deliberations in twenty-six of the forty-two states and can cast tie-breaking votes (*Book of the States, 1998–99:* 48). In addition, they appoint state senate committees in six states—five Southern states and Vermont—and assign bills in twelve states, including six in the South and four in New England. In other words, the lieutenant governor is a legislative player in some states, and the pattern varies by region of the country.

The lieutenant governor of Texas is a good example of a constitutionally powerful lieutenant governor position (Texas State Senate, 1998). The Texas constitution names the lieutenant governor as the president of the state senate, but it also allows the state senate to write its own rules. This gives a great deal of control over legislative decision making to the lieutenant governor. He or she can appoint committees and chairs, rule on parliamentary questions, and set the order of business for voting on bills. By statute, the lieutenant governor is also a member of the legislative budget board and other important administrative boards. There is little that happens in Texas state government that this officeholder does not influence or control.

The presence of a powerful lieutenant governor may signal the constitutional weakness of the governor's position. This is said to be the case in Texas, where Governor George W. Bush was often required to seek the support of the late Lieutenant Governor Bob Bullock (Walters, 1998: 20). In many ways, the Texas lieutenant governor was the more powerful of the two positions, especially in matters related to state policy or spending.

Exploring on Your Own **Visiting the National Governors' Association Web Page**

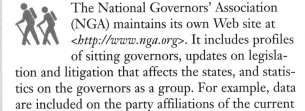 The National Governors' Association (NGA) maintains its own Web site at <*http://www.nga.org*>. It includes profiles of sitting governors, updates on legislation and litigation that affects the states, and statistics on the governors as a group. For example, data are included on the party affiliations of the current governors. This is an excellent resource for discovering the hot topics that face governors at the time you are taking this course. Use your computer to visit this terrific Web site. Explore the leadership in the state where you reside or where you would like to practice your profession after graduation. Your insights will enliven class discussions.

Fran Ulmer, Alaska's Lieutenant Governor, is an integral part of Governor Tony Knowles's cabinet.
Source: © Jim Harrison

The other half of the lieutenant governors are primarily executive branch figures. They may be assigned duties by the governor, take over when the governor is out of the state, and serve as a member of the governor's cabinet if a cabinet system is used. This pattern is clearly at work in Alaska, where Fran Ulmer is lieutenant governor. She is a part of Governor Tony Knowles's team and does not have legislative duties. As a member of his cabinet, she can represent him at official functions and undertake tasks he may assign. Many of the duties of a lieutenant governor may seem ceremonial, yet these officials are able to maintain important contact with the public when the governors are unavailable. As a statewide elected official, they obviously must have excellent "people skills." Governors with their own lieutenant governors can greatly extend their public outreach if their lieutenant is really a part of the team.

If the governor does not have a lieutenant governor available, then he or she will need an inner circle of personal aides who can perform some of the same functions. One way or another, governors must extend their reach. There is no way they can be on a trade delegation to Germany and meet with concerned pork producers back home at the same time. They must have help.

Appointed Agency Heads

The daily administration of state programs requires talented and experienced executives. Governors appoint the chief administrators of most state agencies such as the director of the state corrections department and the chair of the state parole board. In some states, other agency heads are elected statewide. Examples we noted include the attorney general, state school superintent, and secretary of state. It is hard to generalize about which agency heads are appointed and which are elected because practice varies by state.

Many governors meet with their agency heads as a group. We call this a *state cabinet* system. In some cases, the cabinet is described in the state's constitution; in others, it is the creature of tradition or gubernatorial prerogative (see Table 5.5). The cabinet discusses broad issues facing state government. Members exchange information and offer coordinated advice to the governor on matters that affect several of their overlapping jurisdictions. The frequency of meetings is often left to the governor's discretion, and cabinet sessions are closed to the public in all but eight states.

Table 5.5
State Cabinet Systems

Created by	Number (%) of States
Constitution	7 (14)
Statute	19 (38)
Governor	6 (12)
Tradition	7 (14)
No cabinet system	11 (22)

Source: Compiled from *Book of the States, 1998–99: 27.*

Agency heads are responsible for implementing the laws that the state legislature has passed that affect their domains of responsibility. They also are responsible for carrying out the governor's policy directives. These administrators sit atop pyramids of bureaucratic organization. Working through deputy directors, local managers, and operational staff, the director tries to ensure that all agency practices comply with state policy and procedures. He or she is responsible to the governor and hence to the public for compliance. More generally, the agency head is accountable for the efficient and effective operation of agency operations. Any illegal activity, waste, or scandal must be detected and remedied using a military-style chain of command. In this way, everyone who works in state government reports to a manager and the "buck stops" with the agency director or his or her boss, the governor.

To discharge these important responsibilities, the agency heads must be talented and vigilant individuals. Often they have worked their way up through the agency ranks, and sometimes they may have been brought in from private industry. In any case, they must be able to plan and implement agency policies and procedures. They must be able to manage the daily operations and crises of large, statewide departments. These duties require competence in management information systems and personnel and budget management systems. Yet perhaps the most important qualification for these top administrative posts are leadership ability and the governor's trust and confidence. Governors do not want to be accountable to the public for agency operations unless they in turn have reliable chief administrators in control of state government departments.

One additional control is placed on most state agencies. The director of the agency may report to a **governing board** as well as to the governor. Under this arrangement, a governor appoints board members who in turn oversee the actions of agencies and their directors. This additional level of accountability gives a governor some peace of mind. He or she cannot keep up with every action of so many state agencies, but appointees can. Typically, the board will meet monthly, and members will review major programs and policies with the agency director and his or her staff. If political risks are involved, then the board members can advise both the agency director and the governor of their take on the issue.

A great deal of knowledge may guide the more professionally educated state agency heads. Within the study of public administration, extensive literatures are devoted to leadership styles, organization development, and organization theory. Peter Drucker, one of the most famous public administration scholars, has many valuable insights for the state agency director. For example, he observes that while lesser managers may become preoccupied with the agency's operating details, its leader must maintain focus on the agency's contribution to society (Drucker, 1966). For example, the director of the state department of corrections must not only see that prisoners are not allowed to escape, but also must constantly search for effective correctional programs that will help men and women reconcile with society, their victims, and their families. In this respect, the agency's leader is a policy maker, albeit one who must have certain policy decisions confirmed by an elected governor or state legislature.

Dorothy Olshfski studies these state agency executives. She distinguishes the policy leadership in the absence and in the presence of a governor's priority program. If the governor has a major initiative in someone's department, then the agency head will take that lead and support the governor's policy (Olshfski, 1990: 230). On the other hand, most areas of any agency's responsibilities will not involve these high-profile governor's policies. In this large remaining policy domain, the agency head is king or queen.

The responsibility of dealing with a wide range of policy issues brings the agency head into contact with the state's political players. Legislators and interest groups have a stake in the decisions of many state agencies, so agency heads must understand the principles and techniques of the practical political world. The administrators report that they are adept at such skills (Olshfski, 1990), but they are not unanimous in their evaluation of other capital city players. For example, corrections department heads and state equal employment directors around the country report that the media, political parties, governor's staff, and legislators have little interest in corrections and employment policy (Cox, 1997). Only attentive interest groups with a focus on the agency's activities have a sustained interest. Governors themselves are interested only episodically. In other words, life at the top of the organizational pyramid may be lonely, and few agency heads receive credit for the 99 percent of the time their agencies operate legally, ethically, and efficiently.

❧ State Managers

Many well-trained and experienced managers report to agency directors: welfare office directors, Medicaid administrators, state park managers, and prison wardens, all of them responsible for the daily delivery of services. For the average citizen, these managers mean all the difference in service quality, because services get delivered and quality is maintained at this level. Individual problems also get resolved at this level. These *first-line managers* and their professional subordinates meet the public every day. The success of state programs is largely in their hands.

Public administration literature also addresses the interests and concerns of these managers. Considerable research can guide the personnel process from hiring to training, personnel evaluation, and employee discipline. We will have more to say about state employees and their professionalism in the next chapter. Our concern here for policy and program implementation requires that we look at the management systems that enable executives such as the governor and agency directors to make sure their directives are followed.

Management information systems (MIS) are data-rich information flows. Data is collected at the operational level and summarized for the use of different levels of managers. For example, caseload data for welfare offices is collected at the worker and office level, summarized at the district level, and further consolidated for the state at large. A monthly report that shows the number of families that receive public assistance is produced for users all along the way. Of course, more complex data analysis also is used. The average time for benefits of a welfare caseload, the average amount of benefits paid to families, the number and frequency of case payment errors are all data that managers and executives would like to monitor on a regular basis.

Other management systems address the achievement of agency objectives. There are many variations on the classic *management by objectives* (MBO) format for setting goals and monitoring progress toward their achievement. Using these approaches, executives, directors, and managers can set and refine goals, establish benchmarks for certifying their accomplishment, and utilize MIS data to verify goal achievement. The participation by many levels of administration builds teamwork and ensures clear communication about expectations.

Other management systems relate the achievement of goals to budget figures. The *performance budgeting* movement in government focuses on the relationship between budgetary effort and policy implementation success. It stresses efficiency much as MBO stresses effectiveness. It can be a powerful tool in bringing resources to bear on priority programs. It can also identify and reduce the funding for programs that are no longer needed.

Management systems are not the "be all and end all" of state government. They are tools that can effect positive change in the hands of experienced and committed executives, agency heads, and managers. Like all information technology, they are constantly refined. New techniques are always being tried. The twin challenges of efficiency and effectiveness are elusive, but state governments are usually trying to build technology for accountability.

✒ Reforming Executive Branch Government

The history of the executive branch of state government has a few consistent themes: rational organization, making agencies goal-directed, and making government business-like.

Reorganization is an effort to bring reason to the cobweb of interrelated state agencies, offices, bureaus, and boards (Conant, 1988). Many incoming governors wish to restructure state government so that like functions are grouped together and redundancy is eliminated. If state government is to be more accountable, then optimally grouping activities and charting communication flow are important tasks. In twenty-one states, the executive branch can be reorganized by executive order (*Book of the States, 1998–99:* 22–23). In the other states, reorganization requires statutory or constitutional change. The most extensive reorganization might involve moving from a system with many elected agency heads to a cabinet style of government. In that case, basic laws would have to be modified by the legislature.

Given a reasonable consolidation and organization of state operations, a governor should expect the state agencies to be *goal-directed*. States may adopt programs with unclear expectations about what they are to accomplish, but careful crafting of policy plus modern social science tools make it possible to set concrete expectations and measure the effectiveness of state programs. Programs that work can then be reauthorized, and those that are worthless can be abolished. For a middle group of programs that may be underachieving, agencies may fine-tune them to improve their effectiveness. At different times, this type of reform has been included in *management by objectives* and *zero-based budgeting* packages.

Finally, critics have argued that state services should be more *business-like*. By "business-like," they mean that operations should be efficient and minimize waste. Governors from a business background and others who admire corporate culture, as well as many common citizens, would like to see state government get the greatest possible "bang for the buck." This involves improving effectiveness, achieving greater operating efficiency, and changing organizational culture so that citizen "customers" are treated with respect. The use of business-management techniques in state government, however, often seems like the adoption of an endless series of fads. Some recent transplants from business to government are managed health-care benefits for state employees, quality circles for improving service delivery, and competitive hiring and promotion through nonmerit system personnel schemes.

Efficiency, greater effectiveness, and greater consumer satisfaction also are addressed in contemporary *reinventing government* literature (Osborne & Gaebler, 1993). This body of managerial knowledge and creed holds that government should be *catalytic*—that is, set policy direction but be flexible about who actually delivers services. This opens the door for more privatization of service delivery in areas from computer services to prison operation. Private contractors may be able to deliver high-quality services at lower costs. The reinvention literature also calls for more *competitive* government services. Agencies and the offices within them should compete with each other to find improved means of providing state services. Stakeholders in a program—for example, clients and families in the state welfare system—should be *empowered* to make programming choices that affect them. In other words, reinventing government is a whole, integrated package of policy and management tools that are available to make organizations more effective.

Governors, constitutional officers, and agency heads are largely responsible for reforming state government. Although some individual agencies might try to reform themselves on their own, political authority and program

China's Handpicked New Governor of Hong Kong

elsewhere in the world

The city-state of Hong Kong is a densely populated piece of territory that was just outside the reach of China's communist government. The British ruled Hong Kong as a royal colony until 1998 when their long-term lease on the land ran out. Control then reverted to the central Chinese government. With the change in status, Hong Kong's extensive port facilities, docks and warehouses, and well-developed business district came under Chinese control. A committee of four hundred Hong Kong Chinese residents who supported the Chinese government chose the new governor in 1997.

The new governor is Tung Chee-hwa, a Hong Kong shipping tycoon. He also is a politician who was known for many years to be a moderately pro-Chinese businessman.

Local officials who did well under British rule and reformers and who want a liberal administration of the colony and its business enterprises by the Chinese government have been suspicious of the new governor. They are concerned that he will be a puppet of the communists in Beijing. He in turn is worried that reformers and foreigners will antagonize the central government authorities and make matters worse. Clearly, he stands at a strategic leadership moment in history for the city-state of Hong Kong. Governor Tung will have to lead the policy development process in such a way that economic progress is maintained and the People's Republic of China does not have cause to intervene. He will be accountable to the business community and to the Communist Party in walking this tightrope.

funds come from the chief executive, so it is common to find new governors intent on reforming their state government. The packaging of the reform may be administrative in the case of reorganization, programmatic in terms of goal-directed behavior, or business-like in managerial technique. The governor even may plan to reinvent state government altogether. In any case, we should not be surprised to learn that our state's executive branch needs a face-lift.

✒ Chapter Conclusion

In this chapter, we covered a lot of territory. We learned about state government's chief executive—the governor—and something about what it takes to be elected and to govern afterward. From there, we visited the offices of the governor's leadership team, agency heads, senior managers, and the professional employees and contractors who get the job done in state government. In other words, we have covered the waterfront and surveyed the executive branch of state government. The following common themes stand out:

- Governors exercise *policy leadership* in important areas such as corrections and education. In other policy areas, they have been trying to lead individually and as a group. Economic development, welfare reform, and environmental preservation are only a few of the many areas in which the fifty governors have been active. Some policy experiments are more successful than others. The most promising are publicized in magazines such as *Governing* and promoted at meetings of the National Governor's Association. The transfer of innovations eventually trickles down to the agency-operations level.

- State government is *vast*. State services and programs extend into virtually every area of our everyday lives. Governors have to use all of the resources of their personality and all available technology to ride herd on state government. Sometimes a governor can use the budget to reinforce his or her priorities. At other times, a cabinet meeting or a series of one-on-one meetings with an agency director will do the job. In any case, governors are resourceful in promoting compliance with their policy priorities and administrative directions.

- The political system also is *accountable* for results. As we noted in our discussion of capital city players, news media, the public, interest groups, and political opponents are always watching and keeping score. In today's political environment, everyone from the governor down to the line worker in state government is accountable for getting the job done. Many management-technology tools are available to the executive branch of state government. Management information systems and goal-setting packages help monitor the extent to which policy implementation stays on-track.

- Finally, an era of big government is coming to an end at the state level just as it has at the national level. Governors and opinion makers seem intent on introducing more of the features of *free markets* capitalism into state operations. The era of stable, slow-moving state bureaucracies also may be ending. Experiments with catalytic or competitive government administration stimulate new approaches and generate new accountability data.

Recall in our discussion of federalism that we noted the devolution thesis about how power and responsibility for policies and programs are shifting from Washington, D.C., to the fifty state capitals. Today, more is expected of state governments in one sense, and greater economies are expected of them in another. They are caught in a dilemma: how to do more with less. It's a good thing that the state governments attract competent leadership and highly motivated professionals and contractors. They are going to need them.

Key Words for InfoTrac Exploration

gubernatorial elections

National Governors Association

reinventing government

waste in government spending

Sources Cited

Beyle, Thad L. (1994). Unpublished campaign finance contribution data. Pp. 158–159 in Virginia Gray and Peter Eisinger (Eds.), *American States and Cities* (2nd ed.). New York: Longman.

———. (1996). "Governors." Pp. 207–252 in Virginia Gray and Herbert Jacob (Eds.), *Politics in the American States: A Comparative Approach* (6th ed.). Washington, DC: Congressional Quarterly Press.

The Book of the States, 1998–99 (1998). Lexington, KY: Council of State Governments.

Conant, James K. (1988). "In the Shadow of Wilson and Brownlow: Executive Branch Reorganization in the States, 1965 to 1987." *Public Administration Review, 48*(5) (September/October): 892–902.

Cox, George H. (1997). "Tracking Political Variables Across Policy Studies." *Comparative State Politics, 18*(2) (April): 39–46.

Drucker, Peter (1966). *The Effective Executive.* New York: Harper & Row.

National Governors' Association (1998). "1998 Gubernatorial Elections." Online: <*http://www.nga.org/Releases*>.

Nigard, Bill (1998). "Interviews with Press Secretaries and Media Representatives," *Atlanta Week in Review.* Atlanta: Georgia Public Television.

Olshfski, Dorothy (1990). "Politics and Leadership: Political Executives as Work." *Public Productivity and Management Review, 13*(3) (Spring): 225–243.

Osborne, David, and Ted Gaebler (1992). *Reinventing Government: How the Entrepreneurial Spirit is Transforming the Public Sector.* Reading, MA: Addison-Wesley.

Shields, Mark (1998, Nov. 4). "Election Night 1998: Political Wrap-up with Mark Shields and Paul Gigot," *The News Hour with Jim Lehrer.* Washington, DC: Corporation for Public Broadcasting.

Texas State Senate (1998). Online: <*http://www.senate.state.tx.us/*>.

Walters, Jonathan (1998). "The Taming of Texas." *Governing, 11*(10) (July): 18–22.

Bureaucrats and Regulators: Delivering Services and Protecting Consumers

- **The Bureaucracy of Service Delivery**

- **Evaluating State Government Professionalism**

- **Regulators and Consumer Protection**

- **State Public Service Commissions**

- **Regulation: Some Answers**

- **Chapter Conclusion**

What would your lifestyle be like if you couldn't drive? You would have to walk or take public transportation everywhere you wanted to go. For many young Americans, owning and operating an automobile is a major priority. All of us, in fact, must get permission to drive. It is state governments that license drivers to operate motor vehicles. Driving on the public streets and highways is a privilege, not a right. As noted earlier, to get a driver's license, we must appear at a state traffic-safety building, pass a written test, demonstrate good vision and hearing, and perform well on a driving test. If we satisfy all of the requirements, then we will be issued a valid state driver's license.

Have you ever thought about whether you would be treated fairly by the driver's license examiners? Would they single you out because you are African American? Do they give harder driving tests to females? These kinds of questions go to the heart of our public expectations about state employees. Can we count on fair and equal treatment by these bureaucrats?

We have all witnessed the drivers' licensing process. The same written examination is given to everyone. The hearing and sight examinations are standardized. Even the practical driving skills demonstration varies little from one examiner to another. As a matter of course, bureaucracies do such tasks well. They have **standard operating procedures** (SOPs) that describe how an activity is to be carried out. Employees are trained in the SOPs and evaluated in how expertly and consistently they apply them in everyday work. Over a period of years, these same employees develop *expertise*. They know the rules inside and out, and they can answer even the most difficult questions about state law and motor-vehicle operation.

We count on bureaucrats such as those state employees who operate the driver's license office to be capable and fair. If they were not, we would be at the mercy of petty tyrants whenever we used a governmental service. We are quite fortunate in the United States to have a large number of responsible and professional state workers. Ninety-nine times out of one hundred, we are treated courteously and competently when we discharge a duty such as getting or renewing our driver's license. In fact, we count on it!

Given this kind of everyday experience, it is interesting that the word *bureaucrat* has a negative connotation for many Americans. Both conservative and liberal politicians and some members of the media have characterized the men and women who are employed in government agencies as an unproductive drain on the society and the economy. American philosopher George Santayana once remarked, "The working of great institutions is mainly the result of a vast mass of routine, petty malice, self-interest, carelessness, and sheer mistake" (Eigen & Siegel, 1993: 32). Ouch! Stripped of the opinions that sometimes surround the term, a **bureaucracy** is simply "any administrative system, especially of governmental agencies, that carries out policy on a day-to-day basis, uses standardized procedures, has a hierarchy, and is based on the specialization of duties" (Plano & Greenberg, 1997: 221). In this sense, any large scale, well-organized human enterprise could be termed a bureaucracy: the military and large nonprofit

Kansas's state buildings in Topeka are typical of most states' government headquarters, holding the principal offices of major departments and agencies.
Source: © SuperStock

organizations such as the Red Cross, the Boy Scouts, and the Girl Scouts of America. Even large corporations and the administrative offices of church denominations have some of the characteristics of the modern bureaucracy.

In fact, many well-intentioned and highly skilled professionals are employed by state agencies. Engineers, finance managers, and project planners work in the central office of a state agency in the capital. Social workers, highway patrol officers, and park rangers deliver state services at the local level. None of these people are the mindless clerks often panned by bureaucracy's critics.

In this chapter, we will look at two types of state employees: (1) the agency employees who deliver services to the state's citizens, and (2) the regulators who protect consumers from unscrupulous business practices in the state.

Together, these two groups of state employees are the bureaucrats without whom state programs would go unimplemented and state policies would go unenforced. We begin our look at state service delivery agencies with a brief discussion of the principles of bureaucratic behavior and then ask two of the critics' most basic questions:

- Can state government be better organized or even "downsized" to better achieve its purposes?
- Should we try to reinvent public enterprise altogether, making it more like private enterprise?

Then we look at the special duties and responsibilities of state regulatory agencies. We will look at the kinds of threats to the public interest that are posed by unscrupulous business practices. This group of state organizations includes specialized state regulatory agencies such as the state insurance commission. It also includes the state public service commission that oversees utilities such as natural gas and telephone service. Finally, certain regulators manage the licensing of professionals from traditional professionals such as attorneys and physicians to newer professionals such as personal counselors and massage therapists. In the case of regulatory agencies, we will ask two additional questions:

- Who controls the regulators: government, consumers, or the industries who are supposed to be regulated?
- Are excessive burdens being placed on private enterprises when state regulators investigate the complaints of their customers and supervise corporate or professional behavior?

It is a useful fiction to posit that state agencies such as the state public safety and state welfare departments provide direct services to the public while others such as the insurance and public service commissions regulate private behavior. In fact, some state agencies are distinct that way, whereas others such as state departments of natural resources provide both service delivery and regulatory supervision. The distinction we are making is one of function rather than of kind. Service delivery and regulation are where you find them, and the complex administration of state government produces many hybrids. For simplicity's sake, we will discuss service delivery and regulation separately, using examples from the more purely specialized state agencies.

❧ The Bureaucracy of Service Delivery

More than 4.5 million individuals are employed by state agencies in the United States. State employees work in such large departments as higher education, highways, corrections, juvenile justice, social welfare, mental health, natural resources, public safety, financial administration, and legal services. They also work in smaller but important agencies such as industrial development, elementary and secondary education support, state archives, agriculture, assistance to local governments, and judicial administration. These workers are organized into central office operations in the state capital and in direct-service offices throughout the state. Counties are administrative subdivisions of the state and are charged with administering state programs. Many local employees who distribute state services may be titled "county" workers and work in offices with titles such as the "County Welfare Department" and the "County Health Department." The funds are state funds and the programs are state programs, however. In this sense, the local workers report to state administrators and managers in the state capital. Of course, many counties also have their own programs. In that regard, the employees report to county officials. We will have more to say about county government in Chapter 11.

The number of state employees has been steadily increasing for a long time (see Figure 6.1). There could be many causes for this steady and dramatic increase. One certainly is citizens' rising service expectations. Some state agencies such as the department of natural resources provide valued amenities from state parks to hunting and fishing preserves, and demands for these amenities have been rising. Other state agencies—for example, the state highway patrol and the corrections department—are responses to public safety concerns, which also have been increasing. It would be fair to say that the public wants more and more from its state government (Jenks & Wright, 1993), but it is less clear whether Americans are willing to pay for more and better services.

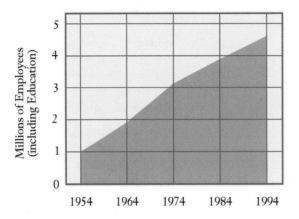

Figure 6.1 Full-time state employees
Source: Adapted from *The Book of the States, 1998-99:* 332.

Another reason for the increase in state employees is the devolution of program responsibilities from the federal government to the states. As we noted earlier, several recent presidents and Congresses have argued that programs such as public health, education, and social welfare can best be organized and managed at the state level. This has meant that state governments have grown while the federal government has shrunk. The shift also suggests that the public is unwilling to see valued services dropped altogether.

One consequence of this climbing trend in state employment has been the impulse to organize very large-scale enterprises. In the 1950s, few states had large agencies that delivered a wide range of services. Increasingly, state governments have felt a need to establish large specialized agencies with large work forces and large budgets. State government in all fifty states has been drawn into the bureaucracy business.

Specialization and Professionalism

The revenue that comes from Washington and the budgets that are voted on by the state legislatures come with strings attached. Government employees must be able to deal with ever-growing policy manuals that prescribe the services to be provided and the manner in which they must be delivered. To comprehend these many thousands of pages of regulations, state employees must become specialists. An ordinary state bureau clerk of the 1950s could not begin to understand and apply highly technical service programs such as Medicaid and Transitional Aid for Families in Need, the new national welfare program.

Professional state employees of the twenty-first century will be well educated, carefully trained in their job responsibilities, and accountable for all of their actions. But this higher level of state programs does not come cheap. Hiring and retaining professionals costs more, and care must be taken that only qualified professionals will be brought into state government. The dramatic rise in state employee salaries is evidence of the increasing professionalism of state workers (see Figure 6.2).

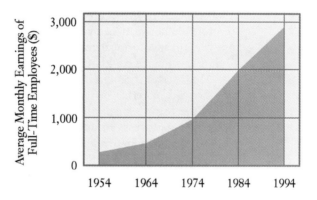

Figure 6.2 Average monthly salary of state employees
Source: Adapted from *The Book of the States, 1998-99:* 332.

There are pockets of blue-collar employment in state government: men and women who maintain the capital grounds, guards who man the walls of state prisons, and clerks who process state documents. These employees are an important part of the overall state government effort, but their numbers have been shrinking for years. More and more of the routine blue-collar work of state government has been automated or contracted out. The employees who remain in these ranks often feel left out of the renaissance in state government. For that reason, unions have made some inroads in recruiting the states' blue-collar workforce. State government has not been enthusiastic about unions, but organizations such as the American Federation of State, County, and Municipal Employees (AFSCME) have argued that they can boost wages and benefits and improve working conditions. Workers who believe they are the state's lowest priority may find these arguments appealing. So, even in an era of shrinking union membership in the United States, some states find their workers wanting union representation.

Civil-Service Protection

Professionalism is also institutionalized in formalized civil-service systems. State **merit systems** were created to protect state employees and public tax dollars from political corruption. Before the enactment of state civil-service laws, elected officials and their appointed allies would hire political friends for state government positions as a reward for personal and partisan loyalty. Under this *spoils system*, state office buildings were crowded with people who knew little about agency responsibilities and whose interests were more in electioneering than engineering. The reform movement that began in the Midwest in the 1920s swept political hacks out of state government and began to organize it around a professional practice of administration.

For many states, the effects of the reform movement were not felt until the 1950s or 1960s. Cynthia Bowling and Deil Wright have measured the shift in professionalism over time by examining the qualifications of state agency heads (Bowling & Wright, 1998: 58). They found that even in the 1960s, agency heads averaged thirteen years of prior state government service in two or more state agencies before being elevated to the position of director or commissioner. They note that 40 percent of agency heads held graduate degrees in the 1960s; currently, the figure is up to 60 percent. These figures show the effects of professionalism as it takes over at the top of state agencies. The challenge has been to institutionalize advances so that state employees' professionalism and independence could be protected.

Merit systems require that each position in state government be concretely described in terms of both duties and the qualifications of a person who would perform them. Merit systems also prescribe the method of screening potential employees: resume review, standardized knowledge test, or both. Only the outstanding candidates from the screening phase are actually interviewed for the position. Personnel procedures also provide for probationary work evaluation, promotion guidelines, annual review processes, disciplinary procedures, salaries by position, and the criteria for raises. To some managers, these *personnel policy requirements* seem to hamstring an agency; to others, civil-service protection is necessary for professional government service (Walters, 1997). The very structure of government service has become a battlefield for politicians with cost-cutting as well as reform agendas.

Several states have ongoing civil-service reform activities. In ten states, the review is wholesale—that is, all aspects of state employment are under review. In thirty-one states, the process is being pursued incrementally (*The Book of the States, 1998–99:* 324). The focus of reform efforts varies by state. Aggregating and ranking the areas gives an indication of the relative importance the states give each area of civil-service procedures (see Table 6.1).

The two top priorities among the states are *classification systems* that adequately describe positions in state government and *compensation*, or plans to pay adequate salaries to attract and retain top-flight professionals in a competitive environment. *Performance evaluation* ranks third. Without a sound performance-evaluation system, employee problems may not be remedied and unacceptable performance may not lead to dismissal from service. *Selection*, or the process of filling vacancies in state agencies, is the fourth most important area. Many criteria are at work in hiring, ranging from competitiveness to affirmative action to veterans' preference. These four priority areas of state civil service are keys to the future success of state government.

Table 6.1
Civil Service Reform in the States, 1998

Type of Reform	Number of States
1. Classification	38
2. Compensation	38
3. Performance evaluation	35
4. Selection	34
5. Recruitment	31
6. Merit testing	30
7. Training	28
8. Benefits	24
9. Employee relations	20
10. Layoffs	20

Source: Council of State Governments Survey reported in *The Book of the States, 1998–99:* 324.

Specialized tasks have led to a large number of state agencies. During the 1970s alone, the number of state agencies in the United States increased by 50 percent (Jenks & Wright, 1993: 82). Within these organizations, even more specialized duties are performed by specially trained state employees.

If the world and its problems would stand still, bureaucracies would probably work well. They have all of the resources needed to repeatedly serve people consistently and lawfully. If a few policy changes were imposed from outside the agency's boundaries, then the chain of command could fine-tune agency procedures. If the nature of the work gradually evolved, then the civil service could reevaluate positions and draw up new specifications and qualifications. Unfortunately for bureaucracy, the pace of change not only is fast but also seems to be accelerating.

Hierarchy and Communications

A well-organized and professionalized state agency has *clear lines of communications*. In terms of detecting problems, communication flows upward on the organizational chart: from the direct service worker to unit managers to the central office in the state capital. In terms of policy interpretations, the communication flow is often downward. The keys to reliable communication are the pathways through which all agency employees know they must communicate (see Figure 6.3).

In the 1950s and 1960s, requirements to use the chain of command were enforced. This led to a problem with improper situations not being addressed. A New York institution for the mentally ill, for example, had deplorable living conditions that were not remedied through the chain of command, and a staff member had to go public to get the situation addressed. This type of **whistle-blowing** draws attention to the limitations of hierarchy. Responses to ineffective bureaucratic communications have included some state whistle-blower protection laws and the creation of ombudsmen or client advocates within state agencies. There also is more delegation of authority to professional workers on the scene so that problems can be solved in less time than it took to cover them up. Client-protection laws also give concerned employees tools for changing policies or procedures that are harming clients.

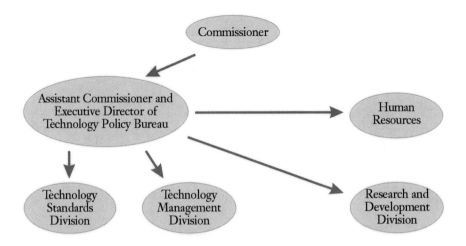

Figure 6.3 Typical bureaucratic organization chart. This shows Minnesota's Technology Policy Bureau in relation to the state's larger Department of Administration.

Carried to its logical extreme, professionalism would lead to buying services in the marketplace. If the state needs computer development, then why not hire a firm with computer systems development experience? By *contracting out* a needed service, a state is not left with employees to consider after the work is done. Compensation and benefit concerns also shift to the company, and state government does not have to worry about salary or raises, medical insurance, or retirement benefits for the contract employees. The idea of contracting out, however, may have been carried to extremes in some states. In Tennessee and other states, for instance, the state has contracted a prison's operation. Guards, counselors, food service personnel, medical staff, and administrators all work for the contractor. This may be extreme because prison employees literally have the power of life and death over inmates. If a prisoner escapes or dies under suspicious circumstances, then the state will certainly be held accountable by the public. If services but not responsibility can be can contracted out, then there may be limits to the usefulness of contracted work.

BOX 6.1   *Privatization Counterpoint*

Not everyone is optimistic about the results of privatizing public services. Three researchers at the Institute for Southern Studies in Durham, North Carolina, have found problems in privatized child-support enforcement in Mississippi, hospital care in Florida, and prison administration in Tennessee (Diehl et al., 2000). Based on their three case studies, the researchers conclude that there is a breakdown in public accountability in privatized services. The public is not included in decision making and cannot obtain information it needs to monitor privatized activities. There is a pattern of preferential treatment in many cases. To maximize profits, providers hike fees and cater to clients who can co-pay or reciprocate. Privatized services also may fail to meet community needs as they cut the total number of jobs and extract profits in lieu of reinvestment in community residents. In fact, promised cost savings may never materialize. Clearly, the privatization controversy has at least two sides. Learn more about this study by visiting the Institute's Web site at *<http://www.i4south.org>*.

CHAPTER 6   Bureaucrats and Regulators: *Delivering Services and Protecting Consumers*

Government, business, and nonprofit agencies are rethinking their positions on organizational structure. Ever-increasing consumer demands, the growth of personal computer technology, and communications advances have all enabled organizations to seek a flatter structure. Instead of being seen as a hierarchy, the organization is increasingly seen as a network of collaboration. People relate as professionals and work in teams to achieve mutually agreed-upon goals. Communication flows around and through all parts of the organization, and control is subordinated to creative problem solving.

Exploring on Your Own **A Trip to the Drivers' License Office**

Earlier in this chapter and in Chapter 4, we discussed the men and women who staff the drivers' license office in your community. In many states, they are attached to the state Department of Public Safety, the same agency that includes the State Troopers or Highway Patrol. Go and observe these bureaucrats in action. How do they exemplify principles of classic bureaucratic organization? What are the advantages to the way they organize and carry out their work? What possible criticisms might you or other citizens have of their policies and procedures? Remember, *bureaucrat* is not a dirty word in and of itself. Bring your notes to class for discussion.

Evaluating State Government Professionalism

Critics have raised the issue of whether large, rigidly structured organizations can deal with the wide variety of problems that emerge when social and technological change is a society's dominant characteristic. A new study of state management practices shows how even the most well-intentioned state government can miss the mark of structuring itself for efficient service delivery.

The Pew Charitable Trust funded an evaluation of state management practices. The Maxwell School of Citizenship and Public Affairs conducted the study at Syracuse University, and the results were published in *Governing* magazine (Barrett & Greene, 1999). The study surveyed the opinions of knowledgeable experts in each state, asking them to evaluate five areas of state government practice: financial management, capital-resource management, human resources, management for results, and information technology.

Financial management—or managing the public's tax dollar—is an important responsibility of state officials. The study included questions about cash management, cost accounting, and preparation of fiscal notes, solvency of the rainy day fund, and Generally Accepted Accounting Principles (GAAP). Overall, the study's experts gave state governments an average grade of B in financial management. Four upper-Midwest states—Minnesota, Michigan, Iowa, and Missouri—scored A's, as did Pennsylvania, Maryland, Washington, and Delaware. New York and Mississippi scored the lowest (D+).

Capital-resource management involves keeping buildings in good repair. It addresses the soundness of government in a state. As a group, the states received a B– on capital-resource management. Minnesota, Michigan, Missouri, Washington, and Maryland again were among the top scorers (A or A–) along with Kentucky and Virginia. The lowest-scoring states were Mississippi (D–), New Mexico (D), and Arizona (D+).

The criterion of *human resources* pertains to the concerns discussed in the civil-service section. The survey asked the experts if a given state maintained a certified list of applicants for positions, paid for performance, or engaged in effective workforce planning. The overall states' score was B–. South Carolina was the only state to score an A. A large and scattered group of states earned B's. Nevada was the only state to get a D, and Rhode Island was the only state to earn an F.

Management for results means that a state uses such techniques discussed in the last chapter as establishing benchmarks for performance or performance budgeting. It also addresses the issue of input, output, and outcome measures for use in executive and legislative decision making. Virginia and Missouri led the pack with A– grades. New York, New Hampshire, Connecticut, Oklahoma, and New Mexico received grades of D+. Arkansas and both Dakotas earned D's, and Mississippi earned an F.

Finally, much has been made of the potential for the Information Age and the communications revolution to reduce our reliance on armies of state employees. The survey asked about *information technology*—the development and maintenance of databases, computer networks, and advanced communications technology. The states averaged a C+ on this criterion, with Washington (A) and Virginia (A–) leading the way. Connecticut, Illinois, Arizona, Wyoming, and Idaho earned D+'s. Arkansas, Mississippi, and Rhode Island scored the lowest (D). Perhaps the greatest shortcoming is that even good information is rarely used to make policy and modify administrative procedures.

What emerges from this study of the effectiveness of state management systems is a *benchmark* for future studies. States know how they stand relative to the overall national average and their neighbors. Few states lead on all or most indicators. California and New York are not pacesetters, according to this approach. Instead, innovators are scattered around the country. In absolute terms, the expert informants consulted in the study perceive that state governments have a way to go before they can boast that they have left the era of bureaucracies and entered the Information Age.

Bureaucracy Conclusion

We are now ready to ask ourselves this question: Can state government be downsized and better organized to achieve its purposes? There is no simple answer. Unquestionably, some state agency offices could be streamlined with new technology, training, or procedures. Certainly, some programs could be eliminated if we want to abandon the goals they seek to achieve. Shall we start with game-preserve programs for hunters? What about child care for working mothers? Or should we eliminate the state subsidy for state universities and have students pay the full cost of their education? The point is that every program benefits somebody.

Similarly, we can address the question of whether we should try to reinvent public enterprise by making it more like private enterprise. U.S. businesses seem to produce fine goods and services and operate at a profit. Should we contract out certain activities to private companies and make other programs more business-like? Many states are trying both approaches. The business community is a constituent just like hunters, working mothers, and college students. By privatizing more services and freezing levels of state employment, perhaps the ever-increasing number of state government employees can be leveled out. Yet it is important to remember that private corporations have their problems, too. Many American corporations have had to fire many of their professional and managerial employees to make a profit. If citizens want more services for less money (lower taxes), then private enterprise may be challenged to deliver just as public enterprise was.

Collecting Your Thoughts *What Would Your Work Requirements Be?*

Jot down the work rights you would want if you were a professional state employee. Consider hours, compensation, benefits, tenure, and disciplinary and grievance rights. Should your hours and compensation be related? Should you be paid more if you had to complete all work regardless of the hours required? How should your annual raises be computed? Would you want across-the-board increases, or would you be happy with raises that were strictly tied to performance? What health benefits would be important to you and your young family? What type of severance pay or retirement package would seem fair? If your work was deemed unsatisfactory, what steps should be provided to ensure that you are treated fairly? Should you have the right to expect continued employment so long as your work is satisfactory? By putting yourself in the place of the state employee, you may better understand the issues surrounding the bureaucracy controversy. Bring your notes to class for discussion.

❧ Regulators and Consumer Protection

States regulate a wide range of corporate and individual behavior for many different reasons. At the heart of the decision to regulate an industry or activity are three fundamental concepts: delegated law-making authority, government support for the regulated industry, and consumer protection. Literally hundreds of state government boards, commissions, and agencies make rules that have the force of law. They also license activities that consumers believe may be dangerous to them if not regulated in the public interest.

First, legislatures grant **rule-making authority** in areas where they feel unable or are unwilling to legislate over and over again. These rules are official public policy and have the full force of law. The utility industry, for example, is a highly technical sector that deals with electrical generation by facilities that burn fossil fuels or natural gas. It involves the engineering capabilities of hydroelectric dams and nuclear plants. Electricity and natural gas are transmitted and sold through complex regional business arrangements. The rates that companies and individuals should pay for electricity and natural gas are part of a sensitive political issue that can affect investors' and consumers' pocketbooks. Utilities can require many dozens of public policy decisions each year. Legislatures would prefer to have specialists deal with most of the utilities industries issues. There would be little political gain from continuously voting on constituents' power bills. Instead, a state legislature typically empowers a public service commission (PSC) to regulate utilities within the state.

Second, many professions and industries *seek* regulation to *limit competition and ensure quality* in the marketplace. A utility company, for instance, will have to invest heavily in construction, machinery, technology, and employees to serve a given population. The company must have a stable environment that ensures its ability to recoup its investments.

Third, there is concern for **consumer protection.** States protect worker safety on the job through industrial regulation, and they screen unqualified and unscrupulous professionals and tradespeople who may harm the public. The standards that define a safe workplace or reasonable workweek are controversial. Organized labor and the federal government regularly champion particular policies, but state agencies are often left to investigate workers' day-to-day complaints. Similarly, consumers have many complaints about insurance companies: Rates may seem unfair, claims may be unreasonably denied, or insurance policies may be canceled after claims are paid. The legislature would have time for little else if it tried to develop solutions to the many problems that arise in overseeing industries such as insurance or utility companies. State regulatory and licensing powers thus are more efficient responses to dealing with the balance between constituents' concerns, be they industries or consumers.

Selecting the Regulators

Regulatory boards and commissioners are chosen by various means in the states. The most senior regulator in state government is the secretary of state. The state's **secretary of state** has many duties, including the chartering of corporations to do business in the state and investigating complaints about the conformity of business practices with those charters. This officeholder is elected in a statewide vote (see Table 6.2). Other important regulators include the insurance commissioner, banking commissioner, consumer affairs director, and members of the state public service commission. The insurance and banking industries draw their own specialized regulators in most states. The public service commissions regulate the utility industries—most importantly, the telephone and electricity companies. In addition, appointed licensing boards decide on the qualifications the state will require for practicing professionals such as attorneys and physicians.

Table 6.2
Method of Selection of State Regulators, 1998

Regulator	Popular Election	Appointed by Governor or Lt. Governor	Civil Service Employee or Appointee	No Agency in State
Secretary of state	45	5	0	0
Banking commissioner	0	24	25	1
Consumer affairs	0	6	33	11
Insurance commissioner	9	27	10	4
Public service commission	7	27	15	1

Source: Compiled from *The Book of the States, 1998–99:* 35–39.

Corporate Regulation

Companies regulated by state commissions and boards do well financially. The purpose of regulating the insurance industry, for example, is not to drive insurance companies or agents out of business but to ensure that the public's interests are protected in these businesses' daily operations. Similarly, utilities are

CHAPTER 6 Bureaucrats and Regulators: *Delivering Services and Protecting Consumers*

Cathy Cox, Georgia's Secretary of State, is responsible for chartering businesses that operate in the state.

Source: Photo courtesy of Georgia's Secretary of State Office

extremely profitable. Their stocks are sold on the national exchanges, and investors are attracted by that profitability. Electrical and natural gas companies can make their target profits in a regulatory environment that supports them as often as it disciplines them. The additional costs of public protection simply are included in the cost of doing business.

The public has little specialized knowledge about many industries such as insurance and utilities and yet depends on them for important services and personal or family security. Legislators are not experts either. Only people who work in the industry everyday are qualified to oversee many corporate practices in a state. A state public utilities commission or a state insurance commission can hire professional staffpeople who are knowledgeable and experienced with utilities or insurance matters. The governor may either appoint the commissioners or they may be popularly elected (again, see Table 6.2). They can then spend virtually all of their time specializing in the laws that govern the industry. Investigators and hearing officers can meet with consumers around the state and try to relieve problems with specific utility companies or insurers.

Not all insurance regulation is routine. Insurance companies insure doctors against malpractice lawsuit awards. As awards by judges and juries have gotten larger and larger, however, insurance companies have both raised their rates and tried to get limits on liability laws. Regulators can deal with the rate issue, but they are powerless to change a state's liability laws. Lawyers often benefit from large settlements against doctors and hospitals, and their associations typically oppose *tort reform* that would place a limit or cap on awards (Williams, 1996: 501). As a result, insurance companies may refuse to write policies in states without realistic liability limits. Where does that leave the doctors in those states? They cannot risk practicing medicine without malpractice insurance, and they were already paying hundreds of thousands of dollars in insurance premiums. States in which such tort reform is in crisis have problems well beyond any insurance commission's ability to solve.

Professional Licensing

Virtually all states license professionals such as architects, engineers, lawyers, physicians, nurses, pharmacists, and veterinarians. Trades such as barbers and cosmetologists are also licensed, as are real estate agents, insurance agents, and funeral directors. All of these occupations involve the public interest because

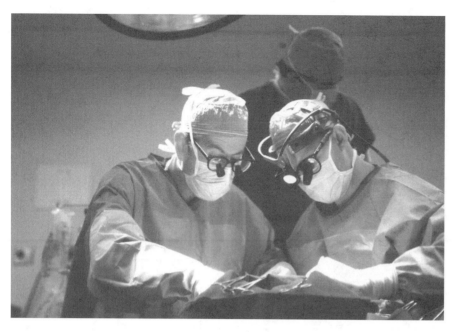
Medical practitioners are among those who are regulated by states and professional societies.
Source: © William Campbell / Corbis Sygma

of malfeasance and misfeasance. *Malfeasance* is unethical behavior, and *misfeasance* is incompetence. Both can threaten the public's health and well-being. The state has a right and an obligation to protect its citizens.

Various professions are increasingly important parts of our national economy and quality of life. Professionals undertake specialized educations at schools or universities that themselves must meet professional accreditation standards (Benveniste, 1987). Following this special instruction, many professions require a *practicum* (teacher education), *internship* (psychology), or *residency* (medicine).

When professional preparation has been completed, the novice takes an extensive and usually quite difficult set of examinations (e.g., bar exams for attorneys). Those who pass the examinations may apply for the state license to practice their profession. After a careful review of credentials (e.g., academic transcripts and exam scores) and a thorough background check, the licensing agency or board will issue the license. Subject to conforming to state rules and professional ethics, the professionals are free to pursue their occupations. Some professions also require continuing education on a regular basis to ensure that practitioners keep current with developments in their profession.

Medical professionals are among the most highly regulated by state governments. Physicians, nurses, and dentists must qualify for and maintain state licenses to practice their professions. Among the many other state-licensed

Collecting Your Thoughts *Professionalism and Your Career*

If you haven't already done so, you and your advisor should have a long conversation about your career. But some pre-advising doodling is probably in order. What future occupations are represented by your classmates' and friends' ambitions? Are you seeking the correct university degree for your preferred profession? Are there standards that dictate what your program of studies should look like? Are internships needed? If so, where? Is there a state licensing requirement? What does it take to pass those exams? You must get your ducks in a row if you expect to enter and succeed in the professional world. Next stop: the library or university placement office. Then get with your advisor and plan how to efficiently map your next couple of years.

health occupations are physical therapists, medical technicians, emergency medical technicians, chiropractors, and dental hygienists. Mental health professionals such as psychologists, social workers, and counselors also are licensed in most states.

Mandatory *continuing education* is required of many professionals in the states. Licensed certified public accountants must take courses in every state except Wisconsin. All but thirteen states require continuing education for attorneys, but those exceptions include the large states of New York, Illinois, and Michigan. There is a great deal of variation by occupation (see Table 6.3).

Table 6.3
Mandatory Continuing Education Regulations by Profession, 1998

Licensed Profession	States Requiring Number (Percent)
Architects	4 (8)
Certified public accountants	49 (98)
Engineers	10 (20)
Nurses	21 (42)
Physical therapists	21 (42)
Physicians	28 (56)
Veterinarians	37 (74)
Psychologists	38 (76)
Dentists	42 (84)
Attorneys	37 (74)
Pharmacists	47 (94)

Source: Compiled from *The Book of the States, 1998–99:* 367.

❧ State Public Service Commissions

Each state regulates many industries that do business within its borders. The type of economic activity that is regulated by a PSC is called a "public service." Some regulated companies are *natural monopolies,* providing public services in the sense that the general public must rely on them for necessities because there are no alternative providers in the marketplace. Electric utilities are a good example: It would be economically irrational to have multiple electric companies running power lines all over the countryside. Other companies provide goods or services that have sensitive externalities or powerful side effects for consumers. An example would be telephone regulation to protect against billing for unwanted or unnecessary services. From these two examples, you will notice that most PSC regulation involves a group of industries that we call *public utilities.* In this section, we look at the organization of these regulatory agencies and the issues that dominate their agendas.

Organization and Powers

Public service agencies consist of a group of commissioners and a staff that works under the commissioners. The method of selecting public service commissioners varies by state. In eight states, the public elects them. The logic behind the election of PSC leaders suggests that consumers need and want to have a hand in their own protection. The candidates must demonstrate their sensitivity to consumer concerns and their independence of the industries they are being elected to regulate.

Louisiana is a good example of a state that elects its commissioners. The state is subdivided into five regions of equal population. A commissioner is elected from each district to serve a six-year term. Montana likewise elects its commissioners from five equally sized districts. They serve four-year terms and choose their own chairperson.

In most states, the governor appoints PSC members. He or she does this either alone or with state senate confirmation, depending on the state. The logic for appointing members of the PSC is that the governor can decide based on the candidates' expertise rather than their popularity. The commissioners are still accountable to the public because the public has elected the governor and can hold him or her accountable for actions by the administration.

Florida is typical of states with an appointed PSC. Joe Garcia is currently the PSC chair. He is accountable to the governor for actions taken by the commission and its staff, and he advises the state legislature on any needed consumer-protection legislation. Garcia is a former executive director of a Cuban relief organization. Commissioner Susan Clark is a University of Florida law graduate who worked as a staff member and manager at the PSC for more than a decade. She has now been appointed for two four-year terms as a commission member.

State PSCs are charged with making rules to control utilities' rates and practices. These rules are made in an open political process in which affected corporations and consumer advocates both have many opportunities to comment. The public may or may not be aware of the rule making depending on how much coverage the capital media give the PSC. Complying with published rules represents one of the costs of doing business in a state. If a complaint is filed against a company, then the PSC investigates it and rules on violations. The commission may punish violators, usually with a fine, although serious or repeat offenses may lead it in some states to revoke the license to operate in the state. In this sense, the regulatory agency functions as a fusion of quasi-legislative, quasi-executive, and quasi-judicial powers.

Staff members who work for public service commissioners investigate complaints and gather information about individual companies. They also help prepare policy information that commissioners will need when making new rules and regulations. The specifics of each regulated industry (e.g., utility and telephone companies) are so technical that staff members tend to specialize. They are commonly organized into divisions that parallel the industries regulated by the PSC.

Wisconsin's staff organization is typical. Its PSC has specialized divisions for electrical, natural gas, and telecommunications regulation. Each division has become expert on a particular industry, but all ultimately report to the public service commissioners. Staff members become efficient in communicating with and about the utility they regulate, although over a long period of time they may become too familiar with the industry representatives with whom they deal. There is danger that they might be "captured" by the industry they were hired to regulate. They may even leave government employment for more lucrative industry positions, taking their knowledge of the regulatory process with them.

Public-Service Issues

Each year, public service commissions receive hundreds of consumer complaints, and the number of complaints has been increasing over the last decade. A visit to the agency home page of the Wisconsin Public Service Commission, for example, reveals that state's experience with customer complaints. The Wisconsin PSC staff now investigates more than two thousand complaints every quarter, or nearly four times what it investigated in the mid-1990s (see Figure 6.4).

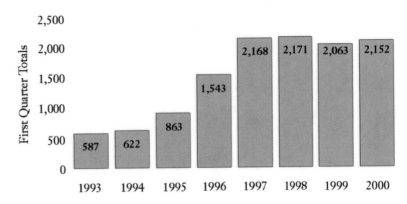

Figure 6.4 Wisconsin PSC consumer complaints
Source: Wisconsin Public Service Commission Online

The types of complaint in Wisconsin also are interesting. Far and away, the greatest cause of consumer complaints has been the telephone industry. The frequency of complaints by industry show that complaints about telephone service dwarf those for the next highest industry, electrical utilities. In Wisconsin, as elsewhere, the bulk of complaints have concerned bills and industry billing practices.

Two issues have developed in regulating the telephone industry—"cramming" and "slamming"—that illustrate how consumers' interests and industry needs sometimes conflict. Consumers resent having charges added to their telephone bills without their approval, which is called *cramming* because extra services and charges are loaded onto customers' bills. Telephone companies insist they have announced such changes on previous bills or through other unobtrusive means. Customers and their advocates respond that any and all customers who are billed for them should explicitly agree to new services or charges. The PSCs of many states have prohibited cramming.

The Florida Public Service Commission has warned consumers to read their bills and all correspondence from their telephone company carefully. Former Florida Commission Chair Julia Johnson advised, "We have heard from consumers about all kinds of charges mysteriously popping up on their bills" (Florida Public Service Commission, 1998a). The PSC also has required telephone companies operating in the state to reimburse charges in cases of consumer complaints. Investigations are now underway that will hopefully lead to stronger Florida telephone customer–protection laws.

The state PSCs have been much tougher concerning the telephone company practice of *slamming*, or changing a customer's long-distance service without his or her permission. More and more state PSCs require that service providers and telemarketers give consumers complete information about who will provide their telephone service and what the charges will be. Failure to do so in Florida requires that the provider change the service to the desired company and charge only the rates charged by that preferred company for up to twelve months thereafter (Florida Public Service Commission, 1998b). Fines also have been levied against slamming violators. The Florida PSC settled with Unidial Incorporated when that company agreed to pay $125,000 to the state's general revenue trust fund. The PSC also fined Phone Calls, Inc., $860,000 for slamming, failing to respond to commission inquiries, and misusing its certificate to operate in the state.

The Future of Public Service Commissions

Many contemporary PSCs describe their missions in terms of *balancing* consumer and industry interests (Public Service Commission History, FL PSC Home page). Customers are more and more aware of their rights and willing to act through official channels. At the same time, technology and shifting federal regulatory policies make the utilities industries an ever-changing economic sector that seeks new opportunities for customers, services, and profits. Other PSCs are using the contemporary jargon of "reinventing government." The Wisconsin PSC, for example, professes to be committed to "removing barriers to the development of competition and spurring the development of customer choices for all utility services" (Wisconsin Public Service Commission, 2000). Regardless of the verbiage, the future of state PSCs looks busy. The numbers of rules, complaints, and adverse actions appear to be rising, so an era of increased state regulation seems at hand.

The future of state public service regulation is likely to be busy. Consumers are increasingly unwilling to allow corporations to take advantage of them. In fact, we now live in a time of consumer rights, and the regulatory environment of the states reflects that reality. We also live in the era of the professions. College graduates are going to work in fields that are professionally self-regulated, so we need to know more about professional regulation as well as consumer protection. Professionals will have to protect themselves from unethical practitioners and unfit competitors. The future of regulation looks bright.

❧ Regulation: Some Answers

We are now ready to answer our basic question, Who controls the regulators? The government, consumers, or industry? The answer is all three. Each entity influences the rules that are made and how vigorously they are enforced. The state legislature can pass a law that preempts a state regulatory rule at any time. Legislators typically choose not to step into regulatory matters, however. Instead, consumer advocates and industry representatives can usually negotiate a solution to the problems that regulators encounter. The role of the regulatory staff members themselves may be to investigate or to arbitrate. Prosecuting the offending industry is a last resort.

Our second question asks, Are excessive regulatory burdens being placed on private enterprise? When a state legislature or a regulatory body concludes that a natural monopoly exists, then the industry that serves the state gains a terrific advantage. It does not have to worry about competitors. Industry members will get to make their case about consumer pricing to a regulatory body. The regulators will consider the industry's needs as well as consumers' ability to pay and study the experience of similar industries in other states. The resulting decision is usually fine with the industry, which is willing to trade a bit on price for a guaranteed and secure market. Of course, a particular utility or other industry may consider using price history or another state's policy as a benchmark to claim unwarranted interference in the free enterprise system. Consumer advocates would argue that the industry would not be in business if not for governmental concessions. The regulator is often left to chart a middle course between the interests of regulated industries and diligent consumers.

❧ Chapter Conclusion

We have talked about two very different types of governmental employees in this chapter: service delivery bureaucrats and regulatory board members and staff. They suffer from a kind of public distrust that has been fostered by politicians of the extreme left and right as well as by the media. Ultraconservative politicians want us to believe that all private enterprise must be unfettered to succeed. We should therefore contract for all services and deregulate all industries. Ultraliberal politicians argue that industry exploits its customers and workers out of pure greed, which must be held in check. They may argue that the state provides essential services for the victims of a capitalism that is red in fang and claw. The media simply love to "investigate" wasteful or ineffective public programs, and it takes little more than a politician's accusation or an isolated case of mis- or malfeasance to get them started. They have nothing to gain from reporting the excellent job that thousands of state service employees and regulators perform every day. State employees suffer this disrespect and have little recourse.

Key Words for InfoTrac Exploration

| civil service | consumer protection | cramming and slamming | whistle-blowing |

Sources Cited

Barrett, Katherine, and Richard Greene (1999). "Grading the States: A Management Report Card." *Governing*, *12*(5) (February): 17–28.

Benveniste, Guy (1987). *Professionalizing the Organization: Reducing Bureaucracy to Enhance Effectiveness.* San Francisco: Jossey-Bass.

Bowling, Cynthia J., and Deil S. Wright (1998). "Public Administration in the Fifty States: A Half-Century Administrative Revolution." *State and Local Government Review*, *30*(1) (Winter): 52–64.

Council of State Governments (1999). *The Book of the States, 1998–99*, Vol. 32. Lexington, KY: Council of State Governments.

Diehl, Kim, Keith Ernst, & Daphne Holden (2000). *Private Gain, Public Pain: How Privatization Harms Communities.* Durham, NC: Institute for Southern Studies.

Eigen, Lewis D., and Jonathan Siegel (Eds.) (1993). *The Macmillan Dictionary of Political Quotations.* New York: Macmillan.

Florida Public Service Commission (1998a). News release. February 4. Online: *<http://www2.scri.net/psc/commissioners.html>*.

——— (1998b). News release. May 19. Online: *<http://www2.scri.net/psc/commissioners.html>*.

Jenks, Stephen S., and Deil S. Wright (1993). "An Agency-Level Approach to Change in the Administrative Functions of American State Governments." *State and Local Government Review*, *25*(2) (Spring): 78–86.

Plano, Jack C., and Milton Greenberg (1997). *The American Political Dictionary*, 10th ed. Fort Worth, TX: Harcourt Brace.

Walters, Jonathan (1997). "Who Needs Civil Service?" *Governing*, *10*(11) (July): 17–21.

Williams, Bruce A. (1996). "Economic Regulation and Environmental Protection." Pp. 478–515 in Virginia Gray and Herbert Jacobs (Eds.), *Politics in the American States: A Comparative Analysis.* Washington, DC: Congressional Quarterly Press.

Wisconsin Public Service Commission (2000). "At a Glance." Online: *<http://www.psc.state.wi.us/>*.

State Courts: The Rules and Boundaries of the Game

~ **American Justice**

~ **Court Structure in the States**

~ **Serving as a State Judge**

~ **The Administration of Justice**

~ **Issues Before the State Courts**

~ **Chapter Conclusion**

Each of the fifty states maintains an elaborate system of civil and criminal courts. Like all of the basic structures of state government, the court systems are defined in each state's constitution and statutory law. All are unique in small but locally important ways, yet they have general features that reflect important overarching principles. These common principles might be called the *American system of justice*. This is where we begin our study of state courts and how the states have engineered court systems that embody those principles. Finally, we will look at the apparent policy priorities of the state court systems. These include important concerns such as controlling crime and civil strife. We will try to answer the following key questions about state court systems:

- Does the close professional fraternity of attorneys serve the public's interest in justice and safety?
- Does adversarial justice actually produce just and reasonable criminal and civil court decisions?
- Do appeal routes and processes offer a satisfactory check on the judgments of individual judges and juries?

Within the boundaries of our federal system of government, the states are free to pursue these priorities. Courts, too, are laboratories of democracy.

❧ American Justice

Your reading thus far has no doubt convinced you that Americans have traditionally favored limited government and protections for individuals' civil liberties. In fact, many people from around the world marvel that our constrained form of government works at all. We are so concerned with the protection of the individual that we have institutionalized an **adversarial system of justice** in which the power of government is carefully balanced with the rights of any accused person. We handicap the power of government in many important ways to ensure that it does not overwhelm and brutalize even one individual citizen. In this way, the courts are the guardians of our liberty.

In criminal cases, the adversaries are the prosecuting counsel and the defense counsel. In civil cases, the adversaries are the attorney who represents the plaintiff and the attorney who represents the respondent. Regardless of which type of case is being heard and the particular court hearing the case, a *level playing field* is promised for both parties. The judge is the neutral umpire for this contest, keeping the contest focused and on-track by enforcing rules of criminal and civil procedure that are known and understood by both attorneys, who are themselves committed to the process. They have been trained by accredited law schools, examined by the state in which they practice, and admitted to the state bar. They are socialized to the rules of the game. They may be disciplined or even disbarred if they fail to observe the standards of practice in their state.

Criminal Trials

The drama that unfolds in the courtroom is familiar to movie and television audiences well beyond the United States. In a **criminal trial,** the state tries to prove its case against an accused person beyond a reasonable doubt. The government's attorney—commonly called the **district attorney**—develops the case against a criminal defendant. The suspect becomes a defendant when the district attorney can establish to a judge's satisfaction that the state has sufficient evidence to bind the individual over for trial. This process is called **arraignment.** In other words, a preliminary hearing leads the district attorney and the court to conclude that they have identified a person who may be guilty of a crime against society.

The district attorney presents the results of the police investigation, questions experts about any physical or forensic evidence, and questions any witnesses to the criminal act. The defendant's attorney, or **defense counsel,** cross-examines the police, experts, and witnesses trying to raise a **reasonable doubt** of the defendant's guilt. It is not necessary to show that the defendant is innocent. It is the obligation of the state to prove its case beyond any reasonable doubt. The *trial judge* keeps the exchanges between attorneys and witnesses within the bounds of the rules of procedure and makes sure that the defendant understands the proceedings at all stages of the trial.

If a **jury** is hearing the case, then its members determine guilt or innocence. The defendant can choose to waive his or her right to a jury trial and have the judge apply the law in the case. Whether or not a jury is used, the judge typically applies a specific sentence or punishment if the accused person is found guilty. The sentence is often determined by state *sentencing guidelines* that have been passed by the legislature or an independent sentencing-guidelines commission. These guidelines have been passed in the states to curtail judicial discretion, to ensure sentencing equity, or both.

Civil Trials

In a **civil case,** two citizens face each other to resolve a dispute. For the purposes of the law, a corporation or organization is a "legal person." One party claims to have suffered a financial or personal loss as a result of the actions of the other party. We call the complaining party the *plaintiff* in the case. The party answering the complaint is the *respondent.* The plaintiff's counsel presents the case: Evidence is introduced, experts are questioned, and witnesses may be called. The respondent's counsel cross-examines the plaintiff's case and presents a responding case. Again, either a jury or a judge may hear the case. The civil court judge is a neutral umpire during the presentation of the case. The burden of proof is lower in civil cases than in criminal cases. Usually, money instead of life or freedom is at stake. The standard in civil cases is that the plaintiff must establish the case against the respondent with a reasonable certainty or by the **preponderance of evidence.** The plaintiff does not need to prove the case beyond any reasonable doubt.

Trial judges frequently consult with and make procedural rulings for attorneys from both sides during a trial: prosecutors and defense attorneys, or attorneys for both plaintiffs and defendants.
Source: © SuperStock

Note the governmental interest involved in each type of case. Clearly, the criminal case is about solving crimes against society. If a society hopes to maintain civil order, then it must have the ability to defend itself and its citizens. The state brings considerable resources to its case. It has investigators, crime labs, and cadres of experts. To fight back, the defense has only the presumption of innocence and the state's responsibility for the burden of proof. Without protections, few individuals could stand up to the suspicions and accusations of the government.

In civil cases, the governmental purpose is to maintain peace among law-abiding citizens. Private disputes can erupt between employers and employees, between neighbors, and between consumers and businesses. Government seeks to control the use of violence in civil society. It reserves to itself the right to employ force to resolve conflict. Private citizens are expected to use the courts to resolve disputes. In court, a jury of one's peers or a well-trained judge will sort complaints and apply the rule of law to a dispute. The courts' decisions are binding—that is, they resolve the dispute.

Civil society must control disruptions whether they are criminal acts or private disputes. Civilization requires a high level of social peace and public confidence. By clarifying and applying the rules of the game, the courts help keep the peace. State courts are society's *primary peacekeeping agents.* In state court, most felony criminal cases are decided. In state court, most appeals from criminal judgments are heard and the most significant civil complaints are adjudicated. Moreover, for all but the most trivial and all but the most nationally threatening law violations, state courts enforce the rules of the game.

❧ Court Structure in the States

Most states have a system of courts that can be clearly understood by the legal community and the public. Courts of **original jurisdiction** hear a case for the first time. They try to establish matters of fact in a case, and then they make their rulings. Courts with *appellate jurisdiction* do not bring back witnesses or add new evidence to a case but rule on matters of law or procedure that are disputed when a criminal verdict or civil judgment has been rendered.

State Trial Courts

Trial courts are called by different names in different states. In Ohio, they are known as the courts of common pleas. A total of eighty-eight such courts are staffed by 372 judges (see **Figure 7.1**). The courts of common pleas hear civil and criminal cases, appeals from the decisions of administrative agencies, divorce and child-custody cases, adoption and mental illness hearings, and juvenile-delinquency cases.

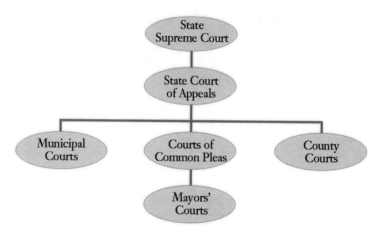

Figure 7.1   The Ohio judicial system
Source: Ohio Court System Online

To serve so many functions for all of their citizens, states carve their territories into *judicial circuits*. The geographic size of these circuits varies because all are designed to serve roughly equal population numbers. In urban jurisdictions, or areas with high population densities, the circuits are compact, and rural jurisdictions may be much larger.

State Appeals Courts

Each state will have a **court of appeals** that hears virtually all disputes with matters that can be appealed. A criminal defendant or the losing party to a civil suit may appeal the judgment of a court of original jurisdiction. The basis of the appeal may be any one of many objections such as improper courtroom procedure, unfair treatment by the trial judge, or improperly secured evidence.

An appeals judge or a panel of appeal judges hears the appeal. These judges do not retry the case but instead review the written transcripts of the original trial and listen to counsels' arguments concerning the case. In most states, the appeals courts have broad discretion to set aside a lower court ruling, modify a penalty, or refer a case back to the lower court for action.

Referring to our earlier example, Ohio has twelve such courts of appeals organized on a regional basis. A total of sixty-six appeals judges sit in three judge panels. They are permitted to hear appeals from common pleas court, municipal court, county courts, and the board of tax appeals.

A **state supreme court** will hear a case only under special circumstances, deciding questions that its justices believe are addressed by the state constitution. For example, a claim on appeal that one's civil rights under the state constitution had been violated might attract the court's attention. In the thirty-seven states with death penalties, the justices hear the automatic appeals of people sentenced to death. In other words, these courts' appellate jurisdiction is highly selective.

Supreme court justices have to be selective, otherwise their single court would be overwhelmed with appeals litigation. The justices sit as a group and deliberate on cases that seem to involve important constitutional or statutory issues. They are under no obligation to take a run-of-the-mill criminal or civil case on appeal. For virtually all cases, appeals end with the appeals court.

The agenda of a state supreme court can be important to businesses, professionals, and consumers. In the three-month period of June through August 1998, for example, Idaho's Supreme Court rendered twenty-nine civil case opinions and sixteen criminal case decisions (Idaho Supreme Court Online). Civil cases that affected business practices in the state included a case on Idaho's Mobile Homes Park Landlord–Tenant Act and one on automobile insurance liability. Professionals were affected by cases involving medical malpractice and the state's Real Estate Licensing Commission. Consumer cases included a shareholders' agreement and buy-back of stocks and spousal maintenance. Criminal cases were just as varied. The Idaho Supreme Court ruled on the search of premises under the open-view doctrine. It also clarified the criminal law on lewd behavior with a minor child, ruled on the meaning of several Idaho drug laws, and reviewed two death-penalty cases.

❧ Serving as a State Judge

States began electing their judges in the early 1800s. Their revolutionary impulse led Americans to distrust political elites. Indeed, they had suffered at the hands of appointed judges during the British administration of the American colonies. Mississippi was the first state to elect judges in 1832 (Crawford, 1931: 308). Now candidates for state trial court judgeships appear on the general election ballots of more than half the states (see Table 7.1). The elections may be either partisan or nonpartisan—that is, the candidates run with or without party labels, depending on the state. The slight preference for nonpartisan elections may indicate that citizens or their legislatures find the sober nature of the administration of justice incompatible with competitive party politics.

Table 7.1
Method of Selecting Trial Judges

Method of Selection	Number of States
Partisan ballot election	11
Nonpartisan election	15
Gubernatorial appointment[*]	8
Gubernatorial appointment with subsequent election	13
Legislative appointment	3

[*]Governor's appointment typically confirmed by another governmental body such as state senate or judicial commission.

Source: Compiled from state court organization, 1995, reported in *The Book of the States, 1998–99:* 135–137.

Most of the other states allow their governors to appoint trial court judges but with two types of restraint on this appointment power. In one group of states, the state senate, a judicial commission, or some other governmental body confirms the governor's choices. In the other group of states, the governor's initial appointment must be confirmed in a subsequent and periodic election. These confirming elections are often nonpartisan. Incumbents have the advantages of a track record and heightened name recognition.

Only three states—Connecticut, South Carolina, and Virginia—allow their state legislatures to select trial court judges. In these and the states with the other types of selection, a judicial qualifications panel typically screens interested individuals and submits a list of prospective judges for appointment.

Candidates for judicial office must almost always be attorneys who are members of the state bar. Only Alabama, Rhode Island, and New Hampshire allow people to serve as judges who have not been admitted to the state bar (National Center for State Courts in *The Book of the States, 1998–99:* 133). Other more informal qualifications may include service as private counsel, district attorney, or public defender.

Appellate court and supreme court justices are typically chosen in much the same manner as trial court judges. Where an election is required to either select or confirm a justice, the elections are more often nonpartisan affairs. Forty-one of the supreme courts are chosen at-large in the state, and nine select their supreme court justices by district. There are odd numbers of justices: five, seven, or nine. Their terms range from six to fourteen years; only Rhode Island selects supreme court justices for life. The most typical terms are six years (thirteen states) and eight years (ten states). Appeals court justices also serve six- or eight-year terms (National Center for State Courts, *State Court Organization,1996* cited in *The Book of the States, 1998–99:* 129–130). Because the workload of this court is sensitive to population size, urbanization, and how litigious the political culture is, the number of appeals court justices is sometimes quite large (see Table 7.2).

Compensation and benefits for judges are established by the state legislature. Iowa's judicial pay scale illustrates that state judges are reasonably well compensated, especially relative to other state employees (see Table 7.3). In 1997, for example, the justices of the Iowa Supreme Court earned six-figure salaries. Most other state judges were paid salaries close to $100,000. Most justices have their own retirement and health-care plans to ensure that they are not forced to return to private practice out of concern for their families' basic

CHAPTER 7 State Courts: *The Rules and Boundaries of the Game*

Table 7.2
The Ten Largest State Appeals Courts, 1996

State	Number of Appellate Court Justices
1. California	88
2. Texas	80
3. New York	66
4. Ohio	65
5. Florida	61
6. Louisiana	54
7. Illinois	42
8. Missouri	32
9. New Jersey	32
10. Michigan	28

Source: National Center for State Courts, *State Court Organization, 1996,* cited in *The Book of the States, 1998–99:* 131–132.

Table 7.3
Iowa Judicial Salaries, 1997

Position	Annual Salary ($)
Chief justice of the supreme court	107,500
Justice of the supreme court	103,600
Chief judge of the court of appeals	103,500
Associate judge of the court of appeals	99,600
Chief judge of a judicial district	98,700
District judge (excluding chief judge)	94,800
District associate judge	82,500

Source: Iowa General Assembly Online

welfare. However, it also would be fair to say that these court members could earn considerably more money in the private practice of the law.

❧ The Administration of Justice

The operations of state court systems involve a great deal of scheduling and paperwork. Every action in a case must be planned, carried out according to legal procedures, and documented as a part of the case record. This requires a statewide courts policy direction and management system that works for judges, district attorneys, defense counsel, and appeals judges.

The states typically have a judicial council and an administrative office of the courts that is charged with the development of a statewide court system. The **judicial council** have representation from all levels of state courts in the state. Judges from the various courts are elected by their peers or appointed by the governor. The chief justice of the state supreme court typically chairs the council. Together, council members represent a potent political force in the capital. For example, they can articulate their courts' budget needs to the governor and the state legislature.

The **administrative office of the courts** (AOC) works under the supervision of the state's judicial council. This type of administrative organization was created in most states during the 1960s and 1970s. The oldest AOC is New Jersey's, created in 1948. The youngest is New Hampshire's; it was created in 1980 (data from the National Center for States Courts, 1997 cited in *Book of the States, 1998–99:* 148). One of the most important AOC tasks is providing a document and procedure structure for the widespread state courts. This state agency may also computerize records needed to track cases. It provides staff services for the state's judges, including statistical studies, strategic plans, and studies of other states' laws and procedures. AOC staff members place the judiciary on a more even plain with executive and legislative staff members who work in the state capital every day. The interests of judges can be protected and their priorities implemented by a diligent staff.

It is not unusual for several judicial *governance commissions* to function in a state at any one given time. In California, for example, the Commission on Judicial Appointments confirms judicial appointments made by the governor. This commission comprises three members: the chief justice of the state supreme court, the state attorney general, and the senior presiding judge of the court of appeals. California also has a Commission on Judicial Performance that deals with judicial misconduct and recommends and implements the censure, removal, forced retirement, or private admonishment of judges. Each governance commission has detailed procedures for discharging its important duties (California Court Information Online). Their existence reflects the need for the state judiciaries to govern and police themselves so that the states can maintain a true separation of powers.

Study commissions are created for special purposes; they are not permanent parts of the administration of justice in the states. One example of the judicial study commission is the Ohio Courts Futures Commission, which consists of fifty member judges, attorneys, political leaders, and private citizens (Moyer, 1998). The commission is to "chart a course" for Ohio's judicial system. Judicial reform commissions, in fact, are a tradition in many states, created in the 1920s and 1930s to study the need for consistent justice. They led to *court unification* in many states—the creation of consistent structure and procedure throughout a state. Today, judicial study commissions look at issues such as how to make jury service more attractive, compensation for jury duty, and how to involve jurors more in the questioning process of trials (Moyer, 1998).

Court administration is also important at the judicial circuit level. Many circuits hire a local *court services administrator* to handle the daily administration of the court. Each of Idaho's seven judicial circuits, for example, has a trial court administrator. One judge serves the circuit as administrative district judge, and a court clerk is selected to maintain the calendar. Together, the administrator, court clerk, and administrative district judge manage the activities at the courthouse (Idaho Supreme Court Online).

To appreciate the *judicial workload* of a state trial–level courthouse, you must understand the traffic that flows through such a building. Attor-

---

elsewhere in the world

Philippine Trial Courts

In the Republic of the Philippines, regional trial courts (RTCs) are the courts of general jurisdiction. There are thirteen judicial regions and 696 RTC branches throughout the country. These trial courts exercise exclusive original jurisdiction over a variety of criminal and civil cases. They also hear appeals from local city courts. In this sense, they are much like our state trial courts. In addition to the RTCs, a set of special Shar'i district courts hear cases involving interpretation and enforcement of Muslim law. Although the Philippines is a largely Catholic country, many Muslims live in the southern provinces.

Source: Philippine Judicial System Online (1998): <http://www.concentric.net/~Almacen/lc.html>.

CHAPTER 7 State Courts: *The Rules and Boundaries of the Game*

BOX 7.1   *A State of the Judiciary Address*

In her State of the Judiciary Address in June 1998, Minnesota Chief Justice Kathleen Blatz challenged her state's policy makers to work on improving the state's courts: "Chief among our challenges is the sheer volume of the cases flooding into our courts. In the last [ten] years, the number of serious criminal cases increased by 70 [percent] and the number of juvenile cases doubled. . . .

The workload of our judges has increased by 40 [percent]. . . . We have learned to better manage our cases and caseloads, we have established case processing time objectives. . . . Even more troubling is the fact that we are spending less time on an increasingly difficult caseload. . . . We have become more efficient, but are we effective?"

Minnesota Supreme Court Judge Kathleen Blatz
Source: Photo Courtesy of the Minnesota State Court System

neys and clients are in and out of the building seeking information. District attorneys, their investigators, and other prosecutorial staff members have offices there. Probation officers are also there to serve the court, supervising offenders whom the judges feel can remain in the community in lieu of incarceration. These people are in and out of offices, courtrooms, jury rooms, and conference rooms. And amid all this human traffic are oceans of paperwork. Keeping the people, facilities, and paperwork organized is no small task. (See also **Box 7.1**.)

Collecting Your Thoughts *Your View of American Justice*

Imagine that you have been arrested for a minor crime. How do you think police and jail personnel will treat you? Will your age or the fact that you are a college student matter? If you actually go to trial, who will sit on a "jury of your peers"? Will the members of the jury *really* be your peers? Would you rather have the judge hear your case without a jury? What concerns might that involve? Save your notes and discuss them with classmates.

☙ Issues Before the State Courts

In addition to the individual justice that our courts offer each citizen, the judiciary is expected to help the rest of state government to achieve important *social policy goals*. Chief among these is **crime control** in the criminal courts and **tort reform** in the civil courts. These two issues illustrate how the state legislature and the governor get involved with judicial matters. After all, the risk of crime and the high costs of civil judgments are of concern to many politicians and interest groups.

Crime-Control Concerns

In their annual reports to the U.S. Department of Justice, police departments reported and calculated steadily increasing rates of violent crime until the mid-1990s when rates began to level out and even drop (see Figure 7.2). Violent crime has been more of a problem in some states than in others. Florida led the country in violent crimes per 100,000 population in 1996 (see Table 7.4) and is one of the three Southern states in the top five. Other states such as California and Illinois are urbanized, so population, poverty, and frustration are more concentrated. Reasonable people have plenty to disagree over about the causes of crime in general and violent crime in particular. Some blame television violence, while others fault our capitalist economic system.

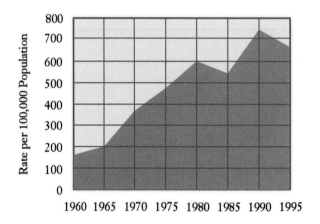

Figure 7.2   Violent crime rates
Source: Sourcebook of Criminal Justice Statistics, 1997: 261

Table 7.4
Top Ten Most Violent States, 1996

State	Violent Crimes per 100,000 Population
1. Florida	1,051
2. South Carolina	996.9
3. Maryland	931.2
4. Louisiana	929.1
5. Illinois	886.2
6. California	862.7
7. New Mexico	840.6
8. Nevada	811.3
9. Tennessee	774.0
10. Alaska	727.7

Source: National Rifle Association cited in the Sourcebook of Criminal Justice Statistics, 1997: 73

There are other sources of crime data, not all of them based on police reports. One way to collect crime information is from the victims. The Roper polling company and the National Opinion Research Center interview random samples of Americans about many issues, including criminal victimiza-

CHAPTER 7   State Courts: *The Rules and Boundaries of the Game*

tion. The consolidation of three such series of data shows another view of the prevalence of crime in our society (see Figure 7.3).

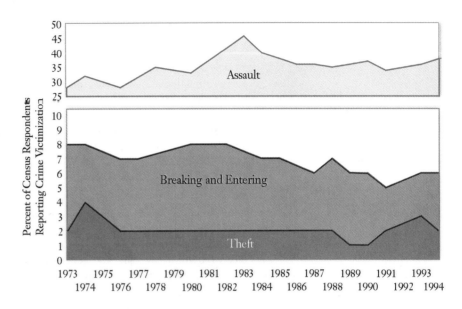

Figure 7.3 Crime Victimization Rates
Source: Sourcebook of Criminal Justice Statistics, 1997

Three survey questions yield interesting responses. In terms of anyone "taking something from them by force during the last years," the figure is only 2 percent to 3 percent and has not changed perceptibly over the past twenty years. Similarly, when asked if anyone had illegally entered his or her home, a steady 6 percent said "yes." The rate is steady over time. Even in terms of violent crime, the survey responses yield provocative findings. Asked if "they had been hit by another person," roughly one-third of those surveyed answered "yes." This rate is high, but many assaultive incidents such as spousal abuse go unreported to the police. In any case, the rate over time has not been skyrocketing in recent years. In fact, it is lower today than in the mid-1980s. So what explains the skyrocketing police numbers?

First, police officials can only report crimes about which they have knowledge. Over time, incidents may be increasingly reported, partly because we Americans have become more litigious, seeking legal remedies to what used to be private matters. Second, the technology of collecting and computerizing crime data has steadily improved. Finally, police are funded based on workload reports; the bigger the workload, the bigger their budgets. Pressure to justify public expenditures may have driven some police departments to report all incidents scrupulously so they don't risk underreporting their workloads.

Crime Control and the Courts

The courts are expected to dispense quick and certain justice so that criminals are punished and people who contemplate criminal acts are deterred from acting on those impulses. If the guilty are convicted and either supervised or incarcerated, then they will not be able to commit additional crimes. If the law enforcement officials gain a reputation for sure and certain punishment, then fewer potential offenders will be tempted to try to get away with criminal behavior.

The role of the courts in crime control is to provide the sure and certain justice that the criminal justice system needs to be successful. Other state agencies must function properly as well. We already have discussed the district attorneys' role as prosecutor. Once the felony defendant is convicted, the state corrections department takes him or her into custody. The trial judge releases the law offender to another agency of state government.

Correctional Supervision and Incapacitation

The state corrections department is responsible for the operation of state prisons. In many states, the department also is involved in supervising both probationers and parolees. In other states, probation has been restricted, and parole may have been abolished. State legislatures write and amend their states' criminal codes and state judges apply them. Corrections employees must deal with the results.

The supervision of convicted law offenders may take place in the community or behind the bars and fences of state prisons (see **Figure 7.4**). If the offender is not violent or habitual and does not seem to be a risk to the community, then the sentencing judge may offer *probation*. A probated sentence offers the offender an opportunity to remain at home and go to work each day so long as he or she obeys all of the court's conditions. These behavioral conditions often include avoiding association with known criminals and hanging out in places such as bars where illegal behavior may be tempting. Probation also may require fines and restitution to the victim of the crime. Failure to check in or meet any of these provisions results in the revocation of probation, with the remainder of the sentence spent in prison.

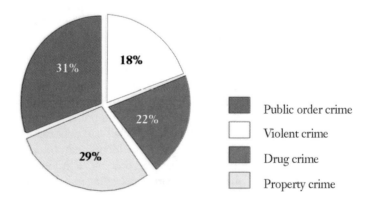

Figure 7.4 Probationers' most serious offenses
Source: Sourcebook of Criminal Justice Statistics, 1997

The likelihood of getting a probated sentence varies with the seriousness of the crime that has been committed. The white-collar crime of fraud draws a probated sentence more than half the time. On the other hand, assault and other violent crimes are rarely probated. For the vast majority of offenses, state judges order some jail or prison time.

Probation officers are professional law enforcement personnel who are trained in supervising convicted offenders. In some states, the officers are employees of the state corrections department; in others, they work directly for state judges. In either case, they are responsible to the court for offenders' behavior. In some jurisdictions, electronic monitoring devices are used to ensure that the offender does not roam from his or her residence during predetermined restricted periods such as after work. In others, probation officers conduct sweeps through local bars and pool rooms to make sure that probationers are not hanging out there.

The state corrections department administers prisons. Incarceration is far more expensive than probation but also far more reliable as a means of incapacitating offenders. Their only victims in prison may be other inmates or perhaps prison staff members. Prisons are extremely expensive to build, however, because architects and engineers must incorporate special materials and systems to keep the facilities secure. Prisons also are expensive to operate because prisoners must be supervised every hour of the day, every day of the year. Other extraordinary expenses of prison operation include medical services, food services, and rehabilitation services. Incarcerating offenders can easily cost ten to twenty times as much as supervising them in the community. However, some offenders are judged as simply too risky to live among us. Incarceration is the only supervision that is appropriate to their crime and their risk to others.

The politics of crime control in the states are mentioned at several points in this textbook because promising the public more personal and home security is politically expedient. If we lock up criminals more often and require that they serve longer sentences, then the average citizen will feel safer. Sometimes in conflict with such expediency, however, is another theme in the policy dialogue about crime control: sentencing fairness. Civil rights activists and social scientists have presented evidence for significant charging and sentencing disparities based on race, with African Americans receiving more severe sentences than whites who commit the same crimes (Bowers & Pierce, 1980). (See also **Box 7.2**.)

In response to this criticism and the general concern that some offenders may get sentences that are seen as too lenient, many states have enacted sentencing guidelines. The guidelines in many states are both *determinant* in

---

| BOX 7.2 | *Race and Sentencing Counterpoint* |

In 1992, a study was conducted of jury trials for serious crimes in the nation's seventy-five largest counties. Researcher Robert Lerner reported that these 55,000 cases showed no discriminatory patterns in their verdicts. For example, white and black murder defendants were convicted 23 percent and 24 percent of the time, respectively. Robbery convictions were 35 percent and 38 percent, and assault convictions were 43 percent and 49 percent. He did find some disparities, however: African Americans were convicted of rape and drug trafficking twice as often as European Americans. Yet the overall disparities were less than expected, perhaps because the trial judge and jury equalize any overly zealous profiling or sweeps conducted in poor minority neighborhoods.

Source: Lerner, 1996.

State prison populations have grown dramatically over the last decade as legislatures and popular referenda have established stricter sentencing guidelines and made probation and parole less attractive and less available to prosecutors and judges.

Source: © SuperStock

requiring fixed sentences for specific crimes and *mandatory* in requiring judges to apply those penalties. **Mandatory determinant sentences** do bring more consistency to sentencing. Although some critics have charged that flexibility has simply moved to the negotiations that precede charging the defendant, most state elected officials seem satisfied with this approach to "sentencing reform." One consequence of more certain and longer prison terms, however, has been the steady growth in states' prison populations (see **Figure 7.5**). In fact, state imprisonment rates more than doubled during the 1990s. Are we becoming a more lawless people or has political tolerance for a measure of criminal behavior vanished?

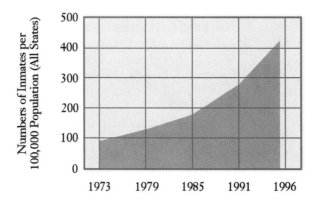

Figure 7.5 States' imprisonment rates
Source: Sourcebook of Criminal Justice Statistics, 1997: 490

During the 1990s, state legislatures piled ever more stringent sentences on the already more severe mandatory determinant sentences. States now boast of "three strikes and you're out" laws that mandate life imprisonment after conviction for a third major felony. Georgia even has a "two strikes and you're out" law. States are abolishing *parole*, supervised release after serving a portion of a court-ordered sentence. This "reform" is often touted as "truth in sentencing legislation." The prospects are bleak for any lowering of the states' prison populations. State legislatures seem willing to fund the new prisons that are required to hold more and more offenders.

The directors of the state corrections departments are willing to go along with the more severe imprisonment policies. They are concerned about prison overcrowding and the threats to staff that develop in today's institutions (Cox & Rhodes, 1990). Many try to maintain a balanced approach to corrections, one that considers prisoners as people with real human needs as well as offenders who have broken the law. Education and counseling programs still exist in most state prisons, families still come to see their loved ones on visitor's day, and men and women complete their sentences and return to live among us. Yet in state policy circles, there is little talk about crime-control policy other than the rhetoric of societal retribution.

Juvenile Crime

Another policy issue related to crime control is how to deal with the growing problem of *juvenile crime*. Increasing numbers of young people are getting involved in ever more serious crimes. This trend is clear. In 1983, the average daily population of juveniles being confined in adult jails was 1,760. Ten years later, in 1994, the average daily jail population of juveniles had doubled to 3,400 (Bureau of Justice Statistics, "Jail and Jail Inmates," in *Sourcebook of Criminal Justice Statistics, 1994*, NCJ-151651). Unfortunately, a significant fraction of young people use firearms to settle grudges. They deal in narcotics, violate curfew laws, and encourage underworld gang violence. Many state policy makers have had enough. They want to draw a new line between delinquency and criminality. To do this, more states are expanding provisions in the law that allow prosecutors to try youthful offenders as adults. If convicted, they serve real prison time instead of indeterminate stays in juvenile rehabilitation facilities. The stakes are high for children, parents, and the criminal justice system, because once a young person has done hard time, there may be little prospect for reconciliation with family, neighbors, and society.

Collecting Your Thoughts *Juvenile Crime in Your Hometown*

Many of you were juveniles not long ago, and some of you have younger brothers and sisters. What pressures do you think young people are under back home? Do their pressures come from society or from their own inner personalities? Should each young person be held accountable for every deed that he or she commits? Or should we take their ages into account? Does the nature of the misdeed matter? Save your answers to discuss with your classmates.

Criminal Justice

Crime-control policies involve legislatures, governors, interest groups, political parties, and media. Such policies certainly are not the exclusive province of state judiciaries. In fact, in many important ways, the judiciary checks the excesses of other players. Nevertheless, the public would like to hold the criminal justice system accountable for the crime problem and the resulting feelings of insecurity. For that reason, judiciaries must strive to restore the public's confidence and peace of mind.

However, state judges also are responsible for the *quality* of justice handed out in their courtrooms. Our general public haste to control crime and its effects on our daily lives can easily lead us to overlook the necessity of affording those accused of crime all of their constitutional protections. When police use offender profiling in their efforts to reduce crime in a city, they risk violating the rights of people who fit the profile but who are innocent of any wrongdoing. When school authorities go through the lockers of school students looking for drugs and weapons, they risk violating the privacy rights of their pupils. The list could go on and on.

We cannot catalog the many balance points that state judges must consider when dispensing justice. We certainly cannot prejudge the legality or constitutionality of issues such as profiling and locker searches, only acknowledge that our adversarial system of justice flushes out such issues. They are not trivial. They cannot be resolved by simple commonsense reasoning. Controlling crime is a wonderful social goal, but protecting ourselves from the potential abuse of government is of equal concern.

Civil Justice

The courts represent more than an instrument of social protection from criminals. They are also the place we go to for **civil justice,** the resolution of private conflicts. In civil cases, we are protected from the excesses of our fellow citizens and large private organizations. To be secure, we also must have confidence that the civil courts will protect our rights of liberty, equality, and property.

Civil Liability. Civil cases resolve conflicts between private parties, be they individuals or corporations. In civil law, liability and not guilt is at stake. As a consequence of being found liable for others' losses, respondents may be required to pay compensatory and punitive damages.

The awarding of *compensatory damages* is based on the concrete losses a plaintiff suffered because of the other person's *negligence*. The amount of compensatory damages is tied to the degree of actual loss suffered. It is not always easy to define the scope of compensatory damages. In addition to direct monetary loss or damage to property, plaintiffs may have suffered injury. Their medical bills should be considered, as might their lost work time and lost wages. The plaintiff may even have suffered mental anxiety, so counselors' or therapists' bills could be considered part of compensatory damages.

Punitive damages are levied against the losing parties to punish them and deter them and others from repeating the negligent behavior. Judges and civil juries set the amount of punitive damages based on their reading of the motivations of the negligent party. If judges and juries perceive that the losers had good intentions, then they may order few if any punitive damages. On the other hand, civil penalties can be extremely expensive if a judge or civil jury believes that callous disregard or vicious negligence caused losses for the plaintiff. In some cases, punitive damages can climb into the millions of dollars.

Defenders of unlimited damage awards point out that plaintiffs and their attorneys may work on a case for several years at their own expense. If they lose the case, they lose all of that money as well; conversely, they will have no trouble covering attorneys' fees and trial costs if they prevail and are awarded compensatory damages. Respondents are often large corporations with staff attorneys and private counsel on retainer to defend them. They have little to lose by stringing out a case. In fact, they may hope that the plaintiffs tire of the struggle and quit. So these questions always must be asked: Has the respondent prolonged the civil trial and intentionally withheld information from a judge or jury? Was the respondent's behavior unfair, an attempt to use the courts to avoid lawful responsibility?

These questions have come up in civil complaints brought by private individuals against U.S. tobacco companies. Individuals and families who have been harmed by the destructive effects of tobacco smoke want these companies to pay damages for the resulting injuries. This is especially the case in litigation that alleges unethical and misleading advertising by the tobacco companies. Did they try to market cigarettes to juveniles, knowing from their own research that tobacco is addictive and causes lung cancer? Were they justified in suppressing the research results even when judges and juries wanted to consider the findings? Should civil penalties not include punitive damages "to teach them a lesson"?

There has been considerable litigation in state courts throughout the United States trying to sort out these issues. In fact, the attorneys general of several states have sued the tobacco companies to recover the Medicaid costs that their states have had to pay as a result of smoking-related illness and disability. The tobacco companies have settled out of court for many millions of dollars. Even these large sums might be dwarfed by the damages awarded by a civil jury were the cases in these states allowed to carry on to completion.

Tort Reform. Many industries are concerned that large punitive damage awards are harming their members' businesses. They argue that only reasonable awards can be considered a legitimate planned expense. If juries award many millions of dollars to plaintiffs, then responding companies may be driven into bankruptcy. Many states' laws forbid driving a respondent into bankruptcy.

Insurance companies are also worried about large settlements and awards. They point out that the cost of liability insurance is continually driven upward by what the insurers see as excessive awards. Pharmaceutical companies, health maintenance organizations, and physicians pass the increased costs of liability insurance on to customers, which means everyone pays for the plaintiffs' financial "windfalls." The insurance companies argue that state legislatures should limit the amount of punitive damages, whether in absolute terms or through some predetermined ratio between compensatory and punitive damages. Perhaps the cap could be defined as ten or even one hundred times the amount of compensatory damages.

At its core, the political fight over *tort reform* is a simple issue: Should states limit the liability of corporations and their insurance companies? The business lobby and insurance companies say, "Yes. Awards are too large and mostly serve to make plaintiffs' attorneys' law firms rich." Insurance companies also argue that excessive awards drive up the premiums for business insurance policies within a state, which ultimately harms consumers because businesses pass along higher insurance costs to them.

The trial lawyers' associations in the states answer, "No. Plaintiffs are entitled to have juries of their peers determine what is appropriate compensation in a case. Plaintiffs have risked time and money on the slim chance that they can defeat the Goliath of big business. Corporations and insurance companies are highly profitable enterprises and can afford the very best legal representation. They also have deep pockets in terms of paying the award amounts." Obviously, both sets of interest groups have vested interests in the issue and their answers.

State legislators are under tremendous pressure from both sides of the tort-reform issue. Although it is difficult to generalize, states in which Republicans control the legislature are more likely to vote tort-reform laws. The Republican Party has traditionally been the party of American business. States in which Democrats control the legislature tend to pass milder forms of tort reform, if any at all. Trial lawyers are a part of the Democrats' political coalition in many states. In both cases, it is pure politics at work. The public interest, however, hangs in the balance.

Ohio provides a good example of the battle over reform. The Ohio Chamber of Commerce worked hard for many years to help elect a governor and legislature that would be friendly to tort reform. They were finally successful. The Ohio legislature passed laws that were more favorable to the state's businesses and their insurance companies. The battle seemed won. Ohio had a comprehensive tort law that limited personal and corporate liability, malpractice, and other awards in civil suits. However, the Ohio Supreme Court intervened. These justices have tended to rule against business interests in general and against lesser 1987 tort reforms in particular (Mahtesian, 1998). The organized business interests have shown a determination to prevail, even if it means helping to elect friendlier judges. Clearly, tort reform is an issue that can dominate a state's political agenda.

France's Inquisitorial Justice System

elsewhere in the world

Some countries have adversarial court systems in which two sides debate criminal and civil cases before a neutral judge. The United States and Great Britain are two countries that use the adversarial system. Other countries use other approaches to address criminal cases. The French use what we call an *inquisitorial model* in their criminal courts. The two approaches illustrate how different peoples try to achieve the same goal using different means.

In the French justice system, an examining magistrate interviews the accused and all witnesses privately before the trial. The magistrate has broad powers to tap phones and consult experts during this investigation. This is allowed because the purpose of the proceeding is to get to the underlying truth. The case only goes to trial if the magistrate is convinced that the accused is guilty. In most cases, the outcome of the case is a foregone conclusion.

Americans would view the judge in an inquisitorial system as a part of the prosecution team. Attorneys themselves have relatively little influence on the proceedings. Yet the French do not believe that guilt or innocence is so relative that only a balanced debate between a prosecuting attorney and a defense counsel can define it. Their system is very different from ours, but they like it. For more on French courts, see Austin Ranney (2001): 335–336, or if you read French, visit the French government Web site <*http://www.justice.fr/justice*>.

❧ Chapter Conclusion

In this chapter, we have learned about U.S. justice, state court structure, and the politics of judicial behavior. Clearly, there is a great deal to know about the third branch of state government, and we have only scratched the surface. Yet we must return to the questions that shaped our inquiry into the courts.

- Is the public's interest in justice and safety well served by the legal profession?

Recall that no one usually speaks in a courtroom other than attorneys. The adversaries are attorneys, and so is the judge. Their language is highly technical and even obscure. Their arguments and judgments are often based on precedents from old court cases that no one but the in-group knows about. It is almost like a priesthood in which only the initiated can comprehend, much less appreciate, the spectacle of the courtroom. Thus, it is only by its fruits that the court system may be judged. This brings us to our second question.

- Does the adversarial justice produce just criminal and civil decisions?

You now know about the careful balancing that takes place in an effort to level the playing field for both parties. The standards for evidence play a key role, especially in criminal cases. The burden to prove a case beyond any reasonable doubt challenges the district attorney to *prove* the state's case. On the other hand, citizens sometimes feel that too many criminals get off on technicalities. A faulty case by the prosecution hurts the public that way. Poorly presented cases and sometimes overburdened courts lead to a lot of plea bargaining, and some Americans dislike this practice as well. Bargaining is even more common in civil cases. You will have to judge these issues for yourself.

- Finally, do appeals adequately and satisfactorily check errors of judgment or interpretation in certain cases?

The right of appeal is meaningful only if a transcript is truly scrutinized. If the case is overturned, then a criminal defendant may go free or a heinous polluting industry may get off the hook. A death-penalty case or a major punitive damages award may be appealed for years. Swift justice is virtually impossible in our legal system. We must weigh the benefits of protected civil liberties against the practical demands of effective public policy. It is another issue that all of us must decide for ourselves.

If you are interested in the practice of law and the drama of courtroom politics, consider taking an upper-division course in judicial behavior or constitutional law. There is a great deal more to discover about our courts and how they affect citizens' daily lives. It is high drama indeed.

Key Words for InfoTrac Exploration

criminal trials	jury duty	state supreme courts	tort reform

Sources Cited

Blatz, Kathleen (1998). *Minnesota State of the Judiciary Address.* Minnesota Court System Online: *<http://www.courts.state.mn.us/home/ndefault. asp?msel=1>.*

Bowers, William, and Glenn Pierce (1980). "Arbitrariness and Discrimination Under Post-Furman Capital Statutes." *Crime and Delinquency, 26:* 4 (October).

Bureau of Justice Statistics (1995). *Sourcebook of Criminal Justice Statistics, 1994.* Washington, DC: U.S. Department of Justice.

Cox, George H., and Susan L. Rhodes (1990). "Managing Overcrowding: Corrections Administrators and the Prison Crisis." *Criminal Justice Policy Review, 4:* 2 (February): 115–143.

California Court Information Online: *<http://www. courtinfo.ca.gov>.*

Council of State Governments (1998). *The Book of the States,* Vol. 32. Lexington, KY: Author.

Crawford, Finla Goff (1931). *State Government.* New York: Henry Holt & Co.

Federal Bureau of Investigation (1993). *Crime in the United States.* Data cited in the *Sourcebook of Criminal Justice Statistics, 1994.*

Idaho Supreme Court Online: *<http://www.idwr.state. id.us/scopins.html>.*

Lerner, Robert (1996). "Acquittal Rates by Race for State Felonies." In *Race and the Criminal Justice System: How Race Affects Jury Trials.* Washington, DC: Center for Equal Opportunity.

Mahtesian, Charles (1998). "Bench Press," *Governing, 11*(11) (August): 18–23.

Moyer, Thomas J. (1998). *Ohio State of the Judiciary Address.* Online: *<http://www.sconet.oh.us/ Futures/sofj.htm>.*

National Center for State Courts (1995). *State Court Organization.* Data cited in the *Book of the States, 1998–99.*

National Rifle Association (1993). Data cited in the *Sourcebook of Criminal Justice Statistics, 1994.*

Philippine Judicial System Online (1998): *<http://www. concentric.net/~Almacen/lc.html>.*

Ranney, Austin (2001). *An Introduction to Political Science* (8th ed.). Upper Saddle River, NJ: Prentice-Hall.

Local Communities: Politics Where We Live

❧ **A Community of Neighborhoods**

❧ **Business and Labor Organizations**

❧ **Civic Clubs**

❧ **Religious Congregations**

❧ **Special Issue Organizations**

❧ **Interpreting Community Groups**

❧ **Chapter Conclusion**

We are born into families, and we grow up in communities. This basic fact of life is so familiar to us that we may not really see the web of social and political relationships that define our daily lives. The study of local government takes us back to these too-often-unexplored relationships in an effort to find out how individuals, families, and neighborhoods try to solve their common problems. At its roots, local government and voluntary associations are about solving the problems of everyday life. We call it "politics at the grassroots."

The sense of community may be a fundamental building block of civil society. Our community is a place and a state of mind. We live among other people, and we form bonds with them over time. Although not permanent, communities need to be stable and supportive, or we move on. When a community meets our personal and family needs, we want to stay put. In fact, we may make personal and career sacrifices so we can remain in a beloved community.

In his recent book *Country of Exiles*, William Leach describes the importance of place to our community identities.

> Boundary and space, place and freedom—these things do not contradict each other but go together. People need to feel a bond to a concrete reality larger than the self, a reality that gives deeper meaning to existence.

They need to be stewards of the concrete places (not the world place or planet) in which they live, because to lose that stewardship is to lose faith in oneself and in one's own society (Leach, 1999: 30).

Our community is the context for our personal and family life. It is the environment that nurtures our educational and professional life. It is the network of people who come to our aid when we need them and who seek our support when they are in need. It takes care of us, and we in turn must take care of it. Therefore, our sense of place is an important part of who we are, how we think, and how we behave.

Community is a truly broad term, and we should probably distinguish it from other terms in our study of local politics and government. In *Habits of the Heart* (1985), the now famous sociological study of contemporary American culture, Robert Bellah and associates distinguish between community and what they term a *lifestyle enclave*. The authors state that "Whereas a community attempts to be an inclusive whole, celebrating the interdependence of public and private life and of the different callings of all, lifestyle is fundamentally segmental and celebrates the narcissism of similarity" (p. 72). A lifestyle enclave may be oriented to leisure and consumption, and people who practice a different lifestyle are tolerated at best and deemed irrelevant or invisible at worst. A community extends beyond one's apartment complex or subdivision. Its boundaries include people with many lifestyles: older and younger people, people of all races, gay and straight people, secure and homeless people, and involved and indifferent people. That is why we emphasize the land and a sense of place in this book.

Neighborhood is too narrow a term. Our neighbors are part of our community, but so are our co-workers, fellow club members, co-religionists, and partners in special interest groups such as environmental protection organizations. Proximity takes on different boundaries according to the different dimensions of our daily lives. We are bound to many groups of people, a network of relationships that binds the community together.

Networks of concerned local citizens can deal with one of the leading problems in civil society today. We have concerns about the environment, homelessness, juvenile delinquency, and many other social issues. Frances Moore Lappé and Paul Martin DuBois, authors of *The Quickening of America* (1994), even use the term *crisis* to refer to the need for local people to address their common concerns: "The biggest problem facing Americans is not those issues that bombard

American neighborhoods reflect their residents' sense of place and often have distinctive characteristics that are based on and reflect the prevailing socioeconomic class and its values.
Source: © Gene Fitzer

CHAPTER 8 Local Communities: *Politics Where We Live*

us daily. . . . The crisis is that we as a people don't know how to come together to solve those problems" (p. 9). Viable communities and a renewed sense of community are keys to social success in the twenty-first century.

In the process of analyzing our communities, we ask the following fundamental questions about people's social concerns and how grassroots politics tries to solve them:

- How do neighbors organize themselves so their political voices will be heard? What are their basic concerns? What are their expectations that local government will be able to help?
- What are the concerns of voluntary associations such as local business groups, labor unions, civic clubs, religious organizations, and single-interest groups that are not neighborhood-based? How do they organize to affect local public policy?
- Does politics at the grass roots create many different nodes of power in the community? Do different groups prevail at different times on different issues, or does a power elite manipulate the community from behind the scenes?

The answers to these questions will help us understand how politics works close to home. We start our introduction to local government in your living room.

∽ A Community of Neighborhoods

Some of us live in apartment buildings, and others in subdivisions. Regardless of the style of housing, we live in proximity with others. A pack of roaming dogs or the failure of garbage pickup affects us both individually and as a group. Prompt solutions to such common problems will satisfy us personally and will ease the concerns of the group.

The *household* or family unit in American society can take several forms. The nuclear family consists of two married adults and their children. Within this group are parents who have borne their own offspring, others who have adopted at least some of their children, and yet others who have combined or "blended" children from their current and former marriages. There are also single-parent households in which one of the parents has died, divorced, or deserted the family. Table 8.1 breaks down the types of households in the United States in 1995.

Although the married couple is the most common type of American household, there are almost as many other types of households when they are

Table 8.1
Household Composition in the United States, 1995

Type of Household	Percentage of Households
Married couple family	54
Male householder, no spouse present	3
Female householder, no spouse present	12
Individual living alone	30

Source: Census Bureau, *Current Population Reports,* P20-447.

added together. These other types of households are increasing in frequency. One thing that most of these households have in common is that they are place-bound. The household either owns or rents shelter. Two-thirds of U.S. households lived in their own homes in 1999 (U.S. Census Bureau Online, 1999). The other one-third rents.

Home ownership varies somewhat by region of the country and by age group. Hawaii has the lowest rate of home ownership of all states: 50 percent. Slightly more than half of all Californians and New Yorkers own their own homes, possibly because of the high cost of single-family homes and the relative attractiveness of apartment living in the more urban parts of those states. Michigan and Minnesota are among a relatively large group of states with home ownership rates between 70 percent and 80 percent. In these states, the cost of home ownership is lower and the cultural value attached to ownership is higher.

Only one-fifth of all heads of household under age twenty-five own their own homes. However, the number jumps dramatically after that age (see **Table 8.2**). Home-ownership rates more than double for the next age group and then increase sharply again. The trend eventually levels off and even reverses itself when older Americans move to supported-living environments such as retirement communities and nursing homes.

Table 8.2
Home Ownership by Age Group, Third Quarter 1999

Age in Years of Head of Household	Percentage Owning Homes
Less than 25	20.4
25 to 29	36.9
30 to 34	54.2
35 to 39	65.1
40 to 44	69.6
45 to 49	75.1
50 to 54	77.8
55 to 59	80.1
60 to 64	81.3
65 to 69	82.9
70 to 74	83.2
75 and older	78.2

Source: Census Bureau Online, *Housing Vacancy Survey.*

Families and individuals rely on their home place, and most Americans will act when they feel that their home is threatened. The defense of self, one's family, and one's space is a fundamental impulse of our species. Publisher Wick Allison once remarked: "You can be fairly tolerant of people's weirdness but you will be less so when it comes to the protection of your family and neighborhood" (Eigen & Siegel, 1993: 204).

There are potentially many threats to our homes and property. Some are social such as crime, unsupervised youth, and stray pets. Other threats are economic: neglected or abandoned property, excessive property taxes, and incompatible land usage. Americans are quick to defend their household and property and are often suspicious of governments' capabilities and intentions.

Neighborhood and Tenants' Associations

The responsibility for solving some of today's problems is proprietary, while the responsibility for others is governmental. Neighborhood associations take action in proprietary and governmental domains. In both cases, there is strength in unity.

Neighbors often come together in **neighborhood or tenants' associations.** These associations are membership organizations that are led by neighborhood people themselves. Membership is limited to people who have proprietary interest in the particular community. In neighborhood associations, people own property and have their primary residence on it; in tenants' associations, they rent their homes or apartments and reside there full time. In many newer suburbs, neighborhood membership and association fees are mandatory.

The neighborhood and tenant groups are typically incorporated, and this makes them "legal persons." Their articles of incorporation will state the purposes of the association and provide for its organization and leadership. In the process of becoming a legal entity, the association secures for itself the right to sue and be sued and the right to raise funds that will make its legal power credible. As a legal person, the association can sue other legal entities such as businesses if the proprietary interests of the group are threatened. Neighborhood associations may have responsibility for enforcing restrictive covenants on property usage. As such, they may act as private governments. They may even have to take legal action against one of their own if the individual acts in such a way as to threaten the property values of the overall neighborhood.

Other key aspects of associations are the social interactions and cooperative services they provide for members. Neighborhood festivals and tenants' street parties are social activities that appeal to many local citizens. A pool or community building may be the focal point for such activities. Once people get to know each other, they often form cooperatives to make their daily lives more enjoyable. Mothers may develop cooperative child-care activities at the community building, and Red Cross volunteers may teach swimming classes at the pool. Social and cooperative interactions are major sources of neighborhood enjoyment for some residents.

Neighborhood associations can bring together residents on a regular basis to discuss issues of common interest and importance.

Source: © Tony Freeman / PhotoEdit

Neighborhood Issues

Neighborhood and tenants' associations and local governments sometimes conduct surveys to find out the concerns of local residents. In fact, universities may help with the design and administration of these mailed surveys (Cox, 1998). The full text of a sample questionnaire is included in Appendix 1. Structured questions probe specific concerns and solicit write-in responses from residents. Interpretation involves tabulating and ranking neighborhood concerns and priorities. The sample questionnaire was completed in a college town, so it may relate to your experience.

One technique for tapping neighborhood concerns is to place the respondent in a familiar situation and ask him or her to visualize how they would respond in such a situation. For example, a scenario might read, "Late in the afternoon or early in the evening, you may want to go for a walk. Maybe you would take your child(ren) or dog, or maybe you just want some time alone." Then a question could ask, "Are you comfortable going out for a walk?" The answers given by 210 neighborhood residents in 1998 appear in Table 8.3.

Table 8.3
Neighborhood Survey Question on Safety, 1998:
"Are you comfortable going out for a walk?"

Responses	Percentage Choosing the Response
Yes, I always feel fine about such things.	56
Occasionally, if not alone or if before dark.	39
No, I'd be afraid.	4

Source: Cox (1998). Neighborhood Survey (unpublished).

A follow-up question can then probe for the source of discomfort for those who feel threatened walking in their own neighborhoods. The most common responses in the 1998 survey were: insufficient lighting, fear of strangers, nervousness about reckless drivers, fear of dogs, and rumors of violent acts. More precise information makes it possible for the neighborhood association to build an agenda for action. Better lighting is something the city can provide, and it also can enforce the unleashed-dog ordinance. Broader issues such as stranger-on-stranger crime and rumor control might be discussed among neighborhood associations and brought before local police officials. Specific information may lead to more effective political action.

Other questions about the quality of neighborhood life can address its appearance, noise levels, and other amenities. Each local community would have its own particular issues, and many communities may share concerns about residential amenities. Some of the issues from the 1998 neighborhood survey illustrate the point.

Modern life is increasingly noisy, and constant noise bombardment can make our lives more anxious and stressful. The 1998 survey asked, "Is there a noise problem where you live?" Fifty-three percent of respondents felt that noise was a problem some or all of the time (see Table 8.4).

The noise that residential neighborhoods endure comes from a variety of sources. The most frequently chosen responses again are illustrative. Automobiles and trucks make residential life near major highways a noisy prospect, and traffic noise was indeed the biggest complaint of the 1998 respondents. Individual neighbors' music, barking dogs, and parties at neighbors' houses were also problems. Industrial and commercial enterprises that crowd residential areas also contribute to the noise pollution.

Table 8.4
Neighborhood Survey Question on Safety, 1998:
"Is noise a problem where you live?"

Responses	Percentage Choosing the Response
No, it's nice and quiet.	46
Sometimes or occasionally.	42
Yes, it's noisy.	11

Source: Cox (1998). Neighborhood Survey (unpublished).

In some neighborhoods, a nearby airport can make city life really noisy. In others, heavy industry or a bus terminal or nightclub is the culprit. Sometimes, local governments can do certain things to abate noise: buying and planting trees on land as buffers for residential neighborhoods, for example, or requiring developers to do so. Local officials also can be more diligent in enforcing the zoning laws that keep industrial or entertainment and residential land uses separated. Although local governments usually cannot reduce noise levels per se, they can take steps to abate the noise that damages the quality of life in residential neighborhoods.

The problem of automobile and truck traffic involves several issues other than noise. Commuters who drive to work often cut through residential neighborhoods and frequently do not adjust their speed accordingly. Residents who have small children waiting for a school bus or who are themselves out walking or jogging must exercise extreme caution when insensitive commuters are hurrying to or from work. Large trucks often cut through town instead of using bypasses and truck routes that were built to keep tractor-trailers out of downtown areas. In dealing with the commuter cut-through problem, local officials may conclude that they need to adjust or more strictly enforce speed limits. They may need to erect caution signs that advise drivers that children are present. Some communities have enacted ordinances that require large tractor-trailers to use alternate routes unless they are making deliveries in the town.

Most people want to live in attractive neighborhoods. The 1998 neighborhood survey asked residents if they were proud of the appearance of their neighborhood. The question read, "When you look around your neighborhood, are you proud of how it looks?" Only 48 percent answered with an unqualified "yes." Those in the other half either thought the appearance could be improved or was simply "ugly" (see Table 8.5).

The most common sources of environmental degradation were unkempt yards or lots. Some absentee property owners allow their land to become overgrown, litter-infested eyesores. They also leave buildings in disrepair, which makes the neighborhood look shabby. Litter from both residents and nonresi-

Table 8.5
Neighborhood Survey Question on Safety, 1998:
"Are you proud of how your neighborhood looks?"

Responses	Percentage Choosing the Response
Yes, the area looks great.	48
Not sure, it could be improved.	44
No, it's an ugly area.	7

Source: Cox (1998). Neighborhood Survey (unpublished).

dents also can mar the landscape. Stray animals "and their leavings" were also problems, as were inappropriately parked or junky cars.

Clearly, there is an agenda here for neighborhood beautification. Association members do a lot of the clean up themselves. An additional public program in some communities requires that convicted drunk drivers and other traffic offenders participate in roadside cleanup activities. City crews also may try to maintain the appearance of roadsides. Although most communities have ordinances that require the upkeep of property, these laws may not be enforced on a regular basis. The association may have to pressure or even sue individual property owners to get action.

Residents also may have questions about the adequacy of their local services and suggestions for improving police protection, solid-waste collection, and road repair. The 1998 survey respondents, for example, were given an opportunity to rate their city services (the details are in Appendix 1). The overall pattern of responses suggests that citizens are satisfied with local government services but that some items needed attention. Bicycle safety concerns might be addressed by clearly marking bicycle lanes, erecting signs to caution motorists that bicyclers are present, and enforcing local ordinances designed to protect bicyclers. Pedestrian safety may require similar measures. Again, each community would need to voice its own concerns.

By using survey research, the associations and the local governments can document the presence and extent of local concerns and then build their plans, budgets, and grants with concrete data on neighborhood priorities. In other words, local government usually can do something when neighborhoods identify specific needs. Officials can react by changing ordinances, enforcing the laws that are already on the books, sending out city workers, and even offering grants to neighborhood and tenants' associations. On the other hand, if there is no mechanism with which to document local needs factually, then little progress may be made in satisfying the needs of residential areas.

Neighborhood Politics

Specific neighborhood problems like those addressed in the neighborhood survey or a proposed zoning change or a road-widening proposal may lead to issue-oriented political action. In such cases, the neighbors will meet on an issue, identify a course of action, pack public hearings, and deluge office holders with letters and telephone and e-mail messages.

One way to think of neighborhood political action on a specific concern is to visualize a committee being set up for each issue. This subgroup of the over-

Collecting Your Thoughts *Quality of Life Problems Where I Live*

Take a few minutes to jot down some of the problems you see at your house or apartment. Feel free to consult the survey in the appendix for ideas, but your own experiences are just as valid. Make a list of "complaints" you would be willing to sharing with the whole class. Are there specific crime, traffic, noise or trash-collection problems where you live? Is pedestrian and bicycle safety a concern for you and your neighbors? What more should local government be doing to help you maintain a satisfying quality of life where you live?

all association gives the rezoning or road-widening proposal undivided attention for as long as it takes to win the issue. They are the community activists who negotiate with government officeholders, grant newspaper interviews, and appear on local cable-television stations to promote the association's legitimate concerns regarding the issue. In the meantime, other routine activities of the association carry on.

A major source of power for neighborhood and tenants' associations is purely and simply political influence (DeLaney, 1995: 17). Many groups advocate voter registration of all members. Incumbents and candidates then will be made aware of the neighborhood's voting clout. The association will hold meetings where local issues, and especially neighborhood issues, will be discussed. Elected association leaders can meet with local government officials, and a monthly newsletter or Web site can be used to provide follow-up information on concerns that have been raised at meetings. In the case of emergency issues, a telephone tree or listserv may reach all neighbors within an evening's time. This type of political consciousness, backed up with leadership and a communication network, makes neighborhood and tenants' associations influential with local political officials. We will have more to say about electoral politics in the next chapter.

Neighborhood and tenants' associations may participate with local government in service delivery in their areas. For example, many neighborhood associations form neighborhood watch programs through which they help local police departments keep an eye out for burglars. The local government encourages this neighborhood self-help activity by orienting watch captains, providing cell phones for walkers and joggers, conducting home security audits, and maintaining statistics and information hotlines about neighborhood crime trends. Another popular joint-service activity is the neighborhood cleanup day. On a given Saturday, neighbors and city workers team up to sweep the neighborhood or apartment development of litter. Residents may also help clean up a vacant lot or fix up a local school playground. When volunteer workers and city employees get to work together on a joint project, they can build confidence in each other in the process. When they cannot, mutual distrust may develop.

By pooling their financial resources and organizing their political and civic resources, neighborhoods become political players. Their concerns become community concerns, especially when several associations band together into a *coalition* or *alliance*. Associations may endorse candidates for public office, and they are often incubators of future political leadership. Neighborhood activists may run for and secure elective office on county commissions or city councils.

Exploring on Your Own **Inventory of Neighborhood Associations**

Working in a team, you and your classmates can compile a listing of neighborhood associations in your community.

The community services planner in your city or county government is a good resource person for this project. Planners deal with neighborhood associations on an almost daily basis. As you build your inventory, be sensitive to the variety of neighborhood associations. You are likely to find that richer and poorer neighborhoods each have active associations. Renters or tenants as well as homeowners form associations. Post your listing on the class's physical or electronic bulletin board.

They may agree to serve on community task forces appointed by mayors or city managers. They may become noted personalities in the game of local politics.

The political venue for displays of neighborhood power varies. On narrow issues such as the location of a commercial building in a residential area, the venue might be the zoning board. On issues related to bicycler and pedestrian safety, the venue could be the traffic committee of the city council. On road-widening proposals, the planning commission might be the place where the political fight takes place. One quality that is needed in the leadership of neighborhood associations is knowledge of the political system and how it works. The structure of local government is highly specialized, and association leaders must be able to pick their field of battle and then show up well armed with facts and figures and well supported by legions of attentive neighbors sitting in the room. Well-organized and well-prepared neighborhood and tenants' organizations are hard to beat in a fair fight. Yet there are other nodes of political power in the community. These interests want to be heard. There are also powerful networks of prominent citizens who work behind the scenes to secure what they want from local government. Neighborhoods are only one of several political bases in the community.

There is relatively little social science research on the effectiveness of these associations. One writer has noted that what he calls "residential community associations" (RCAs) deserve much greater attention because they may be playing a major role in determining the outcome of state and local government decisions. "RCAs have emerged as one of the most potent political forces affecting local government land use decisions in the United States" (Dilger, 1994). He also notes that neighborhood associations also are beginning to influence state policy as they pressure state legislatures for property-tax relief. Future researchers will need to give neighborhood associations more attention.

❧ Business and Labor Organizations

There are bases of civic association other than residence. Employment is a key point of reference for most of us. Almost two-thirds of all Americans work, and the percentage continues to grow. In 1950, 56 percent of the civilian noninstitutionalized population was in the labor force. By 1998, the participation rate had reached 67 percent, where it is projected to remain through 2008. The unemployment rate has been approximately at or below 5 percent for some time now, and fewer and fewer women remain outside of the workforce. We identify with and want the best for and from our companies, agencies, or offices. To a large extent, we see our economic prospects intertwined with

---

Exploring on Your Own **The Local Business Agenda**

Interview someone who owns or manages a local business in your college community or back home. Ask this person how the local Chamber of Commerce or merchants' association helps identify issues that concern the business community. Are all types of private enterprise represented in the association? What type of action does the local group take to ensure that city and county officials address its concerns? To which issues do politicians and bureaucrats seem most responsive? Bring your notes to class for discussion.

those of our employers. It is therefore natural that Americans organize around the shared interests at work no less than we organize around shared interests in our neighborhoods or apartment buildings.

There is great variety in the types of business and professional groups that are organized at the local level. Some of the most common organizations are local Chambers of Commerce, downtown-development authorities or mall merchants' associations, businesswomen's roundtables, labor unions, societies for public administration, and many dozens of specialized professional associations for physicians, attorneys, pharmacists, and so on. All of these employment-based organizations seek to advance the cause of their own enterprises while also promoting the economic development of the community at large.

One of the most popular and most influential business organizations in the United States is the *U.S. Chamber of Commerce*. Membership in the Chamber is local, state, and national. At the local level, members meet on a regular basis, often over lunch. Speakers address the group about issues of local interest, and officials of the local Chamber report the concerns of the local membership. It is common for local public officials to speak at Chamber luncheons. They, in turn, receive input from members about the state of the local economy, prospects for economic development, and civic concerns such as schools that ultimately affect the business community.

Downtown-development authorities are quasi-public organizations that are chartered to promote the economic health of deteriorating downtown business districts. With suburbanization and the flight of business to suburban malls, many downtowns now look deserted. Storefronts may be boarded up, and shoppers hesitate to venture downtown. Special efforts have to be made to retain those businesses that have remained downtown. Other initiatives try to attract new shops and offices to the central city. The development authorities are incorporated and have power to tax members and offer subsidized incentives to prospective new businesses. They can undertake infrastructure improvements such as drainage projects, and they can issue bonds to pay for such improvements. In other words, they mix private and public functions in a focused effort to promote the downtown area.

Mall merchants associations are organizations that address the problems that their members have incurred since moving to the suburbs. Doing business in a mall is different in some respects because the developer owns the structure itself. The merchants who lease space join together to develop and coordinate store policies. For example, what should be the mall's hours of operation? How should merchants coordinate store security? Are unsupervised youths a problem in the mall? Should local police officials be asked to patrol the commons, and should the local government institute a curfew that restricts mall access by underage kids? These are clearly policy issues that would involve the merchants, the developer, and local government officials, but the merchants see strength in unity just as do all of the other associations we have mentioned.

Businesswomen's roundtables have been organized in many communities in response to the growing number of women executives and professionals who have entered the workplace (see Table 8.6).

Table 8.6
Gender of the Workforce, 1960 and 1995

Gender and Marital Status	1960 (%)	1995 (%)
Single males	69.8	73.7
Married males	89.2	77.5
Single females	58.6	66.8
Married females	31.9	61.0

Source: Bureau of Labor Statistics, Bulletins 2217 and 2340.

There has been a dramatic growth in the number of working women, and they find that they also want the benefits of association. Many businesswomen's roundtables use the luncheon-speaker format common to many associations. They also may have a mentors program for new businesswomen, and they may sponsor a variety of special projects such as a special day for daughters to accompany their mothers to work or an internship for women business majors at the local university. Their public policy agenda would include gender-discrimination issues such as the "glass ceiling" that is said to keep women from advancing in companies.

American **labor unions** were once a dominant feature on the local political landscape. In some communities, they still are, particularly in the Northeast and Northern states such as New York, Pennsylvania, Michigan, and Ohio. In 1983, 17 percent of all private-sector workers were unionized; in 1995, the figure was down to 10 percent (Bureau of National Affairs, *Union Membership and Earnings Data Book*, 1996).

The *union locals* are both civic and economic organizations. They sponsor a variety of community events and contribute to local charities. They advocate for the rights of workers regardless of those workers' union affiliations. For example, unions have championed higher minimum-wage laws, even though their own members make far better salaries than the minimum wage. Union support at election time is important. Most union members are registered to vote, and their leadership will usually identify candidates who have supported organized labor and workers more generally.

One interesting *occupation-based association* is the American Society for Public Administration (ASPA). Along with the public-employee organizations, ASPA chapters promote state-of-the-art professional practices in government. They also encourage compliance with national standards for ethical public employment. Local chapters meet regularly, recognize outstanding public servants, and encourage university graduates who enter the public service and speak out on public policy issues of the day.

CHAPTER 8 Local Communities: *Politics Where We Live*

Other professions are organized at the local level as well. The local bar association provides member attorneys with an opportunity to examine issues and speak out on the need for respect for the law. Local medical associations promote vaccinations for school children and volunteer to treat indigent patients at local health clinics. The list of professions and volunteer activities could go on and on. The point is that many professional people donate time and energy to improve the quality of life in the community. Their associations also speak out on issues and lobby informally for what they believe to be enlightened public policies.

Local Business Issues

Economic development represents more jobs and greater profits for the local economy. In many communities, it is considered an unqualified good. To attract and retain businesses, citizens and public officials often are expected to make certain concessions. Local government may offer tax breaks, waive fees for connecting to local water and sewer systems, and waive zoning or building-code restrictions. In the long run, increased payrolls and sales-tax receipts may offset these concessions. However, economic development incentives have drawbacks as well.

Existing local businesses do not get tax breaks and free utilities. They must meet all of the challenges of corporate life and their public obligations. The business community is not of a single mind when it comes to prompting new businesses to locate in town. Similarly, local unionized workers may not be enthusiastic about the relocation of a nonunion shop to the community. They have worked hard to get good wages, benefits, and working conditions, and they do not want to be undercut by the newcomers' depressed wages, weak benefits, and extended work hours. Their employer may decide to peg his or her compensation plan to that of new businesses. In other words, not everyone is happy to see concessions made to new companies.

Another aspect of economic development plans often is *workforce development*. Training new workers at the local vocational technical school can provide an employer with a ready workforce from the day the plant, warehouse, or hospital opens. State and local governments may pay for or subsidize training and actually recruit for the new employer. Ultimately, taxpayers are underwriting another business expense for the sake of possible future benefits to the community.

Finally, economic-development plans are vulnerable to the fads and fashions of contemporary business. Large home-improvement warehouses, for example, offer a wide range of tools, redecorating supplies, and building materials to individual consumers and local contractors. Such warehouse operations need large parcels of land, new utilities connections, and access roads. If local business organizations—in conjunction with a municipal government's economic development department—recruit such an enterprise for the community, then a large initial outlay may be required. Yet how many small local businesses will be affected? Local hardware stores, paint stores, and building suppliers have served individuals and contractors for years. They will suffer if the local development authority endorses the fashion of one-stop shopping for home improvement or if the local government waives its fees.

Recognizing that recruiting new firms is not sufficient for local economic development, some communities have chosen a more *multifaceted approach*. But strategies vary widely from community to community. Business-retention plans are developed alongside business-attraction plans, and small-business incubation is fostered as much as big-business recruitment efforts. In other words, the local economy and local civic culture are considered when economic-development plans use public resources to foster private enterprise. This gives small merchants, labor organizations, and local professionals opportunities to have input into the overall economic-development planning process. The results have been that plans are more diversified (Reese & Rosenfeld, forthcoming; Blakeley, 1991).

Other business issues usually complement the development-planning approach. For example, the business community may favor the building or expansion of a vocational training school. Local business leaders may press for the construction or expansion of a local airport. The local business community usually has a lengthy and quite varied policy agenda.

Business's Political Power

Business owners and managers can tap several resources when it comes to political action. Individually, they may contribute to the political campaigns of elected officials or the challengers who are trying to unseat incumbent officeholders. They can publicly endorse candidates, thereby lending their prestige to a campaign. They may try to convince their workers and those in allied firms to vote for a particular candidate. In any case, the business leader applies resources and prestige earned in the private sector to political careers being established or further developed in the public sector.

One type of civic leader often comes out the business community. A group of economic-development researchers have called them the "civic entrepreneurs" (Henton, Melville, & Walesh, 1997). These men and women possess the entrepreneur's spirit: a willingness to collaborate with others in taking risks on behalf of a better future for the community. They spend the time needed to foster civic activities because they realize that their companies' futures and the future of the community are linked. This idea is reflected in the old adage, "A rising tide lifts all boats."

Another aspect of local business political power is the mobilization of progrowth forces around economic-development efforts. A **progrowth coalition** of business, civic, and labor organizations may square off against neighborhood, special interest, and ad hoc protest groups in the battle over economic development incentives (Feiock & Clingermayer, 1992: 53). Historic preservation and environmental preservation may be powerful opponents of unfettered growth, and concerted prodevelopment efforts may be needed to convince local officials to enact policies that attract business.

Issue politics also interest local business leaders. The road widening that worried a neighborhood association might benefit traffic flow to a new mall. The redevelopment of the downtown area may seem to require the demolition of older neighborhoods so that new commercial enterprises can be erected. There often is a business side to debates on local issues.

Local Labor Union Issues

Working men and women lobby for their interests just as do business owners and managers. Local labor unions are concerned with the working conditions of both public and private employees. They are interested in quality education and vocational training programs. They typically rely on city recreation programs. Unions will seek to defend themselves from the influx of outside, nonunionized companies and from the erosion of workers' rights by local ordinances. They are concerned about illegal immigrants who may take jobs away from U.S. citizens and legal aliens who are unionized. Both offensively and defensively, union members have active local concerns in many U.S. cities.

Labor's Political Power

Public-sector labor unions, including such groups as the Fraternal Order of Police (FOP); the American Federation of State, County, and Municipal Employees (AFSCME); the National Education Association (NEA); and the American Federation of Teachers (AFT) often play particularly significant roles in local governments and school districts. Union power appears to be particularly significant in the largest cities, including New York, Philadelphia, Chicago, Detroit, and Cleveland. In these cities, most if not all local government employees are members of labor unions. They constitute a significant portion of the local population in general and of the active voters in particular. Their numbers enable their unions to be heard when candidates are selected to run for public office and when policy issues are under consideration. Public-sector unions will use their political power to maintain public-sector employment levels, increase their wages, and usually oppose the privatization of government services. (See also **Box 8.1**.)

Teachers' unions and their local chapters are active in promoting policies that they believe benefit their members and communities.
Source: © Joseph Schuyler / Stock · Boston

BOX 8.1   *Unions and Local Change*

In California, the South Bay AFL-CIO Labor Council serves as the communications hub and coordinating arm of all of the unions throughout Santa Clara and San Benito Counties. The council has worked with public and private employees to realize the benefits of its numbers through coalitions of unions: "[W]hen we make the connections between working people's interests and those of the communities we live in, our agenda is broader and our movement becomes stronger."

When the city of San Jose initiated its New Realities Task Force to create a comprehensive plan to move city government into the twenty-first century, the South Bay Labor Council negotiated for labor with one voice. New Realities developed a series of thirty-four measures to both reduce costs and increase revenues so the city could remain financially solvent while continuing to meet the varied demands of its citizens. For more information, check the Web sites for San Jose (<*http://www.ci.san-jose.ca.us/newreal/newreal.html*>) and the South Bay AFL-CIO Labor Council (<*http://www.atwork.org/clc/sol.html*>).

✎ Civic Clubs

Americans lead the world in volunteer activity (Lipset, 1996: 278). We join all sorts of organizations that espouse the principles with which we agree. Any catalog of our civic clubs would miss many groups that are important to some Americans. However, we will mention a few typical groups (see Table 8.7). Each civic club has the word *international* in its title because it has chapters and members in Canada, the Caribbean, or elsewhere in the world. For example, Altrusa International has chapters in nineteen countries. However, the bulk of these organizations' members are Americans.

Table 8.7
Typical American Civic Clubs

Organization	Clubs	Members	Special Focus
Altrusa International	454	14,000	literacy
Civitan International	995	29,400	developmental disabilities
Kiwanis International	8,000	300,000	children's health
Lions International	44,000	1.4 million	blindness
Optimist International	4,000	155,000	youth
Rotary International	29,000	1.2 million	business ethics

Source: Compiled from organizations' home pages.

The Optimist clubs of North America are devoted to the needs of young people. Local clubs meet, often weekly, and hear speakers who are expert in areas such as K–12 schooling, counseling sexually active youth, recreation programs for young people, and programs for children with developmental disabilities. From these speakers and from other sources in the local community, Optimists build service programs that encourage children to have a positive outlook on life. Some of the activities that have become common to Optimist clubs across the United States are "Respect for Law Week," local and statewide oratorical and essay contests, and a "Buckle Up for Safety" project that educates families about the proper use of safety restraints in automobiles. The specific political content of the Optimists' message is hard to distill. Clearly, these clubs advocate adequate funding for education, recreation, and health programs for the community's children. Action and inaction by local officials could be the topic of conversation at their meetings. However, Optimists like most other civic clubs are officially nonpartisan.

The members of these civic clubs volunteer to work—both together and individually—on community projects. For example, representatives from all of the local civic organizations might participate in a March of Dimes Walk-a-

CHAPTER 8 Local Communities: *Politics Where We Live*

Thon to help raise money for that charity. The club might pledge a dollar for every mile walked by one of its members. The clubs can actually compete this way, and the March of Dimes is the beneficiary.

If we ask ourselves what motivates men and women to join civic clubs, we can get as many answers as there are individual members. Some people join to build business contacts. Others are interested in the socializing, and yet others are motivated by the community projects that the clubs carry out. What matters to our analysis is their involvement. People give up some of their precious time for the benefit of the community. They are volunteers who are raising money, educating the public, and providing direct service to people in need.

American civic groups offer members not only a way to contribute to their communities, but also a sense of camaraderie in service.

Source: © Bob Daemmrich / Stock · Boston

Civic Issues

The human development of a community is a multifaceted prospect. Children need guidance. Elderly neighbors need transportation, medical assistance, and adequate shelter. Poor people need to gain confidence in the willingness of the world to provide a working wage for an honest day's work. And they need the compassion of their neighbors when disability, misfortune, and the lack of opportunity cause them despair. We all are related to each other by the bonds of community that define us as a people and unite us as a polity. Civic organizations try to give us a nongovernmental vehicle for pursuing our shared interest in a better community.

Each civic club has its own local projects and its own national and international priorities. These concerns often involve children. The members of civic organizations invest their time and emotional capital in projects that are designed to make a difference in children's lives. Many *youth concerns* fall through the cracks of the governmental, familial, and educational systems. A couple of examples may show how civic clubs fund the needs of today's youth.

A high school might be willing to make education about the responsibilities of parenthood part of its "skills for life" program. But the educators may not have the resources to purchase a set of computerized dolls that act like real babies when they are taken home for the weekend by the teenagers. One such product cries when it is not picked up or changed. It wakes the teenager up in the middle of the night when it needs attention. And it even records the lapse times between crying and getting attention so that the data can be downloaded and evaluated by the teacher. The dolls come in all races, and there is even a special-needs doll that some teachers have called a "crack baby" who is randomly given to an unsuspecting teenager to take home. The baby simulation

Take a few moments to jot down the types of groups that are active on your campus, including those that are social and those that serve the community. What benefits do you think students receive from belonging to campus organizations? Is the service that is rendered to other students or the community more or less important than the socializing that takes place among group members? Are there personal needs that get met by joining and being active in a campus organization? Do you expect to have more or fewer "joining" demands when you graduate and become an active professional? Bring your notes to class to discuss with others.

is highly realistic, and many high school students have been made more aware of the responsibilities that may await them as a result of careless sex.

Civic clubs conduct benefits such as spaghetti suppers, raffles, and celebrity golf tournaments for the expressed purpose of raising funds for just such a worthy project. They have the resources to buy the dolls the school program needs. And they may first have heard about the skills program and the doll when a superintendent or principal or teacher spoke to one of their luncheon meetings. Once they were made aware of the need, they may have voted to make a gift of several dolls to the school. No bureaucracy must be engaged and no lengthy debate held over whether school tax funds or tuition funds should go to this or some other need. A decision is made, the dolls are purchased and sent to the school, and the civic club moves on to the next project.

Sometimes, such civic club initiatives are national rather than purely local. One example has been the campaign to have children buckled into safety seats in cars' backseats. Air bags inflate when an automobile collides with another vehicle or a stationary object. This wonderful invention has undoubtedly saved many lives, but it was not designed for infants and toddlers. The force of the air bag's deployment has broken the necks of small children who were buckled up in the front seats of automobiles or whose safety seats were installed in the front seat. The only safe way to transport infants and toddlers is to buckle them up in a safety seat in a vehicle's backseat.

The automobile industry and several civic organizations have initiated a national public information program about child car safety. Program materials explain the problem and offer safe solutions. At the local level, civic clubs pass out the materials, arrange for local merchants to display information in their businesses, and operate information booths at cooperating malls to spread the word. In the case of this project, a business and civic club partnership is addressing a children's problem in communities throughout the United States.

There are many hundreds of examples of civic clubs working to improve the lives of local citizens without governmental action. The problems may be in the public domain, but they do not always require governmental leadership or involvement. Community members learn that they can come together and help solve problems on their own. The large number of civic clubs in most communities makes this outlet for action available to virtually all citizens. And many civic clubs have university clubs as well, so college students can become involved.

Social service agencies backstop family, school, and volunteer organizations. We will have a lot more to say about these important government agencies later, but at this stage of our study of local government realize that communities are rich networks of private associations. Americans may belong to two, three, or more organizations when we consider neighborhood and tenants associations, business and professional organizations, and civic clubs. Purely private means and methods do much of what needs doing in the community.

Civic Clubs and Politics

The Optimist club and other local civic clubs are nonpartisan, apolitical organizations. They do not support candidates, give to campaigns, or fund rallies in support of referenda items. They do invite politicians and candidates to speak to their members, but only to educate them. They sometimes have programs on referenda issues facing the community at election time, but they typically invite all sides to present their viewpoints. They are a forum for political discussion, but not a vehicle for candidates or causes. That is the official line of American civic clubs. The reality may not be so simple.

While officially open to all people who want to join, civic clubs are criticized as being homogeneous and not always civic-minded. To maintain their memberships, they may shy away from the most controversial public policy issues facing a community. However significant their contributions are, they are but a fraction of the overall public response to social problems. And yet they do make important contributions in many communities.

As a practical matter, many politicians gain experience through their long association with and membership in neighborhood, business, and civic organizations. Politics is about knowing people and having polished "people skills." What better place to meet people and sharpen interpersonal and leadership skills than in a civic club? In fact, many elected officials consider an active record of participation in civic organizations to be a necessary part of the resume of a successful politician.

Another practical consideration is the rich variety of private conversation that takes place around the civic club's luncheon table. Granted, the group takes no official position on a political issue and does not endorse any particular candidate. Private persons, however, make their personal views known to all those who will listen during the chitchat that characterizes many civic club meetings. The more memberships one has, the more opportunities there are to meet people, share ideas, and quietly campaign for one's concerns and political friends.

Rotary Clubs Busy in Indonesia

Indonesia is a large and mostly Muslim nation in Southeast Asia. It consists of hundreds of islands, and these islands and their villages are the basis for what we would call state and local government. Indonesians from the growing ranks of professional and business people have really taken to civic clubs. In 1995–96, for example, one of the five clubs on the island of Bali built a public library in a village that had none. American Rotarians have raised money to help supply books for the new library's shelves. Two women's Rotary Clubs on Bali purchased a traveling mammography machine that will help with the early detection of breast cancer. Civic clubs in Indonesia are welcome to engage in civic projects so long as they do not become political advocacy groups. Thanks to globe-trotter Dr. Faith Willis for this observation.

Religious Congregations

The United States has always been a country of religious institutions. We have active congregations of Jews, Muslims, Buddhists, and Christians. Within the major religions, all of our larger communities and many smaller ones have numerous sects or denominations. For example, we have Orthodox, Conservative, and Reform Jewish congregations. We have Roman Catholic, Eastern Orthodox, and numerous Protestant Christian congregations. Where else in the world do so many congregations practice so many variants of humankind's search for meaning? The liberty of religious belief and practice is another of the hard-won victories of the American political experience. This freedom fits well with other protected liberties such as free speech, the right to assemble, and the freedom to publish ideas.

Freedom of religion in the United States coexists with a First Amendment requirement of separation of church and state. This wall of separation suggests that government actions should not recognize particular religious beliefs or groups. Clearly, this is difficult to define. Laws that provide school vouchers for use in religious schools are currently viewed as constitutionally suspect. Yet construction of a crèche at city hall at Christmas time is thought acceptable so long as religious symbols of other religious groups are in the general area. The wall of separation does not prevent religious individuals or faith-based organizations from exercising their freedom to question and condemn government actions. Even from the pulpit, religious leaders speak to public policy issues. As Martin Luther King, Jr., put it: "The church . . . is not the master or the servant of the state, but rather the conscience of the state" (Eigen & Siegel, 1993: 612).

For many years, the Gallup Organization has polled Americans about their religious affiliations and practices. Consistently, more than two-thirds of all Americans report being members of religious congregations (see Table 8.8). Roughly 40 percent attend religious services on a regular basis—that is, they attended the week preceding the survey. The figures are stable over time, suggesting that we should include religious organizations in our survey of local associations.

Table 8.8
Religious Affiliation in the United States

Year	Respondents Expressing an Affiliation (%)	Now Attending Church (%)
1975	71	41
1980	69	40
1985	71	42
1990	65	40
1994	68	42

Source: Princeton Religious Research Center reprinted in *The American Almanac, 1996–97:* 70.

Religious Issues

Some of the concerns of members of local faith-based organizations and their leaders are common to virtually all religious congregations. Others are specific to only some religions or denominations or even particular congregations. For example, racial harmony is professed as a theme common to all religious groups in the United States. Discrimination in consumer services, employment, housing, voting, school policies, social services, or any other facet of community life may bring condemnation from the same pulpits. Racial discrimination goes against the teachings of our religious groups, and some rabbis, priests, and ministers may feel honor-bound to denounce it. Members also may feel obligated to do something about the discrimination. They may boycott an offending merchant or realtor. They may publicly decry the offense in letters to the newspaper editor, appearances at local business association meetings, or sessions of the city council. In this sense, religious leaders and members are exercising what Dr. King considered the community's conscience.

Other shared issues for religious groups include poverty, especially the suffering of abandoned women and children, elderly citizens, and homeless families. Communities throughout the United States boast faith-based food banks, soup kitchens, homeless shelters, unwed mothers' homes, orphanages, hospitals, and nursing homes. In terms of money donated to easing community problems, religious organizations gave almost $82 billion in 1999 (AAFRC Trust for Philanthropy, 2000). Although the impact of this service and this giving may be evangelical as well as civic, the magnitude of the resources is significant to local social service agencies.

Religious volunteers and church philanthropy are considerable community resources. In the United States, more than half of all college students and two-thirds of all college graduates donate some of their time to community service (Gallup and Independent Sector, cited in *The American Almanac, 1996–97*: 387). Nationally, the service of students and graduates through their faith-based organizations exceeds the individual contributions of arts and cultural groups, environmental groups, or work-related organizations.

Local religious groups also act together to affect community behavior and public policy. They form *citywide ministerial alliances* to seek ways of encouraging religious, racial, and ethnic tolerance. These coalition-styled organizations may be called ministerial associations or councils of churches. Instead of only reacting to sensational events in the community, they work on a routine basis to foster dialogue and understanding. They may sponsor intervisitation across religious or denominational lines, hold joint services for African American and European American congregations, or operate summer youth camps that serve all segments of the community. The Greater Minneapolis Council of Churches is a good example of a coalition of faith-based groups involved in social service delivery and the development of public policy (see **Box 8.2**).

BOX 8.2   *Faith-Based Organizations: Greater Minneapolis Council of Churches (GMCC)*

Programs supported by the Council include:

- Minneapolis FoodShare—food banks for dealing with hunger

- Congregation in Community—services for children and families in poverty

- Paint-a-Thon—housing repair for low-income elderly and disabled residents

- Shared Ministries Tutorial—tutoring for low-income students

- Correctional Chaplaincy—faith communities offering rehabilitation for those in prison

- Congregations Concerned for Children Advocacy Network—political action on issues of child protection, child care, and family welfare

- Handy Works—support for elderly people's housekeeping and minor repairs

- Division of Indian Work—support services for American Indians

- Family Violence Programs—counseling services for American Indian families

Source: GMCC Web site at *<http://www.gmcc.org/programs.html>*.

Working alone, contact a local religious leader or an actively religious family member. Ask this person about the "social ministry" of his or her church. Make notes of the kinds of activities sponsored by the church. Are the services provided without regard to the religious orientation of the person being served? In the same vein, is service offered only locally or is it also offered nationally and overseas? Does the congregation view local government as an adversary or as an ally? Be prepared to write a short and confidential report for your instructor.

Specific denominations may have special concerns of their own. The Roman Catholic Church opposes abortion; Churches of Christ denounce alcohol consumption. These churches can be expected to act on their particular concerns even though not all faiths and denominations choose these issues as their social concerns priorities.

Faith-Based Organizations and Politics

We cannot possibly catalog here all that religious organizations accomplish individually and together. The issues go beyond racial justice and easing the pain of poverty. Proposals to make alcohol or drugs more accessible will draw criticism and opposition from the religious groups. Concessions to gambling casinos and adult bookstores will not go unnoticed. In the 1990s, for example, when the city of Detroit was considering a public referendum to allow casino gambling, local religious groups campaigned against the measure. They lost the battle. Religious leaders and their congregations are vigilant in the community. Religious memberships can be mobilized to express political support or opposition, and they can be encouraged to vote on local referenda. Political officials have learned to keep religious groups in mind when making and enforcing public policy.

The important community role played by *African American churches* deserves special attention. Many black churches have been in the forefront of civic improvement and political reform throughout the United States (Bellah, Madsen, Sullivan, Swindler, & Tipton, 1991: 212). African American ministers are frequently voices of conscience in the community, and many including Martin Luther King, Sr., of Atlanta have become spokespersons for African American citizens. Others such as Martin Luther King, Jr., and Jesse Jackson have gained national prominence leading people of conscience of all races in campaigns to secure social, economic, and political justice. As bases of community action and training grounds for civic and political leadership, black churches have been significant civic institutions in communities throughout the United States.

The African American church has been an avenue for leadership development and a platform for political involvement. Candidates often are endorsed by church leaders. Some churches are heavily involved in economic-development activities, including business development, venture capitalism, and low-income housing. The populations of many central cities have declined over the past few decades, but the African American churches have remained and provided significant opportunities for neighborhood participation (Secret, Johnson, & Forrest, 1990).

❧ Special Issue Organizations

The groups and organizations discussed so far have many diverse issues. A neighborhood association may work on concerns that are close to home such as property, traffic, children, and any number of city services. Business groups foster a prosperous local economy and may address not only taxes, utility infrastructures, and crime rates, but also transportation, schools, and any one of many other topics. The basis for membership in groups so far has been shared characteristics: location, occupation, civic-mindedness, and religion. But what of organizations that are formed to deal with only a narrow range of issues? Special interest organizations are created by like-minded individuals to promote specific positions on a narrower range of issues.

Typical Special Interest Organizations

Environmental organizations are one highly popular example of the special interest group. Members of local environmental groups may be young or old, rich or poor, and religious or secular in motivation. Some are interested in civic development, and others are not. What they share is a concern that the local environment not be degraded. They give their time and treasure to protect land, waterways, and the air we breathe.

Growth management is one broad issue that is shared by environmental interest groups around the country. Commercial and residential growth can be planned or uncontrolled. When development is haphazard, the natural environment takes a beating. In metropolitan areas, any lack of growth management has large-scale repercussions. The flow of streams that drain rainwater is disrupted, concrete parking lots channel runoff, and flooding becomes common. Downtown business districts and neighborhoods are choked with traffic and smog. Farther out from the central city, suburban sprawl consumes land like a disease. One strip mall after another crowds the arteries that lead in and out of the city. Natural vistas are destroyed. Traffic chokes the roadways, and the air becomes dangerously polluted. Bird and animal populations are wiped out. The quality of life steadily dips even as the economic opportunities of new jobs and new services rise.

Another type of special interest group is the *gay rights organization.* Men and women who join these organizations share a commitment to gaining full legal and economic rights for gay men and lesbians. Inspired by the civil rights and women's rights movements, gay rights advocates press for governmental recognition of rights such as protection from discrimination in hiring and promotion, employment benefits for same-sex partners, and protection from discrimination in financial matters such as credit, loans, and home mortgages. Members of gay rights groups are from many different walks of life, live in different parts of town, and work in a variety of occupations. What they share is a commitment to their cause. (See also Box 8.3.)

We have only begun to suggest the many single-issue groups that dot the urban landscape. All of them endure so long as their concerns go unaddressed. They may fade when their major battles have been won. In any case, they are an important part of the community's organizational landscape, providing outlets for social expression and political action for segments of concerned citizens.

Special Interests and Politics

Special interest groups lobby for change. We discussed their lobbying activities in some detail in Chapter 3. Suffice it to say that local interest groups are

The City and County of San Francisco has probably gone further than any other U.S. city in responding to demands for equal rights by lesbian, gay, bisexual, and transgendered citizens, although the process has not always been easy. In the 1970s, the city adopted an ordinance to prohibit discrimination in employment, housing, and public accommodations and elected its first openly gay member of the Board of Supervisors. Throughout the 1980s and early 1990s, the supervisors adopted various domestic partnership ordinances (allowing the registration of same-sex couples and offering the same-sex partners of city employees certain employee benefits) that were challenged and sometimes repealed by voter referenda. Having finally succeeded in adopting a registration process, Mayor Willie Brown now holds and annually presides over a ceremony at which dozens of couples make a public commitment to one another. Most recently, San Francisco has adopted an ordinance that requires any business wanting to contract with the city to offer all of its employees the opportunity to register for domestic-partnership benefits. The nondiscrimination ordinances of the city have been revised to prohibit discrimination on the basis of gender identity, as well as on the basis of sexual orientation.

Thanks to Dr. Charles Gossett for this report.

like their state counterparts in monitoring government decision making and trying to intervene with their viewpoints as decisions are being made.

A local environmental group would have its special issues. It might bring the issues to public attention through information campaigns, perhaps through what are called "teach-ins." The group also might organize highly visible public demonstrations and jockey for good media coverage of such events. Members may even purchase sophisticated advertising to promote their concern.

Some elected and appointed officials openly sympathize with environmental or other special interest groups, and still others could be swayed to a group's viewpoint with good and timely information. If there is a beachhead of local political support, then the interest group will try to get public hearings on the issue. It then will have an opportunity to pack the hearing room and flex its political muscle. The combined votes or administrative support of outright allies plus that of convinced independents could make it possible for an environmental group to win a particular issue over the generally more influential business interests. But win or lose, special interest groups can best compete in local policy making when deliberations are open to the public and well covered by local media.

❧ Interpreting Community Groups

We would be remiss if we also did not point out some of the shortcomings of community organizations within the context of local government decision making. First, everyone does not join or participate in such groups. Higher-income individuals and those with higher education levels are more likely to be joiners. This does not mean that low-income individuals and those without college educations are apathetic, just that they are less likely to participate in many of these groups. Second, not all community groups are civic-minded. What seems to be good for the community to one individual or group may not seem good to others. Certainly the "not in my backyard," or NIMBY, phenomenon is often evidenced by neighborhood groups or associations, which may fight to prevent something they consider undesirable in their vicinity, whether a group home for disabled citizens or a halfway house for ex-offenders. These facilities may, in fact, be considered part of good public policy for the overall community. Finally, some community organizations may reflect a generalized antigovernment bias. Leaders and members may believe that private groups can provide public services more efficiently and more effectively than can government. But this belief may not recognize the important balance between public policy and private actions.

To fully understand community groups, we should view them within a broader context of other participants in local politics. We have looked at types of groups—neighborhood and tenants' associations, business and professional groups, civic clubs, religious groups and alliances, and single-interest groups—but have not exhaustively inventoried local organizations. Nowhere in the world is there more freedom of association than in the United States, and Americans take ample advantage of this right. Many belong to several different types of community organizations, all at the same time. An individual may go to church on Sunday, eat lunch with his or her civic club on Tuesday, attend an evening meeting of his or her professional group on Thursday, and work on projects for a

Proposals such as zoning changes affect local growth-management and environmental policies and often bring strong reactions from citizens in public meetings.
Source: © Bob Daemmrich / Stock · Boston

favorite special interest group on weekends. Sounds exhausting, right? It is the price that Americans often pay for having personal input into the community's decision-making systems. But is all of this involvement effective? Do politicians listen to community groups? Can Americans count on having political institutions and political officials that are open to neighborhood, business, civic, church, and interest group ideas?

Elite Theory

In the 1950s, Atlanta, Georgia, appeared to be dominated by its business leaders. In 1953, Floyd Hunter published a detailed study of Atlanta titled *Community Power Structure: A Study of Decision-Makers.* He presented his case study of local power without disclosing the name of the city, referring to his locale as Regional City; only later did we learn that he had been studying Atlanta. His basic finding was that a wealthy business elite of locally born white men dominated government policy and administration in the city. Elected officials and administrators were simply spokespeople for this behind-the-scenes high society group. Community associations such as the YMCA, the Chamber of Commerce, and the Community Chest (the precursor of the United Way) also carried out the wishes of this business elite. Even African American associations and the city's labor unions followed the direction of this power elite. The relationship was strictly one-directional. Business leaders could reach out and touch any area of public or civic life, and others had little or no influence on the conduct of private enterprise in the city.

Hunter came to these conclusions using a reputational approach to the study of local politics. He went to individuals in prominent positions and asked them who was most influential. They offered the names of those with a general reputation of being powerful, mostly economic leaders. This methodology was later criticized as determining the results in advance of the study.

Hunter's image of local decision making is clear and to the point. A private economic elite dominates public affairs from behind the scenes. It manipulates elected and appointed officials, community activists, and even state lawmakers and regulators. To Hunter, power is concentrated in the hands of a few, and access to power is closed. Public policy reflects the values and wishes of the economic elite, but decisions are made in what only it determines to be "the public interest." What is critical to Hunter's theory is that it is only the elite's interpretation of the public interest that counts. We refer to models such as his as reflections of **elite theory.**

Hunter's study of Atlanta is now quite old. The people he described are gone from the political scene. His observations and conclusions must not be interpreted as exclusively pertaining to the 1950s or to Atlanta or to Southern cities. His case study simply stands as an effort to develop a broad elite theory of politics. In a small rural town, a power elite may be based on family land holdings. In an urban center, people with "old money" may have inherited their seat at the downtown club along with their millions. And in some middle-sized cities in the Midwest, there may be an actual merchant elite along the lines that Hunter described. The principle is the same.

Pluralist Theory

In 1961, Robert Dahl, a Yale University professor, published another landmark study in local power politics. His case study of New Haven, Connecticut, was presented in the book *Who Governs? Democracy and Power in an American City.* In his research, Dahl found a very different pattern of power relationships than Hunter had found in Atlanta. His research looked at specific decisions made by local government. He spoke with a wide variety of local people about each decision and deduced that while some people are politically involved much of the time, others only become involved when they need something from the government. Most of us fall into the second category. Citizen involvement and influence are specialized. Teachers, school principals, and parents (as individuals or as a PTA group) have a lot of say in public school policies, but they may defer to the downtown merchants when it comes to policies about business licenses and local sales-tax collections. Dahl concluded that community power is not the singular preserve of a small elite but is built on many power centers. His perspective therefore is called a **pluralist theory.**

According to Dahl, the average citizen is not politically involved on an ongoing basis. The constant fascination with local politics is left to *homo politicus*, the activist who regularly uses his resources to influence government. The rest of the population is characterized as *homo civicus*, citizens who only become involved in politics when they need something. These citizens then limit their involvement to one relatively narrow sphere. They may have the ability to get what they want in that particular area, but their power is not generalizable to other areas. Power is specialized and dominated by individuals who have some direct interest in a specific policy area or who become involved through a specialized group (Dahl, 1995: 262–263). In fact, this type of power is often exercised through local interest groups such as neighborhood associations and business organizations.

Dahl's theory can be applied in a variety of contemporary settings. African American ministers have had considerable political influence on policies that affect civil rights and human services. Neighborhood association presidents influence many local government decisions on noise ordinances, traffic law enforcement, and road and drainage improvements. College student association officers have influence on public transportation, stranger-on-stranger crime-control efforts, and crowd control policies. Each group has a special niche in which it has some credibility and clout and is prepared to fight passionately for its concerns. We assume that such groups are interested in a "common good," but there is no guarantee.

Over the years, much ink has been spilled debating the topic of "who governs." Both Hunter and Dahl were criticized for using a case-study approach to generalize about local power structures. Both relied on a single city and a single point in time as the bases for their general elitism versus pluralism theories. Studies in other cities and reanalyzed data from the original studies suggest that neither a pure elite explanation nor a purely pluralist explanation fits most cities. Instead, the theories may suggest areas of focus within cities that are constantly changing. Today's local business leaders, for example, may represent national or international interests but not local interests. As American industries merge and ownership changes hands, the substantive position of local business elites could easily change (Harrigan & Vogel, 2000: 221–222).

Another criticism of both researchers is that their theories do not give any attention to how poor citizens and racial minorities are excluded from power. Instead of just looking at what decisions are made, consider all of the issues that never make the agenda of local government. This phenomenon results in a whole class of *nondecisions* on issues that affect the poor, the homeless, handicapped citizens, resident aliens, and many other groups. How can a general theory of local power fail to mention the politics of an economic underclass whose needs and concerns form an important part of today's urban agenda? More recent theorists have suggested that power is not just the ability to get something done but also the ability to prevent something from happening!

Regime Theory

Clarence Stone is one theorist who has responded to some of the gaps in the earlier Hunter and Dahl works. Stone restudied Atlanta and community power in the 1970s and 1980s, and his book *Regime Politics: Governing Atlanta 1946–1988* was published in 1989. His concept of **regime politics** presents an important third view of community power. A *regime* is a relatively durable but informal alliance of elected officials, their political supporters, economic-development interests, property owners, and professional bureaucrats. The regime concept not only recognizes the special role of economic interests in shaping urban policy, but also acknowledges the importance of political factors.

Look at your hometown or the school community from a regime perspective. You can find evidence of the local power structure in the local newspaper's reports on officials' speeches. You may want to attend a local city council meeting—or watch it on public-access cable—and listen to the kinds of issues that are brought up and where officials stand on the issues. Try to identify the governing regime. Is the official "line" coming out of city hall oriented toward growth? Do local officials instead usually talk about maintaining the advances of the recent past? Or is the agenda one of responding to average citizens? Who are the key players in the local governing regime? What policies are they promoting that reflect their underlying orientation to government process and policy? Keep notes on your findings for class discussion.

Cities have different kinds of regimes, and each may vary over time. One regime may focus on developing a city's economic base, while another may try simply to maintain the gains of the recent past. One regime may pride itself on how it responds to the needs and wishes of lower- and middle-class citizens, while another may champion growth by arguing that "a rising tide lifts all boats." Each regime is built on the recognition that money talks. Elected officials need campaign contributions to gain and stay in public office. When there, they need for their city to attract and hold investments in growth and development. They also need tax revenues to pay for city services. Simply being in government does not provide the power and resources needed to govern.

Regime theory takes special notice of business leaders, but countervailing forces may organize and become an out-of-power group opposing a business-led regime. Other interests in the community such as civil rights groups, labor unions, poorer neighborhood associations, and environmental reformers may develop a coalition that will replace a business-oriented regime with one of their own at the next election.

After reviewing a variety of community power theories, contemporary urban scholars have concluded that pluralism is an important contribution to understanding local politics. Certainly, power usually is not held by a few who control everything. Rather, it is dispersed and specific to particular policy areas such as real estate, business regulation, and neighborhood planning. Regimes change with the community's economic and social mix. But equally clear is that the business establishment has exceptional power to influence a wider range of issues than do neighborhood associations. After all, they may move their enterprises out of town if they do not like the way local government treats them. No elected official wants to accept responsibility for abandoned storefronts and empty factories.

❧ Chapter Conclusion

In this chapter, you have learned how individuals come together at the grass roots to engage in civic and political behavior. We have looked at the memberships, concerns, and political activities of neighborhood and tenants' associations, business and labor organizations, civic clubs, religious congregations, and special interest groups. We can now answer our basic questions about local communities and how Americans organize themselves at the grassroots.

BOX 8.4   *Participation Counterpoint*

Robert Putnam gained a great deal of academic attention in 1995 when his article "Bowling Alone: America's Declining Social Capital" was published in the *Journal of Democracy*. He summoned statistics from a variety of sources to support his argument that contemporary U.S. society does not deserve its reputation as a bastion of volunteerism. For example, he argues that organizations as varied as Parent Teacher Associations (PTAs) and civic groups such as the Federation of Women's Clubs reported declining memberships in the 1980s and 1990s.

Mass membership organizations such as the American Association of Retired Persons (AARP) and the National Organization for Women (NOW) grew during the same time period. However, these latter organizations do not require sustained personal involvement and local networking as did the civic organizations of the past. Putnam cited many of the same trends that we discuss here—including employment mobility and technological entertainment—as reasons for this "erosion of social capital."

- So, how *do* neighbors organize themselves so their political voices will be heard, and what are their basic concerns? Citizens organize themselves around their personal and professional interests, and many local people have multiple and overlapping memberships.

- What issues concern voluntary associations? The spectrum of local community issues is broad indeed. Traffic and taxes, schools and sanitation, crime and cosmetology licensing—each one is an important concern to at least some segment of local residents. (For a contrasting viewpoint on volunteerism, see Box 8.4.)

- Does politics at the grass roots create many different nodes of power in the community? Do different groups prevail at different times on different issues, or does a power elite manipulate the community from behind the scenes? The community activism approach to local government helps explain where issues come from and how political players try to resolve them. It focuses our attention on the public to whom government officials are accountable. Taken together, the networks within and between these voluntary associations help define the local body politic. Together with the geographic boundaries of the community, these networks bind the community together. Individuals in the community have crosscutting and ever-changing memberships. Organizations within the community form, dissolve, and re-form as issue coalitions.

Local officials consult with group leaders, and the groups approach government councils, boards, and offices. Interaction between political officials and community leaders is constant. The mixture of these organizations is unique in each community. They blend with the history of each place as well as the structure of government in each area. All this having been said, remember that it is a considerable challenge to really understand the political milieu of any community.

Key Words for InfoTrac Exploration

environmental associations   freedom of religion   gay liberation movement   labor unions

Sources Cited

AAFRC Trust for Philanthropy (2000). Online: <*http://www.aafrc.org/news.htm*>.

Bellah, Robert N., Richard Madsen, William M. Sullivan, Ann Swindler, and Stephen M. Tipton (1985). *Habits of the Heart: Individualism and Commitment in American Life.* Berkeley: University of California Press.

——— (1991). *The Good Society.* New York: Alfred A. Knopf.

Blakeley, Edward J. (1991). "The Meaning of Local Economic Development." Pp. 21–40 in R. Scott Fosler (Ed.), *Local Economic Development: Strategies for a Changing Economy.* Washington, DC: International City Management Association.

Bureau of Labor Statistics (2000). *Labor Force (Demographic) Data.* Online: <*http://stats.bls.gov/emplab1.htm*>.

Bureau of National Affairs (1996). *Union Membership and Earnings Data Book.* Washington, DC: Author.

Cox, George H. (1998). Unpublished data from neighborhood survey. State and Local Government Class, Georgia Southern University.

Dahl, Robert (1995). "Participation and the Problem of Civic Understanding." Amitai Etzioni (Ed.), *Rights and the Common Good: The Communitarian Perspective.* New York: St. Martin's Press.

DeLaney, Ann (1995). *Politics for Dummies: A Reference for the Rest of Us.* Foster City, CA: IDA Books.

Dilger, Robert Jay (1994). "Residential Community Associations: Their Impact on Local Government Finance and Politics." *Public Management,* April: 16–21. Reprinted from *Government Finance Review* by permission of the Government Finance Officers Association.

Eigen, Lewis D., and Jonathan P. Siegel (1993). *The Macmillan Dictionary of Political Quotations.* New York: Macmillan.

Feiock, Richard C., and James C. Clingermayer (1992). "Development Policy Choice: Four Explanations for City Implementation of Economic Development Policies." *American Review of Public Administration,* 22(1) (March): 49–63.

Harrigan, John J., and Ronald K. Vogel (2000). *Political Change in the Metropolis* (6th ed.). New York: Longman.

Henton, Douglas, John Melville, and Kimberly Walesh (1997). "Civic Entrepreneurs: Leaders at the Grass Roots." Pp. 33–68 in *Grassroots Leaders for a New Economy: How Civic Leaders are Building Prosperous Communities.* San Francisco: Jossey-Bass.

Independent Sector (no date). Online: <*http://www.independentsector.org/about/vision.html*>.

Lappé, Frances Moore, and Paul Martin DuBois (1994). *The Quickening of America: Rebuilding Our Nation, Remaking Our Lives.* San Francisco: Jossey-Bass.

Leach, William (1999). *Country of Exiles: The Destruction of Place in American Life.* New York: Pantheon.

Lipset, Seymour Martin (1996). *American Exceptionalism: A Double-Edged Sword.* New York: W.W. Norton & Co.

Reese, Laura, and Raymond A. Rosenfeld (forthcoming). *The Civic Culture of Economic Development.* Thousand Oaks, CA: Sage Publications.

Secret, Philip E., James B. Johnson, & Audrey W. Forrest (1990). "The Impact of Religiosity on Political Participation and Membership in Voluntary Associations Among Black and White Americans." *Journal of Black Studies,* 21(1): 87–162.

Stone, Clarence (1989). *Regime Politics: Governing Atlanta 1946–1988.* Lawrence: University of Kansas Press.

U.S. Bureau of the Census. 1999. *Housing Vacancy Survey.* Online: <*http://www.census.gove/hhes/www.housing.html*>.

Taking the Next Step: Local Political Participation

✎ **Local Elections**

✎ **Variations on the Representative Government Theme**

✎ **Voter Turnout**

✎ **Other Forms of Participation**

✎ **Interpreting Local Participation**

✎ **Chapter Conclusion**

We have provided many examples of community involvement ranging from home to work to your place of worship. The community's civic network is vast! What of all this involvement is actually political? It's a fair question. The answer may not be satisfying: It all depends on the action that the most active people want to take. There is no clear and permanent dividing line between the civic and political worlds. In fact, politics is just one way a community gets things done.

Community groups and organizations are mostly private. They serve their members and provide a civic space for local people to come together to live, work, perform good deeds, worship, or share special common concerns. They only get politically involved when political action is what it takes to achieve their goals. The rest of the time, the members enjoy each other's company and carry out the good deeds of the organization.

America's community life is varied and robust, but citizens acting alone or in concert with their neighbors and co-workers cannot solve every problem. At some point, they must rely on representative government to act in the public interest. For this reason, Americans recognize the need for **general purpose local government.** General purpose local governments are created by state legislation in accordance with the state's constitution. They are given legislative, executive, and judicial responsibilities that are consistent with the state and national constitutions. The citizenry in local elections chooses officeholders, whose power is essentially to act on the wishes of local citizens so long as their enactments do not violate state or federal law. Local governments are far and away "closest to the people."

Three widespread general purpose governments are *municipalities*, *towns* or *townships*, and *counties*. We describe municipal and township government in Chapter 10 and county government in Chapter 11. These types of local government are expected to act on behalf of the community and its citizens. They have broad powers to protect and promote the public interest. For much of American history, general purpose governments seemed able to solve community-wide problems. Each generation has experienced its own challenges, and local governments have evolved to keep up with changing expectations. Elected councils or commissions give voice to public concerns and enact laws that serve the public interest. An elected executive provides overall community leadership and may share the daily administration of local government with a contracted local manager. Local judges enforce community laws and with local grand juries provide a mechanism for the relief of public grievances.

Today, the general purpose local governments are supplemented with various **special purpose local governments.** Special purpose local governments oversee specific local services such as recreation and education. We discuss special service districts and school districts in Chapter 11. These separate government structures are expected to act professionally in the public interest and without interference from community "politics as usual." Governance of recreation authorities and school districts also is vested in representative political institutions. A governing board is either popularly elected or appointed by local officials who are themselves elected by the people. An executive such as a recreation director or school superintendent reports to the board and perhaps is directly elected by the people. Formal written procedures are created to adjudicate grievances against the special purpose local governments. These special purpose governments are less familiar to most Americans, so we give them special attention in separate sections of Chapter 11.

The growth of special purpose local governments has led to *fragmented service delivery* in many communities. Education, recreation, and even water-control and garbage-disposal agencies each has its own minigovernment. Political accountability is difficult without central policy-making authority and an integrated single budget. We are served and taxed by so many different public entities that citizens have difficulty understanding their own local government. We address two approaches to easing the effects of fragmentation. In Chapter 11, we introduce the idea of consolidation, putting some or all services back under one local government. In Chapter 12, we look at metropolitan government, the efforts by large cities to rationalize services that cross city boundaries. So rest assured: We will return to the structure and operations of local government. But first we turn our attention to local politics.

Local political life is enjoyed by activists but generally appreciated even by the less active. In fact, Americans are usually more supportive of local government efforts than they are of national and state politics (National Public Radio, 2000). One reason for this support is that we more often personally know at least some of our local representatives. We are less likely to know state and federal officials. Another reason for support is that we feel more empowered to influence local decisions than we do state or national decisions. For example, the people speak for themselves directly through referendum votes, and local officials try to make their policies and programs acceptable to as many local citizens as possible. In fact, it is an axiom of democratic political life that governments are more responsive to the public the closer they are to them.

In this chapter, we ask ourselves several questions about how the public chooses and then interacts with its representatives:

- Which decisions do we want elected officials to make, and which do we prefer to retain for the electorate?
- Who among us is motivated to seek public office and why?
- Who is willing to participate in the political life of the community by helping candidates, registering voters, voting, or speaking out on the issues?
- Can we evaluate citizen participation in local government in such a way that we can generalize about how Americans perceive their self-government?

To the extent that we can address these political participation issues, we may be able to understand how local governments sometimes satisfy and sometimes frustrate public wishes. We can then estimate the extent to which our elected officials address our private neighborhood, business, civic, religious, and interest organization agendas by ballot measures and representative government. In other words, we can answer the question, How responsive are local governments in the United States?

❧ Local Elections

As we discussed in Chapter 4, the right to vote is a hard-earned civil right for minorities and women. We should not take it for granted, and we should be well-enough informed about local elections to make intelligent decisions about whether to vote and for whom or what we should vote. When it comes to election day, each citizen has the opportunity to choose political leaders and shape local government policy.

The popular ballot allows us to decide some city policies for ourselves. Almost half of all U.S. cities place important issues such as school-bond referenda and sales-tax extensions on ballots for public decision. When the public decides such matters, the process is known as **direct democracy.** More often, we select representatives to decide matters for us; this is called *indirect* or **representative democracy.** Many city officials are elected to hold office during general elections. The mayor, city council members, and city judges are typically selected at the ballot box. Because these officials are the critical policy makers of city government, we must carefully analyze their election.

Local elections are sometimes held throughout the year, not always in conjunction with state and national elections. It might be more efficient if all national, state, and local offices were filled at once. We would not go to the ballot box so often. However, many local officials want city elections to have their own spotlight and local decisions not to be overshadowed by or influenced by national and state elections. The people who staff the polls are city and county employees and community volunteers. The basis of representation is universal suffrage for all legal residents ages eighteen and older. Virtually all localities require citizens to register if they wish to vote; this ensures legal residence and reduces election fraud.

Popular Votes on the Issues

One type of decision that faces voters in local elections is the **referendum.** A referendum vote decides issues that public officials believe should be left to the citizenry. For example, if state law permits a local option sales tax, then the public may be entitled to vote it in. Other common referendum questions include whether to issue a series of school bonds, allow liquor by the drink to be served in restaurants, adopt an annexation plan to extend the city limits, or allow casino gambling. In each case, state law permits localities to decide the issue, and local officials want the public to do so.

Local referenda results are binding in some states and not in others. A study of 3,018 U.S. cities found that nonbinding referenda are found in 40 percent of the cities (Renner & DeSantis, 1998: 41). The nonbinding type of referendum is often found in Northeastern cities and is slightly more common in suburban towns than urban cities and rural communities. Binding referenda are just as common—in 42 percent of sampled cities—and most common in large cities.

One potentially troublesome problem with local referenda is their subject matter. Overall, roughly one-third of all referenda issues pass with public approval. However, three-fourths of all referenda votes that restrict the civil rights of minorities and gays have passed (Gamble, 1997). Public approval of a measure does not mean that it is necessarily the ethically right or constitutionally valid policy. Many referenda results are therefore subject to judicial review by state and federal courts.

Petitions are allowed on the ballot in 36 percent of the cities. The petition has been called a "protest referendum" because it delays implementation of a local ordinance until a future referendum is held (Renner & DeSantis, 1998: 39). This device is more common to middle-sized cities and those in the West.

Initiatives are decisions taken by the electorate to require action by city officials. The initiative is available in 58 percent of the cities and is used most by urban centers and least in small towns. The initiative also is most popular in Western states.

If officeholders are corrupt and have lost the public's confidence, then often they can be removed from office in a **recall** election. Sixty-eight percent of cities use the recall. It is most common in middle-sized and Midwestern cities.

Direct public involvement in policy making will likely increase in the future. Mass media bring issues into everyone's living room, and the Internet makes it easier and easier to poll the public. Proponents of *teledemocracy* foresee a day when many if not most local public policy issues can be decided directly by the people. Critics of teledemocracy argue with equal zeal that policy decisions made by the whim of public opinion may be inferior to those decided by thoughtful deliberation of elected officials. In any case, teledemocracy and direct democracy are obviously interrelated concepts. The integration of cable media with Internet services is already a reality for some high-end media consumers. Over time, such services may become affordable throughout our communities.

Electing City Officials

The election of local representatives opens a whole new line of inquiry for our study of local government. These officials enact public policy on our behalf, often claiming to act "in the public interest." We need to talk about the men and women who seek elective office, why they run, to whom they respond, and how well they represent their constituents.

Council Elections. The **city council** is the legislative body of municipal government. It represents the community and ultimately at least a portion of the community power structure. The members of the city council often are called *councilmen, council members,* or *aldermen.* City councils typically consist of five to nine members, although in large cities there may be thirty or more council seats. Meetings are held weekly or biweekly. The time and place are established in a routine that the public can appreciate and remember. For example, city council in a smaller city might meet on the first Tuesday of each month at 9 A.M. and on the third Tuesday at 6 P.M. By avoiding either all-morning or all-evening meetings, the city government tries to accommodate different peoples' work schedules. Notices of the meetings are made in the local newspaper and on local radio, television, and cable channels.

Election Structures. In the majority of cities, especially small cities, members are chosen in **at-large elections** (see Table 9.1). Large urban cities use a different electoral system: Each member is elected from a **single-member district** or **ward.** Use of single-member districts means that a single person will be chosen to represent a neighborhood or group of neighborhoods. This is undoubtedly a reflection of the continuing need for reforms aimed at ensuring fair ethnic and neighborhood representation (Welch, 1990). As a group, then, the big city council is quite diverse, with representatives from widely differing neighborhoods coming together to make public policy.

Table 9.1
Basis of Representation for Cities, 1998

| | *Percentage* | | |
Population	At-Large	District	Mixed
250,000+	23	32	44
100,000–250,000	40	22	38
50,000–100,000	49	14	37
25,000–50,000	54	17	29
10,000–25,000	60	16	24
5,000–10,000	62	17	22
2,500–5,000	63	19	18
Less than 2,500	81	9	11

Source: Adapted from Renner and DeSantis (1998): 40.

Ensuring diversity in a city that clings to at-large representation requires another approach. If neighborhood associations want to have "one of their own" elected to council, then they must follow a *coalition* strategy. Although one association has relatively few members, a coalition of ten or twelve diverse neighborhood associations can represent a large voting block. Similarly, a single business association, church congregation, or issue organization may be weak in electoral power, but a coalition within or across these groups can be strong. In local electoral politics, there is strength in numbers.

In both at-large and single-member district systems, council members are elected for a *fixed term* in office. A typical term of office for a council member

Council ward map of Bloomington, Illinois. This is typical of the way many cities' wards or districts are shaped as they evolve over time.

can be two, three, or four years, depending on the jurisdiction. Larger communities have begun to impose **term limits** on council members, but the overall percentage of cities with term limits is still quite small, just under 10 percent (Renner & DeSantis, 1998: 38). The council elections are held on a *nonpartisan* basis in three-quarters of U.S. municipalities, which means no party labels are shown next to the names listed on the ballot. Virtually all local council elections of West Coast states are nonpartisan, while mid-Atlantic states overwhelmingly prefer to print ballots with party labels for each candidate.

Collecting Your Thoughts *What Is Fair Representation?*

Put yourself in the position of being a member of your state's constitutional revision commission. Cities in your state now use at-large elections to fill city council seats. A neighborhood activist from your home town has written you asking that the law be changed to require single-member election districts. Draft a brief reply to the request and state your reasons for being for or against such districts. Be prepared to discuss your reasoning with the other "commission members" in your class.

Candidate Selection. City council candidates must operate from some community *power base.* In many cases, the power base includes members from one or more of the community organizations discussed in the last chapter. Because the city council is basically the entry level for people who seek elective office, few candidates other than incumbent council members will have a public-service track record. Relevant experience has to be interpreted in community leadership terms. One candidate may be a successful business owner who claims that his or her private-sector budgetary or management expertise can transfer to the public sector. Or an individual may be a retired neighborhood activist who can claim people skills and leadership abilities that qualify him or her for elective office. In either case, a record of sustained community involvement becomes a major credential for nonincumbents who wish to serve on a city council.

During the first half of this century, city council members were drawn from the ranks of local elites (Prewitt & Eulau, 1971: 301). The franchise was restricted, and political machines could manipulate working-class voters. Today, candidacy is not limited to elites. Many council members come from lower middle-class backgrounds, and virtually all have been active in civic organizations.

Knowledge of a wide range of policy issues is not required to run for city council. This is because the national government and the state governments determine most social policy in the United States. Local governments are usually left with the task of implementing social policies and programs they did not craft. A wide range of eligibility requirements can be found for council office because relatively little policy expertise or professional status is required for service on the part-time, poorly paid city councils.

Council Election Campaigns. Getting on the ballot for a local election usually means *qualifying* through a petition process. A prescribed number of signatures of locally registered voters will have to be filed by a certain date well before the election. A small *filing fee* is paid to the city clerk at the same time. This petition approach is common in communities that use nonpartisan elections. In partisan election jurisdictions, a local political caucus may anoint a candidate, or a primary may be held to decide among several interested persons. In cities throughout the United States, local officials follow the requirements set out in state law for conducting local elections.

The organization and financing of an election bid requires that the candidate creates a *campaign committee* to help him or her get elected. This group of close friends and associates raises funds, contacts prospective voters, and helps advertise the candidacy. Although local council elections are not typically expensive, the costs of media advertising and printing campaign materials can easily outstrip the budget of an individual candidate and his or her family.

The council candidates and their supporters hit the streets as the date for the city election nears. Their tasks are twofold: to make sure potential supporters are registered to vote and make sure that supporters turn out on election day. All campaign activity is related to achieving these goals. It will do a neighborhood activist no good to articulate the issues that trouble many city residents if those residents do not follow through by registering and voting.

There are important differences between campaigning in relatively affluent and poorer council districts. In poor neighborhoods, there are fewer community organizations and financial resources to devote to electioneering. If the election is partisan, then poorer neighborhoods will be tightly organized in an effort to build block voting. If the elections are nonpartisan, then the community institutions that exist—like the African American church and the unionized workers—will be especially important to any candidate who seeks office. The keys are the political resources and leadership skills of community residents (Brady, Verba, & Schlozman, 1995).

If all council seats are elected at-large, then media advertising—the only way to reach the necessary number of prospective voters—will play an important role. In at-large elections, poorer candidates are at a decided disadvantage. They rarely have the wide network of connections needed to build a citywide grassroots campaign or the finances to mount a sustained citywide media blitz.

Role of Incumbents. We have already noted that incumbents have a great advantage in city-council elections: They have a track record, name recognition, and a network of perennial supporters. But *why* would these individuals want to serve another term in office? What are the "perks" (from the word *perquisite*) of office that keep council members motivated and satisfied enough with their job to seek reelection?

The material rewards of council service are modest. Recent data on larger U.S. cities report that thirty-six of the fifty reported council salaries were less than $50,000 per year (*Time Almanac 2000*: 790). Large urban centers such as New York City and Los Angeles paid modestly professional salaries. Many small cities and towns that were not reported in the study pay no more than token amounts.

The satisfactions of public service on city council instead are intrinsic—that is, more psychological than material. One psychic payoff for council service is the perceived significance of the work. Challenging tasks that require a variety of skills present a meaningful use of time for local legislative officials (Lascher, 1993). In smaller communities, the challenge of the work may even outweigh other intrinsic rewards such as public recognition and a desire for public service (Sokolow, 1989). An incumbent who feels that he or she has done a good job and accomplished a great deal in office would seek to remain in office. Incumbents' high reelection rate suggests that voters appreciate a job well done.

Exploring on Your Own **Are City Councils Diverse?**

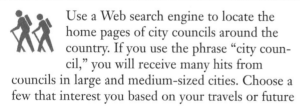 Use a Web search engine to locate the home pages of city councils around the country. If you use the phrase "city council," you will receive many hits from councils in large and medium-sized cities. Choose a few that interest you based on your travels or future professional plans. Many of these home pages will have photographs and names of the current council members. Note how many are African American, Hispanic, and Asian. Also note how many women serve on the city councils you find. Be prepared to discuss your findings with those of your classmates.

Mayoral Elections

The **mayor** is the elected leader of city government. The mayor of a large city is the one very visible elected official. Go to the Web page of any major U.S. city—the mayor's smiling face will be there to greet you. These chief executives of their communities have many significant ceremonial duties. In some cities, they are also the chief administrative officers of city government. In large cities, mayors are well-paid, full-time officials, and they have substantial staff support (Pressman, 1972). They have access to the media and local network connections to keep their visibility high. One recent mayor of New York

Mayoral elections require plenty of person-to-person contact between candidates and voters in addition to skillful use of various media, including television, radio, and newspaper advertising.

Source: © Associated Press / Lenny Ignelzi

City was asked if he would like to run for the presidency. He replied "Why? I'm already the mayor of New York."

The job of mayor is not easy. As regime theory points out, mayors have to maintain supportive relationships with those who control the city's economic development. This means working with the developers, realtors, investors, and business owners of the city who generate jobs and tax revenues. Likewise, the mayor must work with individual citizens, neighborhood associations, unions, environmental groups, and other civic organizations to satisfy their respective policy preferences.

City bureaucracy is another major force that the mayor must accommodate. City employees deliver the services that sustain many contractors and citizens, and they also wield considerable political clout, especially when unionized. If these political challenges were not enough, mayors must deal with intergovernmental relations with the national and state governments. Many of the public policies and fiscal resources that flow into the city are from these sources.

Electoral Structure. In three-fourths of American cities, the mayor is elected directly by the people. In the others, the mayor is selected by the council (Renner & DeSantis, 1998: 35). In some cities, the mayor functions as a chief executive much like the president or governor. In others, the mayor's duties are largely ceremonial. In most cities, the mayor presides over meetings of the city council. We will have more to say about the structure and duties of the mayor's office in the next chapter. For the purpose of our discussion of local elections, suffice it to say that the mayor is elected city-wide and is therefore accountable to all segments of the community.

Candidate Selection. Candidates for mayor usually have been active in the community for some time. They are well connected in the network of voluntary organizations and often have served in leadership posts in neighborhood, business, civic, religious, or special interest groups. They are often recognized leaders in their profession. Many have been elected to city council in the past. Most are articulate and even charismatic figures who perform well in front of the television cameras. Most have photogenic families and are positive role models for the city's youth. In other words, prospective candidates need to be active, clean cut leaders who have many positive hooks to snare the voter.

Election Campaigns. In cities that use partisan elections, the mayoral candidate will likely be a party regular. To be selected by the local party caucus or primary, the mayoral candidate will have to be acceptable to rank-and-file party activists. In nonpartisan city elections, image and ideas play a larger role. The mayoral candidate needs to be able to conceptualize and articulate a positive image of the city's future. In the election itself, the candidates' personas will be compared and their ideas debated. Perhaps most important, the voters must trust the successful mayoral candidate. He or she must appear to be the right person to lead the city in its economic and social development.

Financing a bid for the mayor's office can be a difficult assignment, especially for challengers. The candidate's campaign committee must approach individuals and groups to raise the money needed for political advertising and publications. Most contributors and groups will want the candidate to adopt some position favorable to them. The successful candidate must be agreeable enough to secure that support but independent enough not to be handcuffed once elected.

Local Judicial Elections

City court deals with the enforcement of local ordinances and the settling of minor disputes between citizens. The presiding judges of these "inferior courts" may be known by titles such as *justice of the peace, magistrate,* or *traffic court judge.*

The maximum penalty for violation of a local ordinance is usually a fine, a short term in the local jail, or local probation supervision. These minor infractions are called *misdemeanors.* More serious criminal law violations are called *felonies* and are tried in state courts.

State laws prescribe a dollar value beyond which local small claims cases may not go. Civil cases that involve large amounts of money are heard in state courts.

By and large, we consider inferior court judges to be local officials who are asked to deal with minor crimes and minor conflicts between community residents.

In small cities and towns, local judges are not necessarily attorneys. As part-time local officials, these individuals typically hold court in city hall or even in the judge's place of business or home. In larger cities, the magistrates are somewhat more professionalized. They are trained attorneys with a special interest in criminal and civil law. They work full-time and are paid a relatively modest salary (Blair, 1986: 221). The urban courts are more specialized. One may deal with traffic violations; another may hear juvenile delinquency cases. Although not a prestigious position among lawyers, a local magistrate receives the satisfaction of helping to solve community problems and manage local conflicts.

Local judges are elected, typically for fixed terms on a nonpartisan ballot. In small communities, the election is almost purely a popularity contest. In large cities, the legal community has considerable influence on the nomination and campaigns of the candidates. Incumbent judges are hard to unseat, and few communities have term limits for local judgeships.

Individuals themselves decide whether to run for most local judicial elections. They may feel they have the proper disposition for the bench. Or they may be politically or socially active people who want to contribute to the community. Others may seek the office because they dislike the pressures of private law practice and prefer the security of a regular paycheck. There could be as many motivations as there are different individuals who run for the office of local magistrate.

Voters select between candidates when there is an open judgeship—for example, when a magistrate retires. When an incumbent seeks reelection, he or she is typically returned to office unless some scandal has tarnished his or her reputation. Beyond these basics, winning the election is often a matter of name recognition. By the time the voter reaches the end of the ballot, most of the exciting decisions for council seats and the mayor's office have been made, and the voter is anxious to finish the ballot. Citizens may not appreciate the local magistrate's job until that day when they have to appear in traffic or small claims court.

It is good that the costs for the contest for a magistrate's post are relatively small. The judge has few perks to hand out once in office. Unlike the mayor and council members who can hand out lucrative city contracts, the local judge does not direct much spending. The individual office seeker often bears the costs of his or her election. Nonetheless, the post of local magistrate may be one of the most important—even though most overlooked—positions in local government.

❧ Variations on the Representative Government Theme

We have described the election of city council members, mayors, and judges. A similar process takes place in the election of township supervisors, treasurers, clerks, board members, county commission members, chairs of county commissions, and county judges. American communities also elect members of the school board and, in some cases, the superintendent of schools. Other variations involve the population of the jurisdiction: Distinctions can be made between small rural towns and large cities, as well as between rural and metropolitan regions.

County executives are elected under the commission form of government (explained in Chapter 11). Chair of the county commission is the closest office the county has to that of city mayor. This person directs meetings of the county commission and serves as a weak executive between commission meetings. As more and more urban counties have adopted the commission–manager form of government, the county manager has taken over daily supervision of the county's employees. This leaves the chair with fewer executive duties.

County commissioners are elected at-large in many jurisdictions. In counties where racial discrimination has been asserted, a system of districts may have been created. Even so, counties may mix at-large seats with district seats in composing the overall county commission membership. In all of these situations, the chair is either elected countywide or chosen by the commissioners. Elections for county commissioner follow a pattern that may now be familiar: Incumbents have an advantage based on patronage and a network of relatives, neighbors, and supporters. Challengers have a hard time raising money to run a countywide race. Potential donors do not want to risk offending the incumbent.

School board elections are yet another variation on the elected representatives theme. Elected school boards make policy concerning the education of many community students. The members have broad control over the content and funding of school programs. Candidates are typically concerned parents who have an interest in or strong thoughts about the public schools. Many candidates are professionals, and retired teachers or principals are often elected to seats on the school board.

In county and school board elections and in small town elections, citizens are more likely to know the candidates' personalities. Political relatives are more likely to be helpful. In fact, some smaller communities have generations of "political families" whose members have served in elective office for decades. Local elections in small communities are truly "up close and personal" political experiences. They are part of continuing the "civic memory" that is so often absent in large cities (Dagger, 1981).

Some political scientists and political reformers have advocated a shift from at-large election of representatives to elections based on single-member districts. These reformers argue that neighborhoods in general and minority neighborhoods in particular are best served by having their own council seats (Harrington & Vogel, 2000: 122). Other reformers have argued just the opposite view. They have contended that political machines can easily control particular neighborhoods. It is much more difficult to control an at-large election.

Some of the reforms that were designed to clean up local politics, however, actually have dampened citizen interest in local elections. For example, nonpartisan electoral systems and the council–manager form of government are associated with low voter turnout (Karnig & Walters, 1983; Dye, 1997). Political parties' debates on local issues and an interesting field of mayoral candidates may add interest to a local election. Without partisanship and the debate it brings, local elections may seem so lackluster that citizens fail to turn out to vote.

❧ Voter Turnout

Recall from our earlier discussion of state elections that individuals must register to vote before they can participate on election day. U.S. history is replete with entrenched elites erecting barriers to voting. Still, each generation has expanded the franchise until we now enjoy nearly universal suffrage. The most recent reform was the passage of the National Voter Registration Act of 1993, the so-called Motor Voter Act. Today, registering to vote is not a restrictive process. The individual may register by declaring a local residence and is then assigned a polling place near that residence. Simple voter-registration forms can be picked up at and delivered to government offices and registrars' booths throughout a city or county.

With many offices at stake and with local issues ranking high in the concerns of community residents, we might expect that voter turnout at the polls would be high in city elections. Actually, participation in *off-year local elections* typically is lower than in years in which a U.S. president is elected. On average, only 30 percent of registered voters turn out in these *nonconcurrent elections* compared with as high as 60 percent in presidential elections (Peterson, 1981). On the other hand, local elections that are "piggybacked" on national elections benefit from the higher voter turnout. Georgia elections provide an interesting illustration of this difference (see **Table 9.2**).

In communities throughout Georgia, registered voters went to the polls in November 1996 and November 1998. True to the 1996 national average,

Table 9.2
Georgia Election Returns

Voters	1996 (Presidential) Election Turnout	1998 (Off-Year) Election Turnout
Black females	58.4	45.5
Black males	49.1	38.7
White females	64.2	47.2
White males	64.4	49.3
Other voters	50.9	28.4

Note: Turnout is calculated as percent of registered voters.

Source: Georgia Secretary of State, *Comparative Election Trends*, 1999.

approximately 60 percent of all people who were registered to vote turned out and cast their ballots. The turnout was 10 points lower for African American men and voters who are neither black nor white. In the off-year election of 1998, the turnout fell off by approximately 15 percentage points.

Comparing 1996 and 1998, African Americans retained more of their voting strength than did whites. For example, the turnout for white women fell seventeen points, while that for black women slipped only fourteen points. This resulted in the rough parity of women voters of both races in 1998. White male turnout fell almost twenty-three points, while that for black men slipped only ten points. This still left the turnout rates for black men well below those for white men. Perhaps most notably, voter turnout among Hispanics, Asians, and other nonblack minorities plummeted more than twenty-two points. The turnout was half of what it had been in the 1996 presidential election. There appeared to be little that interested those voters in the off-year election campaigns.

Low voter turnout in off-year elections is found to some degree throughout the world. A study of European countries showed similar trends in off-year elections (Morlan, 1984). The gap between national and purely local election turnout is smaller in Germany and the Scandinavian countries than in the United States, but it is repeatedly there.

In the United States, turnout is even lower in nonconcurrent elections, or those in which not even state positions are being filled. Sixty percent of all cities hold nonconcurrent elections, reasoning that local issues need to be highlighted in local elections (Dye, 1997: 319). In fact, separating local elections leads to lower turnout, and that low turnout probably reflects lessened citizen interest.

Exploring on Your Own **Citizen Access to Local Government Information**

CivicZone.com is an Internet gateway that connects people to their local government resources. Managed from Alexandria, Virginia, the Web site manages databases full of community information for localities throughout the United States. In a recent survey it conducted, CivicZone.com found citizens need and want a wide variety of information about such matters as voter registration, finding lost animals, local crime reports, community calendars, zoning and building codes, and directions to city offices and parks. Explore this interesting new service for busy citizens at *<http://www.civiczone.com/>*.

The critical point is that different people vote in presidential years than in off-year or nonconcurrent years. Citizens must be more motivated to turn out for elections in which the relatively interesting presidential or gubernatorial races are absent. This makes hardcore organization at the civic or grassroots level essential for local races.

We have already noted that candidates and their supporters have to be very active in soliciting votes. However, what motivates an individual to vote in local elections, especially in an off-year election? Longstanding political science research suggests that psychological involvement, partisanship, social status, and age significantly affect turnout in city elections. Some people feel their opinions and preferences are important, and others do not. We refer to this sense of political potency as **political efficacy.** In local elections, more "efficacious" people turn out to vote, while the less efficacious stay away from the polls. While it is true that efficacious people turn out for all elections, it is significant that they continue to vote in local elections even without the luster of a national race (Hamilton, 1971). We therefore must ask, Who are these efficacious citizens? They are disproportionately the most civically involved citizens—by implication, *not* poor, alienated, or transient. In local elections, candidates must spend a disproportionate amount of time appealing to neighborhood association members, active businesspeople and professionals, civic club members, and interest group activists. These are the politically efficacious citizens who will most likely be registered and who will show up and vote.

An important caveat must be added about local elections that *do* coincide with major national and state elections. The 1996 national election attracted a great deal of public attention. A hotly charged presidential race brought many voters to the polls. The Democratic Party was able to activate its base of support among African Americans and organized labor, two constituencies that are important in urban centers. Minority and liberal candidates in local elections benefited from the high turnout as activated voters proceeded down their ballots to consider local races. The Democrats did well again in 1998.

Many active citizens are either political party members or independents who strongly identify with a political party. Because so many city, county, and school board elections are nonpartisan, we must ask, Does **partisanship** matter in local races? The best evidence suggests that "disguised party politics" is at work in many cities that have two-party competitive races at the state level (Dye, 1997: 282). The coalitions of interests—minorities, organized labor, and liberals for Democrats; businesses and conservatives for Republicans—persist to some degree at all levels of U.S. politics. In other words, the partisanship factor spills over from the state level into local politics during election campaigns, even when party labels for local contests are not included on the official ballot.

Some theorists argue that *social status* has an influence on local election turnout. The growth of the U.S. middle class has been accompanied by an increase in the proportion of the electorate that considers itself independent of either major political party. At the same time, we have had a growth of identity politics, a tendency to support and vote for people of our own social class. If candidates can appeal successfully without party labels and if they can rise to elective office primarily on the basis of their race or gender, then social class becomes important. However, identity politics is a game played at all income levels. Wealthy "outsiders" might have just as much trouble attracting inner-city minority voters as African American business owners might have attracting suburban white voters. Local political campaigns may become so compartmentalized under single-member districts that no one on a council can claim to really represent the community at large.

Finally, *age* matters. Voting represents different perceived costs to people at different stages of the life cycle. College students are eligible to register and vote but may not because they do not see how voting benefits them personally or professionally. The same could be said for many young professionals who work extraordinary hours to establish economic security. Young families often have their hands full with two jobs and the demands of young children. In other words, there are disincentives for younger citizens when it comes to political involvement—even the simple act of casting a ballot in local elections.

By contrast, middle-aged individuals and families that are more economically secure have had cause to consider how government might improve their lives. There are economic issues at stake that may benefit the middle-aged voter, who is typically more active in the neighborhood, professional, and civic groups—that is, the places where many political cues are given.

Finally, older people in general and retirees in particular are politically quite active. They have the time and the interest to follow local issues. Candidates actively seek the support of senior citizens because they are almost always registered to vote and do so in large numbers. Special efforts even are made to transport elderly voters to the polls on election day.

✎ Other Forms of Participation

Individuals can offer public service in many ways other than as candidates, supporting candidates, or voting. Local government is replete with boards and commissions that regulate everything from zoning appeals to historic preservation plans to downtown redevelopment. Although the actions of these boards and commissions are usually advisory, elected officials set great stock in their recommendations (Fleischmann & Pierannunzi, 1990).

Research on such local board and commission members suggests that there are several identifiable motivations to serve (Baker, 1994). For many individuals, service to the community is the leading motivation. More personally, volunteers enjoy the social solidarity and personal development that comes from working with others. Some board members even thrive on the attention they receive as associates of local government officials. (See Table 9.3.)

Intergovernmental program mandates may often require the involvement of local citizens from a target population. "Maximum feasible participation" was ordered in many federal programs beginning with the War on Poverty

Table 9.3

Survey of Voluntary Boards in Fifteen Ohio Cities

Motivations for Volunteering	Percent of All Respondents
1. Opportunity to address problems	89
2. Citizen obligation	83
3. Habit of always being involved	64
4. Citizens perceive individual's expertise	57
5. City perceives expertise	51

Source: Adapted from Baker (1994): 124.

during the 1960s and 1970s. Similar citizen-participation mandates have continued in less-intrusive form in the Model Cities Program and today's Community Development Block Grant Program. Clearly, the national government has tried to ensure that local governments are responsive to the people served by federal grants.

In this way, many sectors of the local community are involved in the development and implementation of regulatory policies and social service programs. Middle-class citizens and residents of poorer neighborhoods may or may not serve on many of the same boards. Nevertheless, both groups have been built into the decision-making processes of local government.

❧ Interpreting Local Participation

There appears to be a progression of political participation ranging from total apathy to heavy commitment to civic and political life. The totally apathetic local resident might be described as someone who is not involved with neighborhood, business, or civic groups and who is not even registered to vote. The more involved individual joins groups and votes. The even more politically active person participates in election campaigns and serves on local boards and commissions. The ultimate political activist runs for elective office and sustains a lifelong commitment to community development. Obviously, the range of behavior is broad.

One useful way to track levels of political involvement is to imagine a ladder of citizen participation that individuals and groups must climb to attain real control of their local government (Arnstein, 1969). At the ground level, there is no involvement. At the top of the ladder is meaningful control of the policies and programs of your local government. At regular intervals along the way, people and groups must mobilize to overcome the civic pathologies of manipulation and tokenism. We have adapted Sherry Arnstein's scheme to incorporate the political science concepts and terms already presented.

At different levels of involvement, citizens are subject to varying degrees of *manipulation*. Who benefits from an individual or a group being outside of the election process? Obviously, the people in power in a local community maintain their privileged position by attracting the support of some citizens, overcoming the opposition of others, and enjoying the abstention from politics of yet others. Organizations such as Operation Push try to get residents of underprivileged neighborhoods more involved in the political life of the community. Their motto has been: "If you don't vote, you don't count!" So, one level of manipulation is to keep nonsupporters out of the political arena altogether. Manipulation also can be achieved by organizing blocks of

Local participation and volunteer work in community programs often fill the needs that are not addressed by state and federal programs.
Source: © J. Van Hasselt / Corbis Sygma

voters who just do as they are told and never question officials who are supposed to represent them. That is the essence of machine politics. Finally, politicians can manipulate the public by appointing a handful of underrepresented residents to meaningless campaign posts or the most impotent local regulatory boards. This gives the appearance of involvement without requiring that the politician actually consider the ideas or feelings of local residents.

Tokenism is another step up the rungs of political involvement. Local politicians are adept at knowing when they must take notice of neighborhood, business, civic, religious, or special interest groups. Astute politicians can gain a measure of support by simply informing individuals and groups about issues or decisions that affect them. Speaking to local groups costs the public official little, and the goodwill earned can be valuable. A politician may even go further and specifically consult with the group. By publicly soliciting its members' input, the local official may seem to be building an agenda from the grass roots. Of course, some occasional change in direction is required to prove that the input was more than a gesture. Otherwise, the consultation is merely tokenism.

Finally, the public official may placate an active community group by giving it some small victory on a narrow issue. This *placation* is designed to end the demands of a group without actually building it into the network of political influence. This tactic might work well in the case of local interest groups. Winning the particular issue and then going away might placate an environmental group that is upset over a particular ecological threat. The key to this form of tokenism is to not really include the group in the political system. Some local activists call this strategy "throwing them a bone."

Manipulation and tokenism are present in most cities, towns, and counties. They can present an especially difficult problem when the local government is armed with a large cadre of policy specialists, planners, and career bureaucrats. Smaller cities and nonmetropolitan counties suffer less because local officials need the real and substantial support of local citizens to get the job of governing done. In many ways, smaller jurisdictions enjoy more public accountability.

Some cities—both large and small—recognize and respect the power of citizens and community groups. *Citizen empowerment* takes many forms, and it has been championed by "reinventing government" insiders and activist reformers alike. The central tenant of citizen empowerment is that local residents know the community's problems and have the creative energy and self-interested strength of purpose to solve them. What they often lack are technical expertise and resources, both of which can be provided by government in exchange for the considerable local tax dollars that citizens pay each year.

One approach to citizen empowerment is to form *partnerships* between community organizations and local government agencies or contractors. Neighborhood associations can be partners in cleanup campaigns, pedestrian safety studies, neighborhood watch programs, waste recycling, and many other activities that are important to government and private citizens alike. Local governments and business groups, civic organizations, churches, and special interest groups can conduct similar cooperative efforts. In the partnership agreement, the community group launches significant self-help actions while the local government extends its capabilities through volunteer workers. Both parties benefit in material ways, and both secure each other's goodwill.

A second empowerment approach is *delegated power.* Local governments enjoy a measure of coercive power by virtue of the authority given to them under the state's constitution. For example, local government can build, operate, and police public-housing projects, recreation facilities, and civic center auditoriums. Government sometimes contracts with private businesses to operate some of these activities, and cities and counties certainly can similarly delegate power to neighborhood, business, civic, religious, and special interest groups. An environmental group can operate a nature preserve under contract with city government. A civic club can maintain and operate a baseball diamond complex under contract. And a ministerial alliance can sponsor an after-school program for youth. All of these efforts are examples of delegated power. The community organization makes policy, enforces rules, and serves the public much like a local government agency. They cannot act any way they please, however; they must respect relevant laws that govern such activities. Still, compliance with relevant federal, state, and local laws, along with appropriate financial and evaluation details, can be outlined in the contract agreement between the local government and each organization.

Finally, empowered citizens may actually control an aspect of local power. *Citizen control* of what are usually thought to be public matters is not as common as delegated power. However, in some cases, such control has proven to be the appropriate mechanism for solving a community problem. With citizen control, local government turns over an activity to a community organization. With the exception of ensuring that relevant laws are obeyed, the local officials take a hands-off stance. One illustration of this approach in action is the turning over of a public-housing project to its tenants' association. In some cities, public housing has deteriorated to the point that living conditions are unsanitary and unsafe. In a last-ditch effort to save this important housing resource, adventuresome housing authorities have agreed to requests by tenant groups to let them control the projects. Operating like a private concern, the tenants' association collects rents, undertakes repairs, and hires private police to secure the complex. In many cases, residents are hired to do the repairs and police the facility. Who better knows the needs of that complex? Who has more at stake than the residents themselves? In several well-documented cases, virtual sale of public-housing projects have saved them from total destruction and abandonment. In addition to the material rewards, residents have a feeling of ownership and pride in what they have accomplished. Once restored and made safe, several of these citizen-controlled complexes appear to have good prospects for the future.

There are many degrees of active citizen power, just as there are degrees of tokenism and manipulation. This is why the continuum of citizen participation can be well represented by a ladder metaphor. The progression from passive victim of government to its powerful ally can and does take place. Generally speaking, we can expect community organizations increasingly to act in their own behalf.

This optimistic forecast notwithstanding, we must be cautious about speaking of local communities as if they were all alike. There are many types of communities in the United States. People who live in large urban centers, medium-sized cities, and suburban and rural towns or townships have some of the same social dynamics. However, the variety and magnitude of the problems that locals face are quite different in New York City than in rural Colorado. Because of these differing task environments, governments have developed different approaches to learning about and responding to community needs. We will discuss these differing structural approaches to local government in the next several chapters.

Differences in social realities lead to variations in citizen expectations of government. Urban residents must rely on public services for many of their needs. This leads to ever-rising expectations about the range and quality of services. People who live in rural areas are relatively self-reliant. They have land and space, and they resist taxes, regulation, and government programs. Suburbanites fall somewhere in-between. They like urban-quality services at cheap rural tax rates. As Americans move from place to place over the course of a lifetime, they experience many different types of local government. We cannot begin to describe all of the variations in local public policy, but we will continue to introduce local policy options in the chapters that follow.

❧ Chapter Conclusion

Despite these limitations, we have tried to answer the basic questions of who wants to be involved in politics, how people get involved in politics, and why residents often feel the need to step up and take charge of their own futures.

- We have pointed out linkages between civic life and politics, between public concern and public policy. We have found that some community concerns make their way onto the public agenda. Some issues are resolved by referenda, and some by elected representatives. There are, moreover, several routes to the public resolution of civic concerns.

- We have looked at the motivations and power bases of people who become candidates for local office. Obviously, in a representative democracy, the question of who shall represent whom is critical. Again, there are many different ways in which citizens are represented, many pathways to power.

- We have looked at political participation and found that not everyone is registered to vote and not all registered voters turn out for a local election. Clearly, media coverage and the charisma of local candidates affect voter interest in an election. Yet there are many ways of participating; voting is just one.

The overall picture of local citizen participation in local government is mixed. Different issues activate different constituencies at different points in time. However, we hope that you will agree: Grassroots politics sometimes leads to real self-government. There is little doubt that Americans are competent to govern themselves, but there is concern that we may not be interested enough to bother. We then leave the field of political power to ambitious individuals and the interests they represent.

Key Words for InfoTrac Exploration

local elections	tokenism	voter turnout	women city council members

Sources Cited

Arnstein, Sherry R. (1969). "A Ladder of Citizen Participation." *Journal of the American Institute of Planners, 35* (July): 217.

Baker, John B. (1994). "Government in the Twilight Zone: Motivations of Volunteers to Small City Boards and Commissions." *State and Local Government Review, 26*(2) (Spring): 119–128.

Blair, George S. (1986). *Government at the Grass Roots* (4th ed.). Pacific Palisades, CA: Palisades Publishers.

Brady, Henry E., Sidney Verba, and Kay Lehman Schlozman (1995). "Beyond SES: A Resource Model of Political Participation." *American Political Science Review, 89*(2) (June): 271–294.

Dagger, Richard (1981). "Metropolis, Memory, and Citizenship." *American Journal of Political Science, 25*(4) (November): 715–737.

Dye, Thomas (1997). *Politics in States and Communities* (9th ed.). Upper Saddle River, NJ: Prentice-Hall.

Fleischmann, Arnold, and Carol A. Pierannunzi (1990). "Citizens, Development Interests, and Local Land-Use Regulation." *Journal of Politics, 52*(3) (August): 838–853.

Gamble, Barbara S. (1997). "Putting Civil Rights to a Popular Vote." *American Journal of Political Science, 41*(1) (January): 245–269.

Hamilton, Howard D. (1971). "The Municipal Voter: Voting and Nonvoting in City Elections." *American Political Science Review, 65*(4) (December): 1135–1140.

Harrigan, John J., and Ronald K. Vogel (2000). *Political Change in the Metropolis* (6th ed.). New York: Longman.

Karnig, Albert K., and B. Oliver Walters (1983). "Decline in Municipal Turnout: A Function of Changing Structure." *American Politics Quarterly, 11*(4) (October): 491–505.

Lascher, Edward L. (1993). "Explaining the Appeal of Local Legislative Office." *State and Local Government Review, 25*(1) (Winter): 28–38.

Morlan, Robert L. (1984). "Municipal vs. National Election Voter Turnout: Europe and the United States." *Political Science Quarterly, 99*(3) (Autumn): 457–470.

National Public Radio (2000). "Americans Distrust Government, but Want It to Do More." *Morning Edition* broadcast July 28.

Peterson, Paul E. (1981). *City Limits*. Chicago: University of Chicago Press.

Pressman, Jeffrey L. (1972). "Preconditions of Mayoral Leadership." *American Political Science Review, 66* (June): 511–524.

Prewitt, Kenneth, and Heinz Eulau (1971). "Social Bias in Leadership Selection, Political Recruitment, and Electoral Context." *Journal of Politics, 33*(2): 293–315.

Renner, Tari, and Victor S. DeSantis (1998). "Municipal Form of Government: Issues and Trends." *The Municipal Yearbook—1998*. Washington, DC: International City Management Association.

Sokolow, Alvin D. (1989). "Legislators Without Ambition: Why Small Town Citizens Seek Political Office." *State and Local Government Review, 21*(1) (Winter): 23–30.

Time Almanac 2000. New York: Time-Warner.

Welch, Susan (1990). "The Impact of At-Large Elections on the Representation of Blacks and Hispanics." *Journal of Politics, 52*(4) (November): 1050–1076.

10

Navigating City Hall: How Local Government Is Structured

- ❧ **The Big Picture of Local Government Structure**
- ❧ **Historical Background of Local Government Structure**
- ❧ **Municipal Government Structure**
- ❧ **Townships**
- ❧ **Duties of City Officials**
- ❧ **Chapter Conclusion**

We started our discussion of local government by talking about citizen concerns that are close to home (Chapter 8) and the various approaches citizens take when participating in local government (Chapter 9). Now we are better oriented to the environment of wide-ranging needs and wants around us. Our community organizations meet some of our needs, but they shift into direct political action when an issue or a government decision hits a nerve. As we saw in Chapter 8, such events are important and not particularly rare. Local issues such as traffic safety, economic development, and community race relations present situations in which empowered citizens are concerned and make demands, and local political officials must respond. By electing mayors and council members, and through a wide array of other forms of involvement in local affairs, we express our concerns about how we are governed and which services we receive.

Local governments make dozens of decisions every week, and most of them are routine and noncontroversial. We elect representatives of the public to make these routine decisions in our name. These elected officials delegate tremendous responsibilities to professional city employees to act on their behalf. We expect these elected and administrative officials to deal with the mundane details of matters such as hiring city employees, reviewing departmental budgets, and contracting for construction projects in the community. These officials give local services close attention so that we can enjoy the luxury of paying special attention to only those issues that interest us. This is the essence of representative democracy. But it also is a lot of responsibility for the officeholders.

To the normal mix of challenges that face city government we must add the considerable *antigovernment bias* that many citizens hold today. An often-cited admission from students enrolled in introductory political science classes is something like this: "I just don't like government, so please try to make this course as painless as possible!" In many ways, these students are voicing an old and distinguished line of antigovernment ideas that is directly linked to our expectations and assessment of local governments. The framers of the U.S. Constitution sought a limited government that would not take away individual rights and liberties as had been the case in Europe in the seventeenth and eighteenth centuries. Local governments, like all governments in the United States, are built on a widespread preference for the least government possible, although there is great variation from area to area.

Today, we see a continuation of the antigovernment bias. Big government at any level looks clumsy and wasteful, so many citizens seek to limit governments' abilities to tax us. We move some local government services such as garbage collection, emergency medical care, and school management to the private sector in the belief that greater efficiency can be achieved. Some city managers have responded by joining a *reinventing government* movement, a broadly based reform effort geared to make local government operate in a more business-like manner.

As a result of this antigovernment bias, we are seeing some local government services reduced or eliminated, but we still expect the roads to be paved and cleared of snow, to have police maintain order, and schools prepare our children for the twenty-first century. Our antigovernment bias does not always sit well with our expectation of high-quality, low-cost public services. This can make for extremely interesting local politics.

Starting again with the local activities that are most familiar, we examine city government. We ask ourselves the following questions:

- What is the total organizational structure of the visible general purpose local governments in the United States?
- Why does the structure of local government vary so widely from city to city and state to state? Why does it matter?
- Are there important differences in how small towns and townships deliver services?
- How does organizational politics advance or hinder the responsiveness of city government?

These questions point out how important it is to understand the mechanics of local government. Your time will be well spent if you can learn to navigate the politics of city hall. You then can take your concerns to city hall with the knowledge needed to make sure that they are addressed. You can try to ensure that local government gets the job done.

❧ The Big Picture of Local Government Structure

The structure and powers of local governments in the United States vary widely. Some parts are visible and familiar, such as city governments with their mayors, city councils, and bureaucrats. Some local government employees are quite visible, including police officers, building inspectors, and lifeguards at municipal swimming pools. But other parts of local government are largely invisible, even though their services may be well known. We know that government maintains roads, but we are probably not familiar with the county road commission that decides which roads get paved and when. We know that fresh water arrives on demand at the tap, but we have no clue that a special water commission has responsibility for the water treatment and delivery system. And we are comfortable in our local library, but we are not at all familiar with the library board.

The governments we are most familiar with are the **general purpose local governments:** counties and cities (and, in some states, villages, towns, and townships). These local governments have broad responsibilities for specific geographic areas, although in the case of counties, the geographic area may overlap other general purpose governments. We have reserved part of a separate chapter for county government and its distinctive commission form of government. The other general purpose governments vary somewhat in form, but their major distinguishing characteristic is size.

The governments we are less familiar with—or know nothing about—are **special purpose local governments** that we will discuss more fully in Chapter 11. These organizations may have an elected governing board: for example, the school board of a local school district. However, a board that is appointed by other elected officials—for example, a parks and recreation board or a public housing commission—may instead govern the special purpose local government. The special purpose governments have narrow functional responsibilities and specific geographical jurisdiction that sometimes overlap the service area of several general purpose governments such as cities or counties.

Arrangements for general and special purpose governments are somewhat different in more metropolitan areas of every state. For example, the large metropolitan areas of a state may have a city school district while rural areas have county-wide school systems. Much depends on the size of the community and the state legislature's outlook on differing community needs. This wide variation in state and local practice makes it difficult to generalize about the legal powers of local governments and to provide a simple description of local government structures that applies across the country. To explain the many paths that states and localities have taken, we have to look at the history of local government in the United States.

Before we explore and begin to figure out how to navigate the structure of local government, we should answer the question, Why does it matter? Why should students of state and local government be expected to understand this bewildering array of local government structures?

There are several good answers. First is the idea of citizenship. Being a competent citizen requires some level of familiarity with government institutions. We have a civic responsibility to vote in local elections and support a representative government. If you don't vote, you shouldn't complain! Second, local governments deliver services that affect our day-to-day lives—police and fire protection, emergency medical services, road maintenance, water and sewer services, libraries, parks and recreation, and public education. Citizens are expected to express policy preferences and know to whom to complain when the services do not meet expectations. Knowledge of the structure of local governments enables us to be informed consumers of local government services and to navigate city hall when we are not pleased. Finally, the rules and structure of local governments influence who gets elected and what kinds of policies are adopted. If we want local policies that encourage environmental protection as opposed to economic growth—and sometimes the two are in conflict—we need to elect officials who support our wishes.

⤴ Historical Background of Local Government Structure

Why does the structure of local government vary so widely? The most important part of the answer is found in the U.S. Constitution—which is absolutely silent on local government. Not a word! And the Tenth Amendment to the Constitution states that all powers not delegated to the national government or prohibited to the state governments are reserved for the states or the people themselves. This means that local government is essentially created by the states or by the people directly. The New England townships and the coastal trade centers of the Southern states and the frontier settlements of the American back country were all left to their own devices. And in a federal system that leaves responsibility for local government to the states, we are destined to have at least fifty different sets of rules.

Adding to the variability in structures that existed in 1787 is the fact that states continued to enter the union over time. Some date back to the colonies, while others are creatures of the twentieth century. Some were created when Americans were extremely fearful of the potential abuse that can arise from a powerful chief executive such as a mayor, while others were created when we were fighting corruption and inefficiency that followed rapid industrialization and urbanization. As each new state came into the union, it looked at the forms of local government that existing states had implemented and considered its own innovations. Texans and Californians had local government under Spanish and Mexican law, and Louisiana had experience with French notions of local institutions and laws. These differing historical experiences led to even more variations in the rules for local government in the United States.

Alexis de Tocqueville toured the United States in 1830, ostensibly to examine the new country's prison system. He saw and commented on all types of government activity and civic behavior. Tocqueville viewed local governments as a mainstay of American democracy, but he was told that many were significant failures in the Americans' experiment with self-government.

The development of steam-powered industries and the crowded urban conditions it fostered did not create a healthy environment for good government or civic behavior. Coastal trade centers such as Charleston and Savannah, at least, were planned cities laid out in squares with consideration given to important government buildings, transportation flow, and commercial zones. However, diseases brought on ships docking in the ports ravaged these cities. Illnesses such as yellow fever and cholera swept the coastal cities, and local governments were hard-pressed to control them with the public health tools at their disposal. By the end of the nineteenth century, local governments in the United States compared poorly with their European counterparts. What was the structure of local government that led to this situation?

State governments were of little help to cities struggling to deal with the problems of industrialization and overcrowding. Operating under a stern interpretation of **Dillon's Rule**—the primary constitutional foundation of

In 1868, Iowa judge John F. Dillon stated his doctrine of state–local relations. It became the enduring foundation of local government powers:

A municipal corporation possesses and can exercise the following powers and no others; first those granted in express words; second, those necessarily implied or necessarily incident to the power expressly granted; third, those absolutely essential to the declared objects and purposes of the corporation—not simply convenient, but indispensable. Any fair reasonable, substantial doubt concerning the existence of power is resolved by the courts against the corporation, and the power is denied (Dillon, 1911: 448).

local government power and therefore structure—most state legislatures limited the powers of local officials (see **Box 10.1**). Dillon's Rule places local governments in an inferior position in the broader system of the United States. It limits their powers to those expressly granted, narrowly implied, and essential to declared objectives. Throughout the historical development of urban areas, this language has made it difficult for local governments to respond to the challenges of the day. City officials were not permitted to plan and develop their cities in a rational manner. They lacked the legal tools to adopt and enforce planned development. Instead, city governments were relegated to a status of weak political institutions. Important governmental functions were reserved to the state governments. Services such as public education, barge canal operation, construction of roads and highways, and banking and investment regulation were administered by the states. The counties administered public health, public safety, and solid-waste disposal, acting as administrative arms of the state government. The state preempted virtually all city powers; there was no effective home rule.

Before industrialization, up to perhaps the 1870s, the primary structure of local government was that of a weak mayor with few administrative powers. The fear of executive power that is tied to memories of King George III and the War of Independence led to a powerless mayor who merely presided over a city council. Whenever additional local powers were needed, state legislatures passed special legislation for each city, and often such powers were granted to special independent boards rather than to the mayor or the city council.

This model of state involvement—or, should we say, interference—in local affairs continued as local governments became more and more complicated. New areas of local public services were being established, such as public education, water service, public health, police and fire services, sewage disposal, and public parks (Glaab & Brown, 1976: 162–168). New independent boards were created to oversee individual services, and the general purpose local government had few clear powers to intervene. The quality of these new services was uneven and often poor, while the cost of local government began to rise dramatically. Evidence of corruption emerged, and citizens began to think of the need for a change in local government structures.

Political Machines

As urban areas and local services expanded, political machines began to emerge both before and after the reform efforts. A **political machine** is a highly centralized organization that runs city affairs from behind the scenes. Historically,

THE POWER BEHIND THE THRONE.
HE CANNOT CALL HIS SOUL HIS OWN.

THE TAMMANY KING-DOM

New York City cartoonist Thomas Nast took on Boss Tweed and Tammany Hall in a series of devastating political cartoons.
Source: The Granger Collection, New York, NY

business interests tired of struggling within an unregulated commercial environment. They needed an infrastructure of streets, lighting, water and sewer services, vocational training schools, and other city services. Business interests knew that one rarely gets something for nothing, so some were willing to bribe city officials. Whether called "taxes" or "bribes," such payments to local government were part of getting things done.

At the same time, the flood of immigrants into the cities created large voter pools. By exploiting ethnic politics, corrupt city officials could rig local elections and create their own political machines (Jacobson, 1998). Entire immigrant neighborhoods could be bought off. Sometimes, as little as a bucket of coal or a drink of whiskey could secure a person's vote. With income from corporate payoffs and votes from captive immigrant populations, the big city bosses gained and held control. The political machine had no ideology. Its party label was irrelevant. Its goal was to win votes and stay in power.

The Tammany machine of the nineteenth century is the classic case. This oldest and most famous urban political machine began in 1789 as a New York City social club but evolved into a set of relationships that allowed the newly arrived dirt-poor Irish immigrants to have some control over the city's political affairs. Beginning with the depression of 1837–1842, machine officials distributed fuel, clothing, and food to the poor and were not at all uncomfortable in expecting voter support in the next election. Appropriating the name of Tammany Hall, a perpetually unfinished public building, the machine became the main agency of the Democratic Party in New York, and patronage became central to its success. Candidates for public office were screened and selected by Tammany officials, as were federal, state, and local job seekers. Widespread corruption became the hallmark of the Tammany machine. Jobholders were routinely expected to give a cut of their salary to the organization. In the 1844 city election, 55,000 votes were cast—10,000 more than the number of residents who were eligible to cast them! William Marcy "Boss" Tweed became the leader of Tammany in the mid-1800s. Although Tweed centralized many city services and thus achieved a higher level of efficiency, contractors were required to pay sizable kickbacks to Tammany (also see **Box 10.2**).

One thing that many of the immigrants had in common was their religion (Catholicism and Judaism) and ethnicity (Irish, Italians, and Poles). They were not Protestant, and they were not Anglo-Saxon. By way of contrast, the traditional elites of many states were both. This set the stage for a reform movement that had not only legitimate issues but also a hidden agenda. The reformers could tear control of the corrupt cities from the hands of political machines and gain a stronger foothold for the group they perceived as most deserving to govern: free, white, Protestant property owners (Jacobson, 1998: 17).

As African Americans and Hispanics began to migrate into urban areas in the early 1900s, they had to fight for full participation in the political

BOX 10.2 *The Legacy of a Political Boss and His Machine*

Boss Tweed has gathered mixed reviews over the last one hundred years. On the one hand, he and his cronies were responsible for guiding New York City's growth—new streets, franchises for horse-drawn railways, the planning of Central Park, a new county courthouse, and the inclusion of newly arrived immigrants in the American dream. Patronage, kickbacks, and ballot stuffing, on the other hand, seemed inconsistent with that dream. Unable to appreciate fully his contributions to municipal government, Tweed himself died impoverished and in public disgrace (Glaab & Brown, 1976: 188–191).

machines. Poor African Americans sought political power but were limited when such power conflicted with the needs of ethnic whites, particularly in the areas of public-sector jobs, integrated housing, and integrated schools. Yet, in a few cases, African Americans became crucial elements of machine politics.

Clearly, the political machine played a complex role in the urban United States. It served as a welfare state for poor immigrants when the government and the power structure turned a deaf ear to their pleas for help. It was a channel of social mobility for those who obtained jobs in the local police department or in the schools. It helped businesses cope with the complexities of an unplanned and cumbersome urban government by cutting red tape and facilitating licenses, permits, and contracts. Machines were supportive of city growth through the development of the roads, sewers, and water system infrastructure that was necessary for growth. These infrastructure projects provided opportunities for the machines to let contracts and create jobs. While machines were supportive of organized crime by following a hands-off attitude, they also helped alleviate social conflict by providing a common ground for ethnic groups. Political machines may have been corrupt, but they helped to build the city and helped many citizens make it in an urban environment. These functions of political machines left an important legacy for the urban United States (Ross & Levine, 1996: 156–158).

Progressive Reform Movement

During the late nineteenth century, the Progressive reform movement was born in the Midwest and swept east and west. It changed the rules of local politics. Cities in Minnesota and Wisconsin were home to immigrants from Scandinavian countries. Clean politics and rational government were the hallmarks of their cultural heritage. You will recall that this area of the country was the birthplace of the moralistic political culture, the outlook on civic life that views society as a commonwealth of mutual interest and support. This area of the country was the birthplace of public education, social welfare, and humane crime control.

At the local level, the reform movement was driven by class conflict. Upper- and upper-middle–class businesspeople were unhappy with a political machine based on lower-class immigrant politics. While these good government reformers had a philosophical preference for democratic politics and a concern for the collective good, they also were driven by a desire for direct financial gain for themselves.

One problem city governments faced was a wide array of uncoordinated state laws concerning local affairs. This contributed to a high level of municipal fragmentation and a vacuum of political responsibility. The political machines had evolved to fill the vacuum. By the late 1800s, state legislatures began to pass **general laws** for various size cities. In 1870, Illinois reduced the number of annual laws addressing city affairs from 3,000 to approximately 200. California's 1879 constitution required general laws to govern cities. These general laws dictated both basic structure and operation. In 1875, Missouri allowed cities to write their own charters (Glaab & Brown, 1976: 174). Frank Goodnow, one of the leaders of the municipal reform movement in the late nineteenth century, observed, "the fact that a city is an organization for the satisfaction of local needs makes it necessary that its actions be determined by local considerations. To this end it must have large local powers" (Glaab & Brown, 1976: 175).

The Progressives sought to institute a **civil service,** a personnel system with merit rather than patronage at its heart. Jobs would be rationally described and qualifications would be established for people who wished to hold those offices. Hiring would be based on competitive examinations or other rational bases such as length of experience and professional education. Milwaukee, Seattle, Tacoma, and San Francisco adopted civil-service employment systems in the 1890s. Today, civil service is the foundation of most municipalities' personnel systems.

The **direct primary** allowed citizens rather than political machines to select nominees for local office. **At-large elections** replaced wards or districts, reducing the close personal contact an officeholder might have with constituents. Such elections were designed to shift the focus from individual geographical areas to the city as a whole, thereby promoting the public interest. **Nonpartisan elections** took the convenient party label off the ballot, making it harder for members of voting blocks to identify who they were "supposed to vote for." The official argument for nonpartisan elections was that there should not be a Republican or a Democratic way to provide municipal services. After all, who ever heard of a Republican swimming pool or Democratic streetlights? Today, more than two-thirds of all cities with populations of more than 5,000 have nonpartisan elections.

Progressive reforms sought to strengthen voter responsibility over runaway government through direct democracy. These methods included the **recall, initiative,** and **referendum** (see Chapter 9). San Francisco adopted the initiative and referendum in 1898 along with civil-service reforms, and by the 1930s these reforms were widely adopted, although more commonly in the West than elsewhere.

The Progressive reform movement was driven in part by a desire to bring efficiency and effectiveness to government and to remove politics from municipal affairs. Newly reformed structures for organizing local government developed. The institution of the **city manager** was created in 1908 in Staunton, Virginia, to oversee the administration of local governments. The city manager is a professional administrator who is hired by the city council and given day-to-day responsibility for overseeing city services. The mayor becomes a symbolic figurehead, and the council retains lawmaking and oversight responsibilities. Elections are typically nonpartisan and at-large. The National Municipal League became an advocate of the city manager structure, and it spread quickly, particularly among mid-sized cities.

The **commission form** of local government was another reform created in 1901. Galveston, Texas, had experienced a horrific hurricane and tidal wave

that destroyed one-third of the property and drowned one-sixth of the population. City government was unable to cope with the aftermath and rebuild the city. The Texas legislature responded by creating a five-member commission to act as the legislative and executive branches of government. Collectively, the members were the legislative body with overall budget and ordinance responsibility. Each individual commissioner was given direct responsibility as an administrative head of one or more of the city's departments. One commissioner acted as mayor, but without extra authority. Elections were at-large and typically nonpartisan. By 1917, the commission form of government peaked at approximately 500 cities.

With a variety of local government structures available, the Progressive reforms led to a home-rule movement. Home rule is the opposite of Dillon's Rule. **Home rule** means that local governments have state constitutional or statutory authority to undertake any of a series of reforms on local initiative: reform in structure, functions or services, or revenue sources. A home-rule charter was adopted for the first time in St. Louis in 1875; by the turn of the century, twelve states had some variant of home rule available to their localities. This form was seen as a means to remedy the patronage, corruption, and incompetence that existed in many local governments. It would free localities of interference from state political interests. Ultimately, it was seen as a way to emphasize local effectiveness and efficiency. Home rule allows local governments to set their own direction, but always within the limitations of their state's constitution.

Today, most major cities and more than seventy-five counties have some form of home-rule charter. Still, state or federal actions may limit their powers. Because ultimate legal responsibility for local affairs rests with state government, a delegation of home rule can be rescinded or modified. (See also Box 10.3.)

Conclusion to History of Local Government Structures

We return to some of the guiding questions of this chapter: How does organizational politics advance or hinder the responsiveness of city government? What lessons might students learn from this review of the history of local government structures? Political machines and progressive reforms help us understand how and why city governments are organized the way they are. They explain the rationale behind local government structures with the basic idea that every organizational structure has a history and a bias toward one group of citizens or another. Before industrialization, urbanization, and political machines, local governments were dominated by state legislatures with their antiurban, rural point of view. What emerged was a patchwork quilt of local structures that were unable to cope with the demands of the times. The political machine emerged to fill the void—and it did so quite well. Public infrastructure and public services expanded, and the new immigrant population found its voice in the American landscape. The Progressive reform movement was in part a response to the shift of control to the new Americans. Its emphasis on efficiency and effectiveness in local government services came with a price of reduced responsiveness and equity.

Direct public involvement in policy making is a result of the Progressive reform movement, and such involvement will increase in the future. Mass media bring issues into everyone's living room, and the Internet makes it increasingly easier to poll the public. Teledemocracy and direct democracy are obviously interrelated concepts. As we will see in later sections, the shift in bias continues as urban structures continue to evolve in response to the urban realities of our times.

❧ Municipal Government Structure

Municipalities are one type of general purpose government. Remember that counties, villages, towns, and townships are the other types. They differ from government bodies such as school boards and water quality districts, which only have narrow jurisdiction. General purpose governments are the local

---

| BOX 10.3 | *A Special Case of Home Rule* |

One of the most visible cases of home rule applies to Washington, D.C. For decades, heated debate has raged over the appropriate balance of power between the U.S. Congress and the citizens of the district. Unlike all other localities in the United States, Washington, D.C., is not linked to any state government. It is a creature of the national government. Historically, its citizens lacked even the most basic ingredients of self-government or home rule.

In 1973, President Richard Nixon signed a home-rule charter for the District of Columbia. But years of misadministration by local officials created apathy about self-government, and in 1995 a former member of the Federal Reserve Board was appointed to head a Financial Control Board to oversee city affairs. In exchange for a financial bailout, Congress substantially reduced the powers of the district's mayor.

institutions that are most visible to Americans. The executives and legislative bodies and the services that local governments provide are those known best by most citizens.

Municipal government is constituted under state law for the purpose of meeting the diverse needs of community citizens. As a general purpose government, cities do not need specific state permission to act on the public's behalf. General state statutes permit local citizens to make local laws within a broad framework of state law. For example, local people can decide how much property tax they are willing to pay but cannot pass a local payroll tax unless the legislature makes such a tax a legal option in the state. In terms of local ordinances, cities can regulate individual and corporate behavior for the public good so long as state constitutional protections are respected. In other words, city governments are chartered to meet both anticipated and unanticipated citizen needs. This distinguishes them from special purpose governments such as school districts that are created to accomplish a single, narrower purpose.

The authority for a city's general purpose government is found in its **city charter.** The charter is a grant of general local government powers from the state government. Charters may be amended by local citizens in some states but only by the state legislature in others. A charter amendment might be needed if the city wanted to adopt a council–manager form of government or institute fees for local services. Charter amendments are popularly approved in referenda.

The charter describes the elected officials who will represent the public in governing the city. Each institution of local government—the city council, the mayor, the city manager, and so on—is described in terms of powers and duties. A copy of the city charter is maintained at city hall, and the city attorney is responsible for determining and advising whether specific actions conform to the charter. As a practical matter, states will usually offer a "fill-in-the-blank" charter for cities of certain sizes. For example, there might be a model "small city" charter and a model "large city" charter because relevant state law varies with the size of the city.

There are three types of municipal government: mayor–council, council–manager, and commission. The mayor–council structure is often associated with the nonreformed city, while the latter two types are legacies of the Progressive reform movement.

Strong Mayor Form

The model of the nonreformed city is the strong mayor–council structure. See Figure 10.1. Under the **strong mayor form,** the mayor has broad appointive and veto powers, clear responsibility for overseeing the day-to-day administration of city government, power to set or substantially influence the council's agenda, and significant budgetary influence. The mayor appoints administrative personnel, perhaps with the approval of council. A civil-service system places substantial limits on the mayor's appointive powers for positions below the level of department head. Voters elect a city council by individual geographical districts or wards. Council responsibilities are limited to appropriations, purchasing, and contracts as well as oversight of the executive branch. All elected officials typically are selected in partisan races. Cities with strong mayor systems include Baltimore, Boston, Detroit, New York, Philadelphia, Pittsburgh, and St. Louis.

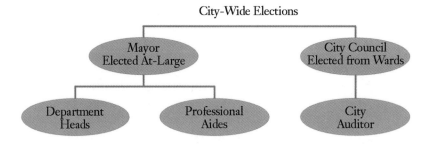

City-Wide Elections

Mayor Elected At-Large

City Council Elected from Wards

Department Heads

Professional Aides

City Auditor

Figure 10.1 Strong mayor form of government

Many cities continue to live out Americans' deep-seated distrust of executive officials. Many mayor–council governments have weak mayors. Under the **weak mayor form,** several city department heads are directly elected by the voters and are independent of the mayor. These officials may include the tax assessor, finance director, and an independent police board. The mayor has few appointive powers, little influence over the budget, and no veto power over city council decisions. In some instances, the city council might select one of its own members to serve as mayor. The weak mayor system is designed to safeguard against the misuse of executive powers, but it makes it difficult for the mayor to run the city and coordinate services. Accountability to the public theoretically exists, but its practical linkages are unclear beyond periodic elections. Nevertheless, we find elements of the weak mayor system in Los Angeles, Minneapolis, Seattle, and many smaller cities throughout the Southeast.

Council–Manager Form

The **council–manager form** of government is found primarily in mid-sized cities with populations of 25,000 to 250,000. The cost of hiring and paying a professional manager makes the system too expensive for many small cities, and the population diversity of large cities makes it difficult for an independent manager to find and maintain support. The reform heritage of the council–manager form may account for the fact that many such cities have councils that are elected in nonpartisan city-wide elections. The council typically chooses the mayor from its members (see Figure 10.2).

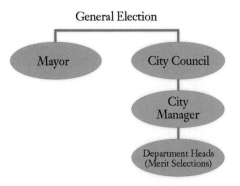

General Election

Mayor

City Council

City Manager

Department Heads (Merit Selections)

Figure 10.2 Council–manager form of government

Frank Fairbanks (center) became city manager of Phoenix, Arizona, in 1990. Management interns such as Lara Cagle can learn about city operations under Fairbanks and Deputy City Manager George Flores.

Source: City of Phoenix. Photo by Bob Rink.

The council–manager model is followed to the letter in few cities. It is not unusual to find city managers in communities with councils elected by districts or a combination of city-wide and districts. Local voters may even elect a mayor. Under the council–manager form, the city council is the policy and legislative body, and it hires the city manager to run city operations. The manager selects department heads and oversees the day-to-day administration of city affairs.

One of the greatest challenges of the council–manager format of local government is found in the balance of power between the city manager and the city council. The job of city manager is a complex one that entails much more skill than simply directing the local bureaucracy. The city manager plays a key leadership role in policy development, working with individual citizens, community groups, the bureaucracy, and members of the city council. A contemporary political scientist has noted four main local government leadership roles; the city manager plays a significant part in three of them:

1. Council dominates the development of a mission, the overall approach to city services.
2. Council and manager share the determination of specific programs and services that will be provided.
3. The manager dominates the administrative function, including the daily working of city government.
4. The manager overwhelmingly controls the local management functions of personnel, budget, purchasing, and data management (Svara, 1990).

In some communities, conflict arises between the city manager and city council over the various roles. City managers typically prefer to play behind-the-scenes roles, but sometimes they become political activists. They try to build their own power bases to force councils to follow their leadership. In other instances, council members may micromanage city government and thus step on the manager's toes. When such conflict occurs, it is not unusual for the city manager to find him- or herself looking for a new city to manage.

The principal strength of the city manager form of government is that administrative responsibility is centralized in the hands of a professional manager who has the support of a majority of the city council. Many theorists believe this should foster a responsible and responsive local government. The principal shortcoming of the council–manager structure is that city managers may be less responsive to citizens than to their own ideas of professionalism. The larger and more diverse a community's population, the more difficult it is for a city manager to find a peaceful middle road that satisfies everyone. Managers know that if their leadership role is too visible, they may find themselves in the midst of conflict in the city. The city manager often follows a "don't rock the boat" course.

Dallas, Phoenix, and Cincinnati are all large cities that use the council–manager form of government. Each has a manager who faces specific challenges in his job. Teodoro J. Benavides is the city manager of Dallas, a community that has grown by 4.5 percent since 1990. Dallas's 1,053,292 residents are a diverse population, with 29.5 percent African Americans and 20 percent Hispanics. In Phoenix, Frank Fairbanks became city manager in 1990. He began his career in the city in 1972, working his way up from management assistant to executive assistant to the city manager, assistant city manager, and finally to his current position. Phoenix has an estimated population of 1,246,712 in 1998, making it the nation's sixth largest city. Cincinnati's John F. Shirey is city manager in a different kind of city from his fellow professionals in Dallas and Phoenix. Cincinnati has an estimated 1996 population of 345,818 and has seen its population drop 5 percent since 1990. In all three cases, the professional city manager's job as chief administrative officer is a huge challenge. Each oversees a multimillion dollar budget, supervises thousands of city employees, and works with a wide array of citizens and community groups. At the same time, each must keep the city council pleased with his performance.

Commission Form

Some reform-minded communities have tried to adapt an old form of government to meet today's challenges. The commission form of government comes from county government; we will have more to say about it in Chapter 11. Briefly, the commission form combines executive and legislative responsibilities in a five- to seven-member body that includes the mayor. Each commissioner is selected in a city-wide nonpartisan election, and each commissioner oversees one or more city departments. Because the commissioners are independently elected, their primary concern may be with the well-being of the departments over which they have responsibility. This can make it difficult to look after the interests of the city as a whole.

Today, fewer than 3 percent of all municipalities use this system of government. Tulsa, Oklahoma, used the commission form of government until 1990 when it switched to a strong mayor form. Portland, Oregon, is the nation's largest city to be governed by a city commission. Portland elects a mayor and four commissioners who together serve as the city commission. The mayor assigns city bureaus to individual commissioners. Voters also elect an independent city auditor. Portland is often included in lists of well-governed cities. It has become a growth center for high-technology manufacturing, stimulating a population growth of 16 percent since 1990 and per capita income growth in the metropolitan area of 16 percent in the same period. The city's services and infrastructure are widely viewed as outstanding. All of this record suggests that a commission form of local government can be effective.

In 1985, Mobile, Alabama, elected a mayor and seven city council members from districts to replace the city commission of three members elected at-large. The process of changing the form of government, which had existed for seventy-four years, began with a federal court order in *Bolden* v. *Mobile*. This case challenged the constitutionality of the city commission to which no black person had ever been elected. By an act of the Alabama legislature, a referendum was held to give the people a choice between alternate forms of government that would meet the approval of the federal court. Today, with a population of 202,581, which is approximately 40 percent African American, three of seven city council members are African American. Clearly, this example shows how important local government structure may be in influencing the nature of representation and policy making.

The Choice of Form

In terms of numbers, the council–manager form of city organization has gradually gained ascendancy over the other types of systems. Today, almost half of all cities employ a professional city manager (see Table 10.1). What is important is that almost half of all American cities have found it desirable to place professional public administrators in charge of their municipal governments. These cities with city managers tend to be smaller and more homogeneous in the makeup of their population. The other half continue to rely on political strategies for their communities. These cities tend to be larger and are populated with a wide variety of racial, ethnic, and political groups. The story of organizing local government does not stop there.

Table 10.1
Current Form of Government, 1998

Organization Form	Number	Percentage of Cities
Commission	66	1.4
Town meeting	238	5.8
Mayor–council	1604	35.2
Council–manager	2207	48.5

Source: International City/County Management Association (ICMA), *Municipal Yearbook* (1998): 31.

Although not all cities have replaced mayoral leadership with city manager leadership, many of them have hired administrators to operate in some capacity. The broad term **chief administrative officer** is sometimes used to describe a professional public administrator who coordinates daily operations (see Table 10.2). The use of professional administrators is certainly not limited to cities that have adopted the council manager form of organization.

Table 10.2
Position of Chief Administrative Officer (CAO), 1998

Metro Status	Percentage with CAOs
Central city	73
Suburban	81
Independent	74

Source: ICMA, *Municipal Yearbook* (1998): 33.

The form of municipal organization varies by city and over time. Communities experiment with newer forms of organization, adapt them to local conditions, and sometimes throw them out and start over again. General state laws typically enable them to modify their charter when a reform is needed. Today, some form of professional management is desired in all but the smallest municipalities. The public also wants a balance of power in local politics, so the council will be balanced against either a mayor or a manager. Political fashions such as term limits and campaign finance reform play a role as well. In other words, success in navigating city government depends on having an accurate road map. But the road map itself is not drawn in stone. Citizens can always tinker.

❧ Townships

Midwestern townships and the towns in New England are geographic subdivisions of counties. They are located in less than half the states. They serve as the principal local government entities outside of incorporated municipalities. Townships are therefore designed as rural local governments. Today, the growth of suburban areas near large cities has resulted in some townships taking on more urban characters.

In Michigan, approximately 45 percent of the population lives in townships. These citizens rely on township government for their local government services. Michigan has both general law townships and chartered townships. The latter have greater home-rule flexibility. Typically, voters elect a supervisor, clerk, treasurer, and two to four trustees. Together, these elected officials act as the legislative body. Individually, the supervisor, clerk, and treasurer have direct responsibility for township functions.

The array of services is limited. Mandated services in Michigan include property assessment, tax collection, and elections. Permitted services include fire protection, law enforcement, and land-use management. Road maintenance is not included because it is a county responsibility in Michigan.

Small town councils like this one in North Carolina more typically rely on their mayors rather than a city manager to do the town's business.
Source: © SuperStock

Canton Charter Township, Michigan, is one such township in the Detroit metropolitan area. Its 1999 population was almost 70,000, and it has grown by 21 percent since 1990. Canton is a bedroom community located near one of the area's many interstate highways. This makes it convenient for residents to travel to jobs all over the metropolitan area. Canton covers thirty-six square miles and is governed by a seven-member board of trustees. The board consists of three full-time administrators: the supervisor, the treasurer, and the clerk. There are also four part-time trustees. The supervisor is essentially Canton's mayor. The township offers a full array of services including state-of-the-art recreational facilities and programs. As a rapidly growing bedroom community,

The New England "town" is the historic home of America's direct democracy town hall meeting. New Englanders still turn out to govern themselves directly. Here all eligible voters can gather and decide tax, service, and policy questions. Between meetings, selectmen and other elected officials are responsible for local affairs. This model of democracy continues in smaller New England towns. In larger suburban towns, the elected representatives govern much like they do in small municipalities.

Canton's public works continuously need enhancement. It appears that the rural township structure has made the transition to an urban form of government. (See also **Box 10.4**.)

In most parts of the United States, what we call small towns are just that: small municipalities. As we have noted throughout the chapter, they have the special challenges of having modest resources to address ever-rising resident expectations. This is especially true in small towns located near big cities. They can be overwhelmed with consumer demands and underwhelmed by the lack of support for local taxes to pay for services. Their problems are unusual, but their form of government is not distinctive. They are simply smaller versions of the municipality that provides general purpose government throughout most of the United States.

❧ Duties of City Officials

There is something of the separation-of-power doctrine at work in local government. Granted, the degree of separateness is not as pronounced as in the national and state governments. Nevertheless, city charters describe the distinctive powers enjoyed by city councils, mayors, city managers, and other local administrators or bureaucrats.

City Councils

City council meetings are held on a regular basis, and notice of the meetings is given in the local media. In small communities and suburban towns, city councils have little need to meet every week. In fact, more than two-thirds of all city councils nationally meet twice each month (Renner & DeSantis, 1998: 36). In large cities, the workload is much heavier. In these larger jurisdictions, the council must meet weekly to keep up with its policy-making responsibilities. To the average citizen and local media, these councils must appear to be in constant session.

The powers of elected city councils are specified in the city charter and in state legislation. Local laws, or ordinances, can be made only within the limits placed by the city charter the state has given the city. In most cases, local councils lack adequate staff to develop policy and funding proposals. They also are unable to monitor the city bureaucracy independently. They simply lack many resources of their own.

Instead, councils typically respond to proposals from the mayor and city department heads. Slightly more than half of all city councils use standing committees in their policy-making processes. These committees usually mirror the organization chart of the city administration. A council committee oversees

The thirteen-member city council is Kansas City's legislative and policy-making body. Its members, including the mayor, are elected to four-year terms. The city is divided into six council districts; their boundaries are revised at least every five years by the council according to population shifts within the city. The mayor and six of the council members are elected at-large. The other six council members each represent a specific district and are elected by residents within those districts. This makes Kansas City one of the cities with a mixed form of representation noted in Table 10.1.

The mayor is the city's chief elected official and president of the city council and enjoys all of the powers and duties of a council member. The mayor appoints most of the council committees and their chairs. He also appoints city advisory boards and commissions. The mayor signs all ordinances and bonds authorized by the council. He or she is an *ex officio* member of the Board of Police Commissioners.

The city council sets the overall policy for the city by adopting ordinances and resolutions. Public hearings are often held to secure public input. The council makes appropriations by approving budgets for all departments and offices. After an ordinance is passed or the budget is adopted, the council continues to monitor the results of its actions through studies, surveys, hearings, and personal contacts.

public safety, while another focuses on parks and recreation, and so on. Council members may therefore see themselves as policy specialists in at least certain concrete areas of local government. In the absence of a strong executive or a professional city manager, this **commission form** of government virtually defines local government. We will discuss the commission form of organization in more detail when we describe county commissions in Chapter 11.

In municipalities where the city council selects and employs a professional city manager, the council members may try to ride herd on the manager's administration. Conflict between managers and council members is common. In fact, most managers require a long-term contract before they will work for a city. If disputes become too contentious, the council will have to find a way to work with him or her, or the latter's contract will have to be bought out.

It would be misleading to present a picture of city councils as being exclusively passive and subservient to the executive branch. Many council members develop a representative relationship with particular interests, neighborhood groups, or city departments. As champions of these narrow interests, they have the ability to hold up executive proposals and the work of the city. (See also Box 10.5.)

City Mayors

Community-power studies question whether elected officials are the most important decision makers. Most of these studies conclude that the mayor and city manager are active and important participants in making decisions that affect local interests. Of course, this varies with the size, location, and history of each community. Leadership in a small Midwestern town may be quite different from that in a major metropolitan center. And mayors and city managers exercise different types of power, one political and the other bureaucratic. We need to look at each type of local executive.

The mayor of the New York City, Rudolph Giuliani, is a highly visible elected executive. So are Mayors Bill Campbell of Atlanta, Richard Daley of

Chicago, Richard Riordan of Los Angeles, and Willie Brown of San Francisco. Each man is by far the most recognized public official in his city as you will see on his city's Web pages.

The mayors are the chief executives of their communities and, as such, have important symbolic responsibilities. They speak out for their cities' political, social, and economic interests. They are also responsible for the smooth administration of government services. In large cities, mayors are well paid, full-time officials. They have considerable staff support, formal policy authority, and great access to the media. Their personal and party political organizations are powerful and increase their visibility and effectiveness among the cities' many interests and neighborhoods (Pressman, 1972). Because our large cities have many problems, it is important that the mayors can mobilize these many resources in support of their policy proposals.

The job of a *big city mayor* is not easy. As the regime theory points out, mayors have to maintain supportive relationships with the city's wealth-producing citizens and institutions. From an economic-development perspective, this means working with bankers, developers, realtors, investors, and the owners of large and small businesses. These players have the private capital and technological resources to generate jobs for city residents and tax revenues for the city. At the same time, the mayor must work with individual citizens, neighborhood associations, and private interest groups, including unions, environmental organizations, and many other segments of the community so that their policy preferences also can be considered.

Within the city government itself, the mayor must work with the large and often independent city bureaucracies. Big city police departments, fire departments, sanitation departments, and welfare agencies are enormous. Each employs thousands of city employees and spends millions of local tax dollars. In the case of many local government organizations such as environmental protection, emergency preparedness, and health and welfare agencies, the bureaucrats serve many masters. They are funded with state and federal funds as well as local funds, so they must be

San Francisco Mayor Willie Brown (right) regularly meets with lobbyists and representatives of various constituencies within the city.
Source: © Mark Richards / PhotoEdit

accountable under several sets of rules and regulations. It is a major job for the mayor to reconcile bureaucratic interests with what he or she perceives to be the public interest. He or she has all of the responsibility for the smooth operations of local government, but rarely does the mayor have the clear authority that would best go with that responsibility.

Big city mayors also must deal with large and diverse city councils. In metropolitan areas, neighborhoods are the basis for representation on the city council. Many of these neighborhoods are homogeneous—that is, they are populated by families that have a common ethnicity, socioeconomic condition, or both. The council persons who are elected from these districts are pressed to deliver on the needs of their constituents. Their relatively narrow concerns can tax a mayor's ability to assist one neighborhood without seeming to abandon the broader public interest. For example, should the mayor support the construction of a major new recreation facility in a Hispanic neighborhood, then the question will arise about why Asian, African American, or working-class white neighborhoods are being slighted. It is sometimes hard to convince council members that the mayor is trying to be everyone's mayor. The council members simply do not share that citywide perspective.

Detroit, Michigan, provides a good example of two men taking very different approaches to the mayorship. In 1993, Dennis Archer took over the job from Coleman Young, the city's first African American mayor. He inherited a city in decline—in population, private investment, and infrastructure (streets, water and sewer lines, and so on). Young's regime had been at odds with private investors, realtors, and suburban officials even though he was responsible for creating generous tax-reduction packages for two major employers—General Motors and Chrysler. The five-term Young had been immensely popular with and responsive to African American neighborhood associations and the city's labor unions. He helped build the self-esteem of African American residents by integrating the police force and other city services. Nevertheless, he had a hostile relationship with local media (see **Box 10.6**). His combative and negative quips always made the news, only adding to Detroit's problems.

Young's attack politics turned off as many Detroit residents as they amused. His regime's goal was not to govern from a broad consensus of community interests but to challenge the preexisting power structure. That strategy and his frank language succeeded in getting him reelected four times. He died in 1997.

Dennis Archer has been a study in contrast. He is prodevelopment and gets along well with the business community. He nurtures the image of Detroit as a sophisticated city with a bright future for all of its citizens. Reconciliation, not confrontation, is the order of the day. Under his leadership, a new baseball

---

BOX 10.6   *Mayor Coleman Young and the Detroit Media*

Consider the following examples of Coleman Young's press quotes from the 1977 files of *The Detroit Free Press:*

- "No other city in America, no other city in the Western world, has lost the population at that rate. And what's at the root of that loss? Economics and race. Or should I say, race and economics."

- "Swearing is an art form. You can express yourself much more directly, much more exactly, much more succinctly, with properly used curse words."

- "I don't know of any other city in the nation where there's such a preoccupation in the suburbs for control. The same people who left the city for racial reasons still want to control what they've left."

Two Detroit mayors. Dennis Archer (left) succeeded five-term mayor Coleman Young.
Source: Photos © Kwabena Shabu

Mayor Dennis Archer has been more willing to work with business and industry leaders than his predecessor to broaden Detroit's economic base. Here Archer stands with the heads of Detroit's "Big Three" automakers—Ford, General Motors, and Chrysler—at the North American International Auto Show.
Source: Photos © Kwabena Shabu

stadium for the Tigers, Comerica Park, opened in 2000, and a new stadium for the National Football League's Lions is scheduled to be built next to Comerica. Three downtown casinos are thriving, and General Motors has moved its international headquarters into the heart of the downtown.

Mayors use all the resources at their disposal in their efforts to be their cities' leaders. At least five leadership styles are commonly used (Kotter & Lawrence, 1974).

The first style of leadership relies heavily on *ceremonial duty* and functions. Although ribbon cuttings at local schools, businesses, and parks may seem ordinary, these duties are an important element of leadership. For generations, the city's mayor may have inaugurated important construction efforts in the city. Today's mayor at a mall opening joins in a tradition that is linked to an earlier mayor's ribbon cutting at the central public library. Citizens today would feel snubbed if their mayor stayed away from the big milestone events of their organization or business.

The second mayoral style is the *city caretaker*. The land, skyline, transportation system, scenic neighborhoods—all are a public trust. Any particular mayor presides over several moments of the city's long-term development. He or she may share the vision of the future developed by others or see a need to amend the vision. In any case, the provision of necessary public services is not mundane when history is being made.

The third style of the contemporary urban mayor is the distinctly *individualistic*. Coleman Young of Detroit was only one of many examples. Some mayors use their personal connections to make modest changes in the city. For whatever reason, they do not seek to broaden the governing coalition. Only the judgment of history can rule on their ultimate contributions.

The fourth style is the *entrepreneur*. These mayors have distinctive policy goals they believe will leave an indelible imprint on the community. They seek to expand their personal and political networks to accomplish these specific goals.

The fifth leadership style is the *executive*. The mayor has strong managerial skills that are used to accomplish specific projects on his or her agenda. Few mayors fall into this category.

Leadership style is a highly individual matter. Some mayors clearly exhibit one or more of the classic styles we have noted. Others are more difficult to categorize. It is much easier for a mayor to tend toward the ceremonial type of leadership than it is to attempt the entrepreneurial type. Many mayors find that they can more easily deliver symbolic rewards to their constituents than real, material benefits. Being a spokesperson for a particular viewpoint is easier than developing stable, good-paying jobs. Suffice it to say that leading the modern American city is an enormous challenge. No man or woman can hope to lead a city and leave an enduring impression on that city without personal strength and endurance.

The vast majority of U.S. cities, 84 percent, are small communities with fewer than 25,000 residents (International City/County Management Association [ICMA], 1998). The mayors of these more than 6,000 smaller municipalities do not lead large governments with legions of bureaucrats and personal staff members. They *are* the local political executives.

The small U.S. city provides many of the same services as do large urban governments, including police and fire, water and sewer, solid-waste (garbage) collection and disposal, street paving and repair, and city parks and recreation programs. Everything is simply done on a smaller scale. The local small city mayor must be resourceful to meet public expectations: services on a par with those of large cities.

Small town mayors also are part-time officials paid on a part-time basis. They usually keep existing businesses to support themselves and their families. This may lead to conflict-of-interest questions. If a local mayor does business with the city, then special arrangements must be made. For example, the mayor may have to recuse him- or herself when a potential conflict of interest arises. This means that the mayor steps aside and does not try to influence a decision that could favor a family's business interests.

Small town mayors also must be careful to avoid favoring friends and associates. He or she must be mayor to everyone, not the leader of a clique or fac-

German Mayors

elsewhere in the world

Local government in Germany has been undergoing radical changes since the Berlin Wall came down and the former West and East Germanies were reunited as the Federal Republic of Germany. An increase in democracy is seen with the introduction of *direct mayoral elections* in all of the country's states. Only Baden-Württemberg and Bavaria had previously provided for the direct popular election of mayors. Almost 90 percent of the directly elected mayors in Baden-Württemberg are trained administrators. In smaller and medium-sized communities throughout Germany, mayors are typically graduates of the universities or applied administrative studies. In cities with populations of 50,000 and more, the mayors are increasingly law school graduates with a specialty in public administration.

The mayors have previous experience in local, county, or regional government or in a federal ministry. German voters believe that their mayors should be professional and therefore not serve in a city where they have many relatives and acquaintances. In addition, mayors should not be involved in party politics. How do you see the differences between American and German mayors?

Denver Mayor Wellington Webb chairs a voting session of the U.S. Conference of Mayors meeting in Seattle in June 2000.

Source: © AP Photo / Elaine Thompson

tion. This is because small towns have little if any political party competition. In larger cities, we expect the mayor's party and the out-of-power party to balance each other, to keep a check on each other's power. But in small towns, the only watchdog on the mayor's behavior may be the local newspaper, and even that guardian may be seen as corrupt if its owners or editor are friends with the mayor.

The political agenda of small town mayors may extend beyond doing their civic duty and serving one or two terms before resuming private life. The agenda may be as simple as community beautification or preserving a local landmark. Like mayors everywhere, however, political problems do not wait to be discovered by the mayor's office. State and federal mandates, statewide partisan realignment, and economic ups and downs bring demands on the mayor, ready or not. Again, the small town mayor may have to deal with many or most of the external demands that big city mayors face.

Finally, mayors are naturally drawn to the company and advice of other mayors. Like all public officials in the United States, mayors have their own *professional associations*. Some of these reference groups are statewide, and others are national. On the state level, big city mayors may be drawn into dialogue with former mayors of the city, or with other mayors of their political party, their own ethnic group, or their own educational background. Nationally, mayors from all backgrounds come together in the United States Conference of Mayors. Through this forum, the nation's big city mayors can try to draw attention to urban problems and promising approaches to solving those problems. They may lobby the U.S. Congress and try to influence state legislatures. In any event, they do not suffer in silence. (See also **Box 10.7**.)

City Managers

The day-to-day operations of medium-sized and large cities are often left to professional city managers. A **city manager** is employed by the city council and may or may not report to the mayor. In fact, in some cities, the city manager *is* the chief executive and the mayor simply chairs council meetings. In other cities, the city manager works under the general supervision of the mayor. It all depends on the terms of the city's charter. The key is to remove some of the politics from the business-like operation of local government.

Managers bring *professional expertise* to local government. They are typically university-trained social scientists with special training in public administration, public policy, or urban planning. Under the terms of the typical con-

BOX 10.7   *On the Web*

Check out the Web sites of a few large cities, and find your own if it has one. How visible is the mayor? Can you identify the mayor's policy initiatives? What kind of staff resources are available to the mayor? Can you make an educated guess about the mayor's role in local policy making? Here are Web addresses of a few large cities:

- Atlanta <*http://www.ci.atlanta.ga.us/*>

- Chicago <*http://www.ci.chi.il.us*>

- Los Angeles <*http://www.ci.la.ca.us*>

- New York <*http://www.ci.nyc.ny.us*>

- San Francisco <*http://www.ci.sf.ca.us/*>

Many smaller cities are also on the Web. What can you learn about the mayors of smaller cities? Are their roles different from those of large cities?

- Asheville, North Carolina <*http://207.4.162.99/avlweb/index.htm*>

- Boulder, Colorado <*http://www.ci.boulder.co.us/*>

Township Web sites often show the differences and similarities between townships and cities. Here are a few important township sites to check:

- Michigan Townships Association <*http://mta-townships.org*>

- Canton Township, Michigan <*http://www.canton-mi.org*>

- Lansing Township, Michigan <*http://lansingtownship.org*>

- Lower Paxton Township, Pennsylvania <*http://lower-paxton.pa.us*>

To find other Web addresses of city governments, check out the U.S. Conference of Mayors Web site and its listing of mayors and their communities' addresses at <*http://www.mayors.org/uscm/meet_mayors/*>.

---

tract, the city manager will use these skills on the city's behalf for the prescribed term of the contract. City managers have their own professional associations, the largest of which is the International City/County Management Association (ICMA). City managers typically move on to positions in larger and larger cities. Once they have managed a large urban government, they may be sought by competing cities—much like the successful CEO of any large organization.

From the perspective of community power and politics, the city manager may be a key player. However, elite theory suggests that the manager is not an important policy maker. Rather, he or she is viewed as the person who implements decisions made elsewhere. The original vision of the city-management movement was that of the talented technocrat. In reality, city managers gradually become the central policy makers in their communities. They have direct access to and control of the very departments of local government. Some city council members defer to a city manager's expertise, while others sympathize with a rational and business-like operation of city government. If a systematic approach to street repair and parks planning leads to better services for previously ignored or neglected neighborhoods, then a city manager may even pick up the active support of community groups. By contrast, former officials and even the mayor may come to be seen as political bosses instead of local government executives. In other words, the city manager may become a player in local politics. (See also Box 10.8.)

The mayor in this type of organizational arrangement is left with relatively few powers and responsibilities. He or she is a figurehead and spokesperson for city government, but the council has most of the real power. By the same

Robert L. Collins was appointed city manager of Kansas City, Missouri, on August 1, 1997. He had considerable professional and educational experience. He served as assistant city manager for economic development and as director of the city's planning and development department, which developed the strategic plan known as FOCUS Kansas City. Collins also oversaw several hotel and manufacturing developments for the city such as the Marriott/Muehlebach Hotel, the Omni Hotel, a civic mall, and a new Harley-Davidson plant. A graduate of the University of Missouri at Kansas City, he holds a Bachelor's degree in economics and a Master's degree in urban planning from the University of Michigan. He holds similar positions on the Landmarks Commission, the Urban Homestead Authority, the Economic Development Corporation, the Civic Council, the Kansas City Municipal Assistance Corporation, the Labor Management Council, the Minority Suppliers Development Council, the Swope Ridge Geriatric Center, and the Mid-America Coalition on Health Care. He is an *ex-officio* board member of the Downtown Council and the Greater Kansas City Chamber of Commerce and holds memberships in the International City Management Association, the American Planning Association, the National Council for Urban Economic Development, the Urban Land Institute, and the American Society of Public Administration.

token, city councils with this much power are usually not interested in sharing it with a strong city manager. If these councils have professionals working with the city departments at all, then they usually will be a weaker form of leader called a *city administrator*. The duties of the administrator might be to coordinate action in city government and provide for consistent operating procedures. However, all really important managerial decisions would be reserved to the council.

The weak mayor form of organization served smaller cities best when they were insulated from the demands of empowered community organizations and intrusive state and federal regulators. In days gone by, city workers expected "politicians" to interfere with their operations. Today, as more and more small cities are forced to live up to the more universal expectations of accountable government, this form of organization has been yielding ground to stronger forms of local governmental organization.

If you live with a weak mayor or commission system and want to get something done for your neighborhood or community organization, then your approach to the local government will be through the council. If the city has a ward system in which a particular council member represents your neighborhood, then that avenue might work. He or she may have control over the area of your concern—public safety or solid-waste disposal, for example—or routinely deal with the council member who does have power over that area. However, you will have to keep the peace with that powerful individual. If you live in a community that uses at-large elections, then you may have to find the "neighborhood-type" politicians on the council and work through them. If your concern is business or professional or you have a special interest, then you will have to find council members who share your concerns. A coalition approach is always an option in an at-large election community.

Mayoral Leadership

Leadership is critical to meeting the increasing demands of local government functioning. Community problems, citizen demands for focused action, and intergovernmental relationships all press city governments to have stronger organizational cohesion. A form of organization is needed that can ensure that a quality job gets done, regardless of the politics of the city council or the quirks of individual council members' personalities. An organizational form is needed that can bring some measure of unity to city government. As we learned earlier, different cities use different forms of organization. The key is that the format "fit" the community's values and its needs.

Relations between the mayor and the council are formalized under several forms of city government. In some cities that use the strong mayor model, the mayor may convene and chair the council, control its agenda, and even veto its actions. The mayor clearly is accountable for the actions of city departments under this organizational model. He or she may hire and supervise city department heads or oversee a city administrator who does so. In any case, major administrative decisions must have his or her approval. Strong mayors in larger cities also have staffs of personal assistants who can help craft the mayor's message and manage communications. Staff assistants may be speech writers, media specialists, pollsters, attorneys, or grant experts. These employees work for the incumbent mayor; are loyal to him or her, and seek to advance the mayor's career. In the largest cities, there may be many dozens of these personal aides, but even in smaller municipalities, strong mayors will need assistants who can extend his or her reach into the community.

If you need action and live in a city with a strong mayor system, then you have several avenues of access, all of them political. Try to interest a member of the mayor's staff in your issue. Use positive press coverage to show the staff member that your issue has public appeal and will not harm the mayor. You may want to look at partisan approaches to your issue. A political party or faction may champion your need, or you may announce a pressing concern for bipartisan support. Use politics, and use the media.

Getting action in a council–manager city requires a good working relationship with the council plus a real appreciation for how bureaucracies work. You will need to get your facts together and work with tools such as issue papers with which bureaucrats can identify. They will ask how they can get you a grant or a budget increase if you cannot document the need. Also, it will be important to find out how the rationalized city government seeks public input under mandates that require them to do so. Your neighborhood or organization may benefit from being included in a special study committee or task force

Collecting Your Thoughts *Does Structure Make a Difference?*

Find the Internet home page for a local government in your area and identify the structural characteristics of its operation. Is it mayor–council, council–manager, or commission? Are elections partisan or nonpartisan? Are council members elected by wards or districts, at-large, or some combination of the two? How do these structural characteristics influence the way local government operates? If these structural characteristics were changed, how might the politics and policies change? Bring your notes to class to discuss.

the city is sponsoring. Short of being co-opted by the bureaucrats, you need to learn to play the game by their rules in this type of organizational system.

Local Government Bureaucrats

Local government bureaucrats are the administrative officials with whom citizens come into contact on a daily basis. They include administrative officials such as city department heads as well as the street-level bureaucrats such as police officers, firefighters, librarians, voting registrars, garbage collectors, and street maintenance and repair workers. Many are professionals, and increasingly most local bureaucrats are selected through a civil-service system on the basis of training and expertise, rather than political connections to elected officials.

Local bureaucrats are responsible to elected officials, but have wide discretion in the services they provide and the manner in which the services are delivered. Examples of local bureaucrats using discretion include the police officer who must decide whether to issue a speeding ticket or the health department inspector who can note a violation in health standards at a restaurant or grocery store. In each case, the local bureaucrat—the police officer and the health inspector—has discretion in how to carry out the law.

Local government bureaucrats are active participants in local politics and elections; they directly benefit from the expansion of local services through their paychecks. In many cities, these workers are members of unions such as the American Federation of State, County and Municipal Employees (AFSCME) and a variety of police organizations.

Bureaucratic power in local politics is the result of several factors. First is the discretion administrators have in carrying out policy that is written in broad, general language, leaving decisions about how the law will be implemented to street-level bureaucrats. Although administrators make individually unimportant decisions, collectively these decisions are important. Second, because city council members and mayors have mostly part-time jobs or only limited staff support, elected officials depend on the permanent bureaucrats or civil servants to develop and carry out public policy. Third, local bureaucrats are often masters in developing supportive relationships with private citizens and local groups that benefit by the services that are provided. These relationships are often used to place pressure on local officials to support particular policies. Finally, the sheer number of local bureaucrats and the citizens who rely on them for particular services can be a significant portion of voters in local elections in which voting turnout is typically extraordinarily low. Thus, the influence of city bureaucrats in local politics and elections may be very significant.

❧ Chapter Conclusion

We began this chapter asking about the structure of city hall and the differences based on size and state mandates. By "city hall," of course, we mean the offices of city, town, and township government. In the next chapter, we will include counties, special purpose governments, and independent school districts. Unless we know the various forms of government and the location of the elected officials within each form, we will have little chance of finding the person who can help us with our concerns. In this regard, we laid a foundation of understanding about general purpose government and the related enabling state laws and city charters for that type of local government. All of this information on local government structure was built on a review of the historical development of localities in the United States.

The structure of local governments in the average metropolitan area of the United States is a complex mixture of governments. Its roots are firmly planted in three different traditions: (1) a distrust of government, especially executive powers; (2) dread of the political machines that evolved during the era of rapid urbanization and the diversification of population; and (3) hopes of a Progressive reform movement that sought to clean up government and turn control over to citizens and professionals. The maze of governments has led to problems of fragmentation, accountability, and performance. These problems are best understood from the perspective of the special purpose government and the entire metropolitan area, the subject of our next chapters.

We can now return to the basic questions we asked at the beginning of this chapter. You should now be able to answer questions about navigating city hall.

- Cities choose the organizational structure that seems to best meet their needs. For some cities, the choice is clear political accountability through a strong mayor system. For others, the professionalism of a city manager is the priority. No one pattern suits all communities.
- Historical experiences are one source of structural variations. Cities that suffered through eras of control by corrupt political machines are more reform-minded. Those communities that embraced the Progressive reform movement will have safeguards against repeats of their bad experiences.
- Small cities and towns use many of the innovations found in major urban centers. A small community may have a city manager and professional local bureaucrats. This is especially true for more affluent smaller communities, including suburban small cities and college towns.
- Regardless of the structure or the size of the city government, local politicians are under pressure to be accountable for results. Business leaders expect efficiency in local government, and articulate local neighborhoods and interests demand effectiveness in local government. On the one hand, virtually any structure can be made to work, although certain organizational forms can do more to address a specific city's problems. We will have more to say on this particular subject when we examine special purpose governments in the next chapter.

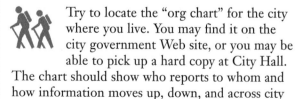

Exploring on Your Own **The City Organizational Chart**

Try to locate the "org chart" for the city where you live. You may find it on the city government Web site, or you may be able to pick up a hard copy at City Hall. The chart should show who reports to whom and how information moves up, down, and across city government. If you want a basis of comparison, you might look at the university's organization chart. It may show different authority and communication patterns. Keep a copy of it with your class notes to reinforce key points that you learned in this chapter.

Key Words for InfoTrac Exploration

bureaucrats   Dennis Archer   municipal government by   political machine
                                                      city manager

Sources Cited

Dillon, John F. (1911). *Commentaries on the Laws of Municipal Corporations* (5th ed.). Boston: Little, Brown & Co.

Glaab, Charles N., and A. Theodore Brown (1976). *A History of Urban America* (2nd ed.). New York: Macmillan.

Horn, Jerry, and Gary Miron (1999). *Evaluation of Michigan's Public School Academy Initiative*. Kalamazoo: Western Michigan University.

International City/County Management Association (ICMA) (1998). *Municipal Yearbook*. Washington, DC: Author.

Jacobson, Matthew Frye (1998). *Whiteness of a Different Color: European Immigrants and the Alchemy of Race*. Cambridge, MA: Harvard University Press.

Kotter, John P., and Paul R. Lawrence (1974). *Mayors in Action: Five Approaches to Urban Governance*. New York: Wiley & Sons.

National Center for Education Statistics (1998). *Inequalities in Public School District Revenue*. Washington, DC: Author.

Pressman, Jeffrey L. (1972). "Preconditions of Mayoral Leadership." *American Political Science Review*, 66 (June): 511–524.

Renner, Tari, and Victor S. DeSantis (1998). "Municipal Form of Government: Issues and Trends." *The Municipal Year Book—1998*. Washington, DC: International City Management Association.

Ross, B. H., and M. A. Levine (1996). *Urban Politics: Power in Metropolitan Areas* (5th ed.). Itasca, IL: Peacock.

Svara, James H. (1990). *Official Leadership in the City: Patterns of Conflict and Cooperation*. New York: Oxford University Press.

CHAPTER

11

Counties, Special Districts, and School Systems: Politics Beyond City Hall

꙳ **States and Their Counties**

꙳ **Special Service Districts**

꙳ **Independent School Districts**

꙳ **Chapter Conclusion**

The study of municipal government only scratches the surface of local government in the United States. We also have county governments, school districts, and various special service districts. The structures, personalities, and issues of these types of local governments differ from those of cities and towns. So while municipal government may be the centerpiece of local government, it is far from the only type of local government to affect our daily lives.

County governments in the United States are created by the states and have powers delegated to them by state government. They are responsible for public policy and government services in the unincorporated portions of counties. Their duties also include the county-wide delivery of state-mandated programs such as public health, social welfare, and medical assistance. They are general purpose governments charged with protecting and serving the public; these duties are carried out by county officials such as a sheriff, a coroner, and a probate judge. The large geographical jurisdiction of counties and the challenges of meeting both state and citizen service expectations make county government a difficult calling in the twenty-first century.

Navigating local government would be difficult without knowing about the sometimes-invisible governments called *special service districts* and *independent school districts.* Over the years, Americans have created many special purpose public authorities, each with its own governing structure. The justification for creating this proliferation of local government authorities flows from the public's continuing distrust of "big government." There are two specific rationales for creating so many independent authorities.

First, the services that special districts and school districts provide should be *apolitical*—that is "above politics." Decisions should be made in the best interests of the consumer and the child and not in the political interests of any politician or regime. For many Americans, the specific service should not be mired in a swamp of local influence peddling and corruption.

Second, the services that the independent authorities provide should be *efficient*—that is, they should be run like a business instead of like a bureaucracy. Revenues for the special district and the school district should be raised by it through special taxes, and all monies should be dedicated exclusively to special purposes. This allows the public to monitor where the money goes more easily. If specialized funds can be applied to a specific problem or service, then concrete improvements may result. Special assessment funds do not get lost in the labyrinth of a local government's budget.

If an important local service can be protected this way, then citizens can live with the special taxes that will be levied for the services. They also can live with a small growth in government regulation over their lives for the sake of achieving a specific and laudable purpose.

As we explore the world of counties and then of special purpose local governments and independent school districts, we must ask ourselves if they are achieving their designated purposes:

- Given their geographic and intergovernmental constraints, do counties deliver quality services in an efficient manner?
- Do special service districts represent a new kind of accountability, or are they just a new way of increasing taxes and expanding government?
- Are school districts accountable to the public, or have they been captured by professionals who are employed in the school system?
- Together, do special service districts and school districts represent more or less democratic control over the apparatus of local government?

The answers to these questions can only be found once we understand the abc's of the United States' historic counties and expanding minigovernments.

❧ States and Their Counties

Federal mandates and homegrown state laws create a large number of programs and services. States could not begin to administer most of the programs out of a single office in the state capital. They must have an organized network of service providers throughout the state who meet the public, deliver the services, answer questions, and interpret policy in individual cases. Like the British before us, we created counties to serve this purpose.

County Geography

There are 3,068 counties in the United States. They vary greatly in size and population. They range in area from 26 square miles (Arlington County, Virginia) to 87,861 square miles (North Slope Borough, Alaska). The population of counties also widely varies: from Loving County, Texas, with 140 residents, to Los Angeles County, California, which is home to 9.1 million people. Forty-eight of the fifty states have operational county governments. Connecticut and Rhode Island are divided into geographic regions called *counties* but do not have functioning governments. Alaska calls its counties *boroughs*, and Louisiana calls them *parishes*. Hawaii and Delaware each have the fewest counties with only three each, while Texas has the most with 254. City–county governments—that is, cities that have consolidated government functions with their surrounding counties—exist in thirty-one jurisdictions, including Denver, New York, San Francisco, and Lafayette, Louisiana (National Association of Counties Online: <*http://www.naco.org*>).

In general, Western counties are quite large because of sparse population. Cochise County, Arizona, is typical (see **Figure 11.1**). Services such as emergency medical care and the sheriff's patrol have greater distances to cover, which sometimes leads to concerns about service quality and the creation of substations at strategic points throughout the county.

Figure 11.1   Cochise County, Arizona

Geography also shapes the kinds of services that a county must provide. A state such as Arizona may have an emergency preparedness plan that stresses heat and drought. California's plan would emphasize wildfires, and Washington state's would require monitoring potential flooding. The land makes demands on counties, especially the areas outside of its municipalities' city limits.

County Demographics

People also shape the kinds of services that counties must provide. Many elderly retired people now reside in Florida, for example. Emergency medical services must deal with strokes, heart attacks, serious falls, and other problems that face elders. Mountainous areas in West Virginia and North Carolina have many isolated, small communities where poor health and alcoholism are problems, while areas of suburban New York and Connecticut have problems with cocaine abuse and HIV. Some areas of the United States are almost entirely English-speaking, while parts of the Southwest are home to Spanish-speaking people and American Indians who speak their native tongues. County officials must be prepared to deal with local people in terms of local demographics and culture.

Suburbanization and migration within the United States have brought many new residents to U.S. counties. New residents seek cheaper land, more amenities, and lower taxes by living outside city limits—and they also bring high expectations with them. This sets the stage for some level of conflict. These new residents want the same quality of services they have received elsewhere, but counties have been accustomed to providing minimal services and charging exceedingly low taxes. Things have had to change. County officials have had to raise taxes so that quality services can be developed, and they have had to meet more often to consider increased demands and needs for action. The typical county commission is no longer a quiet little club where long-term residents get together.

County Authority

States constrain counties in their ability to respond to the demands of general government. To be responsive, counties feel a need for discretionary authority. The U.S. Advisory Commission on Intergovernmental Relations (ACIR) studied the powers of county government in 1981. The commission ranked the states in terms of the amount of discretionary authority granted to their counties. Although a few states such as Oregon and North Carolina offered counties a measure of autonomy, counties in most states were found to "fall short of possessing broad structural, functional, and financing powers, particularly the last" (ACIR, 1981: 60). Although thirty-six states allow their counties some measure of home rule, only a few counties have adopted this option. The consequence is that 95 percent of all U.S. counties are **general law counties** subject to virtual state control (DeSantis & Renner, 1993: 17). Only the remaining 5 percent experience some measure of real independence in making policy and instituting new programs and services.

The Commission Form of Government

The most common governmental structure used by U.S. counties is the **commission form.** Under this form, legislative and executive functions are fused into a single elected **county commission.** The elected commissioners function together as a legislative body, albeit one with quite limited lawmaking authority (see Figure 11.2). County commissioners meet as a group on a regular and publicly announced basis. Between meetings, each commissioner may oversee an area of county government. When problems arise that county employees cannot solve, they will call "their" commissioner.

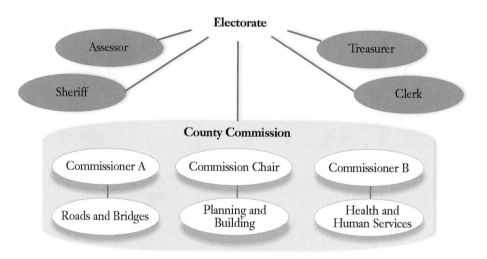

Figure 11.2 Commission form of county government

The **chair of the county commission** is elected as such in some states and selected by the commissioners themselves in others. He or she will chair commission meetings and oversee county government's central bureaucracy, which is responsible for such activities as personnel hiring, accounting, computer services, and courthouse operations.

One example of the commission form of county government is the board of supervisors in San Luis Obispo, California. Serving a county population of 229,000, the board has responsibility for elections, records, social services, public health, planning and building, and tax collection. Each function exists in an administrative department that reports directly to the board.

County Administrators

With so many bosses, county employees may not know who can address their issues and concerns. The commission chair may be in charge from a policy point of view, but he or she cannot oversee the activities of the many offices of county government. Accountability for daily service delivery might be impossible unless someone is responsible for day-to-day operations. For this reason, a county may hire a professional **county administrator** who is a contract employee just like a city manager and accountable to the county commission.

Under the county administrator arrangement, county workers report through a more centralized chain of command (see Figure 11.3). Daily operations are centralized, and elected officials can deal with the public in their roles as representatives of the people. County government becomes more business-like. For example, in Somerset County, New Jersey, with a 1996 population of 260,790, the board of chosen freeholders—yes, the names vary across the country—employs a full-time county administrator, currently Richard E. Williams, who oversees three departments: finance and administrative services, public works, and human services.

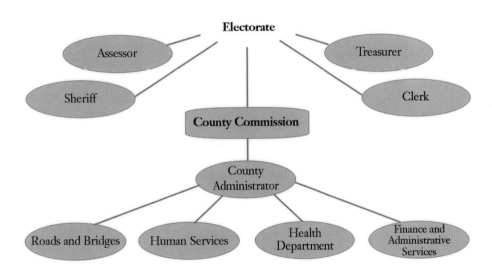

Figure 11.3   County administrator form of government

Other Elected County Officials

Several county officials are elected at the same time as the commissioners. By both tradition and state law, citizens elect the chief law enforcement officer of the county: the **sheriff.** The sheriff's office is responsible for protecting public safety throughout the county, whether geographically tiny or vast. Sheriffs also have increasing responsibilities in fast-growing suburban counties.

Voters also elect a **county tax commissioner,** treasurer, or assessor to administer the county's tax program. This tax commissioner has many responsibilities, including overseeing tax assessments, organizing collection activities, and hearing tax appeals. States extensively regulate county taxation, but the workload is at the local level. Most counties have large departments devoted to these duties.

In many jurisdictions, a **county coroner**—or county medical examiner—also is elected. The coroner is responsible for determining cause of death in any case in which there is some question about a resident's death. The coroner is a trained medical professional who conducts *autopsies*, or investigative operations on dead bodies to determine the cause or causes of death. In some cases, this determination reports foul play; in others, a serious communicable disease may be discovered. In any case, public health and public safety require that this official enjoy the public's confidence.

The sheriff, tax commissioner, and coroner all have legally prescribed duties to discharge. Local residents and state officials count on their professionalism and effectiveness. Along with the broad duties of the county commissioners, these positions reveal many centers of power in county government.

County Executive

A less common structure of county government is the county executive form. In a few counties, voters elect a *county executive* at the same time they elect a county commission (see **Figure 11.4** and **Box 11.1**). Large urban counties often find that placing all of their appointed employees under a single politically accountable executive brings better accountability to county government. The executive prepares a budget and may have veto power over the actions of the commission, which is limited to legislative and oversight responsibilities. In many ways, the county executive in an urban county functions like a big city mayor. The county administrator who reports to the executive manages the daily operations of county government. Recently, several states, including Arkansas, Kentucky, and Tennessee, mandated elected executives for their county governments.

Jefferson Parish (New Orleans), Louisiana, and Cook County (Chicago), Illinois, are examples of the commission–executive county government. Jefferson Parish with a population of 455,043 and Cook County with a population of 5,096,540 respectively elect a parish president and a president of the board of commissioners. These individuals are the chief administrative officers and oversee the main departments of county government.

A common characteristic of all county governments is a high level of *fragmentation;* this is evident when voters directly elect several individuals who

---

| BOX **11.1** | *Suffolk County, New York* |

Robert J. Gaffney is the Suffolk County (NY) county executive. Suffolk County constitutes the eastern two-thirds of Long Island. The office of county executive was created by the county's 1960 charter. A board of supervisors is also elected to serve as the county's legislative body. An attorney and former FBI agent, Gaffney previously served in the New York State Assembly. Under his leader-

ship, Suffolk County has eliminated its $100 million deficit and improved the county's bond rating to investment grade. At the same time, the county has cut general property taxes each year and ended the fiscal year with a surplus. Other accomplishments of Gaffney's administration can be viewed at the county's Web page at *<http://www.co.suffolk.ny.us>*.

Photo courtesy of Robert J. Gaffney.

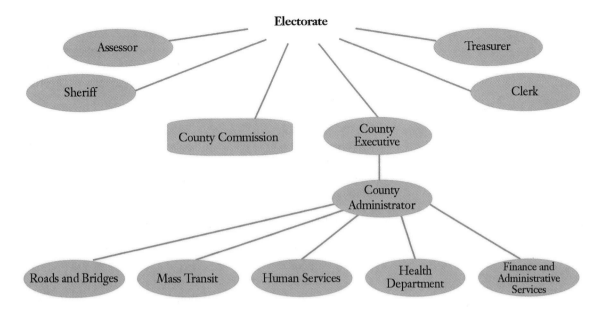

Figure 11.4 County executive form of government

have administrative responsibilities, but no single individual has full administrative capability. Jefferson Parish voters elect the sheriff, clerk of the court, assessor, coroner, and district attorney. In addition to the president of the board of commissioners and the commissioners themselves, Cook County voters elect the county clerk, clerk of circuit court, recorder of deeds, sheriff, treasurer, assessor, and state's attorney.

County Courts

County courts have *limited jurisdiction*. In Florida, they have authority over violations of county ordinances, including traffic violations, and enforce misdemeanor crimes, or relatively minor criminal offenses that carry a penalty of one year or less in the county jail. Civil cases involving amounts of $15,000 or less are also heard in county court. Small claims and landlord–tenant relations are typical civil matters that end up in county court (Florida State Courts System Online, 1998).

Judges of these **inferior courts** sometimes are referred to as *justices of the peace, chancellery judges, magistrates,* or simply as *county judges.* They are elected officials and may serve part-time in smaller jurisdictions. Their qualifications vary, and some may not have law degrees. Their offices are supported by fees and fines levied from the bench.

One allied county official is elected to deal with citizens' legal concerns: the *clerk of county court.* This individual keeps the county court calendar and keeps records of the court's proceedings.

The recorder or *probate judge* is another elected county official and the official who issues deeds, marriage licenses, and gun permits, and processes the wills of individuals who have died. Again, voters may be reassured if they are able to select the individual who will safeguard their privacy in these personal matters.

County courts are not major trial courts. Those duties are usually reserved for state civil and criminal courts. Nevertheless, as local institutions, they facilitate everyday life in communities and maintain important family records. They are "inferior" only in the sense that the concerns of their deliberations are modest. To individuals who need the assistance or protection of local courts, they are not meaningless institutions.

County Services

A county government's elected officials and senior bureaucrats try to provide a clear focus for county services. The 1998 goals of the Kalamazoo County (Michigan) Board of Commissioners are instructive in this regard. The commissioners' goals are to:

> (1) Provide accessible cost effective service delivery to citizens. (2) Improve citizen understanding of the role and structure of county government. (3) Promote effective and responsive Board decision-making. (4) Promote planning and collaboration with other elected officials and units of government. (5) Strengthen the diversity and improve the stability of the community economic base. (6) Develop and implement innovative strategies to mitigate the social conditions which increase demands on human services, law enforcement or other county programs (Kalamazoo County Online, 1998).

County government, of course, does not always operate as smoothly as our diagrams and goals suggest. A typical county has a mixed system in which some services are centralized under the county administrator and others remain under elected officials—another example of the fragmentation of county government. The sheriff is the chief law enforcement official of the county regardless of how he or she receives administrative support. Sheriff's deputies would answer to the sheriff in regard to their investigations and enforcement activities, while their uniforms and equipment might be purchased under a centralized contracting office under the county administrator. If you choose a career in county law enforcement, health administration, or social work, then you will learn a great deal about how supervision and accountability work in the real world of fragmented county governments.

To make service delivery even more complicated, service responsibility sometimes becomes an issue in incorporated cities and towns within the county. County government is responsible for services in the unincorporated portions of the county, but city services usually take over within city limits. Sometimes, two systems of government provide many of the same services. City police duplicate the county sheriff's office. City streets are maintained using much of the same equipment that is needed to maintain county roads. Duplication is found in recreation services, fire protection, and even schooling. Surely, some of these services could be consolidated. (See also Box 11.2.)

Consolidated Services

If a county and a city agree to go together to operate specific services, then we call this arrangement **functional consolidation.** If the two entities go beyond specific services to merge most or all local government services, then we use the term **consolidated government.** Both approaches to providing more efficient and accountable local services are being tried in the United States. Consolidation of services and of governments is discussed further in Chapter 12, "Metropolitan Governments."

County Government Capacity Building

Counties vary a great deal in their capacities to solve problems, govern, and manage government services. Urban counties operate within a milieu of wealth and professionalism. They often have a sound tax base and can hire first-rate workers and managers. Intergovernmental agreements define the roles of municipal, county, and special district governments in their region.

Rural counties typically have weak tax bases and offer few professional services. When people who move into the county bring great expectations of local government with them, they may find that rural county officials are hard pressed to respond to those expectations. *Suburban counties* are somewhere in the middle. They have inherited rural political institutions but face urbanizing service demands. These fast-growing suburban counties are gearing up for change, but the bar of public expectations is often raised faster than they can respond.

Prospects for *rural counties* with rising expectations are not good. State planning agencies try to help them with developing their infrastructures and in attracting new industry. With improved roads, water systems, and waste disposal systems, prospective industries may be attracted to the area. With the new companies come employment opportunities and an improved local tax base (Flora & Johnson, 1991: 51). Yet the economic development of rural areas is at best a hit-or-miss proposition. Some few counties succeed in landing a major industry, while others manage to attract an occasional smaller firm. The resulting modest tax base and lack of highly skilled employees keep the government services capacities of rural communities low.

Urban counties address some service needs that are common to all county governments. For example, they typically operate a solid-waste facility or garbage dump. They provide law enforcement to unincorporated portions of the county and operate the county jail. However, urban counties also have additional duties that distinguish them from smaller counties. Urban counties may provide mass transit, operate airports, coordinate community development and housing programs, and manage sports stadiums. The breadth and the scale of operations is different for the urban county.

The capacity of urban counties to address the demands of modern government depends on their revenue sources and the degree of **home rule** that is authorized by their state governments (Waugh & Streib, 1993). If urban county officials have the money and the power needed to address issues such

Get a map of the county where you now live or where you grew up. Make sure the map has a legend and a scale. Measure the county from edge to edge, from top to bottom. Now convert that measurement (does one inch, for example, equal one mile?) for distance. You may even be able to estimate the total square miles contained within the county's boundaries. How many municipalities are incorporated within the county? What unincorporated area does this leave for the county government to serve? Is the county urban, rural, or suburban? Is it fast-growing? Compare your findings with those of other members of your class. You may have a new appreciation for the challenges that face your county.

as mass transit, then they can hire the professionals to design and operate a commuter rail system. Expertise does not come cheap, but professionals often can bring in extra grant resources as urban county services grow. Overall, urban counties seem to have the resources and alliances they need to succeed.

The fast-growing counties in the suburban areas that surround major cities are a special case of such *capacity building*. These counties must fund and deliver ever-increasing levels of public safety, transportation, and environmental protection services (Benton & Menzel, 1993: 67–68). Traffic and trash dominate the agendas of many county commissions in suburban areas. They must scurry to keep up with increasing demands for good police protection, better roads, and quality solid-waste disposal.

Fortunately for suburbanites, property values are increasing, which boosts property-tax revenues. Sales of goods and service are increasing, which nudges sales-tax receipts higher and higher. Well-trained professionals want to work

---

BOX 11.3 *National Association of Counties*

Throughout this book, we have been careful to remind ourselves and our readers that state and local governments are "not in this alone" when it comes to issues and problems. National associations play a vitally important role in keeping a dialogue open among city and county governments. An important organization in this effort is the National Association of Counties (NACo). One sample activity offered by NACo is its County Model Programs series. Innovative and successful programs in areas ranging from animal control to parks and recreation are posted for officials around the country to study. You can see the series on the NACo Web site at <*http://www.naco.org/counties/models/index.cfm*>. County government does face serious challenges, but local officials can draw on the ideas and support of fellow county officials from elsewhere in the United States.

Michael Hightower, president of the National Association of Counties and a Fulton County, Georgia, commissioner, announces that NACo has launched the nation's first welfare reform clearinghouse on the Internet in October 1996.
Source: © Associated Press

and live in the suburbs, and the quality of the county government workforce has every prospect of improving. In other words, suburban counties may suffer the growing pains of increased county services but have the wherewithal to deal with growth. The only reasonable concern for suburban county officials—other than the unfunded mandates and policy preemption that plague all local governments—is *taxpayer revolt*. If county residents moved out of the city or avoided buying a home inside the city limits because of the perceived tax burden, then they may resent even the most rational county tax plan. While this unwillingness to pay their own way may seem irresponsible, most Americans consistently vote their so-called pocketbook issues. If the county raises the tax rate too much or reassesses property values too often, then local citizens may refuse to support a county's capacity-building efforts. (See also **Box 11.3**.)

❧ Special Service Districts

The creation of special districts is linked to the historic context of local government in the United States. Two apparently conflicting pressures created local governments. First, a distrust of government pervades American culture; second, there remains a belief that government that is closest to the people is preferable to government that is farther away. Not trusting urban areas, rural state legislators designed bare-bones local governments. As urban areas grew and new services were needed, these same state legislators responded by creating special purpose governments. Rather than strengthen general purpose local governments such as counties, municipalities, and townships by granting them new powers, entirely new boards and commissions were established, each with its own responsible officials.

Special districts now have become the most numerous local governments in the United States, with 30,000 specialized limited purpose local governments, excluding school districts (see **Table 11.1**). The number and variety of special service districts has increased in each of the past six decades. The three most common services that special districts deliver are natural resource protection (20 percent), fire protection (17 percent), and housing and community development (11 percent). Of course, even these three total less than half of all special districts in the United States. This dramatizes the great variety of highly specialized purposes for which states and citizens use this type of local government.

Table 11.1
Growth of Special Districts

Year	Number of Districts
1941–42	8,299
1951–52	12,340
1961–62	18,323
1971–72	23,885
1981–82	28,078
1991–92	31,555

Source: 1992 Census of Governments Online (*<http://www.census.gov/prod/www/abs/gc92org.html>*)

Governmental Powers of Special Districts

One principle source of power for special districts is their status as *legal persons*. They can sue and be sued, make contracts, and obtain and dispose of property (Blair, 1986: 141). The powers and responsibilities for each type of special district are outlined in state law. The responsibility for interpreting service policy is vested in a board that is appointed by state or local officials to oversee the district's services. There are also professional and administrative employees who carry out the policies of the district. When special district officials or employees act, they may have to defend themselves in court. Being a "legal person" does not give the special district special advantages in court except for the fact that it operates under a state mandate. For example, a permitting authority may deny an industry a permit to expand its water consumption or increase its discharge of dirty water into area streams and rivers. If the industry's executives believe that the ruling is unreasonable, then they may sue to get it overturned. The special district must be prepared to defend its actions as appropriate and necessary under relevant state law.

A second set of powers comes from the mission given to each type of special district by legislation. To discharge its duties, the state has granted each special district **quasi-governmental powers** such as assessing property taxes, incurring public debt, securing land through eminent domain, and hiring and supervising specially trained enforcement staff. We usually think only general purpose governments levy taxes, but a tax is a tax regardless of what it is called. By the same token, individuals and companies are often surprised to learn that a state government has ceded special districts powers such as eminent domain— that is, foreclosing on property and paying a "fair market price" for land that is needed for a compelling but sometimes heatedly debated public purpose.

Using the example of water use, the permit process requires staff members to review and investigate an industry's plans. This capability in turn requires financial resources. The special district may bill participating area governments, charge for water-use applications, issue and collect fines, and take other actions to protect the underground aquifers that distribute water throughout the state and nation.

The jurisdictions of special districts commonly cross the boundaries of municipalities and counties. Public transportation provides a good example of cross-district jurisdiction. It may once have been all right for each individual city to operate its own bus or metro rail services. At some point, however, duplication proves wasteful. In such a case, the real transportation needs of the area may clearly overlap several general purpose government boundaries. Likewise, it seems extraordinarily wasteful for each city in a metropolitan area to build and maintain its own water-treatment facilities. So in both cases, the area to be addressed by a special district is related to the specific need being addressed not the traditional governmental boundaries. A state might set up a dozen water-quality districts, fifty fire-prevention areas, or twenty economic-development zones.

The rapid growth of special purpose governments reflects Americans' broadening social concerns for the environment and personal well-being. The growth also responds to the antigovernment bias in American political culture. These relatively small and business-like districts solve problems that currently demand solution and without much of the negative baggage of local politicians and bureaucrats. Their revenues are earmarked for special purposes; they are not caught in the property tax wars of general purpose government.

Chicago's Special Districts

The array of special purpose governments is staggering. Illinois tops the list of states with 2,920 such districts, as well as the largest total of all local governments with 6,722. The Chicago metropolitan area is an excellent example of the serious challenges that face large urban communities. It also is a case study in the complexities of special districts. Those with responsibility for public transportation illustrate many of the issues of the invisible governments.

Four boards or authorities govern public transportation in the Chicago metropolitan area: The Chicago Transit Authority controls local transit services within Chicago, the METRA Commuter Rail Board governs commuter rail services, PACE Suburban Bus Board governs suburban bus services, and the Regional Transportation Authority coordinates the services of the other three.

Each organization has its own governing board with members appointed by the governor, Chicago's mayor, or the area county boards of supervisors. In all, thirty-nine individuals hold seats on these various boards. They control services and rates, and they have the power to levy taxes and raise revenue bonds to support their decisions. None of these individuals need be elected officials, and many are not. The average citizens of the Chicago area would probably have difficulty identifying these organizations much less understanding how they function.

Chicago's transportation system and special districts face all of the challenges of any major metropolitan area.
Source: © Kim Karpeles

Water-Quality Districts

Clean water is becoming a major concern in the United States. In many communities, the basic water supply that allows drinking, cooking, and bathing is a system of underground rivers called *aquifers*. Rain, rivers, and streams feed into the underground system. When communities or individuals want to access fresh water, they siphon off above-ground flow or drill a well into the underground water supply.

As progressively more intensive agricultural, commercial, and residential developments have expanded, many areas of the country have run short of water. So much fresh water has been used that local use and downstream supplies are threatened. Along the seacoasts, lowered water levels in aquifers have allowed saltwater to intrude and spoil the underground water supply. Many communities in Florida, for example, must ration water during the driest periods of the year. As a consequence of such problems, many state legislatures are considering limitations on agricultural and commercial access to the water supply.

Florida's water-quality districts are organized to manage local water supply and demand. States establish these special purpose local governments and provide for their structure and powers. The permitting process is one regulatory tool of the water-quality district. A new industry, agribusiness, or mall development would have to apply for a water-use permit. In the application, the business would state its expected rate of water use and outline its water-conservation or supplementation plan. For example, an industry might plan to capture water that it uses in one manufacturing process and use it in a later process. It also would state its plans for cleaning the water residue before the water is returned to the local water system. A special water treatment plant may have to be built to ensure that water-based toxins do not enter the fresh water supply.

If the water-use and release plans are approved, then the enterprise can go forward with its development. On the other hand, if the water-quality district board denies the permit, then the developers will have to change their plans or try to get the board's decision reversed in court. This example reveals some of the operational features of special districts.

Concerns About Special District Government

While special districts may help solve a variety of local service problems, they also create certain challenges. First, the special districts themselves are often invisible to citizens, so holding them accountable to the public is extremely difficult. Second, the individuals who serve on many special district governing boards are appointed rather than elected officials. They may not be well known within a community. Third, a single metropolitan area has so many special districts that there is **fragmentation** among them. One district may not know

Brazilian States as Development Districts

Brazil's experience with federalism has gone full circle. The country has had a federal system of government with regional states and a central government since 1891. Initially, the states had so much autonomy that each became an oligarchy, a political regime in which a small elite held virtually all power. Regionally based elites would compete and even war for control of the central government and the other states. A central presidency and a centralized revenue system would only sometimes dominate regional interests.

Many of Brazil's problems are national in scope but regional in their particulars. Demographically, some regions of the country have large numbers of young people who will be entering the labor market. Vocational education and many new jobs will be needed if these young workers are to be gainfully employed. In other areas, the workforce is aging. The goal is therefore to revitalize the country's social security system and attract younger workers to migrate to the regions with shrinking labor forces. Throughout the southern, agrarian regions, large family estates were just beginning to give way to small farm holdings when large-

scale agribusiness moved in and "rationalized" agricultural production. The new enterprises need neither the old landholding families nor the small family farmers. They need salaried farmworkers who can operate modern machinery.

Brazilian federalism was once a system of political competition for national power and control. In recent years, the national government may have gained a measure of stability and security, but it has now had to turn to the states to tailor economic-development reforms. It is ironic that nationalism succeeds only to have to turn to provincialism for implementing solutions to its economic and social-welfare problems. So now Brazil has come full circle with its subnational states. Today the national government hopes to make the states what we would call economic-development districts. This way the country can have national solutions to its problems while fine-tuning programs according to regional needs. Details of Brazil's political and economic challenges are found at this excellent English-language Web site: <*http://www.mre.gov.br/ projeto/mreweb/ingles/default.htm*>.

what others are doing, and no one is in charge of them all. Fourth and finally, those who are especially aware of a special district government may be a narrow special interest community group that has effectively captured the agency for its own gain without considering other interests. If you want to navigate this part of local government, you'll certainly have to do a lot of homework.

❧ Independent School Districts

School districts are not considered along with the other special purpose governments in the United States because they have a unique history and a common mission. Authority over education is not granted to the national government by the U.S. Constitution. In fact, the word *education* does not even appear in that document. By contrast, education is the only public function that has its own article in virtually *every* state constitution. Clearly, the authors of these documents believed that education was a special government function, because of its links to democracy, participation, and economic survival.

We discussed the widespread interest in state education legislation in Chapter 4. State governments are indeed active in funding colleges, universities, and vocational schools. In many states, education is by far the largest item in the state budget. State funding is also an important part of each K–12 school system's budget.

State Educational Policy

State legislation enables experimentation in school programming. A legislature opens the door to new educational strategies when it authorizes innovations such as charter schools or vouchers. States do not turn over their constitutional responsibility for public education to local governments or school districts. They reserve for themselves permission-granting authority for each specific type of experimental program.

State regulations set general guidelines for school districts, providing consistency in the school calendar, core course content, teacher qualifications, and graduation requirements. A state education department in the state capital enforces these regulations. Written policies are developed, and state employees monitor compliance with state law. A district's failure to comply with state regulations could result in the loss of state funding to local school districts.

Local School Policies

For the development of policies that directly affect children, the power over education is delegated downward to the local level. Local school districts control the content of K–12 teaching within geographical boundaries and administrative parameters created by the state. Teachers are hired and supervised at the local level.

The history of local control of education in the United States has led to the creation and maintenance of more than 14,000 independent school districts. It has been governments' common belief that schools should reflect the values and policy preferences of the citizens they serve. As a result, in three-quarters of the districts, a governing school board is elected directly by voters. In the remaining districts, city councils, county commissions, mayors, or judges appoint board members. A school board itself appoints a professional **school superintendent** who serves as the school system's chief executive.

Amazingly, the number of school districts in the United States declined dramatically in the middle of the twentieth century (see Table 11.2). Today, there is only one-tenth the number of school districts as in 1941. The number of school districts declined because small city and county districts merged into larger, more comprehensive independent school districts. This consolidation of smaller school districts occurred primarily in rural areas where population density is low.

Table 11.2
U.S. School Districts by Year

Year	Number of Districts
1941–42	108,579
1951–52	67,355
1961–62	34,678
1971–72	15,781
1981–82	14,851
1991–92	14,422

Source: 1992 Census of Governments Online (<*http://www.census.gov/ prod/www/abs/gc92org.html*>)

Operating a comprehensive system of elementary schools, middle schools, and high schools requires a fairly large population. A city might have several neighborhood-based elementary and middle schools, but only one or two area high schools may be needed. Athletics, clubs, and specialized curricula can be developed in a large high school.

School District Politics

Even though independent school districts govern our public schools, they are not truly independent of outside influences. Elected school boards work in a particularly dynamic political environment. They must be responsive to public school teachers' unions such as the National Education Association (NEA) and the American Federation of Teachers (AFT). Parent organizations and neighborhood associations are interested in having the very best local and neighborhood schools. Elderly residents of many school districts are resistant to tax increases, partly because they no longer have children in the schools and usually are living on relatively fixed incomes. Business groups want to keep taxes low, but they are aware that the public schools are training their future employees. They also know that a good school system is critical to attracting new businesses and retaining existing companies. State elected officials have ultimate responsibility for education and are prepared to intervene when they believe local school boards are not functioning well. Knowing how to navigate the politics of education is a particularly difficult challenge in the twenty-first century.

Confidence in Public Schools

In recent years, confidence in the nation's public schools has been of great concern. In 1999, a Gallup poll found that only 47 percent of Americans were satisfied with K–12 public schools; 51 percent were dissatisfied (see Table 11.3). This high level of concern reflects a continuing bleak picture of public education in the United States that was painted in 1983 by *A Nation at Risk*, an influential U.S. Department of Education report. The report criticized schools for the decline in discipline and academic standards. Apparently, public opinion seems to reflect this assessment. Or does it?

The same 1999 Gallup poll suggests that the picture of public schools is perhaps not totally grim. In fact, 83 percent of parents are satisfied with the education their children receive in their schools. We like our *local* schools. We are pleased with the job our school district, school board, school superintendent, principal, and teachers are doing. When we look at public education as a national enterprise, we are negative and pessimistic. In education policy, as we move from national pictures of problems and toward local solutions with which we are familiar, our positive assessments increase—and dramatically so.

A good school system can attract business and industry to an area.
Source: © Tom McCarthy / PhotoEdit

Table 11.3
Citizen Satisfaction with Public Schools, 1999

	Nationally (%)	Own Child's School (%)
Completely satisfied	8	37
Somewhat satisfied	39	46
Somewhat dissatisfied	38	12
Completely dissatisfied	13	2
No opinion or no answer	2	3

Source: The Gallup Organization Online (<http://www.gallup.com/online/index.asp>).

Independent School Districts

School Funding

State and local governments primarily finance education (see Table 11.4). Federal, state, and local funds mix in a complex web of financial incentives and regulatory "strings" that are tied to the funds. The three levels of government share a concern that all children have access to quality facilities, quality instruction, and quality technology. All of these important ingredients are costly. The public is generally supportive (National Public Radio, 1999).

Table 11.4
Source of Funds for Public Education, 1998–99

Source of Funds	Percent of School's Budget
National government	6.9
State government	49.8
Local government	43.3

Source: National Center for Education Statistics Online (<*http://nces.ed.gov*>).

Federal Funds. The national government's involvement in funding public education is actually quite limited. This may come as a surprise given the amount of attention education has received recently in national debates and elections. Still, Congress funds less than 7 percent of all K–12 public school expenditures.

The largest federal government *grant-in-aid program* operates under Title I of the Elementary and Secondary Education Act, which was passed in 1965. Title I provides approximately $7 billion to improve education for children who are deemed at risk of school failure and who live in low-income communities. The federal government also funds school lunch programs, Head Start for preschool children, and a wide variety of specialized programs that are targeted to specific needy populations.

In addition to providing limited funds, the federal government's reach into public education is also felt in a vast array of *federal education regulations.* Title IX of the Education Amendments of 1972 prohibits gender discrimination in all school activities, including school sports. Remarkably, in 1971, a Connecticut judge might have stated, "Athletic competition builds character in our boys. We do not need that kind of character in our girls." The Individuals with Disabilities Education Act mandates that all children have access to a free and appropriate education that meets their unique needs. This act requires that individualized plans be created for all disabled children and encourages opportunities for children with disabilities to participate in general education settings and the general education curriculum.

State Funding. State governments have had to be more intimately involved with the financial demands of operating public schools. State legislatures typically fund a *basic grant* for every K–12 child in the state. Local school districts document the number of children they will be serving, and the state essentially writes a check for the basic grant amount multiplied by that number of children.

State funds also come with strings attached. School buildings must meet state standards for safety and cleanliness. Teachers must be accredited under state regulations. Administrative records must be kept that document that state funds are spent appropriately. And these are only the most obvious examples of state regulations.

As we mentioned in Chapter 4, state legislatures have been challenged to make school funding equitable between various locales within their states. Such *funding equity* is concerned with whether students in various independent school districts across a state have access to an education that is comparably funded. The concern is tied to a specific ideal: Education is about giving children a fair start in life, an equal opportunity for political and economic success. Increasingly, wealthier school systems have supplemented their state basic education grants with local tax revenues. This has resulted in pockets of poorly funded schools in sparsely populated rural areas and lower-income urban neighborhoods. Courts in some states—for example, Arizona, Ohio, and Rhode Island—have handed down decisions that seem to require legislatures to equalize educational opportunity within their states. Some states—notably Michigan, Texas, and New Jersey—have responded by overhauling their school-tax laws. Texas "capped" or set a limit on taxable property in any given school district and redirected "excess" revenue to poorer districts. Michigan repealed much of the local school board authority for taxing property and replaced the revenue with increased sales and cigarettes taxes (Lewis & Maruna, 1996: 457). The goal of such legislation is to remove the advantage of localities that have many wealthy residents and valuable property to tax. Of course, such legislation is also of interest to legislators who are concerned with tax reform as a larger issue.

Local Funding. Historically, most public schools have been funded primarily with local *property taxes*. The more valuable the property in a community, the more revenue the school district may raise. A **tax rate** is applied to the **assessed property value,** and the total tax liability is assessed. A community controls the tax rate and the frequency with which property is reassessed. A total property tax bill can increase even when the tax rate is constant if the local tax assessor is allowed to increase the assessed value of the home each year or two. Not surprisingly, there has been considerable resentment of such authority. In Georgia, for example, the state legislature is considering a law that would declare that localities may no longer use this "backdoor" method of raising taxes. Property values could only be reassessed on a state schedule. School boards that want to raise taxes would have to convince local voters to approve an increase in the **millage rate,** the actual tax rate.

In some cases, a lower-income community might tax itself at a rate twice that of a wealthy community and still raise significantly less revenue (National Center for Education Statistics, 1998). The community simply has less valuable property to tax in the first place. In 1971, the California Supreme Court ruled in *Serrano* v. *Priest* that extreme revenue disparities among school districts deprived children in poor districts of equal protection according to both the California and federal constitutions. Two years later, the U.S. Supreme Court ruled in *Rodriguez* v. *San Antonio Independent School District* that relying on local property taxes to fund schools does not violate the Constitution's equal protection clause. This is the case even when the result is wide disparity in the amount of funds that rich and poor school districts are able to raise. These two judicial decisions brought the issue of funding equity for public education into the forefront of education issues. Solutions to the problem of funding equity were then left to state legislatures.

Over the past thirty years, almost all of the states have faced litigation in state courts over their K–12 education financing. These courts led the way in rewriting funding systems either by direct involvement or by ordering legislatures to act. By the time the court actions began, most states had two-part education finance systems. Typically, one part was the basic grant from the state that was designed to meet a minimum level of funding, and a second part was locally generated funds in accordance with a community's individual wish as well as its capacity to tax itself. Even with these dual systems, substantial variance continued to exist among the states.

Looking across the country today, we find a higher level of equity among school districts within each state. But full equity may only be achieved if states take complete control of education financing and deny the heritage of locally run independent school districts. A major problem that many states now face is that to achieve greater equity across districts, they either must substantially increase state revenues for education or "rob Peter to pay Paul"—that is, move funds from one important state program to another. Most states are combining both strategies. One result is that critics complain about the "adequacy" of school financing, some charging that the overall level of expenditures is inadequate, particularly in wealthy suburban school districts where parents are accustomed to having the best schools local taxes can buy.

Inequity in school finances exists across states as well (see **Table 11.5**). New Jersey spends the most per pupil with a 1995–96 expenditure of $9,361, while Utah spends the least at $3,604. Some portion of this variation reflects differences in the cost of living, but a larger portion is a result of each state's policy decisions concerning public services in general and education in particular.

Table 11.5
Per Capita K–12 Spending by State, 1995–96

Ranking	State	Average Spent per Pupil ($)
1	New Jersey	9,361
2	District of Columbia	8,510
3	Connecticut	8,430
4	New York	8,361
5	Alaska	8,189
.	.	.
.	.	.
.	.	.
46	South Dakota	4,220
47	Idaho	4,194
48	Tennessee	4,172
49	Mississippi	3,951
50	Utah	3,604

Source: National Center for Education Statistics Online (<*http://nces.ed.gov*>) (1998).

Education Policy Innovation

A great deal of experimentation and innovation in education is now taking place across the country. Many issues concern professional educators, parents, and politicians alike, including test scores, school violence, the proper role of religion in public schools, the adequacy of funding, teacher salaries, and the apparent failure of many urban, inner-city schools. These issues are being grappled with by fifty state legislatures and governors, thousands of local school districts, and countless community groups.

In spite of the tradition of local control in education, the past twenty years have seen an increase in the role of state governments in local school matters. State governors and legislatures have stepped forward to deal with a vast array of real and perceived problems, including statewide curricula, teacher-certification standards, student performance tests, and funding mechanisms. Two especially prominent issues are school choice and accountability for results.

School Choice. One of the hottest reform issues of public education is that of *school choice*, or providing families with the power to choose which schools their children will attend. In some cases, state-funded tuition vouchers have been proposed that enable students to attend private schools. The issue also includes proposals for *charter schools*, or state-funded nontraditional public schools. These policy proposals are being developed largely outside the public school establishment in general and local school boards in particular.

Publicly funded *tuition vouchers* provide parents with government funding and allow them to shop around for a school of their choice. The cities of Milwaukee and Cleveland, the state of Vermont, and the island commonwealth of Puerto Rico have all experimented with school vouchers. In each case, when religious parochial schools were included in the voucher programs, courts have declared the vouchers unconstitutional because of the current interpretation of the First Amendment's clause establishing a separation of church and state.

More than thirty states have established *charter schools*. Government funding allows students to move from their designated traditional public schools to these nontraditional, nonsectarian public schools of choice. In the 1999–2000 school year, approximately 1,700 charter schools nationwide had enrolled 350,000 students. These numbers appear to be growing rapidly. California, Texas, and Michigan are among the leaders in developing charter schools; together, they are now operating more than 500 schools. Three different groups are creating charter schools: grassroots organizations of parents, teachers, and community members; entrepreneurs; and existing private schools. In the 1996 presidential campaign, Republican candidate Bob Dole endorsed the idea of charter schools. In 1998, President Bill Clinton set a goal of 3,000 charter schools nationwide by 2002 and requested funding to support their growth and development.

Proponents suggest that charter schools will stimulate innovation in curricula and administration, provide choice for parents, encourage parents' involvement in their children's education, and stimulate reform in nearby traditional schools. Opponents argue that funds will be drained from traditional public schools, harming the vast majority of students who are left behind. They worry that charter schools will "cream"—that is, concentrate—the brightest students with the most motivated parents, leaving a still more challenging population for the traditional public schools to educate.

Research on the Michigan charter schools suggests that neither side is completely right. There is little evidence of innovation in curriculum or teaching methods. Neither governing boards nor stakeholders are heavily involved in school governance. There is little evidence of effects on surrounding school districts except that many have created of all-day kindergarten programs in response to charter school competition. At the same time, there is no evidence that charter schools are creaming the best and brightest students. Rather, they are often being created specifically to address the needs of students who have particular learning challenges. Michigan's charter schools are more heavily representative of minority students than the overall state population (Horn & Miron, 1999). Clearly, given the growth of charter schools, they are attractive to parents as an alternative to traditional public schools run by independent school boards. However, the charter schools apparently are draining funds from public school budgets.

Accountability for Results. Another education policy question involves *quality* and *accountability* in public schools. Educational outcomes can be measured in terms of the test scores and employability of students who are schooled in a state. Some observers believe that schools need to compete with each other to improve their performances (Osborne & Gaebler, 1992: 93–104). Open enrollment of students regardless of school district and vouchers that parents may use to purchase the education they want for their children are two competition strategies that many state legislatures have been considering.

To some people, public schools in the United States have an organizational problem that prevents them from achieving the level of success needed for the twenty-first century. This belief suggests that having school districts run by locally elected school boards hampers effective education. They believe that educational excellence can only be achieved by creating a competitive environment where traditional school districts must compete for students with private schools. This variant of the voucher plan would let a parent spend or redeem the voucher at any school in the community, public or private, parochial or secular. The only string attached is that the private school would have to accept the vouchers as "paid in full" tuition for the children. When all parents have the opportunity to chose their children's schools, then quality education would no longer only be available to the wealthy who can afford it. Clearly, this is a controversial issue, for it threatens the very existence of public education as we have come to know it.

Preschool Programs. The education issue for the early decades of the twenty-first century may well be *child-development programs.* As noted in Chapter 4, many states are looking at preschool and kindergarten programs that can better prepare children for entering school. Education may begin in the home, but busy families continue to rely on child-care providers for help. To reassure parents, some state legislatures are looking at licensing child-care providers.

Local Education Policy Making

Within the public school establishment—the independent school district—some communities are developing their own reform proposals such as block scheduling, school uniforms, and back-to-basics curricula.

Block scheduling allows teachers to work with students for longer periods of time in each subject area. The result is that the typical K–12 student's schedule resembles a college student's. Some but not all courses meet daily. Proponents assert that this type of scheduling permits the subject matter in each course to be dealt with more thoroughly.

Many of the distractions and disciplinary problems that plague our schools may be the result of inequity and envy among students. *School uniforms* minimize or remove disparities in status that are often points of conflict between students. Parochial schools have required uniforms for decades. They have found that students attend more to the business of school when the distractions of fashion and cliquishness are removed.

The *back-to-basics curriculum* is a matter of state policy in some parts of the country and within the purview of local school boards in others. When state regulation permits, some communities have moved to institute a curriculum in the schools that produces reliable results in language arts, science, and mathematics. Other elective courses in such areas as fine arts, music, and multiculturalism would be phased out. Sports and social activities would also be curtailed. In some cases, the school day and the school year would be extended. This reallocation of energies is designed to directly affect test scores. The approach is most popular with school officials, teachers, and parents who have faith in testing results.

❧ Chapter Conclusion

We return to our basic questions from the beginning of this chapter. First, we asked whether counties deliver quality services in an efficient manner.

- Although some counties do deliver quality services, they generally lag behind municipalities in service variety and professionalism. Many counties are remote, rural, and poor. Few high-powered professionals work in these counties, which have few resources and amenities to attract such professionals. Economic-development efforts have been an across-the-board response, and development plans occasionally result in new businesses, population growth, and tax-base improvements. The picture is brighter in urban and suburban counties. More cosmopolitan counties are growing rapidly—in fact, too rapidly. If these metropolitan counties can maintain their tax bases against state preemption and taxpayer revolts, then they may well become model service providers.

We next asked whether special service districts were a new form of governmental accountability or a new way to increase taxes and expand government.

- Special service districts now cover the American governmental landscape, and they are by far the fastest areas of growth in the public sector. They are dedicated to many worthy special purposes. Citizens seem to like the business-like way they conduct themselves, even if they sometimes do not seem responsive to questions or criticisms. Professionalism is a powerful value these days, and special service districts hire qualified staff members who know their subject matter. These professionals appear to be getting their jobs done in addressing transportation, water quality, and other types of issues. Indeed, specialized professionals who concentrate their attention on a narrow range of services can accomplish a great deal. In their specific fields of expertise, they are accountable for results. Americans seem to appreciate the quality of these services, and many do not understand why general purpose governments cannot be just as effective. General purpose governments, however, must respond to a far wider range of demands from a more diverse population of constituents.

They must trade off one worthy need against another. They have few dedicated funds to pay for any particular service and must try to keep all public services afloat. It may be unfair to compare the service effectiveness of a special service district with what is possible under a general purpose government.

Our next question asked about the accountability of school districts.

• Independent school districts have their own governance and their own sources of funds. They really are minigovernments unto themselves. Their educational mission is somewhat less narrow than those of special service districts. School boards and superintendents must be able to do several things well if they are to build, maintain, staff, and oversee public schools. Teachers and other school employees are professionals, but citizens do not defer to their judgment to the degree that people defer to the staff of special service districts. Everyone from parents to taxpayers to politicians thinks they know all about educating children. Independent public school districts are reforming, experimenting, and innovating at a frantic pace. They are under so much pressure from state governments and parents that they can leave no potential innovation unexplored. Local private schools and corporate chains of schools are competing with them for the better students, and some parents and politicians are clamoring for vouchers to further fuel the competition. So who's going to win out? Will forces in the community gain control and force school districts to share their best students and tax resources, or will professional teachers and administrators hold onto their positions of trust and public confidence? Public schools are trying to be all things to all people. They are trying to teach both the gifted and the challenged, the well-behaved and the unruly. They want to keep a diverse teacher corps while constantly raising credential and recertification requirements. These and other balancing acts are tough for even the most capable politicians. We cannot say with any confidence that the public schools will win the race against private interests and consumer impatience.

General purpose governments across the country know how they feel. It is a challenging time to be a public servant in local government. Expectations are so high and resources are so limited that creating and running quality public programs sometimes seems an impossible quest. Counties, special districts, and school boards have extremely challenging assignments and unpredictable resources. The politics beyond city hall are rough and tumble. There is no tougher challenge in public service today.

Key Words for InfoTrac Exploration

county executive

education amendments of
1972

elementary school students
clothing

special districts

Sources Cited

Benton, J. Edwin, and Donald C. Menzel (1993). "County Services: The Emergence of Full-Service Government." Pp. 53–69 in David R. Berman (Ed.), *County Governments in an Era of Change.* Westport, CT: Greenwood Press.

Blair, George S. (1986). *Government at the Grass Roots* (4th ed.). Pacific Palisades, CA: Palisades Publishers.

DeSantis, Victor S., and Tari Renner (1993). "Governing the County: Authority, Structure, and Elections." Pp. 15–28 in David R. Berman (Ed.), *County Governments in an Era of Change.* Westport, CT: Greenwood Press.

Flora, Jan L., and Thomas G. Johnson (1991). "Small Businesses." Cornelia B. Flora and James A. Christenson (Eds.), *Rural Policies for the 1990s.* Boulder, CO: Westview Press.

Florida State Courts System (1998). Online: *<http://www.flcourts.org/>.*

Horn, Jerry, and Gary Miron (1999). *Evaluation of Michigan's Public School Academy Initiative.* Kalamazoo, MI: Western Michigan University.

Kalamazoo County Online (1998). Web page: *<http://www.kalcounty.com>.*

Lewis, Dan A., and Shadd Maruna (1996). "The Politics of Education." Pp. 438–477 in Virginia Gray and Herbert Jacob (Eds.), *Politics in the American States: A Comparative Analysis* (6th ed.). Washington, DC: CQ Press.

National Center for Education Statistics (1998). *Inequalities in Public School District Revenue.* Washington, DC: Author.

National Public Radio (1999, Sept. 7). "Americans Willing to Pay for Improving Schools." *Morning Edition.* Washington, DC: NPR/Kaiser/Kennedy School Poll (NPR Online).

Osborne, David, and Ted Gaebler (1992). *Reinventing Government.* Reading, MA: Addison-Wesley.

U.S. Advisory Commission on Intergovernmental Relations (ACIR) (1981). Washington, DC: Author.

U.S. Department of Education (1983). *A Nation at Risk.* Washington, DC: U.S. Government Printing Office.

Waugh, William L., Jr., and Gregory Streib (1993). "County Capacity and Intergovernmental Relations." Pp. 43–52 in David R. Berman (Ed.), *County Governments in an Era of Change.* Westport, CT: Greenwood Press.

Metropolitan Government: Accommodation and Reform

ᴥ **The Growth of the Metropolis**

ᴥ **The Debate over Metropolitan Government**

ᴥ **From Fragmentation to Coordination**

ᴥ **Transportation Policy and Metropolitan Areas**

ᴥ **Chapter Conclusion**

Many of you are residents of a metropolitan area—a large city and its surrounding suburbs. If you *are* a metro resident, then you know how many exciting opportunities urban life provides. Great employment opportunities and recreational adventures are all around you. However, you are also aware of the automobile traffic that chokes the city's arteries in the mornings and afternoons when people travel to and from their jobs. The metropolis has smog and noise as well as stimulation and adventure. You have a vested interest in making U.S. cities work. Each of our personal and family fortunes as well as our common cultural and intellectual heritage are tied to making the metropolitan area work. This great public purpose requires the finest and most effective metro government we can craft.

Residents of Warren, Michigan, are also residents of Macomb County. Depending on where residents live in the city, they might send their children to schools in the Fitzgerald Public School District, the Van Dyke Public School District, the Warren Woods School District, the Warren Consolidated School District, the East Detroit School District, or the Centerline Public School District. All Warren residents are served by the Macomb Intermediate School District and the Macomb Community College District. Finally, Warren citizens are residents of the Huron Metropolitan Authority and the Suburban Mobility Authority for Regional Transportation (SMART) (Citizens Research Council of Michigan, 1999: 12).

Multiple, fragmented, and often overlapping units of local government in the same metropolitan area can create many concerns. First, the average resident of Warren is likely to be confused about which unit of government is responsible for which service. That all of them are also taxing units may raise the ire of citizens when tax bills arrive. In addition to this confusion among residents, the critics of such governmental fragmentation point out that it creates costly and wasteful duplication of public services as well as inequities in service quality and quantity. A resident of a community with exceptionally valuable and desirable property may pay quite low taxes for quite good public services while residents of a neighboring community with less valuable property might pay a lot more for lower-quality services.

This example prompts us to ask the following basic questions about metropolitan government in the United States:

- How did our metropolitan areas become so fragmented?
- For whom is metropolitan fragmentation a serious problem?
- What mechanisms are available to overcome our urban problems?
- Is the public supportive of our metropolitan reform efforts?
- How do metropolitan areas cope with specific policy issues such as transportation that cut across government boundaries?

By answering these questions, we can better appreciate how public officials are tackling the concerns of our large urban areas.

❧ The Growth of the Metropolis

The development of many local governments within a metropolitan area typically occurred over a long period of time and partly as the result of natural changes in technology, especially in transportation. But this development also was spurred, often unintentionally, by federal and state government policies. Basically, the forces that drive the establishment of many different units can be classified into three different categories: (1) technical changes, (2) governmental policies, and (3) cultural forces. Together, these issues changed the landscape of local government in many urban areas across the country.

Technical Change

Advances in transportation—particularly the *automobile*—had unimaginable affects on the nature of urban areas throughout the twentieth century, especially after World War II. With the development of various forms of mass transportation such as trains and rail lines, people were able to live farther and farther from their places of employment in central cities. Residential housing and retail shops also were able to spread from the central city along these transportation routes. The car increased this trend exponentially; people could live quite a distance from and still work and shop in the central city.

Technological changes in the nature of factories also fueled this developmental sprawl from central cities into the surrounding countryside. Initially, factories were built on relatively small parcels of property and had several floors. Indeed, Henry Ford's first automobile factory in Detroit was in a warehouse with many levels. Production would begin on the highest floor, and as the car moved down each floor, more and more pieces were assembled and attached until the vehicle was completed on the ground floor and driven out the front door.

Modern industrial technologies and assembly-line production required larger buildings with production all on one floor. One automobile moving down from floor to floor is easy to envision, but it is hard to picture hundreds of cars doing so in a regular production day. With urban land typically expensive and limited in parcel or lot size, the only areas that could offer the space needed for factories with assembly-line production were the rural lands outside the central city. Thus, changes in technology kept pushing urban development outward.

Governmental Factors

Changes in technology are inevitable, but the policies enacted by both the federal and state governments tended to compound the cities' expansions. More specifically, several policies at the national level allowed people to live farther from work and shopping in central cities. In other words, the policies enhanced urban sprawl. State-level programs and policies, however, often were directly related to the formation of fragmented governments in those sprawling areas.

Federal Policies and Sprawl. At the national level, the Federal Highway Act of 1944 funded the development of 41,000 miles of *interstate highway*. In 1956, a federal tax on gasoline earmarked revenues to extend interstate highways even more. Thus, the federal government funded the construction of roads that not only moved people and goods around the nation but also served to move residents and businesses beyond the limits of the central cities.

The federal *revenue-sharing program* of the 1970s also fueled the development of necessary infrastructure in communities outside of the central cities. Under this program, most cities, regardless of size or economic need, received revenue-sharing funds with few restrictions or guidelines for how they were spent. Many new small and growing local governments used this money to develop water and sewer systems, roads, municipal buildings, and other infrastructural items necessary for their development, expansion, and livability.

Finally, federal *housing-loan programs* after World War II operated in such a way as to favor new over existing housing. Thus, the many soldiers returning from the war were able to purchase homes for their new families under federally sponsored loan programs. However, the loans tended to be available only for new, single family homes that were much more likely to be in areas outside central cities than in already substantially "built" urban areas. In short, federal dollars were used to build new local governments outside of older central cities, many of which would soon themselves urbanize. Legislation at the state levels determined whether the result was simply a larger sprawling city such as Dallas or many separate smaller suburban units ringing a central city such as Detroit.

State Policies and Sprawl. As noted in earlier chapters, laws that regulate how local governments are incorporated, their structures, and their powers are passed at the state level. States also control annexation and incorporation legislation. In other words, states can regulate how cities can come to be—their **incorporation**—and how they can add land to their boundaries—**annexation.**

If an individual state makes it easy for communities to incorporate as cities, then many units of local government will probably be established, some of them quite small. For example, in some states, an area with as few as 100 residents may petition the state for recognition as an incorporated city. On the other hand, if states make it easy for central cities to expand their boundaries by annexing the lands that surround them, then there will likely be fewer very large cities. This has been the case in Texas, where Dallas was allowed to expand into surrounding undeveloped land. The city now covers 378 square miles. In short, states can promote or allow small multiple units of local government by making it easy to incorporate and hard to annex. This has happened in many states.

Along the same lines, states control the laws that regulate the formation of special districts. These special purpose governments are created to provide particular services such as schools, transportation, libraries, parks, and so on. If such special districts are easy to create and have their own funding sources separate from the local government, then they will multiply.

Cultural Forces

We already noted that many of this country's founders shared a strong preference for rural over urban living—an antiurban bias. This has changed somewhat over the years, yet the ideal living situation for many modern Americans has become the single-family detached house in the *suburbs* surrounded by a large, well-treed lawn. By the same token, cities were viewed as dirty, unhealthy, and even unnatural places by many of the founders of the country. Indeed, Thomas Jefferson once said, "I view great cities as penitential to the morals, the health, and the liberties of man." As incomes have increased, Americans have been able to move out of central cities to pursue this suburban dream.

Such preferences have not always been simply lifestyle choices. Many people preferred to live in communities that were racially and economically homogenous. Improved transportation and accumulated wealth made it possible to move out of the central cities. The desire to flee congestion and other urban problems converged with a desire to live in racially and economically segregated communities. There has been much discussion about the extent to which population shifts from central cities to suburbs have represented *white flight* from increasingly racially diverse urban centers. Although research has indicated that many middle-class African Americans also left central cities for the suburbs, racial segregation clearly was a motivating force for many whites. Population and demographic statistics from Detroit, Michigan, and Birming-

---

| BOX 12.1 | *Census Definition of Metropolitan Areas* |

The U.S. Office of Management and Budget (OMB) defines metropolitan areas (MAs) according to published standards that are applied to census bureau data. The general concept of a MA is that of a core area containing a large population nucleus, together with adjacent communities having a high degree of economic and social integration with that core.

Standard definitions of metropolitan areas were first issued in 1949 by the Bureau of the Budget,

the OMB's predecessor, under the designation "standard metropolitan area" (SMA). The term was changed to "standard metropolitan statistical area" (SMSA) in 1959, and to "metropolitan statistical area" (MSA) in 1983. The collective term "metropolitan area" (MA) became effective in 1990. MAs include metropolitan statistical areas (MSAs), consolidated metropolitan statistical areas (CMSAs), and primary metropolitan statistical areas (PMSAs).

CHAPTER 12   Metropolitan Government: *Accommodation and Reform* ham, Alabama, from the last thirty years reveal this demographic shift (see both Table 12.1 and Box 12.1).

Table 12.1
Census Data for Detroit, Michigan, and Birmingham, Alabama

	1970	1980	1990	2000 Estimate
City of Detroit	1,511,336	1,203,339	1,027,974	965,351
% Black	44	63	76	—
% of PMSA*	34	27	24	22
Detroit PMSA	4,490,902	4,387,783	4,266,654	4,473,853
% Black	17	20	22	—
City of Birmingham	300,687	284,413	265,852	252,997
% Black	42	56	63	—
% of MSA	41	35	32	29
Birmingham MSA	737,837	815,286	840,140	908,508
% Black	29	29	29	29

*primary metropolitan statistical area

Source: U.S. Bureau of the Census, *The State of the Nation's Cities: A Comprehensive Database on American Cities and Suburbs.* Center for Urban Policy Research.

Collecting Your Thoughts *Uncontrolled Development Where You Live*

Visualize your drive to the campus each day or the drive to your parents' or a friend's home for the weekend. Do you have to time the trip to avoid traffic congestion? Along the roadside, can cars enter and exit the highway at any point, or is there limited access? What about traffic lights? Are there so few lights that cars continuously dart out into traffic, or are there so many that you can't make it to your destination in a reasonable time? What about billboards, flashing signs, and other distractions? Do you arrive at school or home tired and frazzled? If so, then sprawl is getting to you. If you could get away from it all, what vision comes to mind? Lonely tropical island? Open arid desert? Quiet mountain trail? If yes, then the sprawl is *really* getting to you! Be prepared to discuss your reasons in class.

❧ The Debate over Metropolitan Government

Scholars and local government officials have long debated the advantages and disadvantages of the fragmented metropolis. Is having many local government units in the same metropolitan area a good thing or a bad thing? In large part, the answer depends on your view of the purpose of local government or perhaps whether you live in a suburb or an older central city. Do you see the role of local government as being a vital avenue of citizen participation and representation that is close to the people? Do you feel that the main purpose of local government is to provide basic services at the lowest cost? Do you look to local governments to ensure that citizens of a metropolitan area have equal access to good schools, parks, public safety and other services? How important is it that the actions of one local government not affect the quality of life in another? Your answers to these questions will likely determine where you come out on the debate over the costs and benefits of governmental fragmentation.

Advantages of Multiple Local Governments

The case for maintaining fragmented local governments is usually made as follows. Multiple local governments provide citizens and businesses with choices. This argument rests on the **Tiebout thesis** that likens the multiplicity of local governments to a free market (Ostrom, Tiebout, & Warren, 1961). Potential residents and businesses are able to shop around in the local government *marketplace* and select the location that meets their desires for public services at the prices (tax rates) they are willing to pay. Local governments must then compete with each other in terms of services and tax rates to attract residents. Such a free market should promote innovation, efficiency, and desirability among local governments.

Each small unit of local government can be *administered efficiently* because the service area, need for administrative officials or bureaucrats, and so on will be smaller. Administrative costs to a small area with similar types of residents should be fairly modest. Smaller local governments are closer to the people and hence should be more responsive to the needs and desires of residents. Making your desires known to local officials would be easier in a city of 10,000 than one of 100,000 or 1 million. Indeed, your local officials may live just down the block or even next door in a small community. Having a diversity of smaller units of local government will allow residents to have more control over the form of their local government—mayor or manager, for example—and should increase citizen input on the types and quality of public services provided (Oliver, 2000).

Having smaller, more accessible units of local government is important not just in making it easier for residents to make their service and structural wishes known as noted above. Thomas Jefferson and other founders of this country were clear in their thinking that *citizen participation* in all levels of government was valuable. Such participation not only is a good way to let government know what citizens want, but also brings citizens closer to the government, makes them more aware of how the government is run and of important issues of the day, and allows them to work together for the greater good. In short, participating in government is good for us.

Small local units of government are ideal places for citizens to participate in and learn about government in this country. It is more understandable and accessible, it is easier to run for public office, and it is clearly closer to the people than are the state and federal governments. And the smaller the local units, the more accessible government is. Having smaller multiple local governments will be more likely to preserve and reflect *variations in local culture*. Each community will be more homogeneous, which should lessen conflicts.

In summary, there are many supporters of the benefits of having many, often quite small, units of local government within one urban area. They would say that such an arrangement allows citizens and businesses to have a choice of services and tax rates. It encourages cities to be as desirable and responsive as possible because they have to compete with each other. It allows for government that is closer and more accessible to the people and promotes the development of unique local identities and cultures. In short, we as citizens get a *better choice* of living locations, our cities should be more desirable, and we should be better able to communicate both our desires and complaints in smaller cities where we are more likely to know our local officials. This seems to be quite a persuasive argument. Why then would just as many reasonable students of local government argue just as forcefully that elimination of all these units of local governments, possibly through consolidation into larger units, would be of greater benefit to residents and businesses alike?

Disadvantages of Fragmented Local Governments

As with so many issues, there are two sides, and a strong argument can be made that the current fragmented nature of many metropolitan areas has more drawbacks than potential benefits. The Tiebout thesis noted above, where the marketplace of cities allows residents and businesses to shop for the desired mix of services and taxes, only operates properly under certain circumstances that are often unmet.

First, for the metropolis to operate as a free market, consumers—families looking for homes or businesspeople looking for places to open shop—must have "perfect information." In other words, they must be *fully aware* of all the service differences between communities and the corresponding tax levels.

While most families try to evaluate local school districts before buying or renting homes, finding out about police, fire, sanitation, parks and recreation, and other unseen or hard-to-access services is difficult. Right now, would you be able to describe the quality of your local planning department? How about your local public works department? Even if we as citizens were able to evaluate adequately the quality of services in different communities—that is, to ensure that the free market fully operates—all of us also would have to be completely mobile. That means that everyone would have the resources to move to any community they found most desirable.

The reality is that many people would like to move from cities with poor schools or high crime rates but do not have the money to do so. They lack *mobility.* Taxes in many desirable communities are too high and housing is too expensive. The competitive market works for those who *can* move but not for those who cannot. That lower-income residents of a metropolitan area are less mobile is a problem not just because it limits their ability to choose where they want to live, but also because it creates *tax-base inequities.* Poor residents often have greater need for local services; they may live in more densely populated areas, so sanitation services are more important; or they are not able to join the local country club, so they must rely on public parks for recreation. At the same time that they have greater service needs, they tend to contribute less revenue to the city government simply because what property they do have is likely to be less valuable and thus brings in less property-tax revenue. This creates a perverse situation in which those local governments with the least tax revenues tend to have residents who most need services. Tax-base resources do not always match resident needs in a fragmented metropolitan area.

The uneven distribution of tax base and resident needs creates a great deal of *inequity in service* quality and quantity across the metropolis. Cities with valuable property are able to provide many high-quality services to their residents, including excellent schools, parks with indoor swimming pools, municipal golf courses, and so on. Other cities will not have sufficient tax revenues to provide even very basic levels of services. Again, this is not a problem if everyone can move to any community they want, but we have seen that many cannot. What if you are trapped in a low-resource community?

In a fragmented metropolitan area, the actions of one city often affect citizens in another community. The boundaries of local governments are quite arbitrary, and urban problems and policy solutions often do not stay neatly within those boundaries. For example, most urbanized communities no longer allow residents to burn their yard waste. Not many years ago, however, the smell of burning fall leaves was a normal part of the season. But such burning increases pollution levels when many people do it. In Washtenaw County, Michigan, one community, Pittsfield Township, still allows residents to burn their leaves; none of the surrounding cities do. Will the smoke from the legally burned leaves stay neatly within the borders of Pittsfield Township? Of course not. So the residents of nearby Ypsilanti and Ann Arbor will also experience the smoke from burning leaves in Pittsfield even though they are not allowed to burn leaves.

Central Park is considered by many New Yorkers to be the city's crown jewel.
Source: © SuperStock

Such issues are called negative **externalities**: the negative consequences of the actions of one local government that spill over into surrounding localities. Another example of negative externalities would be one community allowing businesses to dump waste into a local river that runs through several other communities in the area. Lax environmental policies in one city can affect all of the others that share the same watershed. City boundaries and natural watershed boundaries do not necessarily match.

Externalities also can be positive. Many communities have nice parks, and their residents pay high taxes for them. However, most parks are open to anyone who chooses to use them, so residents from neighboring communities—who do not pay taxes for the park—often use them. This is a positive externality where the actions of one community benefit the residents of others. But if many nonresidents do this, then the park may become too crowded for taxpaying residents to use. Having fragmented local units promotes such problems. Having one large consolidated government would help to ensure that all who benefit pay and that uniform rules and regulations apply to the whole urban area.

Multiple units of local government create overlapping, duplicative, and wasteful services. For example, every small community must have a city hall, a police department, and a fire department. Each fire department must purchase and maintain fire trucks, modern radio units, and all of the other equipment

CHAPTER 12 Metropolitan Government: *Accommodation and Reform*

that modern firefighters need. The city of Ypsilanti, Michigan, with roughly 35,000 residents, has two multistory buildings. Because of these two buildings, the fire department must have a truck with ladders and equipment that are capable of reaching the higher floors to fight fires and rescue residents. One quite expensive truck only serves those two buildings. Indeed, if you were standing in downtown Ypsilanti and carefully watched fire trucks go by, you also might notice that some are red and some yellow. This is because the trucks for Ypsilanti and Ypsilanti Township—separate units of local government—must use the same roads to get to fires in their respective communities. Obviously, purchasing equipment for one larger area would be more efficient and would allow local governments to capture the **economies of scale** that come with providing service to many units.

Confusion is another problem with having many overlapping governments. Having many units of government collecting taxes from your property but providing different or even the same services makes it hard to get answers or assign blame if problems occur. With so many government units, citizens actually may be less able to get in touch with their local officials. They will have to spend time just identifying the proper official in the proper unit of government to whom they should complain.

Further, each unit of local government has its own set of public officials who duplicate other sets in other units. Within one metropolitan area, there are many mayors, city managers, police chiefs, and city council members. Many of the elected officials are part-time, and others are not, and certainly the civil servants or bureaucrats within each unit are full-time employees. How many city clerks, city treasurers, and parks and recreation directors are needed within one metropolitan area?

Many of today's most pressing urban problems—crime, poor schools, homelessness, and poverty—are complicated and intractable. How can we expect multiple small units of local government, many with small resource bases, to deal with these issues? Big problems may well require the combined efforts of the whole urban area to muster big and coordinated solutions. Fighting drug and gang problems is a telling example. Many communities enact strong drug-enforcement efforts. In fact, they may target particular areas within the communities for vigorous enforcement. What are the results of such initiatives? Inevitability, drug traffic and its attendant crime goes down in the target area—and often goes up in surrounding communities as drug dealers simply move from one place to another. The problems are mobile, but local government boundaries are not. Coordinated areawide efforts of larger government units with larger resource bases may be the only way to address pressing large problems.

Because most local government revenue comes from local property taxes, the value of the property within each local unit is critical in determining the quality and quantity of services that can be provided. Local units with valuable property will be able to bring in more money to pay for services than units with less-valuable property. Two problems occur with multiple small units of government: (1) There is considerable inequality among the local governments in the amount of money they have to spend on their citizens, and (2) all local units have less revenue separately than they would have if they were together. If we had fewer larger units of local government, then property-tax revenues would be shared or pooled. Citizens across the metropolitan area then would have more uniform services. With greater revenue, the local government would be

The Debate over Metropolitan Government

able to address larger, more costly urban problems. As noted above, many urban problems such as crime and homelessness are complex, and policies to address them are expensive. Local units working with larger revenue bases would be better able to address such issues.

One argument for having a fragmented metropolis is that local units will compete with each other and greater efficiency and choice will result. However, competition among local units also can be bad, particularly for economic development. For the past two decades, local governments have competed with each other to attract industry and other job-producing businesses. This competition has often taken the form of offering breaks from taxes, land development at local expense, subsidy of costly infrastructure, exemptions from local zoning ordinances, and similar incentives. The worst example of this type of competition was when the governors of the states that were competing to attract General Motors' new Saturn manufacturing plant went on the *Phil Donahue Show* to present their packages of incentives to the firms publicly. This type of *Let's Make a Deal* competition among local units of government tends to result in incentive offers beyond what any industry really needs to locate in a community. It costs the "winning" local units tax revenue for years into the future. The excess incentives to business and industry represent a corporate surplus where private firms receive more public tax dollars than they really need (Bachelor & Jones, 1984).

Local governments combined in larger units would be less negatively competitive because they would work together to attract business and jobs to the larger area. They also would be able to pool resources and afford studies that would help identify what an industry really wants and which ones would most benefit the area. They also could determine what incentives they could really afford and hire the consultants necessary to negotiate with industry in a more effective manner. Instead of competing with each other, they would work together to bring jobs to the metropolitan area as a whole. In reality, new jobs created anywhere in a metropolitan area benefit residents from many communities. Despite all of this, a recent examination of city–county consolidations found no increase in manufacturing, retail, or service establishments after consolidations of or coordination of several local units (Carr & Feiock, 1999).

The issue of economic-development policy leads to another argument for combining fragmented local units of government. Clearly, urban problems such as crime, economics, the environment, and so on are areawide issues. When a large new employer locates in a city, residents from many other cities take jobs there. They use the local roads to get to and from work and local emergency services if they have traffic accidents or are victims of crime. The pollution from factories in one community spills over into the air in other communities. Public transportation systems such as subways or busses cross community boundary lines. So, both cooperation and coordinated planning are important and logical for service provision and tax collection.

Comprehensive planning is needed for many issues of local government. Water and sewer systems are an obvious example. It makes little sense for each local community to have its own water and sewer system independently of other local units. First, such systems need to be connected for water distribution and purification and sewage collection and treatment. Second, water and sewage need to flow from higher elevations to lower elevations—that is, downstream. For these reasons, communities must coordinate the flow of water and sewage.

Finally, it is more cost-efficient for local units to share one large purification plant than to have multiple separate ones. Indeed, wastewater purification is an excellent example of an activity where economies of scale accrue. Purifying large amounts of water is much cheaper than small quantities once the facility is built. To coordinate these activities and accommodate both current and future needs, planning needs to take place among communities. And it is much better done on a metropolitan-wide basis than among separate communities. Planning for road maintenance and construction, transportation systems, airports, community health services, and so on is more effectively done for the whole metropolitan area.

In summary, those who support the consolidation of the many local units of government into one larger metropolitan unit point to the benefits of coordinated planning and service provision, including greater tax bases, more equitable distribution of services, enhanced abilities to deal with difficult urban problems, increased effectiveness and efficiency in providing services to a larger area at lower cost, and the avoidance of costly service duplication. But which argument is most persuasive—that supporting the current fragmentation or the one supporting consolidation?

Box 12.2 summarizes both arguments. Indeed, both are quite persuasive, but two points or overriding truths win out. First, there are clear benefits to cooperation among local units in terms of providing services more efficiently and probably more effectively. Second, in most areas, fragmented local units already exist. They are functioning in most cases, and both local officials and residents are resistant to the change required to eliminate local units and create larger governments. In short, there are benefits to consolidation but it is unlikely to happen in most urban areas. So, where does that leave us as citizens

---

| BOX 12.2 | *Should Fragmented Units of Local Government Be Consolidated?* |

No

Having many local units allows residents and business to shop for locations.

Competition among local units will lead to greater efficiency.

Smaller units can be administered more efficiently.

Smaller units will be closer to the people and thus more accountable.

Citizens will have a better chance of receiving the exact service mix they want.

Bureaucracies will be kept smaller.

Local culture will be preserved.

Citizens will have a better opportunity to participate in local government.

Yes

Negative externalities will be reduced.

Positive externalities will be enhanced.

Citizens are not fully mobile; some are stuck in cities with low tax bases and poor services.

Citizens do not have sufficient information to compare alternative local units.

Citizen need and tax base for service are not evenly distributed across the urban area.

Service quality and quantity can be increased.

Larger tax base will allow larger problems to be addressed.

Urban problems spread across the urban area.

Having many small, weak units of government limits options.

Economy of scale in service production will lead to greater efficiency.

Larger tax bases can lead to more service effectiveness.

Benefits of comprehensive planning can be achieved.

and local officials trying to run local governments? Clearly, many avenues for cooperation among local units of government do not require complete consolidation of units. It is these options that we explore in the next section.

❧ From Fragmentation to Coordination

We now turn our attention to possible solutions to the problems of fragmentation in metropolitan areas. Figure 12.1 provides a spectrum of coordination of local government units within a metropolitan area, from complete fragmentation to complete consolidation. The points along this spectrum have been used in different areas across the country and are described below.

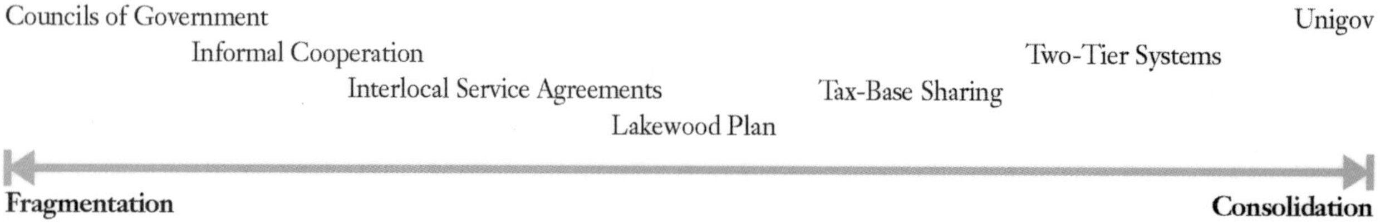

Councils of Government

      Informal Cooperation   Two-Tier Systems

             Interlocal Service Agreements   Tax-Base Sharing

                        Lakewood Plan

Unigov

Fragmentation ←————————————————————————————————→ **Consolidation**

Figure 12.1

Councils of Government

A **council of government (COG)** is a voluntary association of units of local government much like the United Nations is a voluntary association of independent countries around the world. During the 1970s, the U.S. Congress determined that it would be beneficial for local governments to come together to work on common issues, services, and problems that spill from one local unit to another across the metropolitan area. Funds have been allocated at the federal level to support the development of COGs through tying the receipt of federal money to regional planning activities.

Activities commonly addressed by COGs include transportation, planning, technical support, information services, and grant administration. Without consolidating, local units could come together and their officials could work out cooperative solutions to achieve some of the benefits of consolidation. COGs have been limited in their effectiveness because of their voluntary nature. They provide an opportunity to cooperate, but such cooperation remains up to the local units.

An illustration from the Detroit area is telling. The South Eastern Michigan Council of Governments (SEMCOG) has tried to address metropolitan transportation issues for years. The council has been hampered in its efforts to provide coordinated mass transit partly because Detroit is the home of several major auto manufacturers and because of the differing needs and desires of the council's member governments. For example, two completely separate public bus systems operate within the metropolitan area. Detroit Department of Transportation (DDOT) buses operate only within Detroit's central city. Suburban Mobility Authority for Regional Transportation (SMART) buses run within the suburbs and through the city of Detroit, but will not make stops within the central city. To travel to different destinations within Detroit, a rider must change from a SMART bus to a DDOT bus.

COGs often stand as advocates of greater urban cooperation and even consolidation but are not able to force their member units to support such plans. In short, they are able to lead only when member units are willing to follow.

Informal Cooperative Agreements

If the success of local cooperation rests with the willingness of local units to do it, then informal *cooperative agreements* arrived at between local units are perhaps one way to achieve some of the benefits of consolidation. Because these agreements are usually made between just a few units and are based on mutual benefit, they are quite common. One example is a mutual aid agreement in which two or more local units agree to provide police or fire backup for each other. If one unit has a large fire, then fire trucks and personnel come from other units to help out.

Local units often come to agreements to purchase supplies and equipment together. Like buying bulk items at a grocery store, ordering a large amount of office supplies or equipment is usually cheaper than buying small amounts. Local units can easily work together, combine their supply orders, and purchase goods at lower cost. The same system also can work for larger equipment purchases such as fire trucks. The communities of Ypsilanti and Ypsilanti Township, for example, purchase fire trucks together in larger numbers and then have them painted their appropriate yellow or red colors.

Interlocal Service Agreements

Many local units take the service agreement further by either sharing services or having a larger unit provide services for a smaller one. The *interlocal service agreement* is a form of "contracting-out" for services, although the contract is between local units of government rather than between a government and a private provider.

A larger community may provide police service or garbage collection for a smaller one. This is the arrangement between Highland Park and Detroit, for example. Detroit police provide service for the smaller—and completely encircled—city of Highland Park. This invariably is less costly for the smaller unit than providing service on its own; the larger unit can sell its services and also enhance economies of scale from producing larger amounts of service.

The Lakewood Plan

The *Lakewood Plan*—named after Lakewood, California, which gets all of its services from Los Angeles County—extends the above-described service arrangements. The city produces no service on its on but is able to provide services to all its residents at low cost through contracts with the county and other vendors. It does not need to worry about building a police department, buying fire trucks or garbage haulers, and hiring and training building inspectors. The county does all of this. The county is able to produce services at lower cost because it is providing them to a wider area and on a larger scale.

Tax-Base Sharing

The *tax-base sharing approach* to cooperation requires more structural change than just two units agreeing to work together to purchase goods or provide services, and it is thus less frequently used. However, many urban scholars and practitioners are recommending it as a solution to uneven tax bases across an urban area and to competition between local units for economic development.

The best example of tax-base sharing is the Minneapolis–St. Paul, Minnesota, metropolitan area. The state legislature created the Twin Cities Metropolitan Council to address growth issues in the capital area. In 1971, tax-base sharing was added to the council's administration under the state's Fiscal Disparities Law. Under the plan, a portion of any new increase to the tax base as a result of new construction anywhere in the plan area goes into a common pool. The local unit where the development is located keeps 60 percent of the tax-base increase, but the rest must be contributed to the pool. The revenues in the pool are then redistributed to the member governments annually, based on a formula that considers the needs and population of the local units. The plan then accomplishes several of the goals of consolidation. It evens out revenues to provide services across the area because richer areas put greater amounts in the pot and poorer units take more out. It is to the advantage of local units to cooperate in getting industry to locate anywhere in the area because all of them benefit.

Early research on the results of the Minnesota experiment indicated that competition for growth was reduced and the region's poorer communities appeared better off. Over the long term, however, the central cities of Minneapolis and St. Paul apparently contribute more to the fund than they take out, subsidizing growing suburbs with little industry (Ross & Levine, 1996; 333).

Toronto, Ontario, Canada

In January 1998, the Ontario provincial parliament revised the two-tiered government of Toronto and christened it the unified City of Toronto. The movement from a highly fragmented metropolitan area to a unified Metro Toronto began in 1953 with the creation of a federation with independent cities and a powerful regional government. The 1998 reorganization centralized administration and decentralized service delivery. The five formerly independent city councils now operate as community councils with responsibilities for public hearings on planning applications and purely neighborhood matters such as sign and tree ordinances, traffic and parking regulations, and recreational needs. The city council is divided into twenty-eight municipal wards and has fifty-seven members. Still, many important services to Toronto residents continue to be administered through separate agencies, commissions, boards, and other special purpose bodies, each having its own relationship with the city council. For more information go to <http://www.gov.on.ca/MBS/english/its_ontario/cit/to.html>.

Two-Tier Systems

A *two-tier system* is close to a complete consolidation of local government units. By creating two levels of government, however, it preserves the individual nature of local units. Examples of two-tier systems would be Toronto, Ontario, and Miami–Dade County, Florida, although both areas have substantially modified their systems as of late.

Two-tier systems operate much like the relationship between our state and federal units of government. The individual cities maintain their independence, keeping locally elected leaders and continuing to provide and produce many local services. However, each unit also elects representatives to serve in the metropolitan-wide council.

Service functions are then divided between the metropolitan and local levels. The former is responsible for services that require coordination among local units or those that achieve economies of scale. In the case of Toronto, the metropolitan level provides transportation, police, ambulance, social service, planning, parks and recreation, road, and school services. The constituent local units are responsible for fire protection, electrical utilities, property-tax collection, statistical services, and local park and road services. Public works activities are shared.

    CHAPTER 12   Metropolitan Government: *Accommodation and Reform*

This system appears to have worked better in the Toronto area than in Miami, which has considerably more diversity among its residents and the local units that make up the metropolis. Box 12.3 shows the guidelines for determining which level of government would be most effective at providing individual services. These guidelines consider economies-of-scale benefits and the urban issues being addressed as well as political and representation issues.

City–County Consolidation

The most extreme solution to fragmented local units of government is the complete **consolidation** of local units within a county. One notable example of such city–county consolidation is *Unigov* in Indianapolis, Indiana. Although local units of government still exist in name, most services are provided county-wide, and taxes are collected at the county level. All administration is done for the county as a whole.

As of 1996, only twenty-three of 134 city–county proposed consolidations that have gone before voters were approved (Carr & Feiock, 1999: 477). Local officials and residents usually are unwilling to give up their existing local units. The case of Indianapolis is a good example of the conditions that must be met for this to be even possible.

BOX 12.3 *Optimal Assignment of Regional Service Function in a Regional Approach*

Services should be the responsibility of the local unit when:

- A problem, issue, or need can be contained within individual local boundaries.

- The situation cannot be adequately addressed through interlocal action.

- Diverse community or neighborhood values, standards, preferences, or conditions should be recognized and maintained.

- Competition among local units, or among those contracting for the delivery of services, would be likely to produce beneficial results.

- Basic land-use and zoning powers of local governments are affected.

- Citizen participation in decision making and public access to information and decision makers are sought.

- Accountability of public officials in decision making is highly desired.

Services should be the responsibility of a regional unit when:

- A problem, issue, or need transcends the boundaries of a substantial number of local units.

- A comprehensive approach to planning, an inter-local minimum level of effort and standard of service, or a uniform response across local jurisdictions are needed.

- Individual local governments vacate the field.

- A locality through action or inaction does injury to other units or their citizens.

- The situation can be adequately addressed through interlocal action.

- The costs of implementation or delivery are significantly beyond the fiscal capacity of individual local governments.

- Competition among, lack of a unified response by, or inaction on the part of local units will impede resolution of the problem.

- There is a desire to experiment and test the workability of new regional approaches.

From C. W. Stenberg (1999). "Structuring Local Government Units and Relationships." Prepared for presentation at the Symposium on the Future of Local Government in Michigan. Michigan Municipal League Foundation, Midland, Michigan.

The city–county consolidation took place in Indiana for several reasons. The most important is that the state has little tradition of home rule for cities. In this case, the state legislature can and did order the cities and county to consolidate because of political party unity in the state. Local and state officials are predominantly Republican. Both the governor and the mayor of Indianapolis were Republicans, and this party unity made the consolidation vote easier to achieve. Indeed, one central goal was to dilute the voting power of the Democrats within Indianapolis by adding the mostly Republican outlying areas. This made it less likely that Democrats would be able to gain office within the consolidated area.

Consolidation also has been acceptable to residents of the Indianapolis area because the central city is relatively healthy. Its economy was not seen as a drain on the suburbs. Further, in many cases, the city provided superior services to those in the surrounding areas. Many residents viewed coming into the city as an opportunity to receive better services. Much of the land surrounding the central city of Indianapolis was rural. There were fewer pre-existing suburban incorporated units of government than in many urban areas. One critical local service—education—was left out of the consolidation so local units were able to continue running their own schools and were able to maintain an important part of their local identities.

Finally, race was also involved. Indianapolis was becoming increasingly African American while the surrounding suburban and rural areas were primarily white. There was concern at higher levels of government that the city would soon become minority-controlled and that this would have legislative redistricting impacts at the state level. It might also have affected the nature of state legislation and state funding, reducing home rule and state support. Incorporation would dilute black power in the central city by adding many white residents to the population mix. This issue is important to consider. It shows that there are always winners and losers in any governmental restructuring; such changes are rarely neutral. While pushes for consolidation may be framed in terms of effectiveness and efficiency, there are also very real implications for the power balance in urban areas. Clearly, minority residents would have had greater control over the central city if the consolidation had not taken place.

Other Options

Other ideas have been suggested for dealing with local government fragmentation that do not fit neatly on the spectrum we provided in Figure 12.1. For example, some experts have suggested that local governments should periodically review their structures, powers, and services and take the opportunity to consider options that would allow for more coordination or cooperation (Stenberg, 1999).

In states where counties do not currently have many powers, their responsibilities could be enhanced to allow for service provision across the urban area. Such reorganization would allow counties to provide a full range of services for the metropolitan area, including planning, data collection, policy analysis, and problem solving.

State governments can provide incentives to local governments that cooperate in service provision. For example, local units that cooperate in parks or library provision could receive increased state aid.

Elected regional multipurpose districts are another means to increase local government cooperation. Many special purpose governments in the metropolitan area provide services from schools to parks to libraries, but these could be consciously and purposely designed to operate at the regional or county-wide level and along a structural avenue through which local units could cooperate on service provision and gain economies of scale.

The state-mandated Portland Metropolitan Services District (the Metro) in Oregon has members elected from three counties and twenty-four municipalities. It provides areawide planning and some services. This is similar to a two-tier system but offers only limited services.

The Metro (<*http://www.multnomah.lib.or.us/metro/*>) is a directly elected regional government that serves more than 1.3 million residents in the three counties and twenty-four cities that make up greater metropolitan Portland. It provides transportation and land-use planning, oversees regional garbage disposal and recycling waste-reduction programs, and manages regional parks, green spaces, and the Oregon Zoo. It oversees the Oregon Convention Center, Civic Stadium, and the Portland Center for the Performing Arts. This organization reflects the area's interest in regional management. It is governed by an executive officer who is elected regionally and seven council members who are elected by districts. More than a dozen Metro Citizen Advisory Committees advise the council, executive officer, and staff. The committees focus on citizen involvement and substantive policy issues such as Metro's top priority to manage growth through its Region 2040 program. Metro exists along with the city governments of the individual cities such as Portland.

Clearly, many mechanisms are available to overcome the problems associated with uncontrolled metropolitan development. As a practical matter, each state legislature makes some of these options available and refuses to authorize others. If you someday must tackle the intergovernmental problems of metro areas, you will certainly want to familiarize yourself with the relevant state laws for the state in which you are working. In addition to the state's enabling question, you also will also have to consider the preferences and vested interests of the preexisting local governments in the metro area. Coordination is as much a political problem as a legal problem. Many personalities may have to be accommodated before government in the metropolitan area can be rationalized. Perhaps it would be best to take functional approach. The case of transportation is a significant coordination case study in and of itself.

Exploring on Your Own **A Local Government Scavenger Hunt**

Alone or with other members of your class, see how may local government services you can find in your area that are somehow consolidated. To get you started, recreation services are often operated under some form or local intergovernmental agreement. In fact, you may find that recreation has been fully consolidated in your community. Other possible candidates might be fire-prevention and emergency medical services. Good sources of information on this project include any local government directory that your Chamber of Commerce may have published or even the humble phone book. We don't want to give you too many hints! See how long a list you can construct. Bring your list to class for comparison with other students' lists.

❧ Transportation Policy and Metropolitan Areas

Transportation—highway, bus, and rail systems—presents a major policy challenge to local governments. The fragmentation of the metropolitan area into multiple cities, townships, and counties makes it difficult for each community to develop its own transportation policy and operate its own transportation system. We commute, shop, and play across government boundaries. Clearly, transportation is a policy area that is appropriate for a metropolitan solution, and it appears to be applicable to both large and small metropolitan areas.

The Local Government View of Transportation

The Port Authority of New York and New Jersey is a special purpose government dedicated to meeting both states' transportation and port commerce needs in the New York City metropolitan area. The authority operates three airports, a network of bridges and tunnels, a bus terminal, a container port, and a rail rapid-transit system. It also owns the twin towers of the World Trade Center in New York City. With 7,200 employees and a budget of around $4 billion, it is totally self-supporting from tolls, fees, and rents. The Port Authority's existence recognizes that transportation in New York and New Jersey is a policy concern that cuts across government boundaries.

The Port Authority of New York and New Jersey operates much of the metropolitan New York area, including the toll booths at such places as Lincoln Tunnel.
Source: © Charles Arrigo / Sygma

The city of New York's Transportation Department (highway and road maintenance) also operates transportation services in the greater New York metropolitan area through the Metropolitan Transportation Authority (MTA) and Connecticut Rail Commuter Council. The scale of the MTA dwarfs even the Port Authority! Its 1998 budget was $6.4 billion, and it had more than 57,000 employees. The MTA is a *state-created public benefit corporation* serving seven counties and New York City with subways, buses, railroads, and a variety of bridges and tunnels.

The New York Metropolitan Transportation Council oversees planning for much of the transportation services in the New York metropolitan area. Clearly, the scale of transportation concerns that are the focus of the Port Authority and the MTA is much greater than we find elsewhere in the United States. However, perhaps you can begin to see the size and complexity of cross-jurisdictional transportation challenges.

A smaller example of local transportation issues may be seen in Miami–Dade County, Florida. Miami–Dade has a metropolitan planning organization (MPO) that plans for integrated transportation services to the area. Federal and state laws require MPOs. The New York Metropolitan Transportation Council is that region's MPO. MPOs decide what transportation projects are funded with the limited local, state, and federal dollars available, but they do not provide transportation services. The MPO develops both short- and long-range transportation plans and establishes priorities for everything from resurfacing a highway to building or expanding a mass-transit system and building a new runway at the airport.

The Miami–Dade County MPO governing board comprises the Miami–Dade Board of County Commissioners; representatives from the Dade League of Cities, the Miami–Dade Expressway Authority, and the Miami–Dade County School Board; an elected official representing municipalities with populations of more than 50,000; and one at-large member. In addition, the Florida Department of Transportation (FDOT) has two nonvoting members on the MPO governing board.

Transportation planning in the Miami–Dade County metropolitan area is a challenging task. More than 2 million people live in the area, and the population is predicted to soar to 3.3 million by the year 2020. Many visitors to the area also add to these figures. A major role of the MPO is to ensure conformance with federal and state laws and regulations. Virtually every metropolitan area in the United States has some organization with responsibility for developing a transportation-improvement plan and setting metropolitan-wide transportation priorities.

Transportation services—as opposed to plans—in the Miami–Dade area are provided by a wide variety of organizations, including the Miami International Airport, the Port of Miami, Tri-Rail, and Metro Dade Transit. Some of these organizations are operated by Miami–Dade County. Others such as Tri-Rail—a commuter rail system—cross county boundaries into other parts of the huge Miami–Fort Lauderdale area. Miami–Dade Transit Agency operates the area's bus system, the city of Miami's downtown elevated-rail people mover (Metromover), and the county's 21.5-mile Metrorail. In the example of Miami–Dade, the fragmented metropolitan area is sewn together for transportation services by a network of organizations. These services make an integrated transportation system available to area residents and visitors, regardless of their geographical home. No single community could possibly undertake these services unless it covered an entire metropolitan area.

Lest it appear that transportation is a policy issue primarily of large metropolitan areas such as New York and Miami, the case of Des Moines, Iowa, illustrates several similar features. Des Moines has a city population of approximately 190,000 and is part of a relatively small metropolitan area of 435,000. The Des Moines Metropolitan Planning Organization has responsibility for transportation planning for three counties and thirteen communities. In addition, the organization works with the Federal Highway Administration, the Federal Transportation Administration, and the Iowa Department of Transportation. The primary service provider for mass transit is the Des Moines Metropolitan Transit Authority, which operates the local bus system. Transportation services and policy challenges appear to be considerably less complex than those of New York or Miami, but nonetheless they cut across geographical areas and are handled on a metropolitan-wide basis. Federal law requires the metropolitan planning approach, and it appears to be an appropriate fit to the nature of the United States' metropolitan government structures.

The National Government View of Transportation

At the national level, the U.S. Department of Transportation's Federal Highway Administration implements a variety of laws concerning public transportation. The most far-reaching is the *Transportation Equity Act for the Twenty-First Century* (TEA-21) that was passed by Congress in June 1998. The act authorizes federal surface-transportation programs for highways, highway safety, and public transit for 1998–2003. It both requires and provides continuing support for local metropolitan planning programs like those of New York, Miami–Dade, and Des Moines. In fiscal year 1999, TEA-21 authorized $35.1 billion for highway construction, intelligent transportation, bridge repair, and mass transit. It also funds transportation safety programs dealing with seat-belt usage, drunk driving, and railroad crossings. The legislation gives great flexibility to the states and communities to undertake pedestrian programs, build bicycle paths, and operate shared-ride programs. It gives special attention to issues of the handicapped and to expanding opportunities in the Appalachian region. The average fiscal year allocations per state for 1998–2003 are shown in Table 12.2.

Table 12.2

Transportation Equity Act for the Twenty-First Century

State	Average 1998–2003 Allocations ($1,000)
California	2,497,435
Texas	2,022,435
New York	1,378,161
Pennsylvania	1,348,358
Florida	1,273,318
•	•
•	•
•	•
New Hampshire	138,243
Hawaii	138,197
Vermont	122,077
Delaware	118,106
District of Columbia	105,610

Source: Federal Highway Administration Online: <*http://www.fhwa.dot.gov/tea21/funding.htm*>

Transportation Policy Issues for State and Local Governments

States, metropolitan areas, and communities face a wide array of transportation policy issues today. Many of these issues have been around for a long time. How much funding should be allocated for highway maintenance as opposed to new highway construction? What should be the appropriate balance between highways and mass transit? What effects will highways have on neighborhoods and communities? Will they stimulate suburban growth at the expense of older communities? Which highway projects within a metropolitan area should receive priority funding?

With the rapid growth in new technologies, state and local governments face a variety of new policy issues. Public Technology, Inc., is a nonprofit technology research, development, and commercialization organization created by the National League of Cities, the National Association of County Officials, and the International City–County Management Association. Among its programs is the Urban Consortium Transportation Task Force. The task force is trying to help state and local officials work with industry to better introduce technology to improve travel conditions. What kinds of *intelligent transportation systems* should be funded? How can data processing and data communications be applied to surface transportation? The task force also looks at the complex issue of "photo enforcement," or the available technology of measuring speed and photographing vehicles in the act of breaking traffic laws. Should we use the new technology? How do we balance the right to privacy with our need for safe roads? State and local government officials within the context of metropolitan communities also are addressing these policy issues.

Public transportation planning and service delivery is indicative of the importance of local government services to all citizens of a metropolitan area. Regardless of whether we live in New York, Miami–Dade, or Des Moines, in a large or small community, we live and work and play in multiple jurisdictions, and we cross boundaries frequently. Transportation services ranging from road and highway maintenance to bus and rail transit systems require some level of metropolitan cooperation. This cooperation may be imposed on localities by federal or state laws, but for it to work fully, local elected and administrative officials will be the central players. (See also **Box 12.4**.)

❧ Chapter Conclusion

The options for metropolitan government we discussed earlier in this chapter all require state action. This, too, is an important lesson. In many cases, achieving consistent, broad, and ongoing cooperation among units of local government may well require action on the part of state or federal lawmakers. They may either encourage such cooperation through incentives—federally funded metropolitan planning organizations—or legislatively permit or mandate it as in the case of city–county consolidation or regional service districts such as the New York Metropolitan Transportation Authority. At the end of the day, our local government traditions and the existence of many units of local government stand in the way of the more extreme or ambitious cooperative approaches.

Indeed, local officials and residents may need to learn on their own that local government in the future is going to require cooperative solutions to address metropolitan problems. Such efforts can be supported by a strategy that includes three elements: learning, leveraging, and linking.

1. Through *learning*, local officials and residents come together to share information about problems, solutions, and the benefits of cooperation.
2. By *leveraging*, state or federal funding is secured for joint ventures between or among local units.
3. *Linking* creates coalitions of local officials, units, citizen boards, and so on, which can lead to cooperative solutions.

In short, the best opportunities to achieve the benefits of cooperation may well come from the local governmental units themselves.

So where does this leave us in our quest to answer basic questions about how we might govern the metropolitan areas that sometimes seem so ungovernable? You have learned that we did not get into our urban problems overnight.

- Unplanned growth is as American as apple pie. Although there have always been visionaries who could imagine a planned metropolis, our individualistic nature has made implementing any plan difficult. We give our personal and family mobility a higher priority.

- The consequences of uncontrolled growth and fragmented government affect us all. However, middle- and upper-income people have the resources to make choices. They can escape to a lifestyle enclave in the deep suburbs or fortify their gentrified townhouses. Poorer Americans lack such choices. They are trapped in urban centers where service needs are high and tax bases have eroded. Only comprehensive metropolitan planning and programming can meet their needs.

- Many mechanisms are available to metropolitan area governments for use in rationalizing services. If state legislatures will cooperate, then metropolitan government can be made to work.

- Finally, how does the general public view the challenges of metro governance? This is a hard question to answer. Once a service such as a modern metropolitan rail is built, many area residents take advantage of it. Initially, however, many suburban residents would appear to be resigned merely to complaining about auto traffic and smog. This is why public leadership is needed to solve the problems of our metropolitan centers. In the case of metropolitan areas, the political system will have to act where purely private schemes are inadequate to the challenge.

Key Words for InfoTrac Exploration

economies of scale

Port Authority of New York and New Jersey

Transportation Equity Act for the Twenty-First Century of 1998

urban sprawl

Sources Cited

Bachelor, L. W., and B. D. Jones (1984). "Local Policy Discretion and the Corporate Surplus." Pp. 245+ in R. D. Bingham and J. P. Blair (Eds.), *Urban Economic Development, Urban Affairs Annual Review, 27.* Beverly Hills, CA: Sage Publications.

Carr, J. B., and R. C. Feiock (1999). "Metropolitan Government and Economic Development." *Urban Affairs Review, 34*(3) (January): 476–488.

Citizens Research Council of Michigan (1999). "A Bird's Eye View of Michigan Local Government." Prepared for presentation at the Symposium on the Future of Local Government in Michigan, Michigan Municipal League Foundation, Midland, Michigan, June 23–25.

Oliver, J. Eric (2000). "City Size and Civil Involvement in Metropolitan America." *American Political Science Review, 94*(2): 361–373.

Ostrom, V., C. M. Tiebout, and R. Warren (1961). "Organizing Government in Metropolitan Areas: A Theoretical Inquiry." *American Political Science Review 55*(4) (December): 831–842.

Ross, B. H., and M. A. Levine (1996). *Urban Politics, Power in Metropolitan Areas* (5th ed.). Itasca, IL: Peacock Publishers.

Stenberg, C. W. (1999). "Structuring Local Government Units and Relationships." Prepared for presentation at the Symposium on The Future of Local Government in Michigan, Michigan Municipal League Foundation, Midland, Michigan.

Local Government Policy: Decision Making Close to Home

- Local Ordinances

- Code Enforcement

- Mandated Programs

- Raising Public Revenues

- Land-Use Regulation

- Conclusions about Local Policy Making

- Balancing Priorities and Making Trade-Offs

- Development and Preservation

- Public Safety and Social Justice

- Mobility and Sprawl

- Excellent Services and Modest Taxes

- Chapter Conclusion

Throughout this book, you have learned about public policy issues. Each chapter has highlighted one or more major issues in state and local government. You are at least as concerned about what government accomplishes as you are about how it gets it done. That's fair. For example, you are interested in how we maintain a prosperous local economy and protect the local environment. These issues strike close to home. Americans are practical people, and our public life should be about accomplishing noble goals and repairing social ills.

This last chapter begins by focusing your attention on the types of policies enacted by local governments. We also alert you to some of the factors that constrain or limit local decision-making authority. Then we briefly describe the policies that seem to interest young Americans the most, the decisions that directly affect you. We also ask you to stretch your orientation to issues just a little more. As we complete this study of state and local governments, we want you to appreciate how good and worthy goals often conflict with each other. Public life is rarely about knowing the right thing to do and then doing it. More often, government officials have to balance one worthy goal with another.

States grant powers to local governments. Once the powers are given to cities and counties, the state steps back from the process and allows local citizens and their local governments to manage their own affairs. In this chapter, we look at the tools of local governance and examine how public officials use these powers to make and enforce local laws. Of course, nothing in politics is ever as simple as it first seems. So, we have to looks at various types of laws and regulations and the specific purposes for which they are intended.

Where there are grants of power, there are also opportunities to overstep legitimate government authority and threaten individual rights. We must therefore ask ourselves some underlying questions about the legal authority of local governments:

- Should citizens have control over their local affairs despite the fact that the U.S. Constitution does not require it?
- What are appropriate taxing powers for local government and how can unfair tax burdens be remedied?
- How should state and local governments determine if and when it is appropriate to take individual property or control its use?

Answers to these questions will shape our understanding of the legal authority of local officials. Because local government is "close to the people," answers to these questions directly affect us. They can determine how much individual leeway we have versus how much social control the community exercises. Local laws can even determine our standard of living as they encroach on our citizenship and property rights.

❧ Local Ordinances

The popularly elected representatives of the people make the laws for the community. These city council and county commission members are elected for fixed terms and can be reelected if their performance is acceptable to their constituents. Local decisions can take the form of motions, resolutions, or ordinances. **Motions** are used to consider and adopt reports, instruct local officials, or schedule future deliberative action. **Resolutions** express the sentiments of the council or commission about particular matters ranging from local festival recognitions to matters before the state legislature to the retirement of the city manager. They do not initiate any official actions. Local laws that apply generally throughout the jurisdiction are called **ordinances.** These acts can include tax measures, spending measures, changes in local regulations, and new or revised local laws that govern individual and corporate behavior.

Council members introduce draft ordinances by submitting written text and moving to have it adopted. The city or county attorney is available to help draft proposed legislation. After a first reading, the draft ordinance may be referred to a committee for analysis; some councils and commissions use committees, and others do not. Usually, the larger bodies need committees to manage their legislative workload. During deliberations, hearings may be held so that local citizens and organizations can express their views of the proposed ordinances. The matter is scheduled for discussion and debate. Public notice is given about the date and time at which the matter will be initially discussed. This gives the public an opportunity to comment before or during the deliberations.

If council and commission deliberations are televised in a community, then local citizens can tune in for discussions that interest them. Public-access cable television now brings local government meetings into millions of people's homes. Of course, few of us would choose to watch local government activities full-time, but we can use the local newspaper or cable listings to find out when we can watch discussions that concern us most.

The final or third reading of the bill usually signals council or commission action. Public notice is given of the third reading in a local newspaper that is designated as the official record of local government action. Members of the public may request an opportunity to speak briefly before the body about the proposed ordinance. Council members may offer amendments at this time. If the final vote is taken and the bill passes by a majority vote, then it becomes an official city or county ordinance (Blair, 1986: 190–191).

Acts of the council or commission are maintained in an official ledger. The city clerk or the county clerk is the local official who is responsible for keeping this official record of local actions. Some local codebooks date back many decades and are an excellent resource for historical research. Of course, in this day and age, many cities also keep texts of their actions on their official Web pages.

After local ordinances are passed, the agencies of local government develop policies and procedures for their implementation. Local ordinances that regulate personal behavior are forwarded to the police department or the sheriff's office. Others that finance new activities go to such departments as water and sewer and public transportation for incorporation into their budgets. In other words, few actions of local city councils and county commissions are self-actualizing. They require bureaucratic action to become effective laws.

❧ Code Enforcement

Local agencies often have their own notions of the proper way to do things (Rainey, 1991: 44). Some agency employees and even some agency heads may resist new directions from elected officials. In any case, a new or revised local law must traverse the local bureaucracy before it can really take effect. To appreciate how laws take effect, we need to study the leadership and decision-making styles of local agency executives. Without strong leadership, little may change as a result of local lawmaking.

In fact, *selective code enforcement* is a controversial issue. Some agencies and government employees diligently enforce city or county regulations. When a defective piece of equipment, an unsafe bridge, or a poorly maintained roadway harms local citizens, then any failure to enforce the law can be seen as misfeasance in office. The employee and the local government may be civilly liable for damages. On the other extreme, harsh enforcement of local codes can be seen as harassment. Considerable political damage can be done to a local government regime if the harassed party complains in the press. Finally, enforcement of local laws in some neighborhoods and not others may bring charges of discrimination. This type of selective enforcement is political dynamite in communities where racial or economic divisions are deep. We will have more to say about balance in local government activities later in this chapter. For now, suffice it to say that passing a local ordinance or revising a local regulation is only the start in changing a public policy. Without proper enforcement, local policy is impotent.

✎ Mandated Programs

Local governments have to implement decisions of the state and national governments. As we noted in Chapter 2's discussion of federalism, local governments are given unfunded mandates on some issues and preempted from action on others. Local agencies may have to carry out expensive and time-consuming procedures to satisfy the requirements of state and federal officials. A community might refuse to comply with some of these mandates, but the financial costs would be staggering because so many local governments have become dependent on outside funds over the years (see Figure 13.1).

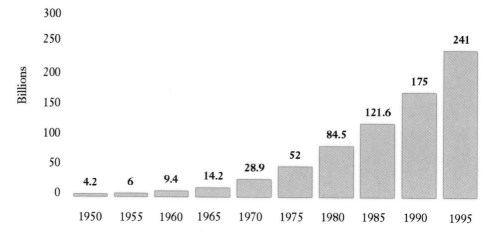

Figure 13.1 State intergovernmental transfers to local governments
Source: The Book of the States, 1998–99: 432

Since 1950, the amount of state revenue being diverted to local governments in the United States has soared from $4.2 billion to more than $250 billion. In terms of the total local revenue available to local governments, state aid now represents almost one-third of all resources that are available to U.S. counties and almost 20 percent of all resources available to U.S. cities (Gray & Eisenger, 1997: 338). Clearly, local governments refuse to comply with external mandates at their peril.

CHAPTER 13 Local Government Policy: *Decision Making Close to Home*

✥ Raising Public Revenues

Without resources, local government can do nothing, and money is the most basic resource. With money, local officials can hire employees to provide services and negotiate with contractors to provide others. This highlights the importance of intergovernmental transfers. It also requires us to consider taxation, the ability of local governments to raise revenue by drawing on the value of local property, sales, or earnings.

Property taxes are usually assessed annually and constitute a substantial part of government funding.

Source: © SuperStock

Ad valorem taxes are levied on land, buildings, and other personal property. This type of tax is a levy based on the value of the item or activity being taxed. In the case of a person's home, the value of the land and the house must be determined. This process is called *property valuation*. In most communities, property values are reassessed on a regular basis so that local taxes can keep up with increases in the value of homes and neighborhoods. The percentage of the value of the property that is to be assessed as tax is called the *millage rate*. The millage rate is quoted in *mils*; one mil equals 1/10th of a cent or 1/1000th of a dollar. If a local government taxes homeowners at the rate of 7.5 mils, then a $100,000 home would owe an annual tax of $750 in property tax. Local governments can raise more **revenue** either by increasing the tax rate or by reassessing property more often.

Sales taxes are levied on the buyers of all retail commodities in the community. A sales tax tries to capture the concept of consumption. In other words, an individual or family who consumes more will pay more in taxes, just as a person or family who owns valuable property will pay more in property tax. Poor people and people living on fixed incomes such as retirees are expected to pay less. To enhance this principle of *progressive taxation*, virtually every state has exempted prescription drugs from the sales tax, and roughly two-thirds of the states have exempted food. Despite these reforms, many political scientists consider taxes on property and sales to be *regressive taxation*, with the burden falling relatively more heavily on poorer citizens.

Local taxation reformers would prefer that earnings be taxed. This would require a local income or **payroll tax.** Most states jealously guard their right to levy income-related taxes, so relatively few cities have been able to enact payroll taxes. Reformers argue that a payroll tax is fair to the poor and helps capture some of the resources of people who work in town but reside outside of the city limits. Some people believe this latter group uses city streets, police protection, and other services without paying its fair share.

Counties and cities differ somewhat in their sources of revenue (see Table 13.1). Because they administer state programs, the counties receive more state funds than do cities. Counties also rely on property taxes as a major revenue source. Cities rely more on **user fees.** In fact, the role of user fees outstrips even that of the property tax. This may be the case because school districts also levy a separate property tax, and there is only so much taxation that the local property owner can bear. After all, the county, the city, and the school board are all levying property taxes on the same land and house. To make matters worse, two-thirds of the states levy a property tax. No wonder the property tax is the one the public "loves to hate" (Snell, 1991).

Table 13.1
Revenue Sources of Local Governments

Revenue Source	U.S. Counties (%)	U.S. Cities (%)
Federal aid	2.2	3.6
State aid	31.3	16.6
Property tax	27.2	17.9
Sales tax	6.8	9.3
User fees	1.3	21.7
All other	31.2	30.9

Source: Adapted from Gray & Eisinger (1997): 338.

❧ Land-Use Regulation

Community residents who own property have rights under U.S. law. To a great extent, an individual may develop and enjoy his or her property without the interference of local officials. But, like any other right, property rights are not absolute. There are constraints on what can be built and how it can be built that are enacted to ensure safety and protect others' property values. **Land-use regulations** consist of a land-use plan, a zoning ordinance, a zoning map, subdivision regulations, building codes, and housing codes.

As a community grows, streets, roads, and transportation flow must be planned. River and stream flood plains must be determined and marked off. Parks and cemeteries must be plotted, and recreational complexes must be sited. In other words, community needs must be considered in land-use decision making. In the early United States, people had a better sense of the need for "commons" as well as private property. Common cow and horse pens, squares devoted to stockades and forts, common spring houses and wells, and many other parcels of property were reserved for common use by everyone. Today, we tend to emphasize private property and the rights associated with developing its full potential. As we have moved away from common law to a more codified legal system, **public property** has come to mean that which belongs to the city, county, or recreational authority. If additional land is needed for common purposes, then we expect local government to buy it at fair market value.

Land-Use Plans

The overall game plan for developing the community is envisioned by its **land-use plan.** The maps that accompany this document note prominent topographical features such as rivers and streams. The downtown business district is laid out in detail, and streets into and out of town are recorded. Existing public uses and private uses are noted on the map. Public utilities such as water and sewer lines are added. In other words, the entire community is plotted in terms of how each parcel of land is being used. The map becomes a plan when the future uses of land are determined. For example, given the growth of young people in the community, where will future recreational facilities need to be located? Considering the direction of new home construction, where should a new school be sited? The future of the community may well depend on how well land-use planning is conducted.

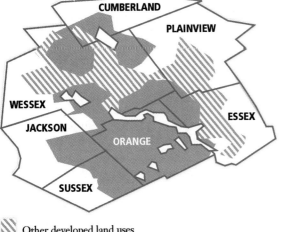

Other developed land uses

Lakes and ponds

Agriculture and forestry

A typical land-use map designates specific uses.

Zoning Ordinances

Once the current nd future use of areas of the community are planned, local government can formally reserve property for consistent use. Zones are laid out for existing and new commercial businesses, high-density apartment buildings, and low-density, single-family home subdivisions. By keeping development within zones that are appropriate to the land and consistent with the community's vision, **zoning** brings rationality to the growth process. People are free to develop property within a zone that is consistent with the zoning designation. If they wish to develop or redevelop a parcel of land in some manner that is deemed inconsistent with the land's zoning designation, then they must seek a *zoning variance.* Otherwise, developers will try to put a noisy night club next to a quiet subdivision or a liquor store next to a school. The decision about whether to allow a variance to zoning therefore can be controversial.

Zoning commissions or boards oversee actual land-use regulation. They zone parcels of land and hear appeals for variances. The *zoning board* takes the credit when the community develops peacefully and rationally, and its members take the heat when individual developers and land owners complain about regulation. If an individual fails to convince the zoning board to rezone a parcel of land or allow a variance to the current zoning, then he or she may appeal to the city council or county commission. Sometimes, people gain from the elected officials what they failed to secure from the appointed members of the zoning commission.

Some communities' land-use maps reflect weak zoning enforcement. Islands of commercially zoned land sit within residentially zoned areas. This *spot zoning* then encourages other nonconforming land use as other developers also want to be made an exception. Land-use regulation can fall apart if developers and land owners do not respect zoning designations.

Subdivision Regulations

Additional guidance is provided to subdivision developers. To protect the value of current and future home owners, a contractor must respect certain regulations when he or she builds. **Subdivision regulations** specify how much setback from the street is required for a house's foundation. Adequate space from the street must be provided so that the city or the developer can install utility services. Some communities also require that the developer put in a sidewalk on the street-side or front setback. Setbacks are also provided for the sides and back of a lot to protect neighboring property owners from encroachment by the developer and the future homeowner. Subdivision regulations try to ensure quality residential development regardless of the area of town where the building is going on. Modest homes and neighborhoods deserve protection just as much as do wealthy subdivisions.

Building Codes

Construction materials are regulated to protect the public safety. Public officials are informed of pending construction when a contractor files for a *building permit*. **Building codes** address materials, plumbing, insulation, and many other aspects of building a structure. Electrical codes, for example, specify the grade of wiring that goes into a home or business building. The local government provides electrical and plumbing inspectors who periodically visit the construction site. Periodically, inspectors must certify—or "sign off on"—key systems at the construction site or it may not be allowed to proceed.

Together, zoning, subdivision regulation, and building codes provide a blanket of consumer-protection regulation. New construction typically is superior to older building because newer and safer materials continue to enter the market and codes are regularly updated. The construction industry itself is instrumental in code development. In fact, some developers consider building regulation to be industry self-regulation. In any case, builders who are unschooled or unscrupulous may be fined and required to rework construction that violates local regulations.

Housing Codes

Controlling the safety and quality of new construction is one thing; regulating existing housing is another. Most communities have laws on the books that require that housing and property be maintained in a safe and sanitary condition. Chapters in local **housing codes** require proper ventilation and heating, screened windows, and properly installed appliances. Home owners and landlords may or may not comply with these requirements, and unless a complaint is lodged, local officials may never know of violations.

Housing codes have not been used effectively to raise the quality of the housing in most communities. Americans are reluctant to submit to governmental regulation of their domiciles, even when safety issues are at stake. Housing code officers in large cities have inspected some privately owned slums. "Slum lords" have been cited for *code violations*, and a few fines have been assessed. However, the individuals and corporations that own low-rent, high-density properties may lack the resources or will to comply with the prevailing housing codes. In extreme cases, the city itself may seize the derelict building for back taxes—and then the city becomes a slum lord. Regulation has proven to be a difficult path to improved housing for community residents who most need better living conditions.

Land-use regulation has a mixed record of effectiveness in the United States. In the newest communities that seem to need it least, it works well. In the older, more substandard inner neighborhoods where it is needed most, it may not work at all. This is frustrating to local officials and the professional associations that promote quality development. Nevertheless, most Americans are gradually becoming better housed. More and more workers are employed in safe buildings. Considering the reluctance of Americans to submit to governmental regulation, perhaps we will muddle through our land-use problems.

In the meantime, some communities are experimenting with new approaches to land-use controls. Minneapolis has decided to let some neighborhoods coordinate their own land use. *Overlay districts* are residential areas in which residents are free to write their own standards (Ehrenhalt, 1998). They can fashion new looks in store fronts and buildings, as well as new approaches to city planning at the neighborhood level. In the early 1990s, the Palm Beach, Florida, Countywide Planning Council authorized a new land trust, the Land Preservation Trust of Palm Beach County, Inc. (Abberger, 1991). Under this regulation, groups of local citizens can acquire and protect natural, historic, or recreational lands. All across the country, local governments are trying to bring land-use controls closer to the people.

Eminent Domain

Americans value property ownership and want government to protect individuals in their lawful enjoyment of their property (Rakove, 1996: 291). The founders of the republic thought of the rights to "life, liberty, and property" as the great freedoms and deliberated before listing "life, liberty, and the pursuit of happiness" in the Declaration of Independence. The concepts of property and the pursuit of happiness were related notions to our forebears.

In early America, communities had "commons," or land set aside for the community's joint use. These common areas were used to graze livestock and drill the local militia. In contemporary U.S. communities, privately owned property dwarfs the amount of public land. If we need access for a new road or a public school, then our public officials typically purchase it from private land owners. But what if the property owner does not want to sell? Does the power of government to regulate land use extend to its seizure from private hands?

The Fifth Amendment to the U.S. Constitution prohibits the seizure of private land without just compensation. When a local government uses the power of **eminent domain,** a legitimate public need must be shown and a fair price must be paid to the land owner. If the owner resists selling, then technically a local government can condemn the property, and a court then may have to arbitrate a truly fair price for the property.

A related "taking" may occur when a local government restricts the use of a piece of property to such an extent that its value is destroyed. Redefining beach dunes to include private building lots near the dunes effectively destroys their value because no building can be raised on them. Recent federal court decisions and state law suggest that local governments should be pressed to demonstrate why particular uses of private property are damaging to the public interest (Wood, 1997). Otherwise, land-use controls may be limited by a doctrine of unlawful takings.

❧ Conclusions About Local Policy Making

At the beginning of the chapter, we asked ourselves several questions about local government policy making. It is now time to take stock of what we have learned about the mechanics of decision making close to home.

- First, local citizens exercise a great deal of control over their local affairs. They have indeed reserved to themselves the power to control city and county government action. This exercise of the Tenth Amendment's reserved powers clause is subtle because constitutional theorists rarely look at political decisions that affect our property, buildings, and egress. In fact, each of us should feel on solid ground when we assert our property rights before local zoning boards or express our opinions before local planning commissions.

- Second, we should feel empowered to speak our piece because of the considerable tax burden we shoulder in support of local government. Home owners and apartment owners pay hefty property taxes, and we all pay local-option sales taxes every time we buy something. If we are going to be asked to shoulder our civic responsibilities every time we spend for housing or food and clothing, then we certainly will not hesitate to speak our minds when public actions might affect us.

- Third, an extreme case of confrontation between the public and our public servants arises when the government wants our property. It is certainly true that a local highway is an important civic project that we all may need and want. But the particular route the road will take is a political decision as much as an engineering decision. If the roadway absolutely must come through our property, then we have a right to be fairly compensated. It is also the case that we should all be vigilant to make sure that poor neighborhoods aren't buffaloed into allowing a right of way while wealthier neighborhoods remain immune. Unlike socialist political systems, we do not automatically subordinate our private interests to just any public purpose. For this reason if no other, we should stay informed, active, and involved in local politics.

When all is said and done, myriad small decision-making bodies dot the landscape of local government. None of us can keep up with what all of them do. That is why we belong to associations. In this way we can each scan a part of the horizon for government actions that may affect us. There is nothing particularly idealistic about the study of associations that we had in Chapter 8 and nothing particularly intimidating about this chapter's look at local government policy making. This is not rocket science! Governing ourselves is something we do, especially at the local level. If we choose to be apathetic, then we will get the decisions we deserve.

❧ Balancing Priorities and Making Trade-Offs

Political decisions are reached through *compromise*. No community group or political party or faction at city hall or the county courthouse gets its way all of the time. Pluralist theories suggest that some groups get some of what they want some of the time. Yet local policy making is more complex than that. Politics often is not a zero-sum game—that is, one player is not a clear winner and another a clear loser, or one player wins everything and the other loses everything. Instead, it is often the case that several parties each get some of what they want. This leaves everyone feeling good about some limited gains, a *positive-sum game*. This result also helps ensure that elected officials preserve some support in various groups in the community. It is simply politically unwise to deny local groups at least some gains in the game of politics.

In looking at how compromises are made in local government, we return to many of the themes that have been developed earlier in this book. We look at the priorities of American citizens, families, and neighborhoods in our effort to see how public officials try to balance different priorities. We ask the following questions:

- How can we have economic development while preserving aspects of the community that we value?
- How can we have public safety while also ensuring social justice?
- How can we enjoy the mobility of our personal automobile and yet avoid the destructiveness of development sprawl?
- How can we enjoy ever-improving local government services while also having modest tax burdens?

These are some of the themes that dominate local politics as we enter the twenty-first century. Most Americans find themselves on both sides of these issues. It is hard to be single-mindedly against either development or preservation, safety or justice, mobility or convenience, or customer service or tax decreases. By examining the merits of many points of view, we may appreciate how difficult it is for local officials to do their jobs while being pulled in different directions by different community interests.

❧ Development and Preservation

Our society is not static. Things change. Much of the change that affects our daily lives is economic and technological. The private sector is a social space within which new ideas are constantly emerging. Innovative business ideas bring new products and new jobs to the economy. Governments at all levels try to nurture this process. Internationally, institutions such as the World Bank try to help economies build foundations for future economic growth. These new economies can become our future trade partners. Nationally, the Departments of Commerce, Treasury, and Labor, the Office of the U.S. Trade Representative, and the Federal Reserve Board foster sustained growth and low inflation. The fifty state governments each have economic development plans that underwrite local efforts to attract and retain industries, foster new small business activities, and train productive workforces. Yet local governments are ultimately at ground zero for new industries, offices of new international trade partners, enhanced ports or airport facilities, or vocational training centers. As the units of government that are "closest to the people," city and county governments must cooperate in the economic-development process.

Economic-Development Strategies

Cities and counties typically have **development authorities** that are chartered to give full-time attention to economic-development activities in the community. Local elected officials are a part of these bodies, but authorities also include local economic leaders such as bankers, land developers, realtors, attorneys, vocational educators, local business owners, and other citizens who have expertise in economic matters. There are four basic approaches to economic development that are used by most local development authorities: (1)

business or industrial attraction, (2) business or industrial retention, (3) small business incubation, and (4) workforce development. Working together, the local public and private partners try to develop initiatives that will stimulate new economic activity and new jobs (Blakely, 1991: 22). To accomplish this goal, local development authorities draft economic-development plans that hopefully dovetail with state and federal plans. Each basic approach to economic development deserves our consideration.

Industrial Attraction. Perhaps the oldest strategy for economic development is the attraction of new industry to the community. The desire for a stronger local economy motivates many communities to entice companies to relocate to their respective cities (Spindler, 1994). If an industrial plant, a warehouse facility, or a services center opens in town, then there will be new job opportunities for local residents, a larger tax base, more spending at local stores, and more training opportunities for local vocational educators. In other words, industrial attraction *incentives* have been historically viewed as positive because everyone in the community seemed to benefit.

During the 1980s, this outlook on economic development underwent some reexamination. The industries that were relocating were mostly from what became popularly known as the Rust Belt, the states and localities of the upper Midwest. They were heading for the Sun Belt, the states and cities of the Southeast and Southwest. Old factories were inefficient to operate, labor costs were high, and the climate of government regulation and taxation seemed unfriendly (generally, see Smith, 1995). If new investments in facilities and technology were to be made, why not build the new plant in the South where land, labor, and taxes were cheap? This meant that Southern states were to compete with each other to attract what was to them new industry. Firms were quite willing to play one state or one community against another in the bidding war. Still, localities were overjoyed when they landed big new companies in their communities.

Communities are now more sophisticated in their approach to industrial attraction (Mahtesian, 1994). They have learned that the *quality of life* in a community is a key criterion for business location. Although cheap land, low-wage workers, and low taxes might get a community onto the short list of relocation sites, the final decision usually involves local amenities. After all, the executives and managers of the company are going to have to live there, too. They want nice housing, natural beauty, convenient shopping, good schools, recreation opportunities, and other amenities just like anyone else. So it really does not benefit a local community to destroy its natural environment and damage the tax base needed for local services. By the same token, development authorities need to take a careful look at prospective industries to weed out flagrant polluters, sweatshop employers, and selfish and self-centered financiers. A community would not seem to gain much by destroying itself in an intense competition to get the least-desirable firms to relocate there.

Business Retention. The many incentives that are offered new enterprises to locate in a community raise another issue. How have existing industries and businesses been shown recently that they are valued members of the community? Are they being slighted by local governments' preoccupation with industrial attraction strategies? The local economic-development effort will be a losing battle if companies leave the community faster than new businesses move in. The local population will have to say goodbye to some enterprises. Economic pressures weed out inefficient and unprofitable enterprises. But many local concerns can sustain themselves if they are given an even playing field with whatever new industries move into the community.

One approach to equalizing development incentives is to offer business expansions the same tax breaks, impact fee packages, and other incentives as new industry construction. Another action might be tax equalization—that is, not discounting local taxes and fees for new businesses. This also will level the playing field. Other benefits that local governments and their development partners can offer existing industries include subsidized employee-training programs, "buy local" promotional campaigns, and local business-appreciation celebrations. The key is to show existing local enterprises that the community appreciates their contributions and wants them to stay in business.

Small Business Incubation. Many local citizens have good ideas and lots of ambition. They strongly desire to open new local businesses and put their ideas into action (Fitchen, 1991: 68–69). Starting a new business, however, can be a scary prospect. Many legal steps have to be followed such as incorporating and getting a business license. New merchants also must master modern business practices, learn personnel law, and feel confident when they write their financing plan for the local bank. A hundred details can intimidate if not prevent enterprising local citizens from implementing their dreams.

A *small business incubator* is a storefront operation that is developed by a university, the local Chamber of Commerce, or an alliance of many skilled groups in the community. People who are interested in starting their own businesses can go to such a center and get printed information, take short courses, or get some feedback on their draft business plans. The staff at the small business incubator has the training, experience, and contacts needed to coach the entrepreneur. Over time, the best of the new ideas find their way into the marketplace. Some of the new businesses make it, and others do not. In the process of finding a niche in the local economy, a new business may open up new jobs and offer new services to local citizens.

Workforce Development. One necessity for any business enterprise is an educated and properly trained workforce. It is one key element in new business attraction and a key to small business incubation. If existing industries are going to modernize, then they need good training capabilities.

The local workforce usually gets its basic reading and computational skills from public schools. Although many school systems emphasize college preparation, more and more of them have realized that many students do not want to go to college. Instead, they want to learn a trade and go to work. To fill this gap in the American educational system, government and business have collaborated in developing state systems of *vocational–technical schools*. In these schools, students can learn marketable skills and train on state-of-the-art equipment. In some cases, they can actually train on equipment provided by a local employer. They can literally walk out of the school and into the shop ready to work.

These four economic development strategies and other innovative ideas may come together in a comprehensive *economic-development plan*. Infrastructural improvements such as new streets, better water and sewer lines, and upgraded communications systems then can be developed. The planning process never ends. Each achievement leads to new insights, and these new insights are incorporated into subsequent development plans. Development authorities are active in virtually all major U.S. cities, and state governments are helping smaller communities produce plans as well. Table 13.2 shows the results of a survey of Georgia's small cities and rural counties. A year after the survey, the state began requiring community-development plans as a condition of state aid. Nevertheless, many of these smaller communities were already actively developing their own plans.

Table 13.2
Georgia Economic-Development Plans, 1991

| | Percent | | |
Provision	Small City Plans	Rural County Plans	Overall
Analysis of local needs, resources	29	35	33
Attraction strategies	24	38	33
Retention strategies	0	17	11
Expansion strategies	18	24	20
Targeted activities	18	21	20
Promotion methods	0	10	7

Source: Cox, Daily, & Pajari (1991): 313.

In all of the rush to develop and implement economic-development plans, some communities forget that they have many treasures to preserve. Development and preservation goals are not incompatible, but they may come into conflict if the planning does not proceed with the end game in mind. The ultimate vision of most communities is to become a place where the best of the old sits side-by-side with the best of the new. It is therefore necessary to balance development with conscious preservation efforts.

Community-Preservation Strategies

All communities have a heritage to protect. That heritage is part environment and part history, part culture and part linguistics. A community is what it is today as the result of a complex evolution of people living on the land and people developing ways to live together. To some community members, development equals modernization, and all of the historical baggage of the community should be swept aside. To others, development is a threat, an assault on their cherished traditions. Most of us want a balance struck that keeps the best of the new and the best of what has gone before.

Environmental Protection. Local people may be loyal to the land because it supported their ancestors. Newcomers may cherish it because they migrated from a place where much of the natural beauty and functioning ecosystem had been destroyed. Young people are said to have an enhanced ecological consciousness, and older people may be nostalgic about the land. In any case, many local residents desire environmental protection for many valid reasons.

Urbanization and then suburbanization have destroyed many natural environments. Streams are polluted, forests are denuded, and open vistas are boxed in. *Ecosystems* that once maintained a natural balance have been disrupted. For example, the forests, grasslands, and savannas can no longer absorb water runoff during heavy rainstorms because they have been replaced with industry, housing, and highways. Pasture lands absorb water; concrete parking lots do not. The runoff cannot collect in natural streams and get carried away to nearby rivers because we have diverted and clogged the streams in the process of building office malls and housing developments. Our urban and suburban air is increasingly polluted with the waste products of industrial production and fossil-fueled automobiles and trucks. What was once a quiet and balanced environment is now stinking, unhealthful sprawl.

Urban governments have tried to preserve some of the natural environment by constructing and maintaining *city parks*. These oases provide playground space for urban children and walk space for the city's retirees—when the city can keep drug dealers and homeless people out of them. Suburban growth-management plans have attempted to set aside land along rivers and streams for passive parks where joggers and cyclists can get outdoors. Of course, suburbanites have to compete with developers for these spots that have natural amenities. Fortunately, many state legislatures have intervened to halt development right up to the river's edge, thereby giving some teeth to local plans that try to preserve a flood plain area for public recreational use. But even rural environments are not safe. Several states have intervened to stop the construction of huge concrete hog farms that spread stench and foul the waters of property owners all around them.

Environmental protection is a challenge for all levels of government. Many national and state regulations try to preserve the integrity of our woodlands and marshes. But local officials again are at ground zero when it comes to policing development efforts. Local governments must face the challenge of refusing to rezone sensitive land, denying building permits near natural treasures, and themselves purchasing and preserving sensitive ecologies. It is not an easy political task, and environmental protection can get expensive. In the end, each city and county decides what priority it will assign to environmental protection.

Historic Preservation. The sense of place that binds us to a community is historical as well as environmental. Communities have stories, just as do individuals and families. Old timers and newcomers alike can appreciate the value of a historically significant city or district within a city. Cities such as Savannah, New Orleans, Boston, and San Francisco boast historic districts that are major amenities of their communities.

A sense of history can be seen in the *architectural preservation* of important old public buildings, churches, businesses, and homes. Historical monuments, museums, and reenactments help residents and visitors interpret the city's past. Schools can teach about local history, and local historic preservation societies can conduct research that leads to new insights into the past. The tourist industry that is growing so rapidly in the United States also plays a role in the politics of preservation. Activities from touring New Orleans' French Quarter in a horse-drawn carriage to visiting a working dairy farm interest Americans who want to make learning about history a part of their vacations.

Cultural Preservation. As we discussed early in this book, the United States is a diverse place. Many peoples from around the world have come to settle here. For some of us, fitting into the American mainstream is of para-

Historic preservation, whether of structures such as this one in New Mexico or of entire neighborhoods, is an increasingly important part of community life.

Source: © Gene Fitzer

mount importance. Others of us need to signal our ethnic and linguistic heritage in order to feel fully self-actualized. Individuals have many shades of ethnic feeling ranging from almost total indifference to deep ethnic identification and pride. The community must therefore be prepared for this range of needs and their expression.

Cultural heritage can be celebrated in *festivals*, enjoyed in distinctive ethnic restaurants, and honored with civic pronouncements. Of course, including all interested ethnic groups can lead to a plethora of celebrations, while leaving out interested groups can cause deep hurt and resentment. For this reason, the local calendar of most communities is full. Given enough notice and a modicum of resources, respect can be shown for African American, Irish, Chinese, Mexican American, German, and Caribbean, as well as many other holidays.

Beyond ceremonial occasions, *cultural tolerance* can be reflected in public policy. For example, should Spanish or other languages spoken in the home be allowed in the public schools, or should only English be spoken by children at school? Should public documents such as birth certificates, marriage licenses, property deeds, and court summons be available in both Spanish and English? There is considerable debate concerning the degree to which French speakers should be accommodated in Louisiana and Florida and the degree to which Spanish speakers should be accommodated in Florida, Texas, and California. One perspective holds that the English language binds us together as a people and should be required. Others hold that most Americans learn to speak English in their own good time, and requirements are unnecessary and disrespectful. This is one of those issues that we must decide for ourselves.

At this point in our study of local government, we have to ask, is economic development being pursued at the expense of our rich cultural and linguistic diversity? At the very moment that our economy is going global, are we failing to appreciate the fact that many Americans speak two or more languages? Are we negligent in not being positive about cultural preservation and balancing our economic ambitions with cultural sensitivity?

Balancing Development and Preservation

Some powerful interests favor economic development, and there often are traditional elites and community activists who promote environmental protection, historic conservation, and cultural preservation. Everyone has a legitimate interest and an articulate point of view. Public officials are caught in the middle, and decisions have to be made. This dilemma leads to a creative give-and-take that brings forward new, heretofore undiscovered options. For example, whole new fields of architecture have developed around the concept of historically sensitive new buildings. New structures can be built that fit in with historic business structures and period homes. From that interest, new products have been developed that look like vintage building materials but have the strength and insulation properties required by today's contractors. Similarly, cities with ethnically diverse populations have built successful festivals such as the Spoleto Festivals in Charleston, South Carolina, that not only showcase the city but also make money. There is virtually no end to the innovative strategies that a community committed to balance can achieve. The results may be that we can have the economic vigor we desire while preserving the amenities that give our communities their distinctive personalities and charm.

❧ Public Safety and Social Justice

We have already noted that personal, family, and neighborhood security are a priority with most Americans. We should not forget that safety is just as important to newcomers as to old-timers, just as important to inner-city residents as it is to suburbanites. Indeed, *personal safety* is a basic human need, and public security is a fundamental responsibility of government. On the other hand, protection must be equitable. Many neighborhoods' residents may feel they are treated as second-class citizens when it comes to police and fire protection. Ironically, many of the neighborhoods that need protective services the most feel least likely to get them.

Social justice requires that people who are suspected of committing crimes be afforded a presumption of innocence. If local governments profile crime cases in such a way that only African American men are scrutinized or if local curfews are enforced selectively in poor neighborhoods, then the cost of security may be too high. There must be a balance between the goals of public safety and our commitment to social justice.

Public Safety Strategies

Public safety involves a wide range of governmental services in areas such as public health, emergency medical services, fire prevention, and police protection. There are hundreds of threats to our person and property that may require governmental action. Emergencies such as canyon fires in California are too severe for home fire-protection devices and even the most modern fire-suppression systems. Garden hoses are no help. Injuries require more than first aid, looting cannot be prevented by burned-out home security systems, and property losses are beyond the capability of personal property insurance to cover. Volunteer firefighters and Red Cross volunteers are examples of community residents who lend important assistance, but only government has the full resources and authority to combat serious emergencies.

Serious threats also can come to individuals and individual households and businesses. Most of us are not prepared to resist force with equal force. We do not go armed so that we can have parity with thugs who wield lethal weapons. We do not spend hundreds of thousands of dollars to make our homes impregnable fortresses, and we do not hire armed guards to patrol the grounds at night. Private businesses and some wealthier citizens may contract with private security companies, but even these services essentially only alert law enforcement authorities when danger is detected. In other words, we expect governmental officials—police officers and sheriffs' deputies—to protect us from harm and severe property loss.

Crime Control. Local governments cannot hope to eliminate all crime and bring utopian bliss to our cities and counties. Were it only true! Human nature being what it is, there will always be people who try to take advantage of others, people who use violence to solve disputes, and people whose reckless behavior places the lives and well-being of others at risk. What laws and law enforcement can hope to accomplish is to *control* the level of crime in a community. By removing habitual offenders to prison; by educating the public about personal, home, and neighborhood security; and by literally standing between danger and the citizen at risk, our police and sheriffs' departments try to "protect and serve."

State laws and state courts govern most of the serious criminal cases in the United States. Property crimes such as burglary and larceny are violations of the state criminal code, as are violent crimes such as assault, rape, and murder. Federal law governs criminal behavior that cuts across state lines, drug importation, crimes on Indian reservations and other actions that are beyond the jurisdiction of state courts. Even though state and federal law govern serious crimes, local law enforcement officers are usually the first contacts for both offenders and victims.

Local ordinances are the basis for a great deal of the regulation that can lead to crime control. For example, loitering ordinances are designed to keep idle males from congregating and getting into trouble. Such ordinances also reassure local merchants, shoppers, and tourists that being out in the community brings minimal risks to personal safety and the security of property. Another local ordinance that may meet local needs is a curfew—this typically affects just teenagers. In 1996, for example, there were almost 133,000 arrests for curfew violations in the United States (Bureau of Justice Statistics, 1997: 333). Again, local residents feel more secure when such an ordinance is enforced.

Crime Prevention. The roots of crime are beyond the scope of this book. Besides, there is little professional or societal consensus about why people knowingly break the law. That is why we try to control that which we do not truly understand. Perhaps if we understood the links between abject poverty and rage or the relationship between self-esteem and drug use we would aspire to win the war against crime once and for all. But we do not. Or perhaps more to the point, we are not free to act on what we do know. Under our form of government, we do not authorize public officials to seize and relocate ghetto children. We cannot confiscate property and reallocate it to homeless people. Our values and our constitutional form of government constrain us. So, our local officials continue to muddle through, and our police try to be as professional as they can be. And we try to control crime.

On the victim side of the prevention equation, some local police and sheriff's departments offer a variety of public services. Officers will conduct a security audit of a home or business and show citizens how to more properly secure their property. In some communities, police officers will accompany business owners as they deposit their cash receipts for each day's business. In others, they will teach firearm-safety programs for citizens who feel they may need to defend themselves and their property. Officers also may teach drug-awareness programs to school children and nonviolent conflict resolution to children and adults, enforce loitering and curfew laws, and sponsor athletic activities for teenagers. The scope of *prevention* programs is limited only by the imagination of police departments and their citizen supporters.

Other Public Safety Strategies. Initially focusing on police protection lets us examine typical issues that arise in balancing governmental priorities. However, many of the same kinds of observations could be made for other public safety services such as public health, disaster relief, emergency medical services, investigation of deaths, and fire prevention. All of these governmental activities are aimed at protecting the public from dangers that individuals, families, and neighborhoods usually cannot handle alone.

All types of emergency services have prevention and response components (Hart, 1994). For example, the county health department immunizes children against infectious diseases and provides disease-control serum when outbreaks occur. Disaster-relief agencies plan for community action in the case of hurricanes, tornados, floods, and other calamities, and they also coordinate emergency services when these disasters actually occur. Emergency medical services and the emergency rooms of local hospitals stockpile medications, equipment, and supplies to use when a citizen calls for an ambulance, and they administer life-saving medical services until the injury or illness can be stabilized. The county coroner or medical examiner examines the bodies of deceased persons who die under questionable circumstances and takes action to notify infectious disease or police officials about the results of any autopsy that is performed. Finally, many fire departments spend as much time preventing fires as they spend fighting them. Special attention is given to advising nursing homes and other high-density residences of the need for fire-suppression systems such as sprinklers, metal fireproof doors, and nonflammable curtains, bedding, and furniture. In each case, the professionals who work to ensure public safety do so first by trying to prevent danger from occurring and second by acting promptly when it does occur.

Ensuring Social Justice

We seek to balance public safety with social justice because public safety can be secured at too high a price. Most dictatorships are remarkably peaceful. If death or dismemberment punishes virtually any crime, then everyone lives in fear of their lives. But the fear is of the government itself. By the same token, we can envision a utopian society of sorts in which we are permitted to take no risks. A paternalistic state cares for us from cradle to grave, feeds us, clothes us all alike, and pumps us full of vitamins and drugs to keep us serene. Americans are not that afraid to live their own private lives. Perhaps the best way to visualize an American style of social justice is to consider the notions of equity and empathy.

In a democratic society, no one citizen is more entitled to public services than any other. Unlike private services where we "get what we pay for," public services are provided for all. Implicitly, then, the same quality of public service should be available to the banker and the poor man, the city elder and the college student. Providing the same courtesy and responsiveness to all citizens is considered to be equitable professional behavior. The codes of ethics of most professions and many local, state, and federal laws insist on *equity* in service delivery.

Americans are compassionate people, and few societies can match the private charitable giving of our citizenry. As Seymour Martin Lipset has noted, "even though the American state now provides more fully for many activities once almost totally dependent on private support, its population, as the most anti-statist people in the developed world, continues to be the most generous on a personal basis" (Lipset, 1996: 71). We have high levels of personal ambition, but we empathize with the individual plant worker who is injured and disabled, the child whose parents are killed, or the illiterate school dropout who later in life cannot find a job. This *empathy* allows us to put ourselves in the disadvantaged person's shoes. We want others to have the opportunities that we have had and hope that they will take advantage of them. We wish others well in striving for and securing the successful middle-class life that most of us enjoy.

Discrimination in service delivery makes us mad. An ambulance should rush to the scene of a heart attack regardless of whether the patient is a financier or a homeless woman. Our whole quarter-century struggle for civil rights was undertaken so that public discrimination might be eradicated. And so we fully expect our public safety organizations to place a high value on the health and lives of all citizens. Because public servants act in our name, we hope that their own natural empathy for the injured and victimized will show through. Or perhaps they will show empathy on our behalf. If they cannot manage either, then they should probably not be employed in the public sector.

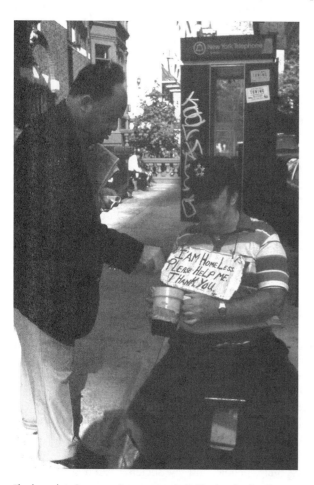

The homeless in our society test our individual and collective beliefs about social responsibility and justice.
Source: © Serge Attal / Corbis Sygma

Many local crime-control ordinances may have a dark side—antiloitering ordinances, for example. We enjoy a constitutionally protected right to assemble and move freely about the community. Singling someone out as a loiterer is a highly subjective judgment. This is especially true if local police single out certain people in certain neighborhoods for selective enforcement of the loitering ordinance. There is little justice in that approach.

Youth curfews are also controversial crime-control ordinances. Residents of upscale suburban neighborhoods would be outraged if police officers brought their children home for being out too late at the movies or at a school function. In fact, most curfew laws have numerous loopholes for "legitimate" reasons for teenagers to be out late. Yet under many curfew ordinances, inner-city youth who have few legitimate places to go in the evening report being hassled by the local police. Again, selective enforcement is an issue.

Roughly 12 percent of the American population is African American, but almost half of all people arrested for vagrancy are black. More than one-third of all arrests for disorderly conduct involve black detainees. And 38 percent of all drug use arrests are of African American users (Bureau of Justice Statistics, 1997: 338). Now it may be that such arrests and such incidents are or are not out of balance. Law enforcers may be objectively and impersonally applying the law. Assuming for the moment that incident rates are that high for African Americans, then the question becomes, how did so many black men become homeless, frustrated, and addicted? Social justice concerns extend beyond the possibility that selective enforcement of the law is disproportionately snaring too many minority citizens.

Other public safety activities can be subjected to the same kind of analysis. Poor families are at greater risk of communicable diseases, household fires, and personal injury. Yet if neighborhood leaders and civil rights activists are to be believed, low-income neighborhoods receive inferior public health, fire suppression, and emergency medical services. Looked at another way, those of us in the American middle class can afford to avoid places where infectious diseases are likely. We can purchase the best in appliances, install fire alarms and suppression systems, and contract for private firefighting services. We have insurance to cover most losses. We can pay for the best in medical care. In other words, the people who most need every kind of emergency service are those who may receive the only the most rudimentary services. Only by admitting possible problems of social justice can we really provide equitable public safety protections.

❧ Mobility and Sprawl

In the early chapters of this book, we made much of the fact that the United States is a vast and beautiful land and that Americans are often a people on the move. We tend to feel that our mastery over nature is complete, and only in recent years have we begun to appreciate that the natural world can be a special space without our technology and us. Perhaps we have gone too far in imposing our will on the land. We may have developed ugly and dysfunctional spaces where beautiful and successful forests once stood. Our science fiction writers have painted a possible future in which humanity stands triumphant in a gas mask atop the slag heap of industrial and commercial waste.

Personal Mobility

We love our automobiles. From their teenage years on, American men and women delight in the freedom that personal transportation affords. We are free to meet friends, go and come from work, run errands on a moment's notice, and explore the countryside on our days off from work or school. No limits. And we are willing to sacrifice in order to have this wonderful freedom of movement. We will give our money, borrow from the bank, or do without other luxuries to buy and maintain our personal automobile. The United States is the land of the personal automobile.

In many countries, public transportation is the basic outlet for mobility. Local people ride buses or trains to work, market, and school. They live relatively close to bus and train lines, leaving more open land. Vacations are planned, and people do not expect to be able to drop everything and take off. Mobility may be more restricted, but life is less hectic.

To accommodate our desire to drive everywhere we need to go, our governments have developed huge networks of highways. The national government has constructed interstate highways, state governments have built state road systems, and our local governments have added even more paved streets. As a result of this government-purchased infrastructure, an *intermodal revolution* (Leach, 1999: 48) has taken place. American commerce has flourished. Goods flow from factory or port to warehouses to malls and shops in ever-increasing numbers. Our consumptive lifestyle if fueled by transportation on both the consumer demand and the business supply ends (see Table 13.3).

Table 13.3
Traffic Volume in Billions of Ton-Miles

Type of Transport	1970	1980	1990
Freight traffic	1,936	2,487	2,895
Passenger traffic	1,181	1,467	1,993

Source: Eno Transportation Foundation in U.S. Department of Commerce (1996), *Statistical Abstract of the United States: American Almanac* (1996): 616.

Urban, Suburban, and Exurban Sprawl

Highways, roads, and streets traverse and dissect the land. That is why we see so many dead animals along the roads and why county and state workers spend so much time removing the carnage. The roadways and parking lots stop rain absorption and cause runoff problems, leading to local flooding and city and county flood-abatement projects. The entire pavement makes cities hotter, and the increasing traffic pollutes the air. Traffic stalls cause delays in getting to work. In other words, even after the construction of roadways is done, we continue to pay a high price for our convenient mobility.

The landscape becomes dotted with hundreds of strip malls. Cars entering and exiting the parking lots at these strip malls clog commuter traffic and cause numerous "fender-bender" accidents. This adds to the already existing frustration of overloaded commuter arteries. As people move farther out of town, old strip malls go downhill. They rent to more marginal businesses or become abandoned altogether. Ring after ring of deterioration spreads outward from the urban center to the suburbs, the deep suburbs, and beyond. Little effort is made to reclaim these neglected and abandoned strip areas.

Balancing Mobility and Sprawl

There are many strategies for working our way out of the problem of sprawl. Some communities adopt *growth-management programs*. They may limit development in some outlying areas while encouraging filling in and clustering development in areas closer to the central city (Florida Department of Community Affairs, 1989). Rapid transit can offer commuters an attractive alternative to driving to work every day. Revitalized parks and improved urban forest canopies can add amenities to city living. Small businesses can be helped if they locate in redeveloped areas of town. In other words, local governments and interested developers can offer residents alternatives to moving increasing distances out of the city.

For individuals who insist on living far away from work and who persist in wanting to commute in their own vehicles, some communities have offered car pooling and ride-share programs. Flexible work schedules and distance-learning education have removed some of the need to commute so much. Electric and natural gas–powered cars offer technological possibilities for the future. Overall, steps can be taken to ease the price we pay for our mobility and the personal automobile. We can bring more balance to the relationship between the two, even if it means lifestyle changes. And local governments can help lead in this adaptive change.

✿ Excellent Services and Modest Taxes

Americans demand first-class public services. Whether the service is fire protection or mass transit, we expect quality and accountability. In that regard, we often demand that government be run on a business-like basis. By this we mean that we want effective services delivered in an efficient manner. Effectiveness pertains to results; efficiency pertains to cost. In this era of general public dissatisfaction with public servants, we want local government to "do more with less." So, in an era of rising expectations, citizens want lower, not higher, tax rates. This is no small task.

Quality Public-Service Strategies

There is no shortage of books written about how to make local government more effective and efficient. You have already learned about one of the most influential reforms: the reinventing government movement. Volumes have been devoted to arguing how elected officials and public employees can be more responsive to local residents. Local governments have placed many reform ideas into practice: clarifying the purposes of local agencies, creating consequences for performance, putting the customer in the driver's seat, shifting control away from the top and center, and creating an entrepreneurial culture (Osborne & Plastrik, 1997).

In a less revolutionary vein, most local governments have upgraded their equipment, hired and trained more educated employees, and incorporated computerized management systems into their operations. The result has been that city and county employees probably are more productive today than they were twenty or even ten years ago. Professional managers have been brought in to manage the activities of local agencies. Many of these managers hold Masters' degrees in either public administration (MPA) or business administration (MBA).

Integrated management systems that fuse better equipment with more-capable employees and information technology make for more-accountable local government. One aspect of a management system is the creation of a clear vision and the articulation of performance standards. The vision statement reminds public servants of why they are there. Performance standards help keep public employees on track. If evaluation information is gathered and analyzed, then local managers can watch trends in effectiveness and efficiency across departments over time. The overall result can be a more focused and streamlined set of local agencies.

One of the reinventing government movement's insights has been that all public services do not have to be delivered by government employees. Many companies are experienced in delivering high-quality services at attractive prices. Contracting out services that can be more efficiently provided by private vendors has several advantages. Companies can be required to submit competitively low bids on local government projects or services. They can be monitored in terms of their performance and costs, and competitor companies may have an opportunity to improve service or reduce costs in the next bidding cycle. Even better, the city or county can be carved up into service districts, and different companies can be given contracts in different service areas. This results in direct head-to-head competition.

Whether a local government professionalizes or reinvents itself or contracts out services, the end game is the same. Citizens want high-quality services. They want an excellent infrastructure of water and sewer lines and treatment facilities so that new economic development takes place. They want police, fire, and ambulance services that respond quickly and act competently when they arrive. They want traffic to flow smoothly along well-maintained streets, even at rush hour. And they want all of these and hundreds of other tasks accomplished at the lowest possible cost.

Keeping Taxes Modest

Local governments are at the low end of the food chain when it comes to revenues. The national government and most state governments use personal income taxes to raise the bulk of their revenues. The federal and most state governments also tax fuels, investments, inheritances, and other sources of personal wealth. Some state governments also tax property and retail sales. The resulting federal income-tax rate in the United States is roughly 30 percent (Johnson, 1997: 44). An additional 10 percent is owed in state and local taxes of all kinds (U.S. Bureau of the Census, 1996: 311). This means that the average American manages to retain something like sixty cents on the dollar of his or her earnings in a typical year. And these are averages. Americans in some parts of the country do much worse.

A *taxpayers' revolt* started in the United States in the 1970s and still continues to some degree. Congress was forced to reform the federal tax code in 1986. Many state legislatures have been pressured to remove sales taxes on food and prescription drugs. And local governments face both hostile state legislatures and organized local home owners in a battle to maintain property tax rates and assessments. No politician in his or her right mind in the 1990s would have run for election on a platform calling for increased taxes.

Cut off from many revenue sources by federal and state preemption, local governments must rely on the sales tax, the property tax, and service fees for locally generated revenue. Of course, they do receive state aid and a trickle of federal aid, but in many respects they are on their own when it comes to financing the services that local citizens demand.

The tax collector comes at us from a lot of different directions in the United States. Our income taxes are usually withheld from our paychecks to ensure that they get paid at the end of the year. The total cost for every gallon of gasoline we put in our vehicles is partially for the product and partially for the taxes. Our property tax bills are either a part of our monthly mortgage payment

Voters can express their opinions and beliefs at each election on a wide range of issues from taxation to social policy.
Source: © Andy Sacks

(escrow account) or are hidden in the cost of our rent. Sales taxes nick our bank accounts every time we make a purchase, but we notice them most when we make a major purchase such as a car or an appliance. In a land of free enterprise where we are expected to make our own way in the world, taxes seem to limit our liberty to do so. And for retired people living on fixed incomes, a tax such as the property tax or sales tax can really hurt. It is fair to say that Americans want government to take a more modest tax bite. The fact that local governments feed last does not ease the pain for taxpayers carrying three levels of government around on their backs.

Balancing Service and Taxation

There is a contradiction in the notion that we want more from local governments but do not want to pay for it. Politicians are no help because they will always promise to *do more with less* (DeLaney, 1995: 143–144). The public administrator will try to "bring efficiency to government," but the effects of reforms are usually short-lived. Government is not a business, so to promise to run local agencies in a business-like fashion may be hollow as well. Perhaps we do need to reinvent government. Inventions make it possible for us to do things in the future that we were unable to do in the past. Maybe the solutions that we seek cannot be found in the institutions that created them.

Again, the problem of balancing services with taxation is not a question of good intentions. Local government workers are like everyone else. They get up and go to work each morning determined to get the job done. Their managers read and study new ideas on how to achieve greater effectiveness and efficiency. Most of the people involved with delivering local services are members of our communities and want them to prosper no less than we do. Perhaps the most that we can hope for is a mix of reforms embedded in an organizational culture that is committed to continuous reform.

Cities and counties are already at work on this agenda. Cost cutting has come first as a means of increasing the efficiency of local government. In tandem with these economizing measures, some services have been contracted out to competitive private companies. Even some whole departments of local government have been privatized. Local neighborhoods help prioritize projects and services. Experimental voucher programs let parents and students pick the school that the youngsters will attend. All around the country, local governments are experimenting with new ways of delivering more satisfactory services at a reasonable cost.

❧ Chapter Conclusion

The larger question of whether we can manage to balance economic development with community preservation, public safety with social justice, personal mobility with livable space, and quality services with modest taxes—all at the same time—is the real challenge of local government in the twenty-first century. Juggling issues with such important social values will require all of our intellectual, political, and administrative skills. A career in local government will witness a fast-paced whirlwind of new technologies, mind-boggling program experiments, and unconventional policy entrepreneurs. Not all of our program experiments will succeed. But some will. And the best will be transferred to localities throughout the country and perhaps throughout the world.

The devolution of power to the neighborhood level is a powerful tenant of the new reinventing government politics that have emerged over the last decade. Just as national leaders saw the value of policy devolution to the state level, state leaders are beginning to return more responsibility to the local level. More powerful home-rule provisions have come slowly because some state legislators are reluctant to give up any of their newly devolved power to local governments (Berman, 1998: 64). However, taxpayer revolts and term-limit drives harken the resurgence of community power in the United States. With local citizens making more of the decisions close to home, city and even county officials can be bolder in structuring local laws that officially empower this already powerful public. In fact, we may look for the gradual development of something like neighborhood-level self-government. The logical consequence of devolving power from distant government structures to decision makers closer and closer to the people is the return of power to the people themselves. As the public sector contracts, the span of private action expands. Perhaps we *can* have effective governance without big government.

Collecting Your Thoughts *Balancing the Priorities of Citizenship*

You have spent your time in this state and local government course developing the knowledge and skills needed for success as both a citizen and an active professional. You have doubtless learned a great deal about how politics and policy making operate at the state and local levels. Take a few minutes and apply the lessons to your own future plans.

- Will you be able to balance the sometimes-conflicting pressures you will face?
- Will you find a balance between the demands of a busy career and the enjoyment of your community's natural and cultural amenities?
- Will you find the middle ground between demanding safety for your person and possessions on the one hand and appreciating the racial diversity and social inequalities of your community on the other?
- Are you reconciled to the trade-off between your mobility in your car and the sprawl that such a lifestyle creates? If not, are you prepared to take some steps to help your community improve the quality of civic space?
- Finally, are you prepared to be an intelligent and balanced taxpayer? Do you realize that we don't get something for nothing in this world? Quality public services are expensive, and you and your contemporaries will have to work out the balance point between private life and civic responsibility.

We wish you the best in finding your own balance.

Key Words for InfoTrac Exploration

loitering   property valuation   state sales taxes   sustainable development

Sources Cited

Abberger, Will (1991). "Growth Management through Land Acquisition." Pp. 66–68 in John DeGrove (Ed.), *Balanced Growth: A Planning Guide for Local Government*. Washington, DC: International City Management Association.

Berman, David (1998). "State–Local Relations: Authority, Finance, and Regional Cooperation." Pp. 62–75 in *The Municipal Year Book: 1998*. Washington, DC: International City Management Association.

Blair, George S. (1986). *Government at the Grass Roots* (4th ed.). Pacific Palisades, CA: Palisades Publishers.

Blakely, Edward J. (1991). "The Meaning of Local Economic Development." Pp. 21–32 in R. Scott Fosler (Ed.), *Local Economic Development: Strategies for a Changing Economy*. Washington, DC: International City Management Association.

Bureau of Justice Statistics (1997). *Sourcebook of Criminal Justice Statistics, 1997*. Washington, DC: U.S. Department of Justice.

Cox, George H., John H. Daily, and Roger N. Pajari (1991). "Local Government Support for Economic Development." *Public Administration Quarterly*, *15*(3) (Fall): 304–327.

DeLaney, Ann (1995). *Politics for Dummies*. Foster City, CA: IDG Books.

Ehrenhalt, Alan (1998). "The Trouble with Zoning." *Governing* (February): 28–30.

Fitchen, Janet M. (1991). *Endangered Spaces, Enduring Places: Change, Identity, and Survival in Rural America*. Boulder: Westview.

Florida Department of Community Affairs (1989). "Techniques for Discouraging Sprawl." Pp. 36–41 in John M. DeGrove (Ed.) (1991), *Balanced Growth: A Planning Guide for Local Government*. Washington, DC: International City Management Association.

Gray, Virginia, & Peter Eisinger (1997). *American States and Cities* (2nd ed.). New York: Longman.

Hart, Bob (1994). "Emergency Management." Pp. 177–194 in James M. Banovetz (Ed.), *Managing Small Cities and Counties*. Washington, DC: International City Management Association.

Johnson, Otto (1997). *Information Please Almanac, 1997*. Boston: Houghton Mifflin.

Leach, William (1999). *Country of Exiles: The Destruction of Place in American Life*. New York: Pantheon.

Lipset, Seymour Martin (1996). *American Exceptionalism: A Double-Edged Sword*. New York: W.W. Norton.

Mahtesian, Charles (1994). "Romancing the Smokestack." *Governing* (8): 36–40.

Osborne, David, & Peter Plastrik (1997). *Banishing Bureaucracy: The Five Strategies for Reinventing Government*. Reading, MA: Addison-Wesley.

Rainey, Hal G. (1991). *Understanding and Managing Public Organizations*. San Francisco: Jossey-Bass.

Rakove, Jack N. (1996). *Original Meanings: Politics and Ideas in the Making of the Constitution*. New York: Random House.

Smith, Hedrick (1995). *Rethinking America: A New Game Plan from the American Innovators*. New York: Random House.

Snell, Ronald K. (1991). "The Tax the Public Loves to Hate." *State Legislatures, 17:* 37–39.

Spindler, Charles J. (1994). "Winners and Losers in Industrial Recruitment: Mercedes-Benz and Alabama." *State and Local Government Review, 26*(3) (Fall): 192–204.

U.S. Bureau of the Census (1996). *The American Almanac: 1997–98*. Washington, DC: U.S. Department of Commerce.

U.S. Department of Commerce (1996). *Statistical Abstract of the United States: American Almanac*. Washington, DC: Author.

Wood, Gwen Y. (1997). "The New 'Takings' Proposals in State Legislatures: Private Property Rights Protection or a New Entitlement?" *State and Local Government Review, 29*(1) (Fall): 188–200.

Neighborhood Survey

We are a city of neighborhoods. For some of us, our neighbors live upstairs in the apartment building or down the lane in the mobile home park. For others, our neighbors are fellow homeowners and renters in single-family subdivisions or condo developments. We all live in neighborhoods.

The purpose of this survey is to find out what our neighbors are thinking about life in this community. The survey may help identify what actions if any our governmental and civic institutions should take to improve the quality of life here. The city government and the local newspaper are sponsoring the neighborhood survey. The questions were developed in consultation with many neighborhood associations. Your answers are anonymous and hopefully will be candid. The results will be presented to the Mayor, City Council, and the City Administrator. They will also be published in the newspaper. The university is paying the costs of the survey. Undergraduate State and Local Government students are doing the legwork.

Please take a couple of minutes and complete the survey questions. Then mail the completed survey to us in the special Business Reply envelope that we have enclosed. The survey is being mailed to a small scientifically chosen sample of local citizens, it is therefore really important that you complete and return the survey to us. Thanks!

Instructions. Please read and react to each of the following questions. In many cases, multiple answers are just fine. There are also spaces provided where you may write in your own answers. Do not sign the survey, and do not write a return address on the envelope that you mail back to us. Thanks again. You'll be hearing from us (in the newspaper and through the neighborhood associations).

Late in the afternoon or early in the evening, you may want to go for a walk. Maybe you would take your child(ren) or dog, or maybe you just want some time alone.

1. Are you comfortable going out for a walk?
    Yes, I always feel fine about such things.   56%
    Occasionally, if not alone or before dark.   39%
    No, I'd be afraid.   4%

2. If you are uncomfortable, why? (multiple answers OK)

Fear of unsupervised youth	11
Fear of strangers	29
Nervous about reckless drivers	20
Insufficient lighting	40
Rumors of violent acts	17
Fear of being burglarized while gone	11
Fear of dogs	19
Nervous about reckless bicyclers, skaters	3
Fear of neighbors	3
Other	9

We all want to live in pleasant surroundings where we would be proud to bring family or friends.

3. When you look around your neighborhood, are you proud of how it looks?

Yes, the area looks great.	48%
Not sure, it could be improved.	44%
No, it's an ugly area.	7%

4. If the neighborhood appearance needs work, why? (multiple answers OK)

Litter, large piles of trash	33
Shabby homes or buildings	32
Stray animals and their leavings	31
Inappropriately parked cars	25
Unkempt yards, lots	65
Other	11

5. Is noise a problem where you live?

No, it's nice and quiet.	46%
Sometimes or occasionally.	42%
Yes, it's noisy.	11%

6. If noise is sometimes or often a problem, why? (multiple answers OK)

Individual neighbor's music	39
Parties at neighbors' houses	30
Barking dogs	30
Excessive traffic	51
Industrial or commercial noise	25
Loud children	7
Neighbors' power tools, mowers	6
Other: loud, fast cars (7); emergency vehicles (4)	22

Many city services are designed to help with problems like safety and the appearance of neighborhoods. Please answer the following questions about how you view the quality of city services this community.

7. How would you rate the quality of each of these city services?

		Excellent	Good	Fair	Poor
a.	quality of drainage services	14%	50%	22%	15%
b.	ease of travel by bicycle	7%	28%	41%	25%

		9%	34%	34%	22%
c.	ease of pedestrian travel	9%	34%	34%	22%
d.	quality of open space	11%	49%	34%	6%

8. If you have had contact with the Police Department, have any of the following been problems for you?

		Yes	No
a.	discourteous person answering call	13%	87%
b.	unfair treatment by officers upon arrival	12%	88%
c.	officers' inability to solve the problem	21%	79%

9. Do you often see a police patrol car driving through your neighborhood?
Yes   62%
No   38%

If yes, does police presence make you feel safe in your neighborhood?
Yes   87%
No   13%

10. In the past 12 months, have you had any problems getting your garbage picked up?

No, never a problem.	87%
Sometimes, but not often.	12%
Frequently a problem.	1%
Always a problem.	1%

11. Have you had a problem with city crews picking up tree limbs, brush, leaves, etc.?

No, never a problem.	66%
Sometimes, but not often.	27%
Frequently a problem.	3%
Always a problem.	3%

12. If you have had a problem with sanitation services, how do you feel that City Hall treated you?

Treated me well.	84%
Treated me poorly.	16%

13. Do you feel that the City is doing enough to promote recycling?
Yes   48%
No   52%

14. Do you believe that the City maintains streets in good condition?
Yes   58%
No   42%

15. Are the City Parks well maintained?
Yes   90%
No   10%

16. Are the public cemeteries well maintained?
Yes   86%
No   14%

17. If you have had contact with employees at City Hall, have they treated you courteously?

Yes 89%
No 1%

18. How would you rate last year's performance by our City Government?

A 16%
B 46%
C 27%
D 7%
F 4%

19. How would you grade the City Council during the same time?

A 11%
B 37%
C 34%
D 13%
F 4%

20. What grade would you give the city's Mayor?

A 35%
B 36%
C 17%
D 7%
F 5%

21. The area of town in which I live is:

Northeast 56
Northwest 46
Southeast 77
Southwest 8

22. My occupation is best described as:

Full-time employed 95
Part-time employed 9
Retiree 70
University student 21
Other student 0
Homemaker 13

23. My neighborhood has its own organization or association:

Yes 35%
No 65%

Thank you for participating in the Neighborhood Survey! Please remember to mail your completed questionnaire. Look for results in upcoming issues of the newspaper.

Glossary

ad valorem tax   A tax that is levied on personal property such as land, buildings, and automobiles. Typically used by local governments and school districts. Unpopular with taxpayers, especially when levied as a property tax.

Administrative Office of the Courts   In state government, an organization created to manage the budgeting, information systems, case-management forms, and other administrative functions for a statewide court system. Typically overseen by a board of state judges (the judicial council) who are chosen from a variety of state courts.

adversarial system of justice   A structure of court procedure in which two parties contest an individual's guilt or liability. Noteworthy for the care taken to balance the powers of the two sides. Contrast with an inquisitorial system of justice.

agenda building   Political officials' acceptance and prioritizing of social issues often performed by political parties. Important in democratic political systems where a wide range of demands for action are always being made.

annexation   Adding territory to a local government unit using policies established by the state government. Important to recapturing a fleeing tax base.

Anti-Federalists   A faction of Founders who favored a weaker national government relative to the state governments and powers reserved to the people. Ancestor of the contemporary Democratic Party.

appropriation   A legislative act that provides revenue for specific public programs. Programs can be authorized but cannot be implemented without the commitment of funds.

arraignment   A formal hearing at which a criminal defendant is charged by the district attorney. Provides an opportunity for the defendant's counsel to challenge basic charges.

assessed property value   Value attached by local government to each parcel of property. Along with the tax rate, it determines the amount of property taxes to be paid.

at-large election   A format for elections in which candidates are elected by voters from throughout the jurisdiction. Contrast with single-member district elections in which candidates run in clearly defined segments of the jurisdiction.

authorization   A legislative act that permits a government agency to operate a specific public program. Only properly authorized programs may be implemented by government agencies.

bicameral   Consisting of two chambers. Most democratic legislative bodies consist of two chambers; the size of each is set by a constitutional provision that states the basis of representation.

block grant   An award of funds from the national to state and local governments for a broad purpose. States and localities are left with significant authority to develop and implement specific programs.

building code   A state or local regulation that prescribes the materials and processes required for residential and commercial construction. Adopted to enhance public safety, often from industry standards.

bureaucracy   A formal, rule-driven organization with specialized duties and a hierarchy of communications. Common to large public and private organizations in the nineteenth and twentieth centuries.

casework   The work an elected official (usually a legislator) does to help constituents with personal, family, or business problems. Distinguished from policy making, which addresses social problems more broadly.

caucuses   Meetings of like-minded political officials at which elections and policy making are discussed. Once the source of candidate nominations in many states and localities, caucuses have now been largely superceded by primary elections. They persist as meetings at which policy is discussed.

chair of county commission   Leader of county government who chairs commission meetings. Under the commission form of government, oversees the county bureaucracy.

chief administrative officer   A professional administrator hired by city governments where the mayor has dominant executive responsibilities. Usually works with the city's mayor in supervising local government services.

citizens   Persons who are born in or naturalized to be empowered members of a particular civil society. In the United States, citizens are the source of all legitimate political authority.

city charter   Constitution-like document for local government that lays out the city's structure and powers. May be amended by local citizens in some states or by state legislatures in others.

city council   The popularly elected policy-making body of municipal government. Council members may be elected from districts, at-large, or from a combination of both.

civil justice   An ideal outcome from an adversarial court procedure in which two private parties try to resolve a dispute. Concerned with the liability of one party for damages to the other.

city manager   Professional administrator hired by city council and given day-to-day responsibility for overseeing city bureaucracy and services.

civil service   Personnel system for hiring bureaucrats at all levels of government that emphasizes merit as the basis for hiring and promoting individuals. One Progressive reform method; replaced political machines' use of patronage to select government bureaucrats.

commerce clause   A provision of the U.S. Constitution of 1787 that empowers the national government to regulate trade and protect interstate commerce among the states. Used as authority for the national government to intervene in the states to protect citizenship rights.

commission form   Most common form of county government. Legislative and executive functions are combined under the popularly elected commission, a legislative body.

community   The societal basis of political organization; the task environment in which social problems arise and policy solutions are attempted. A sociological underpinning of political science's study of localities.

comprehensive planning   Planning activities that take all systems of a community into consideration including land use, housing, and infrastructure improvements. Such planning is often conducted at the metropolitan area level because of the interconnections of many services and laws.

council–manager form   Structure of local government in which an elected council has legislative responsibility, and executive responsibilities are largely given to a professional manager hired by the council.

confederation   A voluntary association or league of political states. A central authority is empowered to address only those concerns delegated by the member states. The United States functioned under Articles of Confederation from 1781 to 1789, and the secessionist states were organized into a Confederate States of America during the Civil War.

consolidated government   Legal combination of city and county government into a single organization. Expected to emphasize efficiency and accountability.

constituents   The citizens served by an elected official. Includes not only those who voted for the official but also those who did not.

constitutional offices   Statewide elected agency head positions specified in the state constitution as popularly elected. Examples include secretary of state and attorney general. These positions are disappearing, however, as governors are given expanding appointment powers.

consumer protection   An activity of state and local government that addresses legal and ethical violations of corporate charters and professional licensing standards. Important in an era of large impersonal organizations and efficacious or empowered citizens.

council of government (COG)   A voluntary association of local government units that works on common issues, services, and problems that spill from one unit to another across the metropolitan area. Federal funds have been allocated to support the development of COGs by tying the receipt of federal money to regional activities.

county administrator   A professional administrator hired by the county commission. Responsible for the daily supervision of the county's bureaucracy.

county commission   The elected legislative body of county government. Under the commission form, commissioners are elected officials who act as both legislators and agency heads for county government.

county coroner   The county medical examiner who has responsibility for determining the cause of death in any case with a question about an individual's death.

county executive form   Structure of county government found primarily in large urban areas. The public elects a county executive who has leadership and managerial responsibilities much like a big city mayor.

county tax commissioner   Official who administers the county's tax program, including tax assessments, collections, and appeals.

court of appeals   A state court that reviews transcripts of criminal and civil cases in which allegations of improper procedure or legal interpretation are alleged. Commonly the last opportunity for reversal of a finding from the court of original jurisdiction.

crime control   A social policy objective that seeks to minimize the threat to public safety and security of property. Typically involved incapacitation and supervision of convicted offenders.

criminal trial   An adversarial legal proceeding in which the state's district attorney tries to prove an individual's criminal guilt beyond a reasonable doubt. May involve a verdict by a jury or one issued by a judge.

defense counsel   In a criminal trial, the attorney who represents the accused. Provided at public expense for indigent defendants.

delegate orientation   A citizen's view of representation that holds that elected officials should vote their constituents' views rather than exclusively their own. An official would be held accountable for voting consistently with the opinions of those who he or she represents.

Democratic Party   The U.S. political party of labor, minorities, and liberals. Descendant of Jefferson's Democratic Republican Party and the faction within the Founders that favored decentralized power and protections for individual liberties.

development authorities   Local associations of government and private-enterprise leaders who promote the local economy.

Dillon's Rule   A principle in constitutional law that holds that a municipality has only those powers expressly delegated to it by state government. Gradually eroding as cities and counties are granted broad home-rule authority by the states.

direct democracy   Methods for enabling citizens to decide policy questions. Includes the referendum and the initiative.

direct primary   Election rule that allows citizens rather than political machines to select the nominees for public office through an election. A reform of the Progressive reform movement.

district attorney   The attorney who represents the state in a criminal trial. Charges and brings the state's case against criminal defendants.

economic development   A shared goal of most polities involving the sustained addition of employment and investment opportunities for communities (and states and nations). In local government, a broadly supported agenda item for elected officials and civic leaders.

economies of scale   The concept that when small units such as local governments decide to act as a single large group, their larger size will enable them to reduce costs. For example, one purchase order for one hundred computers should obtain a lower price than ten purchase orders from separate communities each purchasing ten computers.

electioneering   Efforts by political parties and candidates to win election to public office. Important in understanding expensive U.S. elections and demands for campaign finance reform.

elite theory   A theoretical perspective on local government that holds that a unitary power elite holds substantial control over policy making. Contrasted with the pluralist view of many diverse and narrow elites, each exercising limited influence.

eminent domain   The legal doctrine under which governments may seize private property if a compelling public interest can be demonstrated. Courts require that a fair market price be paid for the property.

executive budgeting   The practice of allowing a governor to draft a proposed budget with input from all state agencies. The legislature can then work at revising and ultimately approving a final budget. Enhances coordinated budget development in the executive branch.

externalities   The negative consequences of the actions of one local government that affect surrounding localities such as automobile pollution from a mall that drifts into a neighboring community.

federal government   A form of government in which constitutional power is divided between a central authority and subnational states. Both the national and subnational governments are empowered by the citizenry and their representatives to act directly on the people.

Federalists   A faction of the Founders who sought a strong national government that could act directly on the people and social needs. Opposed by the Anti-Federalists, who promoted individual and state power and a relatively weak national government.

fiscal notes   In legislative deliberations, analyses that officially estimate the costs of a policy or program being proposed. Important aids in helping legislators appreciate the consequences of their actions.

fixed terms   The constitutional provision that an elected official may serve a specified number of years after first being elected. Sometimes limited to a prescribed number of terms.

floor debate   The phase of legislative deliberations when sponsors, supporters, and critics of a bill speak to its content. Immediately precedes a vote on the bill.

floor leader   A legislator, usually of the governor's party, who speaks for the governor on legislative issues. Provides a communication link between the legislature and the governor on key bills.

fragmentation   A situation in which there are many elected or appointed local governments and government officials with independent responsibilities for public policy over a common geographical area. Fragmentation makes it difficult for citizens to know "where the buck stops."

franchise   The right and privilege of citizens to elect representatives and decide policy issues in conformity with state and federal law. In U.S. history, it is an important civil right that has been expanded to virtually all adult citizens.

functional consolidation   Agreement between county and city governments to combine specific government services under a single unit rather than each duplicate them. Less comprehensive than an overall consolidation plan.

general election   A popular vote on candidates for elective office. Typically includes offices from several levels of government. Distinguished from the primary elections often used to choose party candidates to run later in the general election.

general law county   County government that is governed by state law specifying the structure and powers of all counties in a state. Does not allow local citizens significant home rule.

general laws   State laws that set the governing structure and powers for local governments according to the size of the community. Does not allow local citizens to determine their own rules such as in home rule.

general purpose local government   A broad term that is applied to municipal, county, and other local governments that have been awarded considerable home-rule authority by their states' legislatures. Important to understanding local government officials as policy makers.

governing board   An group of interested citizens appointed by the governor to oversee the operations of a state agency. Empowered in many states to make policy for the agency within established state law.

home rule   The constitutionally recognized authority of municipalities and counties to make laws needed by general purpose local government as long as they do not violate state or federal law. In the United States, home rule is a growing doctrine that has weakened state government control of local governments.

housing code   Local regulations in some cities addressing the safe and sanitary maintenance of residences. In some larger cities, a method of addressing slum lords' neglect of rental property.

identity politics   The practice of acting politically or organizing political organizations on the basis of group identification. A growing trend in

U.S. politics, such action erodes broader senses of civil society such as majoritarianism and commonwealth.

incorporation   The legal status of municipal corporations that gives them distinct powers and responsibilities. Served as model for similar grants of power to unincorporated counties, villages, and so on.

independent school districts   School districts with their own elected governing boards that are independent of city or county government. Independence is intended to insulate schools from local politics.

inferior courts   The lowest level courts with responsibility limited to local ordinances, traffic violations, misdemeanor crimes, and civil cases involving small sums of money.

initiative   A democratic device available in some states that enables citizens to place a matter on the legislative agenda or referendum ballot by securing a requisite number of signatures within a specified time frame. The initiative forces elected officials to deal with difficult issues.

interest organizations   Private associations that try to influence public policy so that it favors their members' economic interests. Regulated to the extent that campaign contributions are tracked and capped in many states.

judicial activists   A group of judges and judicial scholars who hold that constitutions are living documents whose meanings must be refined and even redefined by each generation of citizens. This viewpoint contrasts with strict constructionist or originalist outlooks on constitutional law.

judicial council   A group of judges from various state courts who are selected by their peers to oversee court administration in a state. Serves as a board of directors for the state's administrative office of the courts.

jury   A group of six or twelve citizens who are chosen to sit in judgment in a criminal trial or civil action. Access to a jury trial is constitutionally protected for criminal cases.

labor unions   Formal organizations that represent the economic and political interests of workers. Important interest groups in state (and national) government and local civic activism.

land-use plans   Narratives and maps that describe the current use of residential, commercial, and public property in a community. Enables local citizens and officials to plan compatible future land uses.

land-use regulations   A broad and inclusive term that describes the laws and regulations defining permissible land use in a community. Includes the land-use plan, zoning ordinances, subdivision regulations, building codes, and housing codes.

legitimacy   Public confidence in the government or a belief that the sources and uses of authority are proper. Critical to maintaining respect for political authority.

Libertarian Party   Contemporary U.S. political party that favors small government and maximum protection of individual liberties. Formed as response to perceived weakness of Democrats in promoting individual rights.

lieutenant governor A statewide elected official who takes over the duties of the governor when the latter is disabled. In some states, the presiding chamber official of the state senate; in others, the assistant governor in daily administration.

line-item veto A power enjoyed by the majority of governors that allows them to strike out only specific provisions of passed bills rather than entire bills. Often used to control spending on local projects.

lobbyists Professional employees of interest organizations that try to influence the content of public policy. Important as registered and regulated players in political decision making.

logrolling A particular kind of political cooperation within a legislative body in which elected officials agree to support each others' bills. Important in understanding how a lengthy legislative agenda is expedited.

mandate The claim made by an elected official that success at the polls was due to public support for particular ideas and proposals. The supposed public authority is used to argue for the passage of specific bills.

mandatory determinant sentences In many states, provisions on the criminal code that require specific prison terms for specific crimes. The judge has little or no leeway in considering mitigation or aggravation.

mayor The chief elected official of municipal government. Also the city's chief administrative official in some communities without professional managers.

merit systems Systems of objective employee recruitment, assessment, and advancement used in state government to protect the professionalism and integrity of its workers. An important reaction against corrupt spoils systems of political employment.

millage rate The tax rate expressed in dollars per $1,000 valuation. Applied to the assessed property value to determine the amount of taxes to be collected on each piece of property in a community.

motions Proposals made by state legislators or local council members that seek consideration or adoption of reports, instructions to public employees, or schedule future action.

municipalities The form of government in cities in which the community is incorporated by a city charter that outlines its structure and powers.

national sovereignty The right of a people and their lawful government to hold dominion over a land and its resources. Other nations are obliged to respect such control. In U.S. history, there has been a debate over whether states as well as the national government exercise legitimate sovereign control.

neighborhood A geographical cluster of local residents who share a civic task environment and who may organize to protect and advance the interests of their part of the community.

neighborhood or tenants' associations   Formal organizations that are incorporated to act in the interests of residents. A potentially powerful base for elective office and issue advocacy.

nonpartisan election   Election rule that does not allow a political party label to be formally attached to a candidate's name. Designed to remove party politics from local elections; a Progressive reform.

ordinances   Local laws that apply throughout a jurisdiction. Includes budgetary decisions and regulations concerning individual and corporate behavior.

original jurisdiction   The control exercised over a particular kind of legal case. A state court will be designated as the court of original criminal jurisdiction; another may be named to first hear civil cases.

partisanship   The individual quality of identifying with a political party. Contrast with nonpartisan politics in which party philosophies are absent or ignored.

party leaders   The officials selected within the legislative body to organize and lead a political party's activities. Contrast with chamber officials who serve the entire membership.

party platform   An official statement of philosophy and broad goals by a political party. Important in accommodating a range of interests within a party and maintaining party unity.

party primary   A publicly sponsored election in which citizens are invited to vote their preferences for party candidates who will oppose each other in a later general election. Often organized and financially underwritten by the major political parties, these elections technically choose candidates' electors to party conventions.

payroll tax   A local tax on individual earnings. States allow a few larger cities this kind of income tax because the state governments often tax earnings.

pluralism   Also called *interest group liberalism*, the theory that many diverse groups make political demands and seek public policy benefits. Their interaction with policy makers secures some benefits for most groups over time, keeping diverse players in the game of democratic politics.

political action committee (PAC)   An organization through which an interest group can channel funds to a candidate's campaign. Established to protect the private association rights of the interest groups while still tracking and regulating the money going to election campaigns.

political culture   Politically relevant social mores of a people that shape citizen actions, leadership expectations, and social policy preferences. At times in a country's history, regional political cultures may fragment the body politic and conflict with national goals and priorities.

political efficacy   A sense of personal power or potency in regard to positions on policy issues or political preference. Efficacious people participate more in politics.

political ideologies Sets of consistent political principles or beliefs that bring coherence to otherwise fragmented ideas and proposals. Important among political elites and philosophical movements.

political machine A highly centralized organization that runs city affairs from behind the scenes, often exchanging jobs, contracts and services for votes.

political parties Publicly regulated private associations devoted to securing elective office and governing as a team. A twentieth-century formalization of factions of like-minded elected officials.

politics Behavior that is directed at securing and using power in a society. Winners in the competition for public office shape social policy.

politico orientation The expectation by citizens that their elected officials will act to represent constituent viewpoints sometimes and act in the broader public interest at other times. Contrast with an orientation that an elected official should vote from a single perspective.

preponderance of evidence The standard of proof in civil cases. Contrast with "beyond a reasonable doubt" as the standard in criminal cases.

progrowth coalition A relatively common political alliance in local communities consisting of business and professional interests plus government planners. Tasked to mobilize civic and government resources in support of economic development.

public-interest organizations Advocacy groups such as interest organizations that promote policies that benefit a broad category of citizens rather than a narrow group of beneficiaries. Provide some voice for the interests of women, environmentalists. and consumers.

public property Property deeded to a government or governmental agency. Replaced a common law notion of land held in common for the public good.

quasi-governmental powers The legal authority granted to a special district government that allows it to tax, incur debt, and enforce laws, much like a general purpose government. Because the governing boards of some special districts are not elected by the citizens, these powers are not quite "governmental" powers.

reasonable doubt The standard of proof for states' cases against criminal defendants. Defense counsel need only show a reasonable doubt of guilt to gain the release of the accused. Balances the extensive resources of the state in prosecuting an individual.

redistricting The political process within legislative bodies of redrawing electoral district boundaries to reflect changes in population. Occurs every ten years in response to the federal census of population.

referendum Decision of a policy issue by direct popular vote. A means of decision making outside of the usual representative processes.

Reform Party Contemporary U.S. political party that advocates private-sector action in solving social problems and campaign finance reform.

Formed as a response to perceived weakness in the Republican Party's commitment to small government.

regime politics   A theoretical perspective on local politics that holds that fairly broad coalitions of interests gain control of local government and thereafter accommodate the interests of coalition members. An alternative to the more theoretically "pure" elite and pluralist views.

representative democracy   Democratic government by popularly elected representatives. Contrast with direct democracy by which citizens decide policy issues themselves.

Republican Party   The self-styled party of American business with moderately conservative political ideology. One of two dominant political parties in the United States. Descendant of the Whig Party of the nineteenth century.

reserved powers clause   Constitutional doctrine based on the Tenth Amendment to the Constitution of 1787 that reserves to the states and the people all powers not expressly granted to the national government by the federal constitution. Used at some points in history to enforce state jurisdictions over policies or programs.

resolution   An expression of sentiments by an elected governmental body. Often used to commend civic contributions by individuals and organizations.

revenue   Public funds raised through taxes and fees. Available for budgeting and expenditure by governmental bodies.

revenue estimate   An official projection of governmental tax receipts based on the existing tax law and projected economic conditions. Important for budgeting future governmental expenditures.

rule-making authority   The power of regulatory agencies to make legally binding requirements for corporate operation under a state charter or license. Important as a consumer-protection check on natural monopolies and huge interstate corporations.

sales taxes   State and local assessments on retail and other commercial transactions. Commonly considered a regressive tax because it negatively affects poorer residents more than wealthier residents.

school superintendent   Appointed professional administrator for schools, usually trained in educational administration. Serves as chief executive for the school government.

sheriff   Chief law enforcement officer of county government who is often elected. Typically responsible for investigating crimes outside of municipal city limits.

single-member district   A structure of elections in which the legislative jurisdiction is divided into districts of equal population. Elections are then winner-take-all contests to represent the district. Contrast with proportional representation in which a party gets a number of legislative seats equal to its share of the total popular vote.

Speaker   A legislative chamber official chosen by members of the lower house to organize and lead the body in its deliberations. Contrast with party officials who serve only the interests of their party members.

special purpose local government   Local governmental bodies that have a narrow mission from the state legislature. Limited in the scope of responsibilities; examples include school districts and water-quality districts.

standard operating procedures   The official rules for operation of a public agency. Employees are expected to act in conformity with the procedures manual of their agency.

State of the State Address   A formal address by the governor before the legislature and other dignitaries that outlines a view of issues and priorities for the new session of the legislature. An important opportunity to lead public and elite opinion on the issues of the day.

state secretary of state   An official of state government whose duties vary by state but usually includes the regulation of industries, elections, and official state records. In states where elected, an important statewide political office that may boost future election prospects to other offices.

state supreme court   The highest court in a state justice system. Determines the constitutionality of action vis à vis the state constitution in selective cases. Hears appeals of death penalty cases in states that use that penalty.

statute   A state law that has been fully enacted by the legislature and signed by the governor. The ultimate fate of successful legislative bills.

strict constructionists   A group of judges and judicial scholars who hold that constitutions are the law of the land over time and should not be manipulated to address each generation's shifting opinions or concerns. Only an amendment to a constitution should change its meaning or application.

strong mayor form   Structure of local government in which an elected mayor has extensive executive responsibilities to hire department heads, supervise the delivery of local services, influence the local budget, and veto ordinances passed by the city council.

subdivision regulations   Local regulations that direct the behavior of residential developers and builders. Often crafted by industry standards, state law, and local public opinion.

sunset legislation   A provision in selected state laws that terminates their authorization on a certain date. Laws covered by the provision have to be extended if they are to stay in force past their sunset dates.

supplemental budget   A reprogramming of the current year's budget by the legislature once it has convened. Legislators may add to or supplement a program's funding or cut funding as needed based on revenue receipts.

systems analysis of political life   A model of political life that relates social demands for action to decision making and policy decisions themselves.

Important for understanding the interrelatedness of players and issues in politics.

tax rate   The same as the millage rate.

term limits   Statutory constraints on the number of terms or the number of years that an elected official may serve in office. Enacted to limit the careers of professional politicians but may be enhancing the power of bureaucrats and lobbyists in state capitals.

third parties   Emergent new political parties that do poorly in our winner-take-all, single-member electoral district system. At times in U.S. political history, third parties have been sources of new ideas that get coopted by the two major parties.

Tiebout thesis   The view that local governments should work together much like a free market, achieving coordination and efficiency without central guidance.

tort reform   Efforts in state legislatures to limit the amount of punitive damages that may be awarded in a civil suit. Sought by companies and insurance companies and opposed by trial lawyers.

trustee orientation   An outlook by citizens that their elected officials should exercise independent judgment and serve the broad public interest while in office. Contrast with the delegate orientation that holds that elected officials should vote the preferences of their constituents.

two-party competitive politics   A descriptive phrase for political systems in which public preference and electoral laws favor broad centrist political parties. Contrast with multiparty and single-party systems with more ideologically pure agendas.

user fees   Charges assessed for the use of public facilities such as public golf courses. A means of regulating access and developing sustaining revenue for the facilities.

voter registration   An activity of state government that records a citizen's legal residence and authorizes that citizen to vote in all local, state, and national elections. Originally implemented to retard election fraud, registration laws have been used by some states to keep minorities out of the electoral process.

Voting Rights Act of 1965   With subsequent amendments, the act eliminated restrictions on minority voting that had been instituted in several states. Requires U.S. Department of Justice preclearance of redistricting in affected states and localities.

weak mayor form   Local government structure in which the elected mayor has limited responsibilities. Some city department heads such as the police chief, tax assessor, or finance director are elected directly by the voters and are independent of the mayor.

whistle-blowing   The act of public disclosure by a public employee of information that suggests malfeasance or misfeasance in a government agency. Protected by some state laws to promote accountability.

zoning Public control of the use of property to ensure compatible development in the community. Once land is zoned, nonconforming use is allowed only with a variance issued by local government.

Name Index

Abberger, Will, 299
Anderson, Eloise, 44
Archer, Dennis, 230–231
Arnstein, Sherry R., 206

Baker, John B., 205
Barrett, Katherine, 129
Bellah, Robert N., 22, 162, 182
Benavides, Teodoro J., 224
Bender, Ed, 60
Bennett, William J., 12
Benton, J. Edwin, 250
Benveniste, Guy, 134
Berman, David, 316
Berman, David R., 48, 49
Beyer, Edward, 5
Beyle, Thad L., 65, 66, 110
Bibby, John F., 55
Blair, George S., 200, 293
Blakely, Edward J., 174
Blatz, Kathleen, 149
Bowers, William, 153
Bowling, Cynthia J., 126
Brady, Henry E., 197
Brandeis, Louis, 39
Brown, A. Theodore, 215, 217, 218
Brown, Ron, 36
Brown, Willie, 229
Bryce, James, 34
Buchanan, William, 80
Buckley, William F., 36
Bulloch, Bob, 88, 113
Bush, George W., 113
Bush, Jeb, 105

Campbell, Bill, 228
Carr, J. B., 281
Casey, Linda, 60
Catlin, George, 2

Chi, Keon S., 59
Chiles, Lawton, 105
Clark, Susan, 136
Claude, Richard, 34, 35
Clingermayer, James C., 174
Clinton, Bill, 42
Cloward, Richard A., 36
Cobb, Roger, 69
Collins, Robert, 235
Comer, John, 13, 34
Conant, James K., 117
Cox, Cathy, 133
Cox, George H., 17, 36, 37, 116, 166, 167, 304
Crawford, Finla Goff, 145

Dagger, Richard, 202
Dahl, Robert, 186–187
Daily, John H., 304
Daley, Richard, 228–229
Davidson, Robert E., 34
Davis, Gray, 105
Dawson, Richard E., 17
DeLaney, Ann, 169, 315
DeSantis, Victor S., 194, 195, 196, 199, 244
Diehl, Kim, 128
Dilger, Robert Jay, 170
Dillon, John F., 215
Dole, Bob, 261
Donahue, John D., 48, 49
Drucker, Peter, 115–116
DuBois, Paul M., 23, 77, 162–163
Dye, Thomas, 202, 203, 204

Easton, David, 68, 71
Ehrenhalt, Alan, 85
Ehrenreich, Barbara, 22
Eigen, Lewis D., 33, 34, 36, 122, 164, 180
Eisinger, Peter, 59, 294, 296
Elazar, Daniel, 15, 17

Elder, Charles, 69
Engler, John, 106
Ernst, Keith, 128
Eulau, Heinz, 80, 197

Fairbanks, Frank, 223
Feiock, Richard C., 174, 281
Ferguson, Leroy C., 80
Fitchen, Janet M., 303
Fleischmann, Arnold, 205
Flora, Jan L., 249
Flores, George, 223
Ford, Henry, 268
Forrest, Audrey W., 182
Freeman, Howard E., 44
Freeman, Patricia K., 83

Gaebler, Ted, 93, 118, 262
Gaffney, Robert J., 246
Gamble, Barbara S., 194
Garcia, Joe, 136
Gergen, Kenneth J., 22
Ginsburg, Ruth Bader, 31
Giuliani, Ralph, 228
Glaab, Charles N., 215, 217, 218
Gordon, Dianna, 84
Gore, Al, 111
Gossett, Charles, 184
Gray, Virginia, 59, 62, 64, 294, 296
Greenberg, Milton, 17, 28, 29, 44, 122
Greene, Richard, 129
Gruhl, John, 13, 34

Hamilton, Alexander, 4
Hamilton, Howard D., 204
Hansen, Frederick, 21
Harrington, J. J., 202
Hart, Bob, 309
Henton, Douglas, 173
Hightower, Michael, 250
Holbrook, Thomas M., 55
Holden, Daphne, 128
Howard, S. Kenneth, 86
Hrebenar, Ronald J., 62, 64
Hull, Jane Dee, 107
Hunter, Floyd, 185–186, 187

Jackson, Jesse, 36, 182
Jacobson, Matthew Frye, 9, 216
Jefferson, Thomas, 270
Jenks, Stephen S., 124, 127
Jewell, Malcolm, 55
Johnson, James B., 182
Johnson, Julia, 137
Johnson, Lyndon B., 43

Johnson, Otto, 314
Johnson, Thomas G., 249

Kantorowitz, Ernst H., 3
Karnig, Albert K., 202
Kay, Jane Holz, 19
Kimel, Daniel, 33
King, Angus, 105
King, Jr., Martin Luther, 180, 182
King George III, 3, 215
Knowles, Tony, 103, 109, 114

Labbe, Jill R., 32
Lappé, Frances M., 23, 77, 162–163
Leach, William, 161–162, 311
Lemov, Penelope, 41
Lerner, Robert, 153
Levine, M. A., 217, 280
Lewis, Dan A., 93, 259
Liddy, Gordon, 67
Limbaugh, Rush, 67
Lipset, Seymour Martin, 11, 22, 309–310
Lowenstein, Daniel H., 35, 36
Lowery, David, 62, 64
Lynch, Patrick, 65, 66

MacKay, Buddy, 105
Madison, James, 2, 4
Madsen, Richard, 22, 182
Mahtesian, Charles, 158
Maruna, Shadd, 93, 259
McClory, Robert J., 11
McCormick, Cyrus, 20
Melville, John, 174
Menzel, Donald C., 250
Mfefeto, Nomainda, 316
Mincy, Ronald, 10–11
Morlan, Robert L., 203
Mowzer, Saleem, 316
Moyer, Thomas J., 148

Nast, Thomas, 216
Nice, David, 56
Nicholson, Trish, 33
Nigard, Bill, 110
Nixon, Richard, 220

O'Connor, Sandra Day, 31
Olshfski, Dorothy, 116
Olson, David, 55
Osborne, David, 39, 93, 118, 262, 313
Ostrom, V., 272

Pajari, Roger N., 304
Pataki, George, 107, 111

Perlman, Ellen, 93
Peters, B. Guy, 46
Peterson, Paul E., 202
Pierannunzi, Carol A., 205
Pierce, Glenn, 153
Pipes, Richard, 8
Piven, Frances Fox, 36
Plano, Jack C., 17, 28, 29, 44, 122
Plastrik, Peter, 313
Pressman, Jeffrey L., 198, 229
Prewitt, Kenneth, 197
Price, Reynolds, 12
Putnam, Robert, 189

Rainey, Hal G., 293
Rakove, Jack N., 4, 80, 299
Ranney, Austin, 158
Ratan, Sudha, 139
Reese, Laura, 174
Rehnquist, William H., 31
Reich, Robert B., 22
Reitman, Alan, 34
Renner, Tari, 194, 195, 196, 199, 244
Richardson, Jr., Lillard E., 83
Rigdon, Susan M., 13, 34
Riordan, Richard, 229
Robinson, James A., 17
Rom, Mark Carl, 46
Rosenfeld, Raymond A., 174
Ross, B. H., 217, 280
Rossi, Peter H., 44

Saffell, David C., 84
Sanchez, Samantha, 60
Santayana, George, 122
Schlozman, Kay Lehman, 197
Schram, Sanford F., 33, 42
Secret, Philip E., 182
Shaheen, Jeanne, 107
Shields, Mark, 105
Shirey, John F., 224
Siegel, Jonathan P., 33, 34, 36, 122, 164, 180
Smith, Hedrick, 302

Smolka, Richard G., 36
Snell, Ronald K., 296
Sokolow, Alvin D., 198
Squire, Peverill, 61
Steinman, Michael, 13, 34
Stone, Clarence, 187–188
Streib, Gregory, 249
Sullivan, William M., 22, 182
Swindler, Ann, 22, 182

Taft, Robert, 106
Thacker, Patti, 36, 37
Thomas, Clive S., 62, 64
Tiebout, M., 272
Tipton, Stephen M., 22, 182
Tocqueville, Alexis de, 214
Tung Chee-hwa, 118
Tweed, Willam Marcy "Boss," 216, 217

Ulmer, Fran, 114

Ventura, Jesse, 105
Verba, Sidney, 197
Vilsack, Tom, 106
Vogel, R. K., 202

Wahlke, John C., 80
Walesh, Kimberly, 174
Walker, David B., 86
Walters, B. Oliver, 202
Walters, Jonathan, 126
Warren, R., 272
Waugh, Jr., William L., 249
Webb, Wellington, 233
Weissert, Carol S., 33, 42
Welch, Susan, 13, 34, 195
Whitman, Christine Todd, 65, 107
Wilson, Pete, 105
Wood, Gwen Y., 299
Wright, Deil S., 124, 126, 127

Young, Coleman, 230, 231

Subject Index

administrative office of courts (AOC), 148
ad valorem taxes, 295
adversarial system of justice, 142, 158
age
    jurisdiction in cases of discrimination, 33
    technology's influence on generational changes, 20–21
    voter participation and, 205
agenda building, 69–70
American Indian Movement (AIM), 12
annexation, 260
Anti-Federalists, 4
antigovernment bias, 212
appointments
    of agency heads, 114–116
    by governors, 112
appropriation bills, 95
arraignment, 142
assessed property value, 259
at-large elections, 195, 218
authorization bills, 95
automobile safety, 178

back-to-basics education, 263
Bali Rotary Clubs, 179
basic grants for education, 258
beautification programs, 167–168
bicameral houses, 4, 81
big city mayors, 229–232
Bill of Rights, 4, 32
bills
    appropriation and authorization, 95
    passing in state legislatures, 89–93
block grants, 44
block scheduling, 262–263
Bolden v. *Mobile*, 225
boroughs, 242. *See also* counties
Brazilian development districts, 254
broadcast media, 66–67

budgets
    executive, 111
    governors as state leader for, 110–112
    line-item veto, 111
    oversight in state legislatures, 96–97
    supplemental, 96
    zero-based budgeting, 118
building codes, 298
bureaucrats and regulators, 121–140. *See also* public service
        commissions
    controls for regulators, 138–139
    evaluating professionalism in state government,
        129–131
    overview, 121–123
    regulators and consumer protection, 131–135
    service delivery bureaucrats, 123–129
    state public service commissions, 135–138
Bureau of Labor Statistics, 172
businesses
    economic development and incubation for, 302–303
    local issues for, 173–174
    political power of, 174
    types of local organizations, 170–172

campaign financing, 59–61
candidates. *See also* election campaigns; elections
    for city councils, 196–197
    mayoral, 199
    methods of selecting state, 58
    qualifications of state legislative, 83
    for state judges, 145–146
    state legislative, 80
Canton Charter Township, 226–227
capacity building for metropolitan counties, 249–251, 263
capital city newspapers, 65–66
casework, 83
caucuses, 59
chamber leadership for state legislatures, 88–89

chancellery judges, 247
charter schools, 261–262
Chicago special service districts, 253
chief administrative officer, 225
child-development programs, 262
churches, 179–182
cities. *See also* city councils; local government; metropolitan
      government
    big city mayors, 229–232
    bureaucratic power in, 237
    city charter, 221
    city commissioners, 224–225
    city-county consolidated services, 281–282
    city managers, 218, 233–235
    evolution of nonpartisan elections in, 218
    governmental structure for, 220–226
    historical background of structure, 214–220
    home rule, 48–49, 219, 220
    political machines, 215–217
    scope of government in, 211–212
    small town mayors, 232–233
    strong mayor form of government, 221–222
    structure and power of, 212–214
    structure of municipal governments, 220–226
    townships and, 226–227
    weak mayor form of political structure, 215, 222
citizen control, 208
citizens
    as defined in U.S. Constitution, 34
    difference between subjects and, 3
    empowering, 207
city charter, 221
city commissioners, 224–225
city councils. *See also* local government
    campaigning for, 197–198
    duties of, 227–228
    elections for, 195–196
    incumbents in elections for, 198
    Kansas City, Mo., 228
    selecting candidates for, 196–197
city-county consolidation, 281–282
city managers
    creation of, 218
    duties of, 233–235
    profile of Robert Collins, 235
citywide ministerial alliances, 181
civic clubs, 176–179
civic culture
    involvement in, 22
    race and civic equality, 11
    technology and, 19–22
CivicZone.com, 203
civil liability, 156–157
civil service
    laws regarding, 126–127

Progressive creation of, 218
civil trials, 143–144
clerk of county court, 247
closed primaries, 59
commerce clause, 31–32
commission form of local government
    about, 224–225
    city councils and, 228
    for counties, 244
    origin of, 218–219
communities, 161–190. *See also* local political participation
    assessing levels of local participation, 206–209
    business and labor organizations, 170–175
    civic clubs, 176–179
    community-preservation strategies, 304–306
    county commissioners and school boards, 201–202
    defined, 162
    delegation of power to, 207–208
    gay rights, 183, 184
    general purpose local governments and, 191–192
    neighborhoods and, 163–170
    overview, 161–162
    participation in, 189
    power and influence in, 184–188
    religious congregations and, 179–182
    special interest organizations in, 183–184
    voluntary boards, 205–206
    voter turnout for off-year and presidential elections,
      202–205
Community Power Structure (Hunter), 185–186
compensatory damages, 156
compromises in policy making, 300–301
confederation, 28
consolidated services. *See also* fragmented service delivery
    about, 242–243
    additional options for metropolitan, 282–283
    by councils of government, 278–279
    city-county, 281–282
    with informal cooperative agreements, 279
    with interlocal service agreements, 279
    with Lakewood Plan, 279
    in metropolitan counties, 248
    spectrum in metropolitan governments, 278
    with tax-base sharing, 279–280
Constitution. *See* U.S. Constitution
constitutional federalism, 28–38
    Articles of Confederation and Perpetual Union, 28
    citizenship and voting rights under, 33–37
    conclusions about, 38
    establishment of constitution and federal government,
      28–30
    judicial interpretation of, 30–33
    national supremacy and implied powers clause, 38
constitutional offices, 112
constitution writing, 3

consumer protection, 132
continuing education requirements, 135
corporate regulations, 132–133
costs for gubernatorial races, 104
council-manager form of municipal government, 222–224
councils of government (COG), 278–279
counties, 241–251. *See also* special service districts
    capacity building by, 248, 249–251, 263
    commission form of government in, 244
    consolidated services in metropolitan, 248, 281–283
    county administrator form of government, 245
    county courts, 247–248
    county executives, 246–247
    demographics of, 243
    elected officials for, 245–246
    geography of, 242–243
    governmental authority of, 243–244
    overview, 241–242
    Web sites for, 249
Country of Exiles (Leach), 161–162
county administrator, 245
county commission, 244
county commissioners, 201–202
county coroner, 246
county courts, 247–248
county executives, 246–247
county judges, 248
county tax commissioner, 245–246
court services administrators, 148
court system. *See also* state courts
    American system of justice, 141, 142–144
    civil trials, 143–144
    county courts, 247–248
    criminal trials, 142
    increasing volume in, 149
    role in crime control, 151–152
    structure of state, 144
court unification, 148
cramming, 137
crime control, 149–157
    civil liability and, 156–157
    criminal justice system's role in, 155–156
    discrimination and, 310–311
    for juveniles, 155
    local, 308
    local crime prevention, 308
    neighborhood interests in, 166
    prevalence of violent crime, 150–151
    race and sentencing, 153
    role of courts in, 151–152
    sentencing and prison systems, 152–155
    state legislation on, 94
    tort reform, 133, 157–158
criminal justice system, 155–156
criminal trials, 142

culture. *See also* diversity
    technology's effect on, 22–23
    urban growth and, 270–271

decision making
    state legislatures role in public policy, 76–77
    in state political systems, 67–72
defense counsel, 142
delegate orientation to representative democracy, 80
demand in political systems, 68–69
democracy. *See also* representative democracy
    direct versus representative, 103, 193
    New England town hall model of, 227
    teledemocracy, 194
Democratic Party
    about, 57
    regional support for, 56
    voter realignment in, 106–107
demographics
    census of metropolitan areas, 270–271
    of counties, 243
    federal laws requiring census, 15
    shifting by race, 9–10
Des Moines metropolitan planning organization, 285
development and preservation policies, 301–307
    community-preservation strategies, 304–306
    economic-development strategies, 301–304
    finding balance in, 306–307
    overview, 301
development authorities, 301–302
Dillon's Rule
    about, 48–49, 214–215
    home rule versus, 219
direct democracy
    citizen participation in, 77–79
    representative versus, 193
direct initiative, 79
direct primaries, 218
discrimination and crime control, 310–311
district attorney, 142
districts, city council, 195
diversity. *See also* race
    barriers to voting rights for minorities, 35–37
    cultural preservation and, 305–306
    ethnic violence and, 13
    policy implications of, 13
    South cultural, 15–16
    surveying ethnic, 16
    in United States, 8–9
    various social reactions to, 11–13
    voter turnout by race, 203
dollar limits for campaign financing, 59
downtown-development authorities, 171
dual sovereignty, 29

Ebonics, 13
economic development, 301–304
    attracting industry and, 302
    balancing development and preservation, 306–307
    for communities, 173
    to educate and train workforce, 303–304
    for retaining businesses, 302–303
    for small businesses, 303
economies of scale, 275
education, 258–260
    accountability and quality of, 262, 264
    confidence in public schools, 257
    constitutional basis for school districts, 255
    equity in funding, 259
    federal funding for, 258
    local funding for, 259–260
    local policy making about, 262–263
    local school policies on, 255–256
    policy innovation in schools, 260–262
    school choice, 261–262
    school systems as apolitical, 241–242
    state funding for, 258–259
    state policies, 255
    state requirements for continuing, 135
efficiency of school districts and special service districts, 242
elected regional multipurpose districts, 283
elected state officials, 112
election campaigns. *See also* candidates; elections
    campaign committees for city council, 197
    for city councils, 197–198
    of county officials, 245–246
    financing for state, 59–61
    of governors, 103–105
    for mayor, 200
    for state legislature, 83
electioneering, 58
elections, 193–201. *See also* election campaigns
    of city officials, 194–198
    costs for gubernatorial races, 104
    of county commissioners and school boards, 201–202
    direct versus representative democracy and, 103
    of governors, 103–105
    of judges, 200–201
    mandate from people in, 105
    of mayor, 198–200
    noncurrent, 202
    nonpartisan city, 218
    qualifying for general, 197
    referendums, petitions, initiatives, and recall, 194
    results of recent gubernatorial races, 105–107
    selection of state judges in, 145–146
    of state judges, 145–146
    state-level partisan, 58–59
    voter turnout for, 202–205
elite theory of local power, 185–186

emergency services, 309
enforcing local codes, 293–294
environmental organizations, 183
environmental protection, 304–305
ethnicity. *See* diversity
European home rule, 220
executive budget, 111
executive orders by governor, 77
executives. *See also* state executives
    county, 246–247

federal government
    devolution of policy implementation to state agencies, 124
    establishment of, 29–30
    local administration of mandated programs, 294
    Medicaid as federal-state partnership, 43
    national interest in welfare policies, 43
    policies contributing to metropolitan growth, 269
    state cooperation in policy and program implementation, 42–44
federalism, 27–51
    constitutional, 28–38
    local government home rule, 48–49
    overview, 27–28
    policy preemption and, 47–48
    programmatic, 38–46
    protection of voting rights, 34–35
    revenue sharing and, 47
    Supreme Court views on, 31
    unfunded mandates and, 47
Federalists, 4
Federal Republic of Germany, 85
feedback in state political systems, 72
filing fees, 197
fiscal notes, 92
fixed terms, 81
floor debate, 91–92
floor leaders, 57, 89, 109
fragmented service delivery. *See also* consolidated services
    about, 192
    advantages of metropolitan governments, 272–273, 277
    disadvantages of metropolitan governments, 273–278
    special district governments and, 254–255
France's inquisitorial justice system, 158
functional consolidation, 248

gay rights organizations, 183, 184
gender
    gay rights, 183, 184
    gender-based violence, 31–32
    issues for working mothers on welfare, 42
    voting rights for women, 33, 34
    women in workforce, 172
    of workforce, 172

general law counties, 244
general laws, 218
general purpose local governments, 191–192, 213
generational changes and technology, 20–21
gentrification, 7
geography of counties, 242–243
German mayors, 232
gerrymandering, 82
governing board of state agencies, 115
governors, 102–112
    about, 102–103
    appointments by, 112
    as budgetary leader, 110–112
    election of, 103–105
    of Hong Kong, 118
    inauguration of, 107–108
    as legislative leader, 108–109
    results of recent elections, 105–107
    staff for, 109–110
governor's floor leader, 57, 89
Greater Minneapolis Council of Churches (GMCC), 181
growth management, 183
Gun Free School Zone Act, 31–32

Habits of the Heart (Bellah et al.), 22, 162
history of local government, 214–220
home rule
    defined, 219–220
    scope of laws creating, 48–49
    in urban counties, 249–250
homogeneity of states, 19
Hong Kong, governor of, 118
households
    composition of U.S., 163
    types of, 163–164
housing codes, 298–299
housing-loan programs, 269
human resource management, 130

identity. *See* place
identity politics, 13
immigration, 13–16
implied powers clause, 38
inauguration of governors, 107–108
incarceration, 152–155
incorporation, 269
incumbents in city council elections, 198
independent school districts. *See* school districts
India, public utility regulation in, 139
indirect democracy, 77
indirect initiative, 79
individual and technology, 21–22
individualistic political culture, 17–18, 37
Indonesian Rotary Clubs, 179
industrial attraction, 302

inferior courts, 247
informal cooperative agreements, 279
initiatives, 79, 194
inquisitorial justice system, 158
interest groups
    activities of, 64
    lobbyists, 62–63
    public, 63
    regulating, 64–65
    state-level, 62–64
interlocal service agreements, 279
International City/County Management Association, 225
issues
    addressed by civic clubs, 177–179
    in gubernatorial races, 104
    in gubernatorial State of State Addresses, 108
    for local businesses, 173–174
    local government and public policy, 291–292
    of local labor unions, 174–175
    managed by public service commissions, 137–138
    on metropolitan governments, 271–277
    for neighborhoods, 165–168
    of religious congregations, 180–182
    of state court systems, 149–148

judges. *See also* judicial system
    of county courts, 247
    justices of the peace, 200, 247
    local elections of, 200–201
    salaries of, 146, 147
    state, 145–147
    workload of state, 148
judicial councils, 147
judicial doctrine, 30
judicial system. *See also* judges
    activists within, 30–31
    interpretation of constitutional federalism, 30–33
justice
    administration of, 147–149
    American system of, 141, 142–144
    criminal justice system, 155–156
    inquisitorial system of, 158
    social, 307, 309–311
justices of the peace, 200, 247
juvenile crime, 155

Kalamazoo County Board of Commissioners, 248
Kansas City, Missouri, city council, 228
Kimel Case, 33

labor unions, 170–175
    about, 172
    cooperating for change, 175
    issues of local, 174–175
    local government workers in, 237

labor unions (continued)
    political power of, 175
Lakewood Plan, 279
Landtag, 85
land-use regulation
    about, 296
    building codes, 298
    eminent domain and, 299
    housing codes, 298–299
    land-use plans, 297
    subdivision regulations, 297–298
    zoning ordinances, 297
language and cultural identity, 13
lawyers
    in criminal trials, 142
    licensing and practice of, 77
    roles of in American system of justice, 142
leadership
    of civic leaders, 174
    of mayor, 235–237
    of state governors, 108–109, 110–112
    state legislature partisan, 89
legislative oversight, 94–97
legislative sessions, 84
legitimacy of government, 80
leisure as by-product of technology, 22
Libertarian Party, 57
liberty and property rights, 8
licensing, 133–135
lieutenant governors, 88, 112–114
line-item veto, 111
lobbyists, 62–63
local crime control and prevention, 308
local education funding, 259–260
local government, 211–239, 241–265, 291–317. *See also* city
    councils; counties; metropolitan government; special
    service districts
    about local policy making, 291–292, 299–300
    administering mandated programs, 294
    advantages of multiple governing bodies, 272–273, 277
    bureaucrats and power in, 237
    compromises in policy making, 300–301
    demand for services and low taxes, 313–315
    developing local ordinances, 292–293
    development and preservation policies, 301–307
    disadvantages of fragmented, 273–278
    duties of city councils, 227–228
    enforcing local codes, 293–294
    in Europe, 220
    factors leading to urban growth, 269–270
    historical background of structure, 214–220
    home rule, 48–49, 219, 220
    informal cooperative agreements, 279
    land-use regulation by, 296–299
    local education policy making, 262–263

    local funding for public education, 259–260
    local school policies, 255–256
    mayoral duties, 228–233
    mayoral leadership in, 235–237
    mobility and sprawl, 311–312
    municipal government structure, 220–226
    partnerships between community organizations and,
        207
    policies for public safety and social justice, 307–311
    political machines, 215–217
    Progressive reform movement, 217–220
    public policy issues for, 291–292
    raising public revenues, 295–296
    scope of, 211–212
    special service districts as, 251–255
    structure and power of, 212–214
    tasks of city manager, 233–235
    tax-base sharing approach, 279–280
    townships, 226–227
    transportation policies, 284–287
    views on transportation, 284–285
local government home rule, 48–49, 219, 220
local political participation, 191–210. *See also* elections; local
    government
    assessing levels of, 206–209
    in communities, 189
    county commissioners and school boards, 201–202
    general purpose local governments, 191–192
    local elections, 193–201
    special purpose local governments, 192
    on voluntary boards, 205–206
    voter turnout for off-year and presidential elections,
        202–205
logrolling, 56–57

magistrates, 200, 247
majority leader, 89
malfeasance, 134
mall merchants associations, 171
management
    by objectives, 117, 118
    city managers, 233–235
    evaluating professionalism of state, 129–131
    state managers, 116–117
management information systems (MIS), 116–117, 130
mandatory determinant sentencing, 154
manipulation of local participants, 206–207
Marbury v. *Madison*, 38
mayor, 198–200
    duties of, 228–233
    election of, 198–200
    German, 232
    leadership of, 235–237
    strong mayor form of government, 221–222
    weak mayor form of political structure, 215, 222

mayor *(continued)*
    Web sites for, 234
media at state capital, 64–67
    broadcast, 66–67
    capital city newspapers, 65–66
    news services, 65
Medicaid, 43
merit systems and civil-service laws, 126–127
metropolitan government, 267–289. *See also* local
        government
    capacity building for, 249–251, 263
    census of metropolitan areas, 270
    consolidating services, 248, 281–283
    councils of government, 278–279
    debate over, 271–277
    defining responsibilities for service, 281
    fragmented local governments, 272–278
    governmental factors leading to, 269–270
    informal cooperative agreements, 279
    interlocal service agreements, 279
    Lakewood Plan, 279
    spectrum of coordination in, 278
    tax-base sharing approach, 279–280
    transportation policies and, 284–287
    two-tier systems of, 280–281
    uncontrolled growth and, 268–271, 288
    Web sites on, 288
Metropolitan Transportation Authority (MTA), 284
Miami–Dade metropolitan planning organization, 284–285
migration, 13–16
millage rate, 259, 295
minority leader, 89
misfeasance, 134
mobility
    regional identities and, 6–7
    urban sprawl and, 311–312
moralistic political culture, 18–19, 37
motions, 292
Motor Voter Law, 36, 37, 202
multiculturalism. *See also* diversity
    controversy over, 12
municipal government. *See* local government
municipalities, 220–221

National Association of Counties, 250
National Center for State Courts, 147, 148
National Governor's Association (NGA), 42–43, 113
National Voter Registration Act (NVRA), 36, 37, 202
natural monopolies, 135
neighborhoods, 163–170
    defined, 162
    households and home ownership, 163–164
    issues for, 165–168
    neighborhood or tenants' associations, 165
    political action in, 168–170

New England town hall, 227
news services at state capital, 65
noblesse oblige, 17
noise control, 166–167
noncurrent elections, 202
nonpartisan elections, 218
nouveau riche, 17

occupation-based associations, 172
off-year local elections, 202
open primaries, 59
ordinances, 292
original jurisdiction, 144
overlay districts, 299

parishes, 242. *See also* counties
participation. *See* local political participation
partisan politics. *See* political parties
party whip, 89
passing state legislation, 89–93
payroll taxes, 295–296
personal property, 7–8
personal safety, 166
petitions, 194
philanthropy, 181
Philippine trial courts, 148
placation, 207
place, 1–25
    diversity in United States, 8–9
    homes as sense of, 164
    immigration and migration, 13–16
    mobility and, 6–7
    overview, 1–3
    personal property as, 7–8
    policy implications of diversity, 13
    political culture and, 16–18
    principle of constitutions and sovereignty, 3–5
    race and racial consciousness, 9–13
    regional loyalties and, 5–6
    role of urbanization and mass culture in, 6–7
    sense of place in politics, 5
    sketching a sense of place, 8
    technology and civic culture, 19–22
plaintiffs in civil trials, 143
pluralism, 71
pluralist theory of local power, 186–187
policy. *See also* programmatic federalism; welfare
    about local policy making, 291–292, 299–300
    compromises in local policy making, 300–301
    diversity's impact on, 13
    enforcing local codes, 293–294
    federalism and preemption of, 47–48
    innovations in education, 260–262
    issues for local government, 291–292
    school districts and local education, 262–263

policy (continued)
    state legislatures and decision making, 76–77
political action committees (PAC), 60
political action in neighborhoods, 168–170
political culture, 16–18
political efficacy, 204
political parties, 54–62
    campaign financing for, 59–61
    campaign financing for state, 59–61
    character of, 57–58
    effectiveness and discipline of, 56–57
    effectiveness and discipline of state, 56–57
    impact on local elections, 204
    organization of, 54–56
    partisan elections, 58–59
    party leadership of state legislatures, 89
    party primaries, 58
    platforms for, 56
    in state legislatures, 87
    state-level organizations, 54–56
    in Switzerland, 55
    teamwork in, 61–62
    teamwork in state, 61–62
political power
    of businesses, 174
    comparison of lieutenant governor versus vice president, 113
    elite theory of local, 185–186
    governmental authority of counties, 243–244
    of labor unions, 175
    of local bureaucrats, 237
    in local governments, 212–214
    pluralist theory of local, 186–187
    political machines, 215–217
    of public service commissions, 135–136
    regime theory of local, 187–188
    religious congregations and, 182
    of special interest groups, 183–184
    of special service districts, 252
political support in political systems, 69
politico orientation to representative democracy, 80
politics
    about state politics and political systems, 53–54
    around state legislatures, 86–87
    identity, 13
    sense of place in, 5–6
pork barrel projects, 111
Port Authority of New York and New Jersey, 284
Portland Metropolitan Services District, 283
poverty, 39–42
    ethnicity and, 39–41
    evaluating welfare programs and policies, 44–46
    state welfare and workfare solutions, 41
    working mothers and related issues for welfare recipients, 42

preponderance of evidence, 143
preschool programs, 262
preservation policies
    community-preservation strategies, 304–306
    for cultural preservation, 305–306
    historic preservation, 305
president of the senate, 88
president pro tempore, 88
press secretary to governor, 109–110
principle of constitutions and sovereignty, 3–5
prison systems, 152–155
privatization of public services, 128
probate judge, 247
probation, 152
professionalism
    evaluating for state government, 129–131
    professional licensing and, 133–135
    required of state bureaucrats, 125
program evaluation for welfare policies, 44–46
programmatic federalism, 38–46
    development of social programs, 39–42
    federal and state cooperation in policy and program implementation, 42–44
    overview, 38–39
program review in state legislatures, 95
Progressive reform movement, 217–220
progrowth coalitions, 174
property
    changing definitions of, 7–8
    public, 296
public education legislation, 93
public interest groups, 63
public opinion in political systems, 69
public property, 296
public safety, 307–309. *See also* crime control
    emergency services for, 309
    local crime control, 308
    local crime prevention, 308
public service commissions, 135–138
    future of, 138
    organization and powers of, 135–136
    public-service issues managed by, 137–138
    public utilities and, 135
    regulation of, 138–139
public utilities
    in India, 139
    regulating, 131, 132
    role of state public service commissions in, 135
punitive damages, 156

qualifying for general elections, 197
quasi-governmental powers of special service districts, 252
Quickening of America, The, 162–163

race, 9–13. *See also* diversity
    civic equality and, 11
    common racial terminology, 9
    comparison of sentencing by, 153
    crime control and discrimination, 310–311
    federal protection of voting rights, 34–35
    local government structure and representation by, 225
    poverty and ethnicity, 39–41
    reactions to diversity, 11–13
    shifting demographics, 9–10
    social mores and segregation, 16–17
    unclear social definitions of, 9–11
    voter turnout by, 203
    white flight to suburbs, 270–271
racial gerrymandering, 82
reasonable doubt, 142
recall, 194, 218
redistricting, 82
reduction in force (RIF), 111
referendums, 78, 194, 218
reforming
    campaign financing, 60
    civil service, 126, 127
    corrections and sentencing, 153–154
    local governments, 212
    municipal governments by Progressives, 217–220
    public education, 260–262
    public service strategies and costs, 313–315
    state government, 117–119, 129–131
    welfare, 94
Reform Party, 57–58
Regime Politics (Stone), 187–188
regime theory of local power, 187–188
regions
    loyalties to, 5–6
    migration and growth of, 14–16
    support for political parties by, 56
regulation, 131–135
    controls for, 138–139
    of corporations, 132–133
    of interest groups, 64–65
    of land-use, 296–299
    professional licensing and, 133–135
    of public utilities, 131, 132, 139
    regulatory oversight of state legislatures, 97
religious congregations, 179–182
    citywide ministerial alliances, 181
    issues addressed by, 180–182
    political involvement of, 182
Religious Freedom Restoration Act (RFRA), 32
representative democracy, 80–86, 193
    election campaigns, 83
    legislative sessions, 84
    profile of legislators, 84–86
    public expectations of, 80–81

    representation in state legislatures, 81–83
    selecting candidates and legitimacy of, 80
    state legislatures as, 80–86
Republican Party
    about, 57
    regional support for, 56
    voter realignment in, 106–107
Republic of Philippines, 148
Republic of South Africa, 316
reserved powers clause of Bill of Rights, 4, 32
residential community associations (RCAs), 170
resolutions, 292
respondents in civil trials, 143
revenue estimates, 96
revenue-sharing programs, 47, 269
roll call votes, 92–93
Rotary Clubs in Indonesia, 179
rulings, 77

salaries
    of court judges, 146, 147
    of state employees, 125
sales taxes, 295
school boards, 201–202
school districts, 255–263
    accountability of, 262, 264
    confidence in public schools, 257
    constitutional basis for, 255
    education policy innovation, 260–262
    local education policy making and, 262–263
    local school policies, 255–256
    policies of, 256–257
    school funding, 258–260
    state education policies and, 255
school superintendents, 256
school uniforms, 262–263
"second thirteen" states, 29
secretary of state, 132
selective code enforcement, 293–294
sentencing, 142, 152–155
service delivery
    balancing services and taxes for local governments, 313–315
    by counties, 248, 249–251, 263
    for counties, 249–251, 263
    county demographics and impact on, 243
    defining local and regional responsibilities for service, 281
    for metropolitan counties, 249–251, 263
    in Western counties, 243
service delivery bureaucrats, 123–129
    fragmented service delivery, 192
    hierarchy and communications among, 127–129
    increases in state employees, 123–124
    merit systems and civil-service laws, 126–127

service delivery bureaucrats (continued)
    privatization and, 128
    specialization and professionalism required of, 125
sheriff, 245, 248
single-member districts
    for city council, 195
    for state legislature, 81
slamming, 138
Smart Air Transport System (SATS), 21
social justice, 307, 309–311
social mores, 16–17
social policy. *See* programmatic federalism
South, migration and diversity in, 15–16
sovereignty
    defined, 3
    dual, 29
    state claims to, 30
speaker of house, 88–89
special interest organizations, 183–184
special purpose local governments, 192, 213
special service districts, 251–255
    about, 251, 263–264
    as apolitical, 241–242
    in Brazil, 254
    in Chicago, 253
    concerns about fragmented service, 254–255
    governmental powers of, 252
    water-quality districts as, 253–254
sprawl. *See* urbanization
staff for governor, 109–110
standard operating procedures (SOP), 121–122
state agencies. *See also* state employees
    appointed agency heads, 114–116
    hierarchy and communications among, 127–129
    increases in state employees, 123–124
    merit systems and civil-service laws, 126–127
    privatization of public services, 128
    reforms in, 117–118
    specialization and professionalism required from, 125
    standard operating procedures (SOP), 121–122
state appeals courts, 144–145, 147
state cabinets, 114, 115
state courts, 141–160. *See also* crime control
    about, 141
    administering justice, 147–149
    American system of justice, 141, 142–144
    crime control and, 149–157
    increasing volume in, 149
    state appeals courts, 144–145
    state judges, 145–147
    state trial courts, 144
    tort reform, 133, 157–158
state employees
    hierarchy and communications among, 127–129
    increases in state employees, 123–124

    merit systems and civil-service laws, 126–127
    privatization and, 128
    specialization and professionalism required of, 125
state executives, 101–120. *See also* governors; lieutenant
    governors
    appointed agency heads, 114–116
    governors, 102–112
    lieutenant governors, 88, 112–114
    overview, 101–102
    reforming executive branch government, 117–119
    state managers, 116–117
state funding for public education, 258–259
state legislators, 84–86
state legislatures, 75–99. *See also* state executives
    budgetary oversight in, 96–97
    chamber leadership for, 88–89
    creation of general purpose local governments, 191–192
    crime control legislation, 94
    direct democracy, 77–79
    election campaigns, 83
    governor as leader of, 108–109
    legislative sessions of, 84
    organization of legislative life around, 86–87
    overview of, 75–76
    party leadership of, 89
    party politics in, 87
    passage of general laws for, 218
    passing state laws, 89–93
    profile of legislators, 84–86
    program review in, 95
    public education legislation, 93
    public policy decision making by, 76–77
    regulatory oversight, 97
    representation in, 81–83
    representative democracy, 80–86
    rule-making authority granted to regulators, 131
    types of legislative oversight, 94–97
    welfare reform legislation, 94
state managers, 116–117
State of the State Address, 108
state public service commissions. *See* public service
    commissions
state regulations, 77
states, 53–73. *See also* political parties; state executives; state
    legislatures
    about politics and political systems, 53–54
    constitutions of, 2
    decision-making model for political systems, 67–72
    dual sovereignty and, 29, 30
    education policies and school districts, 255
    federal policy preemptions, 47–48
    home rule laws and, 48–49
    implementation of federal welfare laws, 44
    increasing imprisonment rates in, 154
    interest groups, 62–64

states (continued)
  jurisdiction in age discrimination cases, 33
  local administration of mandated programs, 294
  media at state capital, 64–67
  Medicaid as federal-state partnership, 43
  methods of selecting state regulators, 132
  model of political systems, 68–72
  with most registered lobbyists, 63
  most violent, 150
  policies contributing to urban sprawl, 269–270
  policy and program implementation with federal
    government, 42–44
  referenda laws for, 78
  rights under Articles of Confederation and Perpetual
    Union, 28
  role in voter registration, 34
  "second thirteen," 29
  state-level political parties, 54–62
  welfare and workfare solutions by, 41
state supreme courts, 144, 145
state trial courts, 144
statutes, 76
statutory referendums, 78
strict constructionists, 30–31
strong mayor form, 221–222
subdivision regulations, 297–298
sunset legislation, 92
supplemental budget, 96
Switzerland
  federalism in, 49
  political parties in, 55

Tammany Hall, 216
taxes
  collection by county tax commissioner, 245–246
  consolidating services with tax-base sharing, 279–280
  costs of local services, 314–315
  demand for excellent services and low, 313–315
  raising public revenues via, 295–296
  tax-base sharing, 279–280
  tax rate, 259
technology, 19–22
  effect on place, time, and culture, 22–23
  generational changes and, 20–21
  influence on culture, 19
  influences on individual, 21–22
  influencing urban growth, 268–269
  leisure as by-product of, 22
teledemocracy, 194
tenant's associations, 165
term limits
  for city council members, 196
  for gubernatorial terms, 103
  for state legislators, 81
third parties, 57

Tiebout thesis, 272
time as affected by technology, 22–23
Title I of Elementary and Secondary Education Act, 258
tokenism, 207
Toronto, Ontario, as two-tier metropolitan system, 280
tort reform, 133, 157–158
town hall meetings, 77, 227
towns and townships, 226–227, 232–233
traditionalistic political culture, 17, 37
traffic court judges, 200
transportation, 284–287
  interstate highways and urban sprawl, 269
  issues for state and local governments, 286–287
  local government views of, 284–285
  national government's view of, 286
  personal mobility versus urban sprawl, 311–312
  Smart Air Transport System (SATS), 21
  transit authorities, 253
  urban growth and, 268–269
  Web sites for issues on metropolitan, 288
Transportation Equity Act for the Twenty-First Century, 286
trial courts
  in Republic of Philippines, 148
  state, 144
trustee orientation to representative democracy, 80
tuition vouchers, 261
two-party competitive political systems, 103–104
two-tier systems of metropolitan government, 280–281

uncontrolled growth
  forces contributing to, 268–271
  overview of, 288
unfunded mandates and federalism, 47
unions. See labor unions
United States of America
  American system of justice, 141, 142–144
  establishment of Constitution and federal government,
    28–30
  principle of constitutions and sovereignty, 3–5
  two-party competitive political system, 57
  viewed originally as confederation, 28
urbanization
  cultural contributions to, 270–271
  interstate highways and, 269
  local government factors leading to, 269–270
  mass culture and, 6–7
  mobility and, 311–312
  state policies contributing to, 269–270
  technological changes and, 268–269
U.S. Advisory Commission on Intergovernmental Relations
  (ACIR), 243–244
U.S. Bureau of the Census, 164
  constitutional requirements of, 15
  data on state of birth and residence, 7
  defining metropolitan areas using census data, 270

U.S. Bureau of the Census *(continued)*
    regional growth data, 15
U.S. Chamber of Commerce, 171
U.S. Civil War, 6, 30
U.S. Constitution. *See also* constitutional federalism
    establishment of federal government and, 28–30
    interpretations of commerce clause of, 31–32
    on local governments, 214
    national supremacy and implied powers clause, 38
    reserved powers clause of Bill of Rights, 4, 32
    revisions of, 79
    school districts as government function, 255
user fees, 296
U.S. Immigration and Naturalization Service, 14
U.S. Office of Management and Budget, 270
U.S. Supreme Court, 30–31

vice president, 113
violent crime, 150–151
voluntary community boards, 205–206
volunteerism, 181, 189
voter realignment in political parties, 106–107
voter registration
    Motor Voter Law, 36, 37, 202
    patterns of, 37
    states' role in, 34
voter turnout, 202–205
voting rights, 33–37
    Constitutional protection of, 33
    contemporary barriers to, 35–37
    federal protection of, 34–35
    patterns of voter registration, 37
    state's role in voter registration, 34
Voting Rights Act of 1965, 35

wards, city council, 195, 196
Washington, D.C., 220
water-quality districts, 253–254
weak mayor form, 215, 222
Web sites
    for cities, 234
    for counties, 249
    for issues on metropolitan government and
        transportation, 288
    links to diverse interest groups on, 21
    for Swiss Confederation, 49
welfare
    Medicaid as federal-state partnership, 43
    national interest in policies, 43
    program evaluation and, 44–46
    state implementation of federal laws, 44
    state solutions for, 41
    Swiss program for, 49
    working mothers and related issues for recipients, 42
Welfare Reform Act of 1996, 44
welfare reform legislation, 94
whistle-blowing, 127
Who Governs? (Dahl), 186
women
    issues for working mothers on welfare, 42
    voting rights for, 33, 34
    in workforce, 172

youth, civic clubs involvement with, 177–178

zero-based budgeting, 118
zoning ordinances, 297